Access to Knowledge

Access to Knowledge

The Continuing Agenda For Our Nation's Schools

**John I. Goodlad
and Pamela Keating,**
Editors

With a Foreword by
Donald M. Stewart

College Entrance Examination Board
New York 1994

Copies of this book may be ordered from: College Board Publications, Box 886, New York, New York 10101-0886. The price is $16.95.

Editorial inquiries concerning this book should be directed to: Editorial Office, The College Board, 45 Columbus Avenue, New York, New York 10023-6992.

Library of Congress Catalog Card Number: 94-072433

ISBN: 0-87447-502-3

Printed in the United States of America.

9 8 7 6 5 4 3 2 1

Contents

Foreword

When we discuss education in the United States, we often touch on issues of principle—and sometimes even strike a nerve. Questions of academic preparation, equity, national standards, and institutional mission translate into concerns for a modern democracy. Who do we wish to be? Based on what principles do we wish to define ourselves? On what grounds will we construct a common schooling and a shared existence? The education issues that endure most frequently spring from tensions left unsettled, from questions difficult to answer, or from challenges left unmet. That we still feel the need to speak of equity and excellence as poles of a debate, or of the need to balance the two, indicates an unresolved dichotomy that still limits our vision of education reform.

It is to such pivotal issues that the authors of this volume have turned their considerable skills and varied insights. In this collection of essays, some of your top education researchers and practitioners face the difficult issues that access to knowledge entails.

In the years since the book was first published, the urgency of the subject has only grown. While wealthy suburban schools consider the best ways to incorporate technology into their curricula, half of the African-American males who enter high school in Detroit do not graduate; more go to jail than go to college; and murder remains the leading cause of death for those in the fifth grade and above. As Professor John Goodlad, editor of this volume, and the other contributors have documented, the inequities are also painfully evident in the level of curriculum, quality of pedagogy, and school environment. Recent research has also revealed some frightening facts, first dealt with in this volume by co-editor Pamela Keating, about how our schools fail women and girls. By the middle school years, girls' performance frequently lags behind that of boys. At the same time, girls suffer a severe loss of self-esteem.

It is not only race and gender that limit access to knowledge. According to a report in the September 1993 issues of *Postsecondary Education Opportunity*, 94 percent of students in the highest income quartile graduate from high school, as compared with 64 percent in the lowest quartile. The inequity is more dramatic in postsecondary education. There, an estimated 76 percent of students from high-income families will complete bachelor's degrees, as opposed to 4 percent of their low-income classmates.

Undergirding the original publication of *Access to Knowledge* were two basic premises: lack of academic achievement is not the fault of the student, and education reform must begin in the classroom. Certainly in the years since, these ideas have gained some credence, as witnessed by such College Board initiatives as EQUITY 2000. The EQUITY initiative is not only based on the assumption that all children can succeed in a rigorous college-preparatory program, but also entails training and support for teachers, guidance counselors, and principals.

Federal support for educational excellence—as embodied in the 1994 passage of Goals 2000 legislation—is also a heartening sign. And again the Board has responded to these efforts with the Pacesetter initiative, intended not only to define education standards, but also to give students the materials they need to achieve and teachers the pedagogical tools to reach these standards. The impetus is there. But the movement toward education reform should be viewed as a beginning.

The introduction to the first edition of *Access to Knowledge* stated that "this book is conceived as a work in progress." Certainly that is no less true of this revised edition. Teaming up sound vision with cogent research, the essays that follow tackle the complex issues of success from a variety of vantage points; from the anthropologist to the school principal, from psychologists to school reformers. It is my sincere hope that their fine research and insights will assist us in furthering this essential conversation and allow us to wrestle anew with the unresolved challenges of equity and excellence.

I am delighted that the College Board's Office of Academic Affairs has decided to reissue this extremely valuable collection. The insight that it brings to the resolution of issues defining the future of education in this nation are perhaps even more important today than they were when the first edition appeared. Moreover, no one speaks more clearly or forthrightly to the issues of education than John Goodlad. This revised edition has provided him with an opportunity to comment on how far we have come and, more critically, where we must yet go. I warmly recommend to readers "Retrospect and Prospect," the commentary he has prepared especially for this new edition.

Many individuals contributed to the making and remaking of *Access to Knowledge*. I am delighted to have this opportunity to thank them.

Acknowledgments

This book is the work not of one individual, but of many. As a result, the pages that follow are the craft of different hands and the sound of several voices: teachers, scholars, administrators and policymakers, parents, and community leaders. The College Board wishes to thank all of the individuals and organizations that contributed to both the original edition and *Access to Knowledge: The Continuing Agenda for Our Nation's Schools*.

Of the many people to whom we are indebted for contributing to this book, special recognition should be accorded to the authors of two papers.

Although their names appear elsewhere with more complete identifications, I wish to mention them here as well: John I. Goodlad, James P. Comer, Martin E. Orlando, John U. Ogbu, Pamela Keating, Virginia Richardson and Patricia Colfer, Robert L. Sinclair and Ward J. Ghory, Asa G. Hilliard, Kenneth A. Sirotmik, Jeannie Oakes and Martin N. Lipton, Suzanne Soo Hoo, Carol Wilson and Lance Wright, Linda Darling-Hammond with the assistance of Joslyn Gree, Charles M. Hodge, Jose A. Cardenas, Robert H. Slavin and Jomills H. Braddock, Joan Kernan Cone, Susan Murphy, and Myra Sadker, David Sadker, Lynn Fox, and Melinda Salata.

This book could not have been undertaken without the leadership of John Goodlad both in his role as editor and in his thoughtful conceptualization and formulation of the overarching theme "access to knowledge," a common theme that represents our shared belief that more Americans must come to understand the great stake all of us have in changing the outcomes for those most disadvantaged. Our hope is that this book will help all of us to address the questions of quality and equity in a broader perspective and perhaps clearer light. Pamela Keating's editorial contribution was also invaluable in bringing the original project to fruition several years ago.

The contribution of the College Board staff was equally important, particularly that of Robert Orrill, executive director of the Office of Academic Affairs, whose vision kept this project alive through a second edition. Our thanks, too, to Dorothy Downie and Peter Nelson for innumerable contributions, large and small.

Without these important contributors, this book would not have been possible. The College Board owes much to their efforts. The following chapters, while representing many viewpoints and offering diverse recommendations, are one voice in what we view as an unfinished agenda for everyone interested in achieving quality education for all students.

DONALD M. STEWART

1.

Common Schools for the Common Weal: Reconciling Self-Interest with the Common Good

JOHN I. GOODLAD

Précis
Our failure to educate a sizable number of young people not only represents a waste of the talent and energies of these individuals but also constitutes a crisis for the nation. Contributing to this crisis are certain institutionalized features of America's educational system, which function as barriers to knowledge, especially for poor and minority students.

John Goodlad, having recognized and described these conditions, holds that we should return to the belief of the nation's founders that each citizen's self-interest involves the public good. Serious support for school reform follows from a deeper understanding of the idea that what is truly good in the long run for each individual citizen comes about when people choose the common weal, the overarching public good, as their first priority in making decisions about schools and other social issues, rather than considering only what will benefit their own group the most.

Goodlad also asserts that school reform should be addressed as a set of changes that must be worked on together, since schools ought to be understood as institutions composed of interlocking parts. Attention should be given to the interaction of the parts as well as to the nature of each separate part. Systemic reform needs to proceed in ways that will be mutually reinforcing for various aspects of education, and not result in proposals that are at cross-purposes.

To bring about changes deemed critical, six areas are identified for specific consideration. The dropout rate is at the top of the list. Other issues include the haphazard distribution of knowledge in the curriculum, limited instructional repertoire of teachers, persistent misperceptions about the distribution of ability among students, organizational arrangements that have prejudicial consequences for children, and two university-level activities—teacher preparation and research—that perpetuate problems of inequity.

Goodlad indicates that school personnel should take into account all these areas as they develop plans for reform. Their discussions should include a dialogue about what equity means, what practices deny equal access to knowledge within a particular school, and what steps might be taken to promote full access for all students.

Only through measures such as these can schools provide for the future of the democracy by fulfilling the obligation, articulated by Thomas Jefferson, of each generation to render its youths fit to govern the next.

John I. Goodlad, former dean of the graduate school of education at the University of California, Los Angeles, is professor and director of the Center for Educational Renewal in the College of Education at the University of Washington in Seattle. He is the author of an influential critique of American schooling, *A Place Called School,* and is currently directing a national examination of the education of educators.

—*The College Board*

The schools to be supported by special tax assessments in the early settlements of what is now the United States were not intended to be common. Nor did they reflect a belief in the individual's right to gain knowledge. Nor were they intended for the Indians whose claims to this land ran longer and deeper.

These public schools were "common" only in the sense that they were to serve the immigrant commoners—those who could not provide privately for their children's education. And their purpose was to assure the values and beliefs the settlers brought with them, through teaching the literacy skills required for learning the laws of the land and the religious precepts. The schools to be provided by the householders' assessments were self-serving, whether or not their own children attended, in both a personal and a community sense.

Strong arguments can be advanced for the observation that, even as the public school became more commonly attended, it served best those whose educational needs and interests could be well served without it. The economically advantaged, if they so chose, could add their tax dollars to other dollars, seek or create private schools, and leave those of less affluence to fend educationally for themselves. It is difficult to assess all the ways the public schools have deferred to the well served either to keep them in or to assure their continued support through taxes. It is difficult to effect reforms unless these can be portrayed either as not threatening the interests of the well served or as benefiting them and the poorly served at least equally.

One can argue that virtually every major effort designed to improve the school's capacity to serve has resulted, at least early on, in improving or extending the options of those already best served. The Smith-Hughes Act of 1917 is a case in point. Intended to broaden the school's appeal to students marginally involved in a largely college-preparatory curriculum by adding agriculture, home economics, and mechanical trades, the more vocationally oriented curricula initially attracted very few of the students performing poorly in academics.[1] One of the predictable outcomes of school reform is that improvements motivated at the outset by the need or desire to serve better the disadvantaged are incorporated first into schools and school districts or segments of schools populated disproportionately by the advantaged.

Nature of the Malaise

A person interested in change but discouraged by these observations might join the social reformers (including historical revisionists and curriculum reconstructionists) in concluding that reform focused directly on the school itself is futile. School reform, they say, must follow fundamental social reform. The question then arises as to whether we are willing and able to effect the economic policies many people believe to be part of social reform. A reduction in economic inequities, it is argued, would ease the school's task of reducing inequities regarding access to knowledge. Progress toward economic and social reforms probably would accelerate if increasingly large numbers of people in advantaged positions perceived change to be compatible with— indeed, necessary to—their self-interests. It is cynical but realistic to observe, once again, that the common welfare is likely to advance when the advantaged see their self-interests and the common weal to be entwined.

Two far-reaching conditions of our society pose increasing threats to the self-interests of the economically advantaged. First, as James B. Conant so trenchantly observed,[2] this country was born with a congenital deformity: namely, the enslavement of a portion of its people. Second, it already has within it a growing population of children, youth, and adults who simply will not manage to take advantage of the yellow brick road to an acceptable standard of living, let alone fame and fortune. The Horatio Alger stories of my own childhood, with their bootblack-to-riches scenarios, had a bit of a hollow ring even then. They are fairy-tale folklore today.

However compelling the history of our black people, from slavery to candidacy for the presidency, blackness still carries its special burden of inequities, including the status of inferiority within segments of the white population and, sadly, even the black. This status and this burden are reflected quite obviously, as well as in a variety of subtle ways, in our schools.

The population born into poverty that cannot take advantage of the yellow brick road is black and brown and white and growing rapidly in numbers. This population carries with it quite different disadvantages from those of the groups absorbed into the United States so successfully at the turn of the century and subsequently. And color (for some) is only one of these. The other disadvantages include generations of poverty, the benefit of only one parent, malnutrition, lack of sensory stimulation, and lack of a language having instrumental or social value in the surrounding culture. And then there is that staggering statistic. We are not talking about socializing, accommodating, or rehabilitating 10 percent or 15 percent of our total population but perhaps 35 percent or more.[3] Not included in these percentages are estimates of "at risk" children and youth for whom the demographics of birth raise no danger signals.

We are, in hard fact, confronted with phenomena we have never faced before, phenomena which could overwhelm us—and which will, indeed, overwhelm us in one way or another unless we undertake a direct attack on them and their otherwise inevitable consequences. Bold ideas are needed as never before. Throwing money at the problems will not suffice. But large sums of money are required to support ideas of promise, some of which undoubtedly will fail.

I turn now to the intellectual and strategic view that positions itself somewhere between the stagnation of cynicism (and perhaps ultimate resort to "lifeboat" theory and action) and the chaos likely to ensue if we fail to recognize the significance of these changing circumstances. The position is one of anticipating the reconstruction of society through a process driven by necessity and enlightened self-interest, however idealistic and selfless the accompanying rhetoric may be.

For a decade or two, we have been drifting as a nation into deeper and deeper trouble, without any widespread awareness of or agreement on the nature of our malaise. Several different kinds of much publicized, self-imposed conditions or external forces have distracted us from hardheaded self-examination and, to a degree, have served as scapegoats: "too much government," "Japanese ingenuity," and "Russian imperialism," to name some of the major ones. These slogans turn our attention away from ourselves, especially when some evidence to support them is mustered.

But more and more people are taking off their eyeshades, focusing more sharply, and seeing the emperor's new clothes. They are beginning to realize that preparing technicians in our schools to fit the demands of business and industry oriented to the short-term bottom line is not enhancing our economy. They see, too, that increased sales per square foot of space may attract rather than divert takeover by a company not primarily interested in the welfare of the community or the morale of the workers. "Better schools mean better jobs"[4] not only begins to sound a little hollow but also deludes us in our expectations for what schools can and cannot do and, especially, should do. Yet when Harvard president Derek Bok looks critically at the responsibility of the Business School for attending to the ethics of its students, and *The New York Times* picks up the theme, our faith in what we fear is gone from both our educational institutions and their social context is renewed a little.[5]

The context of interviews with citizens of England conducted by *The Wall Street Journal* in London presents us with disquieting views.[6] As a nation, we are trusted no more than the USSR as keepers of the peace; as a people, we are depicted as preoccupied with the pursuit of money. But, encouragingly, we are viewed by many of those interviewed as freedom loving and freedom pursuing. Without the United States, some said, the people of the Western world would be far less free. Our responsibility to maintain and to extend this freedom is clear.

The important word here is "responsibility." There is no freedom without sustained attention to the personal and collective efforts required to maintain it. This requires, as Jefferson and others forging the Republic argued, a well-educated *citizenry*, not merely a much-educated elite. Maintaining our freedom requires not merely educated leadership but an educated polity capable of judging whether this leadership deserves our trust and continued support. There must not be, then, two kinds of education for our citizens. "We cannot . . . provide at public expense these advanced educational opportunities for X because his father is a banker, and practically deny them to Y because his father cleans the streets of the city."[7]

On the deficit side, many of us either turn our backs on what should be central to our personal and political lives or resort to a variety of modes of denial. One of the most dangerous of these escapes is the narrowing of our sense of community to family, social group, or religious sect, to the degree that self-interest no longer connects with the common weal. When this occurs, as it has for many of us, our freedom is endangered. And when these self-interests dominate the culture of our public schools, the schools are agents of freedom no longer.

On the positive side, significant numbers of people are coming in from their oases of denial, or shaking themselves out of inexplicable ennui, in growing realization that their present and future are being shaped in their absence. Even if skeptical of idealism, they realize that their own self-interests, to be served, must be joined productively with the self-interests of others. To a considerable degree, self-interest and the common interest must become one.

Returning to where this paper began, the so-called common school always has served special self-interests. While doing so, however, it also has been driven by a sense of serving the common weal. Consequently, through the nineteenth century, the prevailing rhetoric emphasized development in the young of moral, ethical, religious, political, and economic responsibility. McGuffey's Eclectic Readers once offered fare for both character and intellectual development. Whereas young people encountered in the Readers the real-world issues depicted by Shakespeare, Webster, Thackeray, and Cooper, today's students encounter "an unrealistic image of a society where all the battles are in the past, where racism is history and where women and minorities have nothing left to strive for."[8] But failure to open up the mind to battles of the present is a charge now being leveled at more than elementary and secondary schools. Allan Bloom addresses this charge to that citadel of intellectuality, the university, to those whose controversial, authorized opinions on our malaise presumably require the protection of academic freedom.[9] As a thoughtful graduate dean once said to me: "I am less concerned about the state of academic freedom on this campus than I am about whether there are any professors who need it."

But the promising concomitant of Bloom's book on higher education and the closing of the American mind is public reaction to it. What might have been, a decade ago, a stimulating treatise read by segments of academe and a handful of "intellectuals" outside the university, became an overnight best seller. The publisher must be at once surprised, elated, and puzzled. The book touched a sensitive nerve which most of our politicians and political observers, normally confident in their awareness of the public pulse, scarcely sense. The eyeshades are coming off; the emperor is less than handsome.

Is this critique merely a momentary tweaking of our moral sensitivities? Are most of us to sink back into that "heavy lethargy . . . [that] drowsy reverie interrupted by nervous thrills"?[10] We must assume not, even though cynicism comes easier. As a people, we often come to the brink before we act. We are nearing the edge.

The Common School Malaise

It is difficult to disagree with those social reformers who believe that reform of the school without reform of the larger society is futile. My argument is that the two must proceed simultaneously. Time and time again in the past, school reformers have been out of sync with a largely content or unsympathetic society. Certainly, they are again today. But growing awareness of malaise in the larger society and of the need to address our ills on all fronts is encouraging. And so is the idea that the Harvard Business School has a moral responsibility to deal with business ethics in its curriculum. Likewise, emphasis on the concept of universities making a contribution to critical thinking is heartening. (Let us not pause too long on the question of when and why we began to think otherwise!) And it is even reasonable to hope that "Better schools mean better jobs" is prudent rhetoric for arousing public interest in schooling and leading people into serious reflection on the aims of education and the functions of schools. If not, of what use is hope?

If it is feasible and perhaps even promising for us to address simultaneously the shortcomings of both our society and our schools, what most deserves our attention in regard to the latter? The following constitutes an agenda to command our time and energy and direct our financial resources. The components of this agenda link commonly with the issue of equal access to knowledge, an issue now looming larger in significance than the issue of equal access to schools.[11] First, although there is tacit agreement that the completion of both elementary and secondary schools (the new common school) is necessary to both the common weal and individual effectiveness as parent, worker, and citizen, and full participation in the bounties of life, we fall short by about 25 percent. Second, the generally casual and haphazard approach to determining and arranging the distribution of knowledge for those who complete the K-12 curriculum results in unacceptable differences in the quality of *what* students learn, regardless of their color or socioeconomic status. Third, limited conceptions of what intellectual and character development mean and require by way of nurturing, accompanied by the limited instructional repertoire such conceptions reflect, seriously restrict the quality of *how* students learn. Fourth, deep-seated myths and prejudices about the distribution of ability to learn contribute significantly to differentiating students' access to the array of knowledge schools provide. Fifth, the internal organization of schools, partly reflecting these myths and prejudices and partly designed to make the school's job easier, usually serves to create sharp differences in the educational opportunities enjoyed by students. Sixth, programs for the education of teachers and administrators, focused as they are on individual skills and competencies and on the institutional conditions to be established and maintained, fail to prepare educators whose abilities and priorities are directed toward school renewal. As one's attention moves toward the negative end of all these conditions and circumstances of schooling and as one encounters increasing fallout of students, or evidence of inequities or deprivation, one simultaneously encounters a growing proportion of minority and economically deprived white children and youth. How one best goes about addressing this critical agenda is itself an agenda item of great significance.

The Agenda

Pushing Students to and beyond the Margins

If our conception of excellence in schooling truly embraced an assumption of a K-12 education for all, we might accurately depict it in the shape of a rectangle, thus:

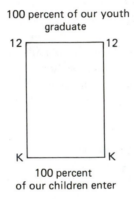

But this is not the mental picture most of us hold. Rather, what we have come to expect looks more like this:

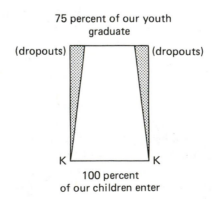

In each instance, close to 100 percent of all 5- and 6-year-olds enter. In the second—closely representing reality—75 percent graduate within the normal or close-to-normal span of years. Nationwide, about 72 percent of students entering the ninth grade graduate four years later. But the statistics are quite different for cities such as New York and Chicago where the dropout rates are over 40 percent. Although the percentage of school-age blacks, Hispanics, and native Americans graduating from secondary schools has been growing, the dropout rates are consistently higher than for whites and Asians.[12]

The stabilization of graduation rates for white students over more than a decade is puzzling; there are disturbing signs of this stabilization beginning also among some minorities. The changing demographics noted earlier warn us that stabilization will deteriorate to regression unless we soon learn a great deal more about motivating and creating compelling environments for large numbers of students not now likely to be meaningfully engaged in the ethos of schools.

There is no question that circumstances outside schools—such as family mobility—have much to do with student dropout rates. But it is also true that most schools simply do not provide environments congenial to students who fail to adapt to the conventional expectations and regularities of schooling. Many teenagers find themselves at the margins of their school's culture. From here, it is easy and sometimes compelling to walk permanently into the world beyond these margins, more often than not with negative consequences for both the individual and society.

The casualness with which school authorities and segments of the community have accepted this drift toward the margins is scandalous. Schools rarely gather data on the course of the drift and steps to alleviate it are almost always absent or, if the data are available, they still require collation and interpretation. The follow-up of those who have drifted beyond the margins is spotty at best and absent at worst. The idea that the school may have failed in its responsibility runs counter to conventional wisdom. However, it is not unreasonable to propose that if achievement test scores are a major indicator of a school's quality, the scores of those in the high school age group who have dropped out should be included with the scores of those still in school. But this proposal usually is met with nervous chuckles and not taken seriously.

Describing a fully comprehensive program for addressing the school dropout problem is beyond the scope of this writer and this paper. A *minimum* list of imperatives includes the following:

1. Acceptance of the proposition that institutional pathology is a significant correlate of the "at risk" classification assigned to large numbers of school-age children and youth.

2. The joining of families and all our social agencies—health, education,

welfare, etc.—into a network of support for children, especially during the prenatal and early childhood years.

3. A philosophical shift away from the question of whether the child is ready for school to the question of whether the school is ready for the child, and an accompanying broadening of school expectations to accommodate the individual and social differences inherent in cohorts of children.

4. An expectation, reflected in daily practice, that each child has responsibility for *both* his or her learning and that of all others in the peer group.

5. Implicit understanding among all school-based adults that the school environment is to be completely free of muted or spoken language, actions, structures, and circumstances conveying to children that they cannot learn and particularly that this inability is associated with circumstances of birth.

6. Organizational arrangements designed to maximize teachers' knowledge and understanding of children and the peer teaching strengths of heterogeneous groups of students. These include:

- Teams of teachers associated with cohort groups of students over several years rather than just one,
- Utilization of special resource personnel in regular classroom settings,
- Cooperative learning and peer tutoring,
- Schools-within-schools, characterized by intimate and cooperative arrangements for reducing the anonymity and isolation of students, particularly at the junior and senior high school levels.

7. Organizational arrangements designed to promote optimal progress of all students, not merely grade-level attainment; continuous progress through a nongraded structure is recommended. [13]

8. Internal processes of data gathering and contextual evaluation sensitively geared to signals that denote students' actual progression in gaining access to knowledge and that warn of any individual drift toward the margins of the school's culture.

9. A shift away from norm-referenced testing to both criterion-referenced and domain-referenced testing for diagnostic purposes, to accompany this recommended contextual evaluation.

10. Classroom-centered counseling programs designed to bring together teachers, counselors, and students in common bonds of understanding, trust, and mutual growth.

Casual Distribution of Knowledge in the Curriculum

The distribution of time and teachers to the subjects of the K-12 curriculum speaks to both some values in the surrounding society and to casual, haphazard curriculum planning. In *A Place Called School,* I report the enormous range in time spent on instruction in the elementary schools and in allocation of teachers to subjects in the secondary schools of our sample.[14] But whether an elementary school managed only 19 or as many as 27 hours per week of instruction, the language arts and mathematics received substantial attention, the two fields together gaining about 54 percent of all instructional time, averaged across schools. At the junior and senior high school levels, 39 percent and 31 percent, respectively, of teacher assignments were to classes in English and mathematics.

These averages disguise school-to-school variations, of course. But what stands out in the school-to-school data is the enormous range in commitment or lack of commitment to subjects beyond the language arts (including reading), English, and mathematics, from paying virtually no attention to subjects such as physical education and the arts to giving the latter more time than science and the social studies. At the senior high level, attention to foreign languages ranged from none offered in the curriculum to three in several schools and four in one school in our sample. Allocations of teachers to vocational subjects ranged from 13 percent to 42 percent of the total. Adding to these school-to-school differences are the extraordinary within-school differences in the courses taken by students within subject rubrics and the content of courses with similar titles. (This latter problem will be discussed in a subsequent section.) The metaphor of "the shopping-mall high school"[15] certainly fits our data although, as I point out later, some of the options are barred to some of the students. Clearly, students' encounters with knowledge differ widely because of the happenstance of attending this school or that and because of the choices made available to them in the schools they happen to attend.

If we need a common school to provide a common literacy, a common awareness of our democracy and the responsibility for it, a common understanding of the diversity of our heritages, and a common induction into civilized conversation, we have much to do. First, we must rid ourselves of the dangerous notion that individual differences such as in interests and rate of learning call for significantly differentiated curricula. I am not calling, however, for a curriculum that will be the same in all schools. In *A Place Called School*, I recommend a curriculum balanced among the major fields of knowledge and knowing. Students would have choices in literature or among the visual arts, for example, but the courses offered would be judged *of equal value*. Second, we must come to understand and then act on the fact that the K-12 curriculum represents, for most students, the last and only chance they will have to experience a broad, balanced, and common formal general education. Less than half of those graduating will go on to college. And, for those who do go on to higher education, there is no assurance that they will experience a liberal education. At all levels of the public school system, much attention has been directed to the reduction of major educational goals to specific competencies but little to the question of what is worth knowing and, therefore, worth teaching. This lack of attention and action suggests intellectual bankruptcy in curriculum planning. We talk about getting students into the educational mainstream as though it were both clearly defined and worth getting into. The first of these attributes clearly is missing; the second is debatable, at best.

Misconceptions about Learning and Their Impact on Teaching

Teaching that simply endeavors to pour knowledge into the heads of students is based on false premises; teaching must assist students in deriving meanings from and about phenomena. But these conceptions of learning, education, and teaching are not the ones most dominant in the actual conduct of schools. Indeed, the nature and arrangement of topics to be covered in the grades, laid out in textbooks, and included in achievement tests consistently reflect the empty vessel theory so routinely rejected in enlightened educational dialogue and so venerated in practice.

Even though most teachers reject the image of passive students patiently having their vessels filled up and are familiar with a variety of teaching modes, study after study reveals the dominance of telling, lecturing, and questioning the class and monitoring seatwork. Skillfully varying teaching techniques and individualizing time allocations are virtually the only ways available to teachers for meeting the admittedly large range in individual differences and aptitude for learning. Regardless of considerable contrary rhetoric, we do not yet know enough about the varied ways humans learn to warrant a science of teaching specifically addressed to such variations. But we do know that differences in both the nature of what is to be learned and the ways learning occurs necessitate a broad and varied repertoire of teaching techniques: lecturing, demonstrating, coaching, tutoring, symbolically representing, role playing, and more.

Ironically, in seeking to cope with individual differences, particularly at the secondary level, educators have relied heavily on differentiating the curriculum. What they should have been concentrating on is the creation of settings for learning offering the widest possible array of ways for students to acquire understandings or skills. The guiding admonition to teachers should be: Exercise great caution in varying the curriculum to meet individual differences but be as creative as possible in varying the ways of teaching and the modes of learning.

Misconceptions about Individual Differences

Recognizing cultural or individual differences is accompanied by value judgments. The more noticeable the differences—in language, skin color, gender, dress, and economic advantage—the more likely are negative comparisons. The influx of immigrants, early in this century, speaking languages other than English, was accompanied by fear on the part of English-speaking settlers that the culture would be watered down. The use of the Binet test by H. H.

Goddard at Ellis Island led him to the bizarre conclusion that large percentages of the foreign-speaking immigrant population were feeble minded. [16] This kind of thinking accompanies the myth that native Americans and blacks are intellectually inferior.

The advent of near-universal schooling, and the equating of education with schooling, contributed significantly to misunderstanding about individual differences in learning and about different kinds of intelligence. To be intelligent frequently was equated with doing well in school. School, in turn, valued and rewarded boys and girls who took readily to the language-oriented abstractions of schooling. Hand-oriented children, including the artistically gifted, not only found little in school to accommodate their learning styles but also often experienced repression of their gifts and talents.

The school's general failure to provide for, let alone capitalize on, different kinds of intelligence and styles of learning resulted in clearly prejudicial practices. Children most needing the enrichment of early childhood education were denied admission to kindergarten because they failed to make the necessary score on standardized tests. [17] Grade failure of boys, with accompanying labeling as failures in the primary grades, exceeded grade retention of girls by two or three times. Children not admitted to kindergarten or retained for another year at grade level were disproportionately from low economic and minority groups. These practices, and others like them, are still evident in schools today.

In effect, many school practices reflect rather than compensate for shortcomings in the conventional wisdom of many adults. Professional preparation is intended to provide those who complete it, and are certified or licensed, with understandings likely to counteract and overcome these social disparities. Clearly, increased professionalization of schoolteachers and administrators has not yet removed the barriers to learning resulting from long-standing, outmoded practices in our schools.

Organizational Arrangements in Schools

Nowhere in schooling is this generalization about schools reflecting social shortcomings more applicable than in the grouping and tracking practices commonly found in schools. And perhaps nowhere else in schooling are the negative, prejudicial consequences for access to knowledge so clear and so severe.

The patterns are readily discernible and are, regrettably, more the rule than the exception. For at least two generations, first-grade children have been organized into subgroups, usually three, for reading and some other subjects, each group presumed to be differentiated from the others on estimates of "ability." However, since these estimates are made early in the year and since there is much confusion in the field regarding the difference between ability and achievement, the estimates once again reflect home and family circumstances, especially the level of schooling attained by mothers and fathers. Poor and minority children are disproportionately represented in the low groups. Children in the lowest groups rarely are moved to the highest groups; the disparity between the attainment of the highest and lowest groups grows greater over time.

Teachers in junior and senior high school are dismayed by the enormous range in academic achievement presented by their students. They usually resort, not surprisingly, to tracking—the separation of students into curricular patterns wherein the courses taken by different students vary widely in expectations, teacher enthusiasm, methods of teaching, classroom ambience, and content.[18] Most senior high schools are characterized, also, by a rather sharp division into a vocationally oriented curriculum and an academically oriented curriculum with a further division into the tracks just scribed. Students in the lowest tracks and the vocationally oriented curriculum are disproportionately poor and disproportionately from racial minority groups.

Teachers of the upper tracks tend to prefer this arrangement. They derive support from those parents in the community who see their self-interests best served by a tracked school. Reasons for this system frequently are argued as common sense; contrary research findings are pushed aside. Arguments for mixed groupings are rejected as impractical, as not confronting the reality of the range of individual differences in talent and achievement.

Clearly, large numbers of children and youth are denied access to knowledge reserved for those who take readily to the customs and regularities of schooling. These customs and regularities, in turn, are advantageous for students whose backgrounds prepare them for and support them in what schools do. Under these circumstances, the kinds of arguments based on research not favorable to tracking fade in relative importance to moral arguments. It simply is immoral for schools to perpetuate practices that clearly discriminate against poor children, many of whom also are from minority groups. Unless schools rid themselves of these practices, the courts will become the point of recourse for those seeking equitable treatment in schools. Although legal action may still become necessary, it will be, to a degree, unfortunate since court decisions might well outlaw those thoughtful processes of meeting individual differences that are not discriminatory. The courts often are unable to make the subtle distinctions called for in addressing schooling wrongs.

The Education of Educators

The foregoing sample of ways in which the school's role in providing equitably for its clientele is corrupted reflects, in large measure, some questionable assumptions about the mission of our schools and, indeed, about the nature of education. The instructional, curricular, and organizational shortcomings enumerated above are symptoms of these questionable assumptions. The shortcomings result from both omission and commission.

Omission occurs in what we largely leave out of teacher education programs. First, the part of teacher education believed to have the most impact is student teaching wherein, almost always, the future teacher is assigned to an experienced teacher and inducted into practice. In effect, the student learns the established ways of schooling even though many of these ways are under severe attack and lack a defensible knowledge base. If we set out to erect a system designed to keep things the way they are, it would be difficult to improve on how most teachers are now prepared. Little wonder that teachers teach as they were taught during their years as students in the schools.

Second, serious questions are being raised as to whether the so-called liberal college provides undergraduates, some of them future teachers, with the broad understanding and canons of assessment they need to participate critically in human affairs extending much beyond earning a living.[19] Future teachers get a modest introduction to the history of our educational system and to some of the philosophical issues associated with it. One cannot conclude, however, that graduates possess the understandings and tools requisite to enculturating the young into a political democracy and developing in them the necessary moral sensitivities. And, even if they did, it would be necessary to possess extraordinary fortitude in seeking to offset the contrary forces in the social context of schooling.

We are back to where we began—namely, to reinforcing the argument that reform in society and reform in schools must go hand-in-hand. And so, teacher-preparing institutions should be doing everything possible to select future teachers committed to the enculturating role of the common school and the concepts of equity associated with it. These institutions should then develop in teachers the necessary understandings and skills. It is fair to say, I think, that attention in these programs to the implicit attributes is, at best, casual. The shortcomings appear to be more on the order of omission than commission.

Third, the commission extenuating the effects of the omission is the centrality of attention on how to teach rather than on the issues of what and whom to teach. That this emphasis on how is conducted badly and needs to be improved sidesteps the issue of whether sufficient attention is given to first questions. My conclusion is that *most* teachers begin their teaching preoccupied with questions of what to do in the classroom today and tomorrow and think scarcely at all about what the school in which they teach is for, their responsibilities to children as moral beings, or the conflicts and incongruencies among their varied relationships to child, parent, and state. It is most unlikely that so-called staff development activities in which they will engage in subsequent years will do much or anything to change their preoccupation with what works. And the voice of the teaching profession on the

moral issues of schooling, including such matters as the right to learn and
the right to equal access to knowledge, is almost mute.

One need only study the preparation programs of school administrators
to see how preoccupation with what works and neglect of central educational
issues extends upward into the professional orientation of superintendents.
And, in spite of recent exhortations regarding the central role of the principal
in school improvement, the emphasis in training programs, both pre-service
and in-service, is on process, not the substance of schooling, let alone the
issues raised here. Administrators like to be referred to as leaders, but they
often are hopelessly caught up in the values and routines of management.
Many tell me that they have little or no discretionary time and that such
discretionary time as is available goes to things other than reading and
thinking about the enterprise that is their life's work.

In some fields, this need to bring a more reflective, inquiring mode into
action-oriented human endeavors is being accommodated through collaboration between practitioners and researchers. Agriculture, engineering, and
urban planning provide examples of professional schools in universities effectively and appropriately connected with practice. A similar joining of
schools and schools of education could appear to be rather natural. But the
Review Committee for Education of the University of California found little
of this kind of collaboration on the several campuses, and few incentives for
faculty members to become involved beyond using schools to provide human
subjects for research, which usually is published in journals not readily
accessible to practitioners.[20]

There is now a considerable store of research on the issues addressed
here, most of it undertaken by university professors. But neither the processes
nor the outcomes connect very meaningfully with educational practice in
schools.[21] Consequently, my colleagues and I have been promoting for several
years an intensive collaboration in the form of school–university partnerships,
with a view to bringing the real problems of the schools into the purview of
university professors and the deliberative processes of the universities into
the culture of practitioners.[22] One of our hopes is that the preparation
programs of both teachers and administrators will be fundamentally redesigned.

It is evident that the spotlight on educational reform has broadened
beyond schools to include the education of educators. This was the sequence,
too, in the cycle of attention to educational reform following the launching
of Sputnik in 1957. But past preoccupation with teacher education has
repeatedly exposed the same problems and posed the same solutions,[23]
suggesting the hypothesis that the necessary changes have not occurred.
Extrapolating from the past, one can be only cautiously optimistic. There are
signs, nonetheless, that the teacher education community is acutely sensitive
to the need for reform.[24] There is some awareness that preparing teachers for
the changing problems of our schools complicates teacher education pro-

cesses, but the full magnitude of the efforts required has not yet been grasped by either educators or the general public.

Addressing the Agenda

The agenda for gaining equal access to schools has been driven largely by court actions and seriously hampered by housing patterns. The solutions have been essentially noneducational, even though school districts have been at the center largely because of tensions surrounding the busing issue.

Although the courts may very well enter into the agenda regarding access to knowledge, such as in regard to tracking, the legal course is a slippery one. It can be argued, for example, that there is no point in students gaining access to what they do not understand, that it is inhumane to expose slow-learning students to repeated failure. Such an argument sidesteps, of course, the school's responsibility to prevent annual deficits in learning and to provide the varied institutional procedures, emotional support, and time required by slower students. Laws against discriminatory arrangements in schools are not likely to put an end to them; too many subtle ways to subvert such laws are available. And laws are unlikely to increase understanding of human learning and sound educational concepts, change attitudes and values, and develop moral sensitivities pertaining to human rights.

These limitations on the role of the courts aside, it is helpful for the public and school people to understand that the present, general laws of the land imply equal access not only to schools but to the education schools are supposed to provide. Further, state documents on schooling almost always include the concept of equity in some form and admonish school boards and educators to eschew practices likely to discriminate against students because of their race, ethnicity, or religion. This kind of legal, ethical, and moral framework provides educators with the justification they need for pursuing rigorously every avenue likely to make knowledge equitably available in schools.

The importance of the issues and the seriousness of the problems necessitate taking action in schools even *before* the attitudes and values of the community reflect the spirit of the laws of the land and the directives of state and local education authorities. In effect, school personnel are obliged to eliminate whatever arrangements and practices serve as barriers to access to knowledge and replace these with arrangements deemed more equitable. In a comprehensive study of schools most effectively desegregating and subsequently integrating, the researchers discovered consistent adherence to policies and practices reflecting the above obligation.[25] The schools did not wait for teachers to change their values and attitudes; they simply did not tolerate discriminatory behavior.

The individual school, then, is the center of attention and change. The principal and the teachers take responsibility for translating the meanings of equal access to knowledge for all into the entire culture of the school. Doing so requires a considerable amount of dialogue about what equity means, what practices deny equal access, and what practices promote it. Then, a plan of action must be devised that deliberately sets out the steps to be taken and the kinds of assessments deemed necessary to the evaluation of progress.[26] It is essential that the principal and teachers be joined in all phases by students and parents. The IDEA organization, with headquarters in Dayton, Ohio, has developed and refined a useful process of collaboration based on research, development, and a good deal of experience with schools and school districts.

The concept of the school as the center of change must not be interpreted to mean that the school can do alone what is necessary.[27] The school exists as part of a larger ecosystem that often hampers the school's efforts to become a renewing culture in which the very best educational and social values permeate daily life. The 1987 Yearbook (Part 1) of the National Society for the Study of Education addresses the requirements of a supportive infrastructure involving the surrounding community, the district office, colleges and universities, and the several divisions of state educational governance and leadership. What Calvin Frazier writes about these requirements is particularly relevant to gaining full equity with respect to access to knowledge, perhaps the most compelling educational issue of this century:

> The opportunity now exists for states and the education community to fashion a collaborative arrangement that will enhance American education for the remainder of this century. It is a time for selflessness and a willingness to forgo those elements geared to enhance or protect any one group. . . . [28]

It is a time for self-interest and the common weal to join in assuring us that all schools educate uncommonly for a common understanding of our heritages and full participation in a democratic society.

Notes

1. Ralph W. Tyler, "Marginality in Schools," foreword to Robert L. Sinclair and Ward J. Ghory, *Reaching Marginal Students* (Berkeley, Calif.: McCutchan, 1987), xii.
2. James B. Conant, *Slums and Suburbs* (New York: McGraw-Hill, 1961), 8.
3. L. Scott Miller, "Nation Building and Education," *Education Week* 5 (May 14, 1986): 42, 52.
4. National Governors' Association, *Time for Results: The Governors' 1991 Report on Education* (Washington, D.C.: National Governors' Association, 1986).
5. Bernard R. Gifford, "Prestige and Education: The Missing Link in School Reform," *The Review of Education* 10, (Summer 1984): 186–189.
6. James M. Perry, "An Ocean Apart," *The Wall Street Journal* 116 (June 3, 1987): 1, 24.

7. George S. Counts, *The Selective Character of American Secondary Education* (Chicago: University of Chicago Press, 1922), 156.

8. Diane Ravitch, "Where Have All the Classics Gone? You Won't Find Them in Primers," *New York Times Book Review*, May 17, 1987, 46.

9. Allan Bloom, *The Closing of the American Mind* (New York: Simon and Schuster, 1987).

10. Irwin Edman, *Arts and the Man* (New York: Norton, 1928), 15.

11. John I. Goodlad, "Equality of Educational Opportunity: A Values Perspective," in *Equality of Opportunity Reconsidered: Values in Education for Tomorrow*, ed. M. Dino Carelli and John G. Morris (Hamburg: UNESCO Institute for Education, 1979), 23–41.

12. Robert L. Sinclair and Ward J. Ghory, *Last Things First*, this volume, chapter 7.

13. John I. Goodlad and Robert H. Anderson, *The Nongraded Elementary School* (New York: Harcourt Brace Jovanovich, 1963; reprinted with a new Introduction, New York: Teachers College Press, 1987).

14. John I. Goodlad, *A Place Called School: Prospects for the Future* (New York: McGraw-Hill, 1984), 198–204.

15. Arthur G. Powell, E. Farrar, and D. K. Cohen, *The Shopping Mall High School* (Boston: Houghton Mifflin, 1985).

16. Thomas K. Gilhool, "From the Education of All Handicapped Children to the Effective Education of Every Child," unpublished manuscript, 1984.

17. John I. Goodlad, "When to Begin: Dimensions of the First Grade Entrance Age Problem," *Childhood Education* 32 (September 1955): 21–28.

18. Jeannie Oakes, *Keeping Track: How Schools Structure Inequality* (New Haven: Yale University Press, 1985).

19. Ernest L. Boyer, *College: The Undergraduate Experience in America* (New York: Harper and Row, 1987).

20. Review Committee on Education, *The Role of the University of California in Precollegiate Education* (Berkeley, Calif.: University of California, 1984), 27.

21. An array of related issues has been presented by Theodore R. Sizer, *High School Reform and the Reform of Teacher Education*, Ninth Annual DeGarmo Lecture, Society of Professors of Education, University of Minnesota, Minneapolis, 1984.

22. Kenneth A. Sirotnik and John I. Goodlad, eds., *School–University Partnerships in Action: Concepts, Cases, and Concerns* (New York: Teachers College Press, 1988).

23. Su Zhixin, *Teacher Education Reform In the United States, 1890–1986*, Occasional Paper No. 3, Center for Educational Renewal, College of Education, University of Washington, Seattle, 1986.

24. See such reports as California Commission on the Teaching Profession, *Who Will Teach Our Children?* (Sacramento, Calif.: The Commission, 1985); Holmes Group, *Tomorrow's Teachers* (East Lansing, Mich.: Author, 1986); National Commission on Excellence in Teacher Education, *A Call for Change in Teacher Education* (Washington, D.C.: American Association of Colleges for Teacher Education, 1985); Task Force on Teaching as a Profession, *A Nation Prepared: Teachers for the 21st Century* (New York: Carnegie Forum on Education and the Economy, 1986).

25. Garlie A. Forehand and Marjorie Ragosta, *A Handbook for Integrated Schooling* (Washington, D.C.: Department of Health, Education, and Welfare, 1976).

26. For a description of the processes and their use in 18 schools, see Mary M.

Bentzen, *Changing Schools: The Magic Feather Principle* (New York: McGraw-Hill, 1974); and John I. Goodlad, *The Dynamics of Educational Change* (New York: McGraw-Hill, 1975).
27. Kenneth A. Sirotnik, "The School as the Center of Change," paper for the Southwestern Bell Invitational Conference, *Restructuring Schooling for Quality Education: A New Reform Agenda*, The Brackenridge Forum for the Enhancement of Teaching, Trinity University, San Antonio, Texas, August 18–20, 1987.
28. Calvin M. Frazier, "The 1980s: States Assume Educational Leadership," in *The Ecology of School Renewal*, ed. John I. Goodlad, Eighty-sixth Yearbook, Part 1, National Society for the Study of Education (Chicago: University of Chicago Press, 1987), 99–117.

Selected References

Bentzen, Mary M. *Changing Schools: The Magic Feather Principle*. New York: McGraw-Hill, 1974.

Bloom, Allan. *The Closing of the American Mind*. New York: Simon and Schuster, 1987.

Boyer, Ernest L. *College: The Undergraduate Experience in America*. New York: Harper and Row, 1987.

Conant, James B. *Slums and Suburbs*. New York: McGraw-Hill, 1961.

Counts, George S. *The Selective Character of American Secondary Education*. Chicago: University of Chicago Press, 1922.

Edman, Irwin. *Arts and the Man*. New York: Norton, 1928.

Forehand, Garlie A., and Marjorie Ragosta. *A Handbook for Integrated Schooling*. Washington, D.C.: Department of Health, Education, and Welfare, 1976.

Frazier, Calvin M. "The 1980s: States Assume Educational Leadership." In *The Ecology of School Renewal*, edited by John I. Goodlad, Eighty-sixth Yearbook, Part 1, National Society for the Study of Education, 99–117. Chicago: University of Chicago Press, 1987.

Gifford, Bernard R. "Prestige and Education: The Missing Link in School Reform." *The Review of Education* 10 (Summer 1984): 186–189.

Gilhool, Thomas K. "From the Education of All Handicapped Children to the Effective Education of Every Child," unpublished, 1984.

Goodlad, John I. "When to Begin: Dimensions of the First Grade Entrance Age Problem." *Childhood Education* 32 (September 1955): 21–28.

Goodlad, John I. *The Dynamics of Educational Change*. New York: McGraw-Hill, 1975.

Goodlad, John I. "Equality of Educational Opportunity: A Values Perspective." In *Equality of Opportunity Reconsidered: Values in Education for Tomorrow*, edited by M. Dino Carelli and John G. Morris, 23–41. Hamburg: UNESCO Institute for Education, 1979.

Goodlad, John I. *A Place Called School: Prospects for the Future*. New York: McGraw-Hill, 1984.

Goodlad, John, I., and Robert H. Anderson. *The Nongraded Elementary School*. New York: Harcourt Brace Jovanovich, 1963; reprinted with a new Introduction, New York: Teachers College Press, 1987.

Miller, L. Scott. "Nation Building and Education." *Education Week* 5 (May 14, 1986): 42, 52.

National Governors' Association. *Time for Results: The Governors' 1991 Report on Education.* Washington, D.C., 1986.

Oakes, Jeannie. *Keeping Track: How Schools Structure Inequality.* New Haven: Yale University Press, 1985.

Perry, James M. "An Ocean Apart." *The Wall Street Journal* 116 (June 3, 1987): 1, 24.

Powell, Arthur G., E. Farrar, and D. K. Cohen. *The Shopping Mall High School.* Boston: Houghton Mifflin, 1985.

Ravitch, Diane. "Where Have All the Classics Gone? You Won't Find Them in Primers." *New York Times Book Review,* May 17, 1987, 46.

Review Committee on Education. *The Role of the University of California in Precollegiate Education.* Berkeley, Calif.: University of California, 1984.

Sinclair, Robert L., and Ward J. Ghory. *Last Things First,* this volume, chapter 7.

Sirotnik, Kenneth A., and John I. Goodlad, eds. *School–University Partnerships in Action: Concepts, Cases, and Concerns.* New York: Teachers College Press, 1988.

Sirotnik, Kenneth A. "The School as the Center of Change." Paper for the Southwestern Bell Invitational Conference, *Restructuring Schooling for Quality Education: A New Reform Agenda,* edited by Kenneth A. Sirotnik and John I. Goodlad. The Brackenridge Forum for the Enhancement of Teaching, Trinity University, San Antonio, Texas, August 18–20, 1987.

Sizer, Theodore R. *High School Reform and the Reform of Teacher Education.* Ninth Annual DeGarmo Lecture, Society of Professors of Education. University of Minnesota, Minneapolis, 1984.

Tyler, Ralph W. "Marginality in Schools." Foreword to Robert L. Sinclair and Ward J. Ghory, *Reaching Marginal Students.* Berkeley, Calif.: McCutchan, 1987.

Su, Zhixin. *Teacher Education Reform in the United States (1890–1986),* Occasional Paper No. 3. Center for Educational Renewal, College of Education, University of Washington, Seattle, 1986.

2.

Home, School, and Academic Learning

JAMES P. COMER

Précis

When schools were an integral part of stable communities, teachers quite naturally reinforced parental and community values. At school, children easily formed bonds with adults and experienced a sense of continuity and stability, conditions that were highly conducive to learning. Today a different environment prevails in many areas. Children from low-income families must function under conditions of social disintegration (of neighborhoods, home life, and the family itself). Many suffer stressful racial and ethnic tensions. Instead of developing a sense of belonging, such children may come to believe at an early age that their opportunities are limited and lose their motivation at school.

According to James Comer, one possible solution is for the school to work toward building a stable community for such children. All school personnel should work to establish bonds between students and teachers and between home and school. Comer maintains that each child must be socialized before he or she can be taught; hence the need for students to establish bonds with school staff and for schools to serve as stable, anchoring settings.

To help schools achieve this goal, Comer presents a model that emphasizes the role of nurturance in all human affairs and that uses existing school personnel in new ways. He calls for a school-based governance and management team of 10 to 15 people, led by the principal and including representatives of all the adults in school, from teachers to nonprofessional support staff, as well as a child development specialist such as the school psychologist or social worker, along with parents. Although the team would try to solve existing behavior problems, its main focus would be on *preventing* problems. The point is to consider the needs that children bring to school, rather than just the problems created because the school system is not functioning well. By applying principles for building relationships, the school gradually comes to be regarded by a widening circle of families as a place to be trusted, a place where they can receive help, resulting in dramatic increases in school involvement.

This model was initially applied in two New Haven elementary schools with the lowest academic achievement levels in the city. Today one of the original schools and another in the project are in the city's top five percent in achievement, with no change in the makeup of the student population (which is 99 percent black and poor).

Comer is now extending his research and recommendations to middle schools and high schools.

James P. Comer, M.D., is director of the School Development Program of the Yale Child Study Center at Yale University. He is associate dean of the Yale Medical School, where he is also Maurice Falk Professor of Child Psychiatry.

—The College Board

A first-grade teacher in the New Haven, Connecticut, school system greeted her new students on the first day of school and gave them a general orientation on what to expect, and how to succeed, in the classroom and in the school. A 6-year-old raised his hand, as instructed by his teacher, and said, "Teacher, my mama said I don't have to do anything you say." The incident reflects a problem in the quality of relationships between home and school that interferes with teaching and academic learning. This problem is more widespread than generally acknowledged, is not well understood, and, therefore, is often deplored but receives little effective intervention.

Educators, in general, recognize the importance of parent support for teaching and academic learning but consider it a parental responsibility—something the school cannot do much about. We often limit our responsibility and mission to teaching. We think of learning as the students' responsibility, as something we cannot do much about other than to teach. But effective parental support, teaching, and student learning are an interactive process with delicate interrelationships which must be understood and nurtured—more actively today than 40 years ago when natural conditions created communities that promoted acceptance of mainstream values set among parents, school staff, and students alike.

Severe and expressed difficulties in home–school relationships are a reasonably recent phenomenon, dating from the 1950s. Because there has been a decline in the sense of community everywhere, home–school relationships are more often a problem among all groups. But the problem is most prevalent among families with children at greatest risk for school failure. At the same time, a high quality of relationships between home and school is often the only chance many such children have for finishing school and for leading reasonably successful lives.

In this chapter, I attempt to show how difficult relationships between home and school present a barrier to academic learning for all children, but particularly for low-income children from families under stress and for certain minorities. To do so, I first review learning in the context of development and include certain misapprehensions about how academic learning takes place. Next I consider how scientific and technology-based changes over the past 150 years have changed the nature of community and/or social networks, family functioning, and individual development. I then discuss the way in which the peculiar history of several groups creates potential and real barriers to successful home–school relationships. I close with a discussion of what individual schools and systems—as well as educators and other relevant policymakers—can do to promote desirable home–school relationships.

Academic Learning and Development

Interest in, some of the capacity for, and all the motivation for learning academic material is a function of social relationships and overall develop-

men[...] biological potential for learning can be realized
or s[...] uality of relationships the child experiences in
the [...] network, in school, and in social networks of the
larg[...] anding development in these several social context[...]

The basic task of all human beings is to provide for themselves and their families. In modern society this is most easily made possible by acquiring education and training and, as a result, qualifying for a job or career that permits the individual to satisfy fundamental needs and experience the sense of well-being associated with being able to do so. This increases the individual's potential for living successfully in a family, being motivated to rear his or her children well, and serving as a responsible member of a community and the larger society. Never before in the history of the world has academic or formal education been so necessary for individuals to meet basic human needs; thus never before has the kind of development that facilitates academic learning been so important to understand and promote.

Children are not born with the fully developed capacity to acquire academic learning or to meet any of their adult tasks. They are born totally dependent and will die without the care and attention of mature, responsible adults. They are born with a set of biological potentials which must be developed. Their aggressive or survival energy must be chaneled into the constructive energy of work and play, or it can become harmful to them and to the people around them. They are born with the capacity to form a relationship with others which must be promoted by their caretakers. As parents care for children, an emotional bonding takes place between them which enables parents to aid child growth and development along multiple developmental pathways. The experience of this first relationship is the template for all future relationships.

There are many developmental pathways, but at least five are critical to facilitate adequate future academic learning: social-interactive, psycho-emotional-affective, moral, speech and language, and intellectual-cognitive. The last-named most directly facilitates school or academic learning. Academic learning is, in large part, a function of the quality of development across all the critical developmental pathways. It is not—as many of our school organization, management, and teaching methods suggest—an isolated cognitive, mechanical procedure. School success is as much a function of development in the social-interactive, psycho-emotional, and moral areas as it is a function of development in the speech, language, and cognitive development areas.

Caretakers and parents, without being self-consciously aware of it, are members of primary social networks made up of extended families, friends, and institutions selected by them, and more or less accepting of them. Each primary social network has a set of attitudes, values, and ways of behaving (or culture). Parents transmit these attitudes, values, and behaviors to their children in the process of rearing them. The young child accepts and receives the culture of the parent's social network with even less self-consciousness. With no "road map" or previous experience to guide his or her actions—and driven to action by biological imperatives—a child imitates, identifies with, and finally internalizes the attitudes, values, and actions of the primary caretakers. Because this process takes place in the absence of previous experience and knowledge, it is extremely powerful. It shapes personality development as well as lifelong style and behavior.

Parental Interaction

Mainstream parents read to their children and take them on trips which promote and stimulate their curiosity—to the circus, zoos, museums, theatrical programs, and so on. They usually talk to the children about what they are experiencing, clarify misconceptions, and help them understand more and more about the environment around them. Even in everyday activities— shopping at the supermarket, playing, watching television, and so on— mainstream parents often promote learning. They usually reward learning through appreciation and approval (as opposed to a great deal of criticism and punitive behavior). Misconceptions and errors are viewed as natural and necessary aspects of learning and not as a basis for ridicule or low expectations. This general approach encourages the child to explore and take the chance of being wrong without fear. It eventually leads to confident and competent learners willing to take chances to learn more and more. Such children eventually develop rich and vast experiences and knowledge prior to entering school.

As mainstream parents interact with their children, they also model and promote social and interactive behavior that is considered acceptable in school and other mainstream institutions. These children are taught to say, "Good morning," "Thank you," and "Please," as well as all the other niceties of social interaction. They are taught the rules and understandings of the mainstream game of life. They are taught to negotiate to have their needs and rights met, and to fight only as a last resort, and when there is cause. They are taught to delay immediate gratification in order to achieve longer-range goals. They are encouraged and supported in doing so—again, more often through clear statements of expectations and approval than by punishment.

The power of parents in establishing desirable behavior is often greatly underestimated. Thus children do not want to anger and "lose" parents—the only protection they have—as they traverse unfamiliar territory. The young child, unlike most adults, does not have a reassuring, successful record of task completion.

The child also picks up the social network culture—a powerful influence on behavior—from the parents. In religious experiences of one kind or another the child develops a belief system and is often taught to be reflective and thoughtful, and to meditate about the nature and purpose of life and his or her role in society. The celebrations, concerns, and causes embraced by members of this social network are often eventually internalized by the growing child. The perceptions of social network members about themselves, their group, and other groups are also internalized by the child. And, most important, the attitudes about learning or education, and its relevance to their lives and future, are internalized by the child.

I am not suggesting that the destiny of a child is determined entirely by the first few years of life. Most children gain developmental experience that will permit them to function adequately in school even when they are from social networks different from that of the school. Nonetheless, it should be obvious that children who grow up in social networks with attitudes, values, and ways of behaving closest to those of the school are best prepared to meet the expectations of the school. Extreme differences and poorly functioning schools pose the greatest problem.[1]

Unfortunately, many social and behavioral scientists have labeled mainstream behavior as middle class, as if it is inherent only in certain groups, particularly middle-income, well-educated people, and only certain minorities. The confusion leads many to suggest that behaviors that lead to school failure are desired by, even genetically determined by, individuals who display them. Mainstream behavior is necessary to permit respectful interactions among individuals as children, and as adults. It promotes a level of development and kind of behavior needed to function well in this complex scientific and technology-based postindustrial society, as opposed to the past agricultural and early industrial age society. Among every income, racial, and ethnic group, such behavior is *more often* found in individuals who succeed in school. I have deliberately used the term "mainstream" in describing the average expected developmental experience, as opposed to middle-class and middle-income, to emphasize this point.

There is also a widespread notion that nonmainstream behaviors are not modifiable and are willfully engaged in as a deliberate fashion of rejection, without cause; that these are desired, even cultural or racial, norms. The confusion between what are class, racial, and ethnic issues and behaviors and what are developmentally determined behaviors and issues often leads to the charge that institutions dominated by the middle class impose their attitudes, values, and ways on helpless persons from other classes, with the implication that that's not right.[2] The outcome of such a perception, however—and in some cases the motive—is that by not helping children develop well, and gain mainstream skills, schools serve to lock them into poorly functioning networks with limited future economic opportunities, and to limit their opportunities to master adult tasks.

On the other hand, ethnic and racial differences do exist. But these differences are largely in the context of experiences, style, and expression.

They do not preclude developmental experiences that will promote academic achievement. Much behavior that is called "cultural" or "racial" (as if it were deliberately created within a group or genetically determined) is really the consequence of past and present public policy that denied some groups political, social, economic, and educational opportunities in the mainstream of the society. For historical reasons to be discussed here briefly (and because of cultural differences), the social networks in which some children grow up vary from the mainstream social network the school represents—from marginal variance all the way to antisocial, chaotic behavior reflective of major social disintegration.

Unresolved differences between families and children in the spectrum of social networks and the people and expectations in the school constitute formidable barriers to school success. The inability of schools—for whatever reason—to adjust and facilitate the achievement of children from social networks that are different puts the final nail in the coffin of academic and life success for too many such children.

Most families in nonmainstream social networks care deeply about their children but do not take them on trips that promote and stimulate their curiosity. Some do not talk a great deal to their children about what they are experiencing or attempt to clarify misconceptions. The children often learn from other children and other immature persons around them. Some parents see no benefit in helping their children learn to manage their everyday environment. Many children are not taught the social niceties, manners, or interaction skills necessary to function well with other children and adults in or out of their own social network. And some children grow up in families in which their lives and their causes are not celebrated and emphasized—in some cases they are a source of despair and hopelessness. Parents cannot serve as models of hope, confidence, and competence; nonetheless, they want their children to succeed in school and in life.

Many nonmainstream children enter school without having mastered the skills and behavior necessary for academic success. Some fight because they do not have negotiation skills. Some are unable to control their impulses, sit still at the appropriate time, show spontaneity and curiosity at the right time and in acceptable ways, or display the discipline necessary to invest in a learning task. They often have skills and are curious about things that may lead to success outside school, but that lead to failure in school. Some children have not learned to use language well. Some have never used scissors and other materials they are expected to use in school. And, as a result of this lack of preparation, these children present themselves to the school in such a way that they are viewed as "bad" or "dumb."

Our cultural or societal response is to punish badness and to have low academic expectations for children who do not appear to be highly intelligent. Healthy children can respond to school life in troublesome ways. They often act up and act out even more, attempting to control the teacher or the class, in the long run provoking more punitive responses. Children expected to show low academic performance will often do so. Even children from backgrounds where they have received a great deal of support need continued support in school in order to perform in a confident and competent fashion.

When the staff view children as bad or as having limited potential—or view parents as uncaring or incompetent—it is difficult for the kind of positive emotional bonding to take place between student and teacher that is needed to promote optimal academic learning. It is not possible for parents to support the work of the school. And because of class, racial, and other struggles over the years—and the fact that people no longer completely accept the authority of teachers and other leaders—difficult interactions and reactions cause or intensify antagonism between home and school. This kind of attitude and behavior can be seen in the words of the mother who told her 6-year-old son that he did not have to do anything the teacher wanted him to do.

Positive bonding is needed for the child to imitate, identify with, and internalize the attitudes, values, and ways of the teacher and the school. It is this relationship process that gives positive meaning to academic learning, that motivates the child to sustain interest in abstract materials that are not inherently interesting or immediately useful. After all, what is the difference between a scribble and a letter of the alphabet to a child? The only reason the letter of the alphabet is meaningful to the child, and worth learning and remembering, is because a meaningful "other" wants him or her to do so.

Because children under 8 or 9 years of age are easily influenced by adults—note that the 6-year-old quoted above raised his hand, as instructed by his teacher, to say that he didn't have to listen—they accept the authority and leadership of important adults around them. For this reason teachers are able to help many children who are underdeveloped make significant progress in the first two or three years of school. But around age 8 or 9, two developmental conditions begin to erode the ability of teachers to do so.

Cognitive development reaches a stage that enables the child to understand that he or she is different in some ways from the staff in school, sometimes from other children. Their feelings about themselves and other people then become an issue they must struggle with. "Do they like me?" "Do I belong here?" "Do I have a right to be here?" The answers depend a great deal on the quality of relationships between home and school, teacher and student. Also, around second or third grade the level of abstract thinking required to be successful in school increases. Children who have not had the kind of developmental experiences that will enable them to continue to achieve at this higher level of expectation will now have more academic difficulty.

The combination of increased academic difficulty and questionable or difficult relationships forces the child to begin to choose between the culture of the school and the culture of the social network. Parents, home, and the social network are the source of the child's self-affirmation, much more important than the people and culture of the school. At this point—without unusual intellect, talent, or other circumstances—many children begin to drift away from the culture of the school, even before they leave physically. This process is hastened by the developmental need to begin emotional separation from adults in late preadolescence and early adolescence. Many children are then set adrift without the kind of relationship experiences and support they need and without the kind of internalized value set that will lead to continued desirable academic and social performance, achievement in and graduation from secondary school, and reasonable opportunities in life.

More troublesome negative forces outside the marginal and mainstream social network often become attractive to young people seeking to belong and develop personal adequacy and actualization. Involvement in the drug culture, teenage pregnancy, delinquency, and crime increase and become more attractive possibilities as the probability of school and mainstream success fades. This troublesome course is more likely today than before the 1950s.

Scientific and Technological Changes

Academic learning problems were not pressing social or economic issues prior to the 1960s. Most heads of households could find work, or otherwise provide for themselves and their families, and meet all their adult responsibilities without a high level of individual development and formal education. And the nature of community was such that it promoted adequate social and individual development for most individuals. But after World War II, scientific and technological developments began to affect the economy, the nature of community, and the family in a way that has made academic learning necessary; and academic learning problems are our nation's number one social issue. In order to promote adequate academic learning among most students, we must understand better the effects of scientific and technological change and their relationship to individual development and academic learning.

Before World War II, we were a nation of small towns and rural areas, and even the cities were collections of small towns. Transportation was slow, and rapid communication was still limited. Most people worked reasonably close to their homes. Leisure-time activities were usually local and communal—a part of religious or social club activities. Information and stimulation from outside sources did not have great and pervasive impact.

As a result of these conditions, adult authority figures—parents, teachers, employers, religious and community leaders—often interacted with each other in the course of daily activities. A shopping trip, a visit to the post office, and similar errands often brought adults and young people in contact with the powerful people in their family social networks and in the social networks of the larger community. These authority figures were the "source of all truth" and more or less in agreement—or unable to fully express disagreement and effect change. Under these conditions the most powerful leaders were able to establish the expectations of, and one's "place" in, a community.

The "place" of various groups was often unfairly limited. But at the same time, the clear expectations and sense of place also provided most people with a predictable social environment, a sense of belonging, and community. These conditions permitted neighbors and friends to share the responsibility of helping children grow and perform as the community expected.

The school was a natural part of the community, and of the past, and as such, a beneficiary of the authority of the home and community. And the nature of community usually promoted behaviors that were acceptable in school. At the same time, the "place" of particular children and families provided or limited their motivation for education. Thus many children did not receive the preparation and motivation to achieve well academically and to finish school. But most such children did not act up and act out in school in troublesome ways. They simply left when it was possible. And again, it was not a problem, because the agricultural economy through the turn of the century and industrial development through the 1950s could absorb such dropouts.

After World War II, however, education increasingly became the ticket of admission to a job paying a "living wage," or to the primary job market, whether the position truly required an education or not. And since the late 1970s job opportunities more often require formal academic skills. In addition, modern jobs require a higher level of social and interaction skills, psychological development, and a higher level of thinking skills. Educators adjusted the curriculum to scientific and technological changes. And recently a great deal of attention has been given to teaching strategies and student achievement standards. But there has been an inadequate response by educators to the massive changes in relationships that science and technology wrought, decreasing the ability of many families and school staffs to support the education of children. Raising and enforcing higher standards—without a concomitant response to relationship conditions—can increase achievement test scores without significantly improving higher-level academic learning, school completion, and future life functioning among young people. A brief review of the changed relationships in the society after World War II is needed here.

After the 1940s we became a nation of metropolitan areas. Modern transportation made it possible for people to live long distances from where they worked. Leisure-time activities are now more often distant and less often communal than in the past. Television brings massive amounts of information, numerous images, attitudes, values, and ways of behaving from around the world directly to children. All these conditions serve to decrease the power of, trust toward, and agreement among authority figures. Young people often observe attitudes, values, and behaviors that are different from those their parents are trying to promote.

In many ways these conditions are liberating in that the will of the most powerful authority figures cannot be imposed on all as easily as in the past. On the other hand, the security of a predictable social environment, a sense of place and of community has been lost. And school is no longer a natural part of the community with an automatic transfer of authority from parents to school people. The changed conditions permit distrust and alienation, and their expression. This makes it more difficult for neighbors, friends, and even kin to share the responsibility of helping children grow and perform adequately at home and at school.

But although the world of the child is more complex than ever before, children are no more mature than they ever were. They are in greater need of interactions with mature, emotionally meaningful adults who can help them manage, integrate, and use the complex knowledge and information they receive into their developing psyches. But because of changed community relationships, they have fewer such interactions. The changed conditions of community and society have put more stress on families, in turn, more often weakening their structure and functioning, further reducing the support that children need for overall growth and development and academic learning.

Students from low-income families—more often experiencing economic and other stresses—are more adversely affected under these circumstances. And although all children benefit from positive social relationships, children from families under greater stress are least likely to develop fully and achieve at an adequate academic level without significant parent–school collaboration. A disproportionate number of such children are from families and groups who had an atypical and more traumatic historical experience in this country. And at the same time, the obstacles to home–school collaboration are greatest among these groups.

Today, in a postindustrial society, young people without academic credentials, higher-order thinking skills, and good interpersonal skills are less able to participate in the primary job market. Opportunities in the secondary job market less often enable people to take care of themselves and their families and meet other adult tasks. Thus students who drop out of school are more likely to be on a downhill course in life and to contribute to the social problems in our society.

Group Experience and Academic Learning

Heads of households are expected to work, care for themselves and their families, experience the well-being related to being able to do so, and be motivated to be responsible childrearers, citizens of the community and society. Thus it is critical that most people be able to participate in the primary job market of the economy or otherwise earn a "living wage." Most immigrant groups in America underwent three generations of development that roughly paralleled stages in the economy of this country—agricultural prior to 1900, heavy industrial through the 1940s, late and postindustrial through the 1980s. Most groups experienced a reasonably high degree of cultural continuity in the transition from the old country to the new. Many retained the same religion, used the same language, moved from the same place, and lived together in the new country until they were assimilated. This experience promoted cultural and social cohesion, and facilitated family functioning.

In addition, most were able to vote almost immediately. This participation enabled the groups to gain political, economic, and social power and opportunity in the mainstream of the society within one generation. These experiences, and the community conditions described above, facilitated desirable family functioning and promoted an interest in academic learning among many immigrant families. Because massive immigration occurred before 1915, most families could gain mainstream opportunities and develop the dominant lifestyle through participation in an economy that, before 1900, rarely required education or training. The strength of the family unit during that period made it possible for immigrant families to prepare their children for the moderate level of education and training needed between 1900 and World War II, and in turn, for the high level of education and training needed to be competitive in the job market since then. Blacks, Hispanics, and native Americans, in particular, had a different experience. I will describe only the black American situation here.

Blacks experienced extreme cultural discontinuity after arriving in this country. There was a loss of stabilizing cultural institutions and the imposition of a degrading slave culture. Without a protective culture, a significant number of blacks experienced social, and sometimes psychological, trauma. And among a small group, the negative effects were transmitted from generation to generation during slavery and beyond.

After slavery, a strict racial caste system emerged. Most blacks were denied the vote in the eight southern states where they would have had the greatest political power. Without political power, it was impossible to gain economic and social power in the mainstream of the society. Because of the resultant powerlessness, the black community was greatly undereducated during the pre–World War II period when most of America was gaining the education necessary to participate in the last stage of the industrial economy, 1945 to 1980 and beyond. For example, in the nine states that had 80 percent of the black population in the 1930s, four to eight times as much money was spent on the education of a white child as on that of a black child; a disparity of as much as 25 times in areas that were disproportionately black.[3] As late as the mid-1960s, one-half of the endowment of Harvard was equal to more than that of the endowments of all the 100-plus black colleges combined.[4]

Despite the obstacles and adverse conditions blacks experienced, much of the group was protected from extreme ill effects by black churches and the rural, small-town cultures of the pre–1950s. In fact, even though most black families were not able to undergo the three-generational progression of other groups, most did reasonably well, although employed at the bottom of the economy right up to the 1950s. More than 70 percent of all black families were two-parent families as late as the 1950s, and most black communities were safe.[5]

But as education became a "ticket" to the primary job market and agricultural laboring jobs began to decrease, pushing much of the community into urban areas (with consequent cultural dislocation), many families that had once functioned well began to function less well. The loss of church and small-town culture left many with a sense of exclusion and alienation from the mainstream of society. Because blacks had been denied an opportunity to gain political and economic power, even educated blacks were denied opportunities. As a result, blacks lacked the cultural cohesion, powerful institutions and individuals in the mainstream of the society necessary to exert a pull on the attitudes, values, and behaviors of much of the nonmainstream black community. And, after the 1950s, the nonmainstream black community grew at a more rapid rate than the more mainstream community.

When the civil rights movement reached its peak in the 1960s, the nation was already into the last stage of the industrial era. By this time a reasonable opportunity to participate in the mainstream of the society required a high level of education, as well as good social and interpersonal skills. Families traumatized and denied an education in the past were most closed out by the requirements of the primary job market. Many were unable to give their children the preschool experiences needed to prepare them for academic learning. At the same time, the civil rights movement heightened their awareness of, and reaction to, denial and exclusion.

Anger and alienation increased vis-à-vis mainstream institutions and individuals. Thus developed the conditions that led the black youngster discussed previously to announce to his teacher—also black but a mainstream person in a mainstream institution—"My mama said I don't have to do anything you say." Differences of all kinds—income, education, race, style, and class—are all potential barriers to desired home–school relationships. Without a careful and systematic effort to reduce these barriers, they persist and interfere with academic learning.[6]

Reducing Barriers

Understanding the effects of structural change on various groups, communities, families, and education helps us to conceptualize and appreciate the complexity of the home–school relationship problem. Fortunately, it is not necessary to respond to all the past and present factors involved to reduce barriers to desirable home–school relationships. A focus on creating relationships that permit both parents and school staff to promote student growth along the critical developmental pathways provides direction and reduces superficial and harmful interactions. A mechanism is required that recognizes the complexity of both the home and school as social systems, with real and potential problems, and that works to minimize them on a continuing basis and to foster cooperation in the interest of children. The school is one of the most complex social systems in our society.[7] It contains people of mixed interests, ages, abilities, backgrounds, styles, and so on. Its facilities, materials, and supplies must be utilized in an efficient and effective way. At the same time, school staffs, like parents, lack the degree of authority born of their relationships under pre-1940s conditions. This situation often leads to a troubled school environment in which neither staff nor students flourish and parents do not feel welcome.

On the home side of the equation, parents across the socioeconomic spectrum are often apprehensive about, even afraid of, interactions with school people. Many view problems their children have (or might have) in school as negative reflections on their childrearing skills or as signs of future difficulty for their children. Parents under stress are often having difficulties in other areas of their life, sometimes feeling like failures, and a child's difficulty in school represents another failure. Some parents avoid school because they had trouble in and bad memories about it themselves. And often parents are called to school only when their children are in difficulty. Many low-income parents send their children to school with mixed feelings— hoping the school will provide them with skills and a better opportunity, but believing that school people will not do so and, in fact, have no interest in doing so. Moreover, school failure is much more problematic today than ever before.

Again, without positive parent–staff interactions, students who are underdeveloped, or most different from the school culture in style and interest, are least likely to receive the preparation and support needed for bonding, imitation, identification, and internalization of the attitudes, values, and ways of school people, adequate overall development, and the resultant desired level of academic learning. Yet trust of and affection for school staff is not automatic. Thus the home–school interface is highly charged emotionally.

Schools—more than parents—are in a position to create the conditions needed to overcome difficult relationship barriers.[8] School staffs can be motivated to do so when they fully understand the connection between home–school relationships, child development, and learning. They are further motivated to do so when mechanisms are in place that permit them to work closely with parents while enhancing, not losing, their status or power. Adjustments in organization, structure, and management based on knowledge about child development, human behavior, and social systems can create conditions which minimize relationship barriers and promote student development.[9]

School-Based Management

First, a mechanism is needed to facilitate cooperative interactions between all the players—at home and at school.[10] Programs must be coordinated and the facilities, materials, and supplies utilized in a way that promotes trust between home and school, among school staff, and between staff and students. The school must make a conscious effort to create a social climate, or ethos, in which parents feel not only welcome, but needed. A school-based governance and management team—with input and support from a group representing all parents, and a school team with knowledge of child behavior and relationships—is an important way to achieve these conditions in today's school.

Such a team should be led by the principal and should be representative of all the adults in a school—and in the middle or high school, of students as well, whenever possible. Such a group works best with no more than 10 to 15 members. It is most effective when teachers select their own representatives (approximately four people representing different grade levels), and parents select approximately the same number from among themselves. The parent group should include representatives of the various ethnic groups, residential areas, and other different perspectives in the school where possible. A person from the nonprofessional support staff—custodial, cafeteria— can also serve on this group. A person with knowledge of child development, relationships, and institutional functioning—social worker, psychologist, special education teacher—should serve on the governance and management team. This makeup creates a relationship mechanism sensitive to child development and capable of considering the concerns of all the players in the educational enterprise in an orderly way. It also permits everyone to be a party to meeting the challenge of a particular school.

Such a group must operate within guidelines reviewed and supported by the central office administration and at the building level. Several suggestions may be particularly useful. First, the participants cannot undermine the authority or paralyze the leadership of the principal. At the same time, the principal cannot use the group as a "rubber stamp" for ideas or approaches he or she wishes to impose. There are also obvious areas where the principal must have full authority. Second, a "no fault" approach—not blaming parents, teachers, administrators, or students for the problems but focusing on solutions—should be used, thus decreasing the likelihood of group conflict. This permits a focus on problem solving. Third, decisions should be made by consensus rather than by voting, with an agreement to try other approaches if the one selected does not work. Finally, it is helpful for the group to delegate tasks to others in the building so that all feel involved, while keeping all activities coordinated. The guidelines for service on the governance and management group should allow for continuity of experienced members as well as for change and "new blood."

The group should develop a comprehensive school plan. The plan should include strategies needed to create a desirable school climate and to reach academic achievement goals. Staff development needed to facilitate both should be in the third component of the plan. While activities in these areas can take place simultaneously, improving the social climate or ethos of a school is often needed before sustained academic gains can be realized. In many low-income areas, parents are more comfortable participating in activities designed to improve the social climate than in supporting the academic program of the school. With this initial focus, their strengths are utilized rather than their weaknesses exposed. A good social climate allows staff and parents to acknowledge deficiencies that they would not have acknowledged in a school climate that promoted distrust and defensiveness. This openness permits the kind of staff development that helps school people examine their interactions with parents and students and overcome their weaknesses.

It is in such a climate that the staff can better understand the manifestations of student underdevelopment or development in areas that do not lead to school success. They can develop skills that will permit them to modify and aid the growth of their students in both behavioral and academic areas. This ability leads to improved interactions between staff and students, and increases parents' trust in and desire to interact with school people.

Parental Support

When the development of a desirable social climate is a part of the comprehensive school plan, parents' participation can be built in as an integrated, important (rather than peripheral and superficial) activity.[11] Parents can sponsor workshops in which teachers help them understand what the school is trying to accomplish in child development and academic areas, and how to help their children make the most of available opportunities. In the process parents provide staff with information and understanding of themselves and their children which permits the staff to be more effective.

The professional support staff team—social worker, psychologist, special education teacher—should help all the groups plan and interact in a way that reduces home–school conflict or avoidance. Programs should be planned so that parents are invited during good times as well as bad times. Parents should be supported in their work in the school so that they fully understand what it is they are trying to accomplish and that it is truly important, and they should be helped to achieve success in their initial activities in particular so that they will not be turned off and withdraw. Sometimes a classroom teacher can work with the parent leader and group in the school to provide such support, reducing the possibility of an adversarial relationship and increasing the likelihood that the parents' contribution will be meaningful and successful.

The resultant improved performance of the children, and the perception that they or their representatives are working in a meaningful way with staff, create a good feeling among parents about the school, which then permeates the community. More apprehensive and reluctant parents are thus encouraged to become involved with the school program. Even greater sensitivity to the barriers between home and school emerges as parents and teachers get to know each other as people sharing goals rather than as people who are different because of race, income, education, or class. The barriers between home and school are further eroded, and a good relationship can develop.

The New Haven Experience

Our Yale Child Study Center worked in collaboration with the New Haven School System and designed a parent participation program (as described) from 1968 through 1980.[12] Initially, in each of two schools serving up to 350 children, only 10 to 15 parents turned out for even the most important activities (such as the Christmas program). Eventually, as many as 400 parents, friends, and relatives attended a Christmas program, and an average of 250 participated in most activities sponsored by parents and staff. Parents' participation increased significantly in most of the more than 40 elementary schools in which we used this approach. Through a school calendar sponsored by parents and staff, the various schools have supported projects as diverse as "Welcome Back to School" potluck suppers, "Little Olympics," book fairs, gospel choirs, mock elections, and on and on. In all cases, these projects are designed to bring parents and staff together in a way that enables both groups to promote the overall development of the children and improve academic learning. Highly significant gains in academic learning were made in our initial project schools—from being 18 months below grade level on fourth-grade language arts and mathematics tests (among the lowest in the city in 1968) to being tied for third and fourth highest achievements in these areas among the 26 schools in the city in 1984.[13] The schools were among the top in attendance and experienced greatly reduced behavior problems. There was no significant change in the socioeconomic makeup of the areas the schools served. We have now observed improved performance in most of the schools in which these methods were used to overcome the barriers to positive home–school relationships.[14]

Nonintegrated Parent Programs

Some people are achieving similar results without changing the organization and management of their schools. In such cases the change is dependent upon the skill level and energy (or motivation to use it) of particular administrators and individuals. And it is my impression that almost anything that is done in schools, or most social systems, that is systematic enough and done with great energy can bring about change. But improved conditions can disappear quickly when such individuals leave the setting or are no longer able to expend the high level of energy needed on an ongoing basis.

To sustain desirable home–school relationships, student growth, and achievement at a desired level, the attitudes, values, and behaviors that promote these conditions must be institutionalized or become part of the school structures and ethos. This makes it possible for "average good efforts" and "average good people" to accept and live up to "the way it is and must be"—high standards of achievement and behavior—in a particular building or social system. When the entire school supports parent involvement—or any other shared attitude, value, or behavior—it is easier for the individual teacher to work with parents in a constructive way. This close cooperation requires a mechanism that generates and maintains the desired school ethos and behavior. And it is only when the parent participation activities are integrated into the work of the school—not peripheral and unimportant—that the barriers to parent–school relationships can be reduced on an ongoing basis.

In our work, we have observed a synergism in which the benefits—real and psychological—for the entire building are greater when activities are part of a building strategy rather than isolated and unrelated. These outcomes grow out of a sense of community and a sense of common cause. It is in such a climate that families under stress gain the support, confidence, and competence needed to help themselves and their children. At least seven parents who were involved in our initial project schools (who had themselves not finished school) went back and did so, went on to college, and are now professionally employed. A number were able to accept jobs they did not have the confidence to take before participating in the school program. Most of these parents credit the environment or ethos of the school for energizing and giving them direction and support. We believe that motivated and empowered, more confident and competent parents are better able to support the development of their children and, in turn, academic learning.

Again, I acknowledge that barriers to parents' participation can be reduced without the kind of change in school organization and management and close attention to the child development and relationship issues that I have mentioned. But such a result is often temporary, less internalized, and less powerful in positively affecting the attitudes, values, and behaviors of parents, school staff, and students.

Summary

Children are not "learning machines" that can be turned on and off, or tuned to various levels by parents or by teachers. Academic learning is both cognitive and relational-affective. It requires emotional bonding to parents first, and to others—including school people and programs. This interaction is optimal where home–school attitudes, values, and ways of behaving are similar. But historical and contemporary conditions have created differences and often barriers to desirable home–school relationships for children, families, and schools most in need. Knowledge, skills, and sensitivity based on social and behavioral science can be applied to change the social system of a school in a way that facilitates desirable home–school interactions and, in turn, that adequately promotes student growth and development, and academic learning.

Notes

1. S. L. Lightfoot, *Worlds Apart: Relationships between Families and Schools* (New York: Basic Books, 1978).
2. E. W. Gordon and C. C. Yeakey, "Policy Implications of Status Variables in Schooling," in *Policy Making in Education*, ed. A. Lieberman and M. McLaughlin (Chicago: University of Chicago Press, 1982): 105–132.
3. D. Blose and A. Caliver, *Statistics of the Education of Negroes, 1929–32*, Bulletin No. 13, U.S. Office of Education (Washington, D.C.: Council for Financial Aid to Education, 1936).
4. Council for Financial Aid to Education, *1964–1965 Voluntary Support of America's Colleges and Universities* (New York: Council for Financial Aid to Education, 1967).
5. Bureau of the Census. *Statistical Abstract of the United States: 1958* (Washington, D.C.: U.S. Government Printing Office, 1960).
6. D. Davies, ed., *Schools Where Parents Make a Difference* (Boston: Institute for Responsive Education, 1976).
7. J. I. Goodlad, *A Place Called School* (New York: McGraw-Hill, 1984).
8. W. G. Winters and C. M. Schraft, *Developing Parent–School Collaboration: A Guide for School Personnel* (New Haven: Yale Child Study Center, 1977).
9. C. M. Schraft and J. P. Comer, "Parent Participation and Urban Schools," *School Social Work Quarterly*, 14 (1979): 309–325.
10. J. P. Comer, *School Power* (New York: Free Press, 1980).
11. J. P. Comer, "Parent Participation in the Schools," *Phi Delta Kappan* (February 1986): 442–446.
12. J. P. Comer, "Home–School Relationships as They Affect the Academic Success of Children," *Education and Urban Society* 16 (May 1984): 323–337.
13. J. P. Comer, "The Education of Inner-City Children," *Grants Magazine* 3 (March 1980): 20–27.
14. J. P. Comer, "The Yale-New Haven Primary Prevention Project: A Follow-up Study," *Journal of the American Academy of Child Psychiatry* 24 (1985): 154–160.

Selected References

Berry, M. F., and J. Blassingame. *Long Memory: The Black Experience in America.* New York: Oxford University Press, 1982.
Biber, B. "Integration of Mental Health Principles in the School Setting." In *Preven-*

tion of Mental Disorders in Children, edited by G. Caplan, 323–352. New York: Basic Books, 1961.

Billingsley, A. *Black Families in White America.* Englewood Cliffs, N.J.: Prentice-Hall, 1986.

Blose, D., and A. Caliver. *Statistics of the Education of Negroes, 1929–32.* Bulletin No. 13, U.S. Office of Education. Washington, D.C.: Council for Financial Aid to Education, 1936.

Bureau of the Census. *Statistical Abstract of the United States: 1958.* Washington, D.C.: U.S. Government Printing Office, 1960.

Cohen, D. *The Learning Child.* New York: Pantheon, 1972.

Comer, J. P. *School Power.* New York: Free Press, 1980.

Comer, J. P. "The Education of Inner-City Children." *Grants Magazine* (March 1980): 20–27.

Comer, J. P. "Home–School Relationships as They Affect the Academic Success of Children." *Education and Urban Society* 16 (May 1984): 323–337.

Comer, J. P. "The Yale–New Haven Primary Prevention Project: A Follow-up Study." *Journal of the American Academy of Child Psychiatry* 24, (1985): 154–160.

Comer, J. P. "Parent Participation in the Schools." *Phi Delta Kappan* (February 1986): 442–446.

Council for Financial Aid to Education. *1964–1965 Voluntary Support of America's Colleges and Universities.* New York: Council for Financial Aid to Education, 1967.

Curry, N., ed. *The Feeling Child: Affective Development Reconsidered.* Binghamton, N.Y.: Haworth Press, 1986.

Davies, D., ed. *Schools Where Parents Make a Difference.* Boston: Institute for Responsive Education, 1976.

Goodlad, John I. *A Place Called School: Prospects for the Future.* New York: McGraw-Hill, 1984.

Gordon, E. W., and C. C. Yeakey. "Policy Implications of Status Variables in Schooling." In *Policy Making in Education,* edited by A. Lieberman and M. McLaughlin, 105–132. Chicago: University of Chicago Press, 1982.

Hansen, M. L. *The Immigrant in American History.* Cambridge, Mass.: Harvard University Press, 1940.

Lightfoot, S. L. *Worlds Apart: Relationships between Families and Schools.* New York: Basic Books, 1978.

Schraft, C. M., and J. P. Comer. "Parent Participation and Urban Schools." *School Social Work Quarterly* 14 (1979): 309–325.

Winters, W. G., and C. M. Schraft. *Developing Parent-School Collaboration: A Guide for School Personnel.* New Haven: Yale Child Study Center, 1977.

3.

Demographics of Disadvantage: Intensity of Childhood Poverty and Its Relationship to Educational Achievement

MARTIN E. ORLAND

Précis
The longer a child is in poverty, the more deleterious the effect on his or her educational growth. Furthermore, the concentration of poverty within a school can be shown to be harmful to *all* students in that school whether or not an individual student comes from a poor background. For instance, a student who is not poor but goes to a high-poverty school is more likely to be a low achiever than a student in poverty who goes to a low-poverty school.

Martin Orland reports these associations derived from the National Assessment of Chapter I of the Educational Consolidation and Improvement Act. The Assessment was commissioned by the U.S. Congress to provide policy perspectives on the major federal assistance program for educating students who at the time the legislation was initiated were called "the disadvantaged." The findings will challenge policymakers as well as teachers and administrators to question longheld assumptions about how to meet the needs of such students.

Policymakers determining how to distribute funds should note that not all poverty is equally associated with poor school performance. Any fund allocation arrangement that looks only at whether families are poor at a given point in time will be less efficient than one that takes into account the intensity of students' actual experience of poverty (that is, both its "longevity" and "concentration" in schools).

Teachers and administrators, deciding how to use these funds, should see the school as the key unit of reform and change because certain conditions at the school level appear to be responsible for depressing the general academic performance of students. (A school's performance can be predicted by its overall socioeconomic level better than a student's performance can be predicted by individual socioeconomic status.)

Widespread practices that may seem inappropriate in the light of these findings include special programs at the school level that isolate some students in separate classrooms because they are designated to be "disadvantaged" on some dimension; the insistence at the school district level that those who are labeled most in need of help be kept isolated in special classrooms and programs so the district can more easily monitor federal funding; and the distribution of funds as though the student is the relevant unit of change, rather than investing in improved school conditions.

The challenge to practitioners is to develop understanding of why it is important to develop schoolwide options for improving education and to design programs that change school conditions to respond to the circumstances of disadvantaged students.

Martin E. Orland is a senior associate, National Center for Education Statistics, and a coauthor of the *Preliminary Findings of the National Assessment of Chapter I.*

—*The College Board*

Since 1974, children have constituted America's poorest age group. According to a recent joint report to Congress by the Congressional Research Service and Congressional Budget Office, the number of poor children in the United States was close to 14 million in 1983.[1] This figure represented about 22 percent of all Americans under 18 years of age. Further, the incidence of childhood poverty increased substantially in the early 1980s; in 1979 the number of poor children and the childhood poverty rate stood at about 10 million and 17 percent, respectively.

How does this condition of childhood poverty affect a student's academic performance? This was one of the central questions addressed by the National Assessment of Chapter I in a study commissioned by the Congress to assess the federal government's major assistance program for educating disadvantaged children: Chapter I of the Educational Consolidation and Improvement Act.[2] In its formula for allocating monies to school districts and its provisions for delivering services to school buildings and students, Chapter I and its longstanding predecessor program—Title I of the Elementary and Secondary Education Act—at least implicitly assume that poverty and educational achievement are significantly related.[3]

This paper, which summarizes some of the key findings of the Chapter I National Assessment, investigates the merits of that assumption. To do so, I go beyond reporting about the mere existence of childhood poverty and its relationship to academic achievement. I explore the *longevity* of childhood poverty as well as its *concentrations* within schools—conditions which can be said to represent the magnitude or "intensity" of a child's poverty experience. The paper also identifies the kinds of students most likely to experience these more "intense" forms of poverty and shows how strongly these conditions are related to student academic performance.

Following a background discussion presenting a rationale for the approach to this topic, I report separately on the two measures of poverty intensity used in this study: poverty longevity and school poverty concentrations. The kinds of students most likely to experience each type of poverty are described, and data revealing the relationship between each condition and student academic achievement are presented. The paper concludes with a brief discussion of the implications of these findings for educational policy reform.

Background

Education researchers have known for years that a weak but statistically significant relationship exists between student poverty and academic achieve-

This paper is the work of the author alone and should not be interpreted as necessarily reflecting the findings, opinions, or policies of the U.S. Department of Education. Special thanks go to Richard K. Jung and Mary Kennedy, much of whose work for the first interim report of the Chapter I National Assessment is reflected in this manuscript.

ment. One reviewer of the literature on this topic, while noting the different definitions used in analyses of this type, concluded that a poor child was roughly twice as likely to be a low academic achiever as a child who was not poor.[4] Studies attempting to correlate poverty and/or family-income conditions with student academic performance have generally found simple correlation coefficients of around .2 to .3, which is indicative of a modest statistical association between the two variables.[5]

Looking at these past studies attempting to associate demographic conditions (including poverty) with academic performance, we see two findings that are especially noteworthy. First, the factors that explain most of the variation in student achievement are not parental income levels or other measures of socioeconomic status (parents' education, occupation, etc.), but rather measures of "home atmosphere" such as parental aspirations for their children, the amount of reading materials in the home, and family attitudes toward education.[6] Given this finding, it is not surprising to learn that a onetime measure of a family's poverty status correlates only weakly with academic performance. Family economic circumstances often change rapidly in this country, and, as such, a diverse cross section of citizens could be expected to be classified as "poor" at any single point in time. Among the poor, for example, are those who are temporarily ill, between jobs, or gaining a needed education credential at one extreme, as well as the low-skill, "hard-core" unemployed at the other.

A student's "home atmosphere" (and therefore expected academic performance levels) might systematically differ among children residing in households experiencing very different types of poverty. A poverty measure that merely assesses whether a person is poor at a given time, however, would not capture much of this relationship. It would be roughly akin to trying to predict a person's life expectancy by asking whether that individual was currently ill, but without distinguishing whether he or she was suffering from the flu or cancer.

The second finding of interest from past research on this topic is the statistical relationship between poverty and achievement at the *school building* level. Correlation coefficients of .5 and above were consistently found when the poverty and achievement characteristics of schools were analyzed.[7] These coefficients were much higher than those found at the student level. In other words, you could predict with considerably more accuracy a school's academic performance by knowing its overall rate of poverty than you could an individual student's achievement by knowing whether he or she was poor.

This increased predictive value at the school level could mean the existence of an educational effect associated with high concentrations of school poverty that is independent of a student's individual poverty status. Such a finding would be consistent with some of the recent research literature on the importance of such school factors as peer influence, parental involvement, and school instructional characteristics (i.e., "effective schools") on academic performance; factors that might well be associated with school poverty conditions. However, the finding could also be little more than a statistical artifact that can occur when aggregated data are analyzed.[8] Previous studies on the subject have not attempted to disentangle student from school poverty effects on individual student achievement.

The above findings and the issues they raise reveal a need to go beyond previous examinations of poverty and student achievement, and investigate the "intensity" of childhood poverty experiences—as reflected in both the longevity of student poverty and school poverty concentrations. Specifically, it is important to learn about the kinds of students most likely to experience these more intense forms of poverty and how these conditions relate to students' educational achievement levels. In order to do this, we conducted two separate secondary analyses of existing data bases: one to investigate the incidence and effects of poverty longevity, and a second to address identical questions about school poverty concentrations.

Poverty Longevity and Student Achievement

One likely reason that the relationship between the length of time students experience poverty and their academic achievement has been unexplored is the absence of much available data on this question. An imperfect but nevertheless useful data source for investigating this issue is available from a study called the Panel Survey of Income Dynamics (PSID). Since 1968, this survey (sponsored by the University of Michigan's Institute for Social Research) has been annually tracking the income conditions and other circumstances of about 6,000 nationally representative families.

Table 1 presents information from the PSID on the average length of time that children of different races and with other distinguishing characteristics are poor.[9] It is clear from the table that the length of time a child is likely to be poor is related to several demographic conditions. The most important of these is probably race. Black children in the PSID are poor for an average of 5.4 of their first 15 years of life, whereas nonblack children are poor for an average of less than one year. Roughly 1 in 4 black children surveyed is poor for 10 years or more, and one half are poor for five years or more. The comparable percentages for white children are 1 in 200 (poor for 10 years or more), and 1 in 20 (poor for five years or more). Other characteristics associated with increased durations of childhood poverty include living in a single-parent household, having a disabled head of the family, living in a rural area, and, for black children, living in the South.

Because the PSID study was designed primarily to follow the behavior of the labor market over time rather than to analyze relationships between family income and student educational attainment, it contains little information about academic achievement. However, the study did collect information between 1978 and 1983 on the grade levels attained by 16- and 18-year-old

Table 1. Expected Number of Years in Poverty during First 15 Years of Life, by Race

	Non-black	Black
All households	0.8	5.4
Characteristics of household at birth of child		
Never married mother	6.2	6.0
Teenage mother	1.2	5.4
Education of head		
8 years	1.2	5.6
12 years	0.7	5.3
Characteristics of household throughout childhood (15 years)		
Head disabled	3.3	10.9
Lived in south	0.8	6.4
Lived out of south	0.7	4.3
Large city	0.7	3.9
Rural area	1.1	8.1
One parent	3.2	7.3
Two parents	0.5	3.0

children in the sampled households. In our study, these data were compared to an "expected grade level" for children of that age. (The expected grade level for 16-year-olds was tenth grade and for 18-year olds twelfth grade.) First we noted whether a student in the sample was behind his or her expected grade level; then we determined whether the length of time that the student was poor was associated with his or her grade attainment.[10]

The findings from this analysis are summarized in Table 2 for both black and white students who were 16 and 18 years old.[11] They show a clear association between the length of time students were poor and the likelihood that they would be behind their expected grade level. For each age cohort and among each ethnic group, the proportion of students behind grade level increased with the number of years in poverty. Among black 16-year-olds, for example (who had not experienced any time in poverty), about 1 in 6 was behind the expected grade level. This likelihood doubles to about 1 in 3 for those who had spent eight or more years living in poverty.

It is also informative to learn whether the length of time children experience poverty is associated with grade-level attainment *after* other aspects of the students' backgrounds are taken into account. To examine this question, a multivariate statistical model was constructed that measured the independent contributions of length of time in poverty as well as other student and family characteristics in explaining grade-level attainment. The results of this analysis are reported in Table 3.[12]

Table 2. Percentage of 16- and 18-Year-Old Students below Expected Grade Level, by Race and Years in Poverty

	Black Students	White Students
16-Year-Olds		
Less than one year in poverty	16.4	22.0
One–two years in poverty	16.6	20.5
Three–seven years in poverty	24.7	26.0
Eight or more years in poverty	35.7	48.3
All time spent in poverty	25.2	22.9

	Black Students	White Students
18-Year-Olds		
Less than one year in poverty	34.4	25.4
One–two years in poverty	27.5	31.3
Three–seven years in poverty	48.5	42.8
Eight or more years in poverty	50.9	85.7
All time spent in poverty	46.6	28.8

The findings reveal several factors that are significantly associated with the likelihood of a student falling behind grade level. They also show some that are not related to this condition once other factors are taken into account. Being male, for example, increases the probability that a student would be behind his expected grade level by 14 percent. Similarly, having a mother who did not finish high school increased this likelihood by 6 percent. On the

Table 3. Relationships between Student and Family Characteristics and Falling Below Grade Level for 16- and 18-Year-Old Students (N = 1,380)

Characteristic[a]	Likelihood of falling below grade level[b]
Gender (being male)	*Increases* likelihood by 14 percentage points
Mother did not finish high school	*Increases* likelihood by 6 percentage points
Mother attended a PTA meeting while student was in elementary school	*Decreases* likelihood by 10 percentage points
Average family income during the 15-year period of the study	*Decreases* likelihood by 4 percentage points per $1,000 of income
Number of years living below official poverty line	*Increases* likelihood by 2 percentage points *per year* in poverty

a. Characteristics tested but found unrelated to students falling below grade level were:
   • Whether the student was black.
   • Whether the family lived in the South.
   • Whether the mother was less than 20 years old when the student was born.
   • Whether the mother was single at any time during the PSID study.
b. Nationwide average proportion of students below grade level is 23.9% of 16-year-olds and 32.0% of 18-year-olds.

other hand, being black did *not* increase the likelihood of being behind grade level once other factors such as gender and mother's education were statistically taken into account.[13]

Of particular importance for purposes of understanding the relationship between poverty and achievement is the finding that, even after controlling for other factors, the length of time a student experiences poverty is statistically associated with the likelihood of falling behind in grade level. For each year of student poverty, the likelihood of falling behind in grade level increases by 2 percent. Thus, according to these data, a student from a family that had been poor for 10 years is almost 20 percent more likely to be behind in grade level as one whose family was poor only for a single year. This outcome would be expected even if these two students were both equivalent with respect to their gender, their mother's high school attainment, and whether she had ever attended a PTA meeting.

These findings should not be construed to suggest that increased time in poverty "causes" lower student achievement. We are still relatively ignorant about the complex processes which are actually responsible for differences in educational attainment among groups with different characteristics, be it poverty or some other attribute. More than likely, the length of time in poverty is strongly associated with some other feature of the home, or perhaps school environment, which is not present in this statistical model but which nevertheless has a direct effect on student academic performance.

For purposes of some public policy decisions, however, such as where to target remedial education resources, the absence of a causal specification of the relationship between poverty longevity and achievement is less critical than the mere fact that an association is present. It is reasonably clear from the above findings, for example, that any allocation system based on poverty that ignores poverty longevity will target remedial resources less efficiently than one that attempts to take this circumstance into account.

Concentrations of Poverty in Schools and Student Achievement

To analyze the characteristics and achievement levels of students attending schools with high concentrations of poverty, two principal data bases were used. The Sustaining Effects Study (SES) contains nationally representative information on student and school poverty, certain other demographic characteristics, and standardized achievement test scores. The SES data used in our reanalysis were originally collected between the fall of 1976 and the spring of 1979 and provide information about the poverty concentration/achievement relationship among elementary school students (grades one through six).[14] In addition to the SES, we also used the 1980 census to provide other demographic information about high-poverty schools.[15]

Table 4. Racial and Ethnic Characteristics of Poverty Concentrations in Elementary Schools

	Poverty Concentration		
Variable	Low (< 7% Poor)	Medium (7–24% Poor)	High (> 24% Poor)
White (%)	94.57	82.26	52.50
Black (%)	2.99	9.42	31.74
Hispanic (%)	1.17	6.00	11.56
Primary language other than English (%)	5.81	10.88	19.37

Table 4 presents findings from the Sustaining Effects Study on the racial/ethnic composition of students attending low-, moderate-, and high-poverty elementary schools in 1976.[16] Clearly, minority student representation is much greater in schools with the highest concentrations of poverty than for those with lower poverty rates. Among school districts with the highest rates of student poverty, a similar pattern is found. Based on 1980 census information, the average percentage of nonwhite and non-English-speaking students residing in the nation's highest-poverty districts is about three times that of students living in lower poverty areas.[17]

The size, urbanization, and location of school districts with high poverty concentrations (and therefore containing most high-poverty schools) were also obtained by analyzing census data.[18] They show that the districts most likely to contain the highest concentrations of poverty are very small rural systems and quite large urban ones. They also reveal much higher proportions of high-poverty districts in the South than in other geographic regions, as illustrated in Table 5.[19]

Overall, students served in schools with high rates of poverty share many of the characteristics of students experiencing long-term poverty. Both types of students are far more likely to be black, to be living in rural areas, and to reside in the South than are students not experiencing these poverty circumstances. Because the data bases used for these two sets of demographic analyses were necessarily different, it is not possible to determine the extent to which the same students who experienced long-term poverty also attended schools with high poverty concentrations. Nevertheless, the similar demographic profiles of both types of students suggest that many of the same children may be subjected to both types of intense poverty experiences.

To assess how concentrations of poverty in schools are related to student academic achievement, we reanalyzed data originally collected for the Sustaining Effects Study (SES). The first analysis compares the prevalence of low-achieving students among schools with varying rates of poverty. To do

Table 5. Distribution of High Poverty Districts and Other Districts among Regions

Geographic Region	High Concentration Districts (Top 25th Percentile)		Other Districts (Lower 75th Percentile)	
	No.	%	No.	%
Northeast[a] (3,128 districts)	359	11.5	2,769	88.5
North Central[b] (6,159 districts)	1,215	19.7	4,944	80.3
South[c] (3,445 districts)	1,676	48.7	1,769	51.3
West[d] (2,931 districts)	687	23.4	2,244	76.6
TOTAL	3,937	25.1	11,726	74.9

a. Connecticut, Maine, Massachusetts, New Hampshire, New Jersey, New York, Pennsylvania, Rhode Island (U.S. Census).
b. Illinois, Indiana, Iowa, Kansas, Michigan, Minnesota, Missouri, Nebraska, North Dakota, Ohio, South Dakota, Wisconsin (U.S. Census).
c. Alabama, Arkansas, Delaware, District of Columbia, Florida, Georgia, Kentucky, Louisiana, Maryland, Mississippi, North Carolina, Oklahoma, South Carolina, Tennessee, Texas, Virginia, West Virginia (U.S. Census).
d. Alaska, Arizona, California, Colorado, Idaho, Montana, Nevada, New Mexico, Oregon, Utah, Washington, Wyoming (Hawaii was not included) (U.S. Census).

this, we divided our elementary school sample into high, low, and "average" poverty schools and then noted the percentage of both poor and nonpoor students in each type of school who were low achievers. The findings are presented in Table 6.[20]

Several things are worth noting from this table. Most obvious (and least surprising) is the fact that school poverty rates and achievement rates are associated. The percentage of low achievers is clearly much higher among

Table 6. Percentage of Students Whose Achievement Scores Fall below the Twenty-Fifth Percentile Rank, by Student and School Poverty Status

Student Poverty Status	School Poverty Status			
	Low Poverty (< 7% Poor)	Medium Poverty (7–24% Poor)	High Poverty (> 24% Poor)	All Schools
Nonpoor	11.0	20.7	36.9	18.7
Poor	27.6	39.2	56.0	46.7
All students	11.9	23.9	47.5	25.0

groups of schools with the highest poverty rates than for those with lower poverty concentrations.

More interesting is the fact that the percentage of low achievers appears dramatically higher for schools in the highest poverty grouping compared with other schools. That percentage grows by about 12 percentage points (from about 11.9 to 23.9 percent of all students) for schools grouped in the moderate (as opposed to low) poverty ranges. It increases by nearly 24 percentage points, however (from 23.9 to 47.5 percent of all students), between schools in the moderate poverty group and those with the highest poverty rates. These findings indicate that the association between school poverty and student achievement becomes especially strong in the nation's highest-poverty schools. What's more, this relationship is apparent for both poor and nonpoor students. In fact, according to these data, a nonpoor student in a poor school is actually *more* likely to be a low achiever (36.9 percent) than is a poor student in a low-poverty school (27.6 percent).

This finding that the likelihood of both poor and nonpoor students being low achievers varies depending on the poverty concentrations in their school suggests the existence of a unique "school effect" on student achievement which is associated with school poverty rates. However, this need not necessarily be the case. It could be that other individual or family characteristics of students in high- and low-poverty schools differ and are responsible for the differing proportions of low achievers. For example, even nonpoor students in high-poverty schools may be more likely to have mothers who failed to finish high school than poor students in low-poverty schools. As we have seen earlier, this characteristic has a significant association with student achievement and could help explain the school poverty–achievement relationships previously described.

A multivariate statistical model was again employed to examine whether school poverty rates were associated with student achievement after taking into account other individual and family characteristics of students. The findings show that part of the apparent relationship between school poverty rates and student achievement is, indeed, an artifact of differing student and family characteristics among enrollees of high- and low-poverty schools. However, after controlling for these characteristics, a statistically significant association remains between the proportion of poor children attending a school and student academic performance levels. That is, there are differences in student performance in high- and low-poverty schools that are not explained solely by the different types of students attending these schools.

As was the case in attempting to explain how poverty longevity relates to student achievement, the ways in which school poverty concentrations might affect student achievement are not well understood. More than likely there are several features of the school environment that both differ, on average, among high- and low-poverty schools and contribute to differences in student achievement. Examples of such factors, which have been cited in the research literature, include the influence of peers on student academic norms, the resources available for educating students, the quality of supervisory and instructional staff, and the presence of school characteristics such as shared goals, high teacher expectations for student performance, and strong levels of parent involvement.[21]

Again, for some public policy purposes, it is less important to identify the "causes" of this relationship than to merely recognize its existence. For whatever reason(s), a child attending a school with high poverty concentrations has a greater likelihood of performing poorly in school than a child with a similar socioeconomic background who attends a school with a lower poverty rate.

Summary and Implications

The purpose of this paper has been to report on the kinds of students most likely to have more "intense" poverty experiences and the relationship between this condition and student academic achievement. Two types of poverty intensity were identified for separate analysis: the length of time a student is poor, and the poverty concentration of the school a student attends.

Students experiencing long-term poverty are more likely to be black, to come from single-parent households or ones with a disabled family head, to live in rural areas, and (among black children) to reside in the South than are students who are poor for shorter periods. They are also significantly more likely to experience academic difficulty, as evidenced by data showing the relationship between the number of years of student poverty and the proportion failing to attain the expected grade level for their age. Even after controlling for other student demographic characteristics, each year of student poverty was statistically associated with a 2 percent increase in the likelihood of falling behind expected grade level.

Students attending schools with high poverty concentrations are also more likely to be black, to come from rural areas, and to reside in the South than are other students. The fact that these characteristics are also prevalent among students in long-term poverty suggests that many of the same students may be subjected to both kinds of "intense" poverty experiences. The percentage of students who perform poorly on standardized tests was found to be dramatically higher in schools with very high concentrations of poverty compared with other schools. Statistical techniques designed to separate the effect of individual student poverty (and other student and family characteristics) from that of school poverty concentration on student performance revealed a significant independent relationship between school poverty rates and student achievement.

The findings reported here provide at least three major insights about education disadvantage and its relationship to demographic factors that should be kept in mind by researchers, policymakers, and others interested in improving educational opportunities for the disadvantaged. First, it's clear from these analyses that all student poverty is not equal. Students experiencing long-term poverty or who attend schools with high poverty concentrations are much more likely to have educational difficulties than students from families whose duration in poverty is short or who attend schools with low poverty rates. To the extent that student poverty continues to be treated as a simple dichotomous characteristic (you're either poor or you're not), the result will be less useful research insights and less efficient targeting of programs and resources to areas of highest need.

Second, these findings suggest that many of the same students who experience long-term poverty also attend schools with high poverty concentrations. Black students, students from rural areas, and those who live in the South would appear from our data to be particularly likely to experience these multiple disadvantaged conditions. Perversely, the likely overlap of students experiencing both forms of intense poverty may make it easier to design improved resource allocation policies. Policymakers, for example, could allocate more monies to schools with high poverty concentrations and, in the process, also reach many students in long-term poverty. Better data and more comprehensive analyses are needed to address this issue of overlap among students experiencing intense forms of poverty.

Finally, the findings from this study reinforce the notion that there are independent school factors that depress the academic achievement levels of all students attending high-poverty schools. Thus initiatives aimed at enhancing the quality of these schools hold promise for enhancing student achievement. Policymakers and researchers need to seriously examine school-based reform options as a means of more effectively serving students attending schools with high poverty rates.

Notes

1. U.S. House of Representatives, *Children in Poverty* (report prepared for the Committee on Ways and Means by the Congressional Research Service and Congressional Budget Office), Government Printing Office, 1985.
2. The first report of the Chapter I National Assessment is published as M. M. Kennedy, R. K. Jung, and M. E. Orland, *Poverty, Achievement, and the Distribution of Compensatory Education Services* (Washington, D.C.: U.S. Government Printing Office, 1986). It contains a more detailed presentation and complete documentation of the research findings discussed in this essay. The congressional mandate for the Chapter I National Assessment can be found in Appendix A of that volume.
3. The Chapter I legislation expresses this premise more directly in its "Declaration of Policy" (Section 552), which states that children from low-income families have "special educational needs."
4. A. Wolf, *Poverty and Achievement* (Washington, D.C.: National Institute of Education, 1977), 1.
5. Ibid., 3–5.

6. K. R. White, "The Relationship between Socioeconomic Status and Academic Achievement," *Psychological Bulletin* 91, No. 3 (1982): 461–481.

7. Wolf, *Poverty and Achievement*, 12–15.

8. This phenomenon of statistical relationships varying solely because of the unit of analysis employed is commonly referred to by researchers as the "ecological fallacy."

9. This table is from Greg J. Duncan and Willard L. Rogers, "A Demographic Analysis of Childhood Poverty," unpublished paper, University of Michigan Institute for Social Research, Ann Arbor. Cited in *Children in Poverty*, report prepared for the Committee on Ways and Means, U.S. House of Representatives, by the Congressional Research Service and Congressional Budget Office, Washington, D.C.: U.S. Government Printing Office, 1985, 47.

10. The specific procedures employed in this analysis as well as more detailed findings can be found in Kennedy, Jung, and Orland, *Poverty, Achievement, and Distribution*, D–1 to D–15.

11. The table is derived from the reanalysis of Panel Study of Income Dynamics (PSID) data conducted for the Chapter I National Assessment.

12. The table is derived from the reanalysis of Panel Study of Income Dynamics (PSID) data conducted for the Chapter I National Assessment.

13. Interestingly, although race was not found to be independently related to whether a student would fall behind expected grade level, the extent to which other factors were related to grade-level attainment differed substantially by race. For whites, number of years in poverty was significantly related to grade attainment, as was the age of the mother when her first child was born and whether she had ever attended a PTA meeting. For blacks, on the other hand, none of these factors was significantly related to the likelihood of falling behind in grade level, but the mother's education, whether she lived in the South, and whether she was single were all related. These findings suggest that demographic characteristics, including the length of time in poverty, affect the academic achievement of blacks and whites differently.

14. Other analyses were performed for high school students using data from the study *High School and Beyond* (Chicago: National Opinion Research Center, 1983). Because of space limitations, findings from these analyses are not reported here. The general patterns, however, are quite similar to those noted in the elementary school findings.

15. A detailed description of these data bases, the analytic models employed, and the results of the analyses can be found in Kennedy, Jung, and Orland, *Poverty, Achievement, and Distribution*, D–17 to D–60 and E–47 to E–62.

16. The table is derived from a reanalysis of data from the Sustaining Effects Study (SES) conducted for the Chapter I National Assessment. School poverty groupings were determined by dividing the nationally representative sample into four equal-sized "quartiles" of poverty. Schools with poverty rates in the highest quartile of this distribution (with poverty rates of 24 percent and above) were labeled "high-concentration" schools, those in the lowest quartile (poverty rates below 7 percent) were identified as "low-concentration" schools, and those in the middle were considered "moderate concentration" schools. See R. Hoepfner, H. Zagorski, and J. Wellisch, *The Sample for the Sustaining Effects Study and Projections of Its Characteristics: Report #1 from the Study of the Sustaining Effects of Compensatory Education on Basic Skills* (Santa Monica, Calif.: Systems Development Corporation, 1977) for a full description of the SES sample and its characteristics.

17. This and subsequent analysis of school district demographic characteristics are based on data taken from the Census Bureau's STF-3F file. District poverty designations were obtained by dividing all school districts into poverty "quartiles" in a manner similar to that described earlier for obtaining school poverty designations. Further information on this data base and the analytic procedures employed can be obtained from Kennedy, Jung, and Orland, *Poverty, Achievement, and Distribution,* Appendix E.

18. The school district rather than the school building was employed as the unit of analysis for investigating many of the demographic characteristics of students attending high-poverty schools simply because no national data bases existed at the time of this study that allowed us to analyze these characteristics at the school-building level. The implicit assumption in an analysis of this type is that most high-poverty schools are located in high-poverty districts and that most low-poverty schools can be found in low-poverty districts. Recent analyses conducted by the Chapter I National Assessment using newly available data confirms the accuracy of this assumption. See B. F. Birman, M. D. Orland, et al., *Preliminary Findings of the National Assessment of Chapter I* (Washington, D.C.: Office of Educational Research and Improvement, U.S. Department of Education, 1987), Table 1.5 for these findings.

19. The table is derived from a reanalysis of 1980 Census Data (STF-3F file) conducted for the Chapter I National Assessment.

20. The table is derived from a reanalysis of data from the Sustaining Effects Study (SES) conducted for the Chapter I National Assessment.

21. A few of these factors have been explored further in subsequent activities of the Chapter I National Assessment and have revealed relationships that are consistent with these hypotheses. For example, the National Assessment found that high-poverty school districts tend to raise less money than other districts in their state (M. E. Orland, "Relating School District Resource Needs and Capacities to Chapter I Allocation: Implications for More Effective Service Targeting," paper delivered to the Convention of the American Education Research Association, Washington, D.C., April 1987) and that administrators in high-poverty schools are least likely to report high general levels of parental involvement (Birman, Orland, et al., *Preliminary Findings*).

Selected References

Birman, B. F., M. D. Orland, et al. *Preliminary Findings of the National Assessment of Chapter I.* Report prepared for the U.S. House of Representatives Subcommittee on Elementary, Secondary and Vocational Education. Washington, D.C.: Office of Educational Research and Improvement, U.S. Department of Education, 1987.

Hoepfner, R., H. Zagorski, and J. Wellisch. *The Sample for the Sustaining Effects Study and Projections of Its Characteristics: Report #1 from the Study of the Sustaining Effects of Compensatory Education on Basic Skills.* Santa Monica, Calif.: Systems Development Corporation, 1977.

Kennedy, M. M., R. K. Jung, and M. E. Orland. *Poverty, Achievement, and the Distribution of Compensatory Education Services.* Interim report from the National

Assessment of Chapter I. Washington, D.C.: U.S. Government Printing Office, 1986.

National Opinion Research Center. *High School and Beyond: 1980 Sophomore Cohort First Follow-up (1982)*. Chicago: National Opinion Research Center, 1983.

Orland, M. E. "Relating School District Resource Needs and Capacities to Chapter I Allocation: Implications for More Effective Service Targeting." Paper delivered to the convention of the American Education Research Association, Washington, D.C., April 1987.

U.S. House of Representatives. *Children in Poverty*. Report prepared for the Committee on Ways and Means by the Congressional Research Service and Congressional Budget Office. Washington, D.C.: U.S. Government Printing Office, 1985.

White, K. R. "The Relationship between Socioeconomic Status and Academic Achievement." *Psychological Bulletin* (1982): 461–481.

Wolf, A. *Poverty and Achievement. 91, No. 3:* National Institute of Education, 1977.

4.

Overcoming Racial Barriers to Equal Access

JOHN U. OGBU

Précis
A previously underexamined aspect of race relations, overlooked both in explaining the variability of school achievement and in trying to equalize access to knowledge in schools, is the relationship of involuntary minority group populations to the dominant cultural group. John Ogbu distinguishes between voluntary and involuntary minority groups to explain success in American society and schooling.

Ogbu notes that cultural studies reveal that race alone does not explain variability in school achievement. Being a member of a racial minority group neither explains school success nor lack of it, in this country or elsewhere. Asian-Americans, for example, have done well in U.S. schools and so have some other immigrant minority groups. Blacks, Hispanics, and American Indians, on the other hand, have done less well.

To understand relevant differences between these groups, Ogbu develops a structural picture of racial stratification. That is, when races are assigned different rungs on the social ladder, two types of barriers enforce that assignment. One, Ogbu calls instrumental barriers: fairly overt and visible exclusionary activities like discrimination in jobs, housing, and education. Other barriers he terms expressive: conscious and unconscious derogatory treatment of a minority group by members of the dominant group that satisfies the latter's psychological needs such as scapegoating. Members of these minority groups, in turn, develop coping and survival strategies that represent responses to the instrumental and expressive behaviors of the dominant group. These behaviors become culturally folded into the traditions of the minority group and are passed on from one generation to the next. Even if the dominant group takes action to eliminate these instrumental barriers and curbs its negative expressive behavior, imbedded minority group responses tend to persist because they are learned early in life and are not easily given up. These behaviors represent a cultural defense to derogatory treatment, and can foster a counterculture in opposition to the dominant group. Some black teenagers, for example, display negative attitudes toward school success: achieving success in school may seem like joining the oppressors. Minority group members themselves may not consciously recognize these behaviors for what they are, Ogbu believes.

Educators are asked to explore the history and nature of racial minority groups' coping responses, especially their expressive behaviors, which Ogbu says policymakers and reformers often are not fully aware of and do not adequately address as a barrier to school success. He focuses primarily on black students as examples but emphasizes that American Indians and Hispanic Americans originally from the southwestern United States are others for whom expressive responses to earlier domination and derogatory treatment by the mainstream group function as a barrier to school success. Ogbu distinguishes their experiences from those of other immigrant groups and shows how children from these involuntary minority cultures must fight against their own culture to be successful in schools. Schools are urged to develop programs that take these behaviors into account, understanding this critical dimension to removing racial barriers to knowledge.

John U. Ogbu is professor of anthropology at the University of California, Berkeley. He has written extensively on issues of minority group status, class, and caste in American society.

—*The College Board*

Variability is a common feature of the school performance of racial minority students in the United States and in other urban industrial societies, such as England, Israel, Japan, and New Zealand. In these and similar societies children from *some* racial minority groups do well in school, whereas children from *some other* racial minority groups do not. In the United States, for example, it is well known that Asian-Americans do well in school, but most American Indians, black Americans, and Mexican-Americans do not. In New Zealand the indigenous Maoris do less well in school than Polynesians from other islands, although the two groups belong to the same "race." Membership of minorities and the dominant group in the same "race" does not necessarily translate into equal school performance. Consider the case of Israel where Oriental Jews consistently lag behind the Ashkenazi Jews in school performance; consider, too, the case of Japan where the Buraku outcastes massively continue to underperform the dominant Ippon Japanese.

My conclusion from comparative research is that race is not a significant variable in determining school success or school failure except where racial groups are *stratified*. But then, racial minorities are not all equally affected by racial stratification, owing to differences in their initial terms of incorporation into the social arrangements under which they exist. Another conclusion emerging from comparative research is that racial barriers to school success are not captured by such popular concepts as "at-risk," "disadvantaged," and "the underclass" that are in their various definitions largely applied to black Americans and similar minority youths in the United States.

This chapter is more about the nature of racial barriers against minority school success than about how to overcome such barriers. The reason is that my own comparative research has focused on identifying and clarifying the nature of the barriers, in the belief that the first step toward overcoming the barriers is to understand them.

In the next section I explain what I mean by racial stratification and its relation to minority status. Then I describe the case of black Americans as an example of a racial minority in a stratified society. This leads to an analysis of the racial barriers to equal access to knowledge, or how racial barriers affect school adjustment and performance for blacks. A brief section follows on educational strategies of black youths. The concluding section makes some suggestions about how to reduce the barriers identified in the chapter.

Racial Stratification

Racial stratification exists when members of different, publicly recognized and named racial groups are not treated alike in the economic marketplace, for social positions, and for other purposes even when the persons involved have similar social-class background or similar training and ability. It is customary for American social scientists and other scientists to think of racial stratification mainly in terms of prejudice and instrumental discrimination *against* the minorities. I suggest, however, that racial stratification also involves the adaptive or coping *responses* of the minorities. Each of these components of racial stratification has two faces: instrumental and expressive barriers *against* the minorities, on the one hand, and instrumental and expressive *responses* of the minorities, on the other.

Instrumental barriers are those that yield tangible gains for the dominant group, such as gains resulting from job, wage, and housing discrimination. Consider the case of AT&T that was investigated by the Equal Employment Opportunities Commission: in 1974 the Commission reported that the giant company "saved" about $362 million a year by not paying women, black, and Hispanic workers what they would have earned had they been white males (DeWare 1978). Expressive barriers are the conscious and unconscious treatment of racial minorities by members of the dominant group that satisfies the latter's psychological needs. They include scapegoating as well as personal, intellectual, and cultural derogation of the minorities. Instrumental responses of the minorities consist of the various ways they try to cope with their limited access to jobs, decent wages, education, housing, and the like, including efforts to circumvent, reduce, and eliminate those barriers. Expressive responses are conscious and unconscious responses the minorities make to their treatment that satisfy their own psychological needs, such as the need to maintain their sense of self-worth and integrity. In a racially stratified society such as the United States the expressive barriers and expressive responses are institutionalized as emotionally held beliefs that justify certain attitudes and behaviors toward members of the outgroup (DeVos 1967).

Racial stratification is maintained by the persistence of the instrumental barriers and instrumental responses as well as by the persistence of what DeVos (1984) calls "socialized feelings of aversion, revulsion and disgust" toward the minorities (i.e., expressive barriers) and socialized distrust and opposition of the minorities toward members of the dominant group (i.e., expressive responses).

In view of some claims about the declining significance of race in determining the life chances of black Americans, it is important to point out here that the expressive dimensions of racial stratification may persist after instrumental barriers have been eliminated or after racial minorities have gained more opportunities to hold traditional white middle-class jobs and other positions. DeVos (1967, 1984) has suggested that the expressive dimensions are more resistant to change because they have usually taken on a life of their own as "cultural solutions" to recurring psychological problems facing dominant-group members as well as recurring psychological problems facing racial minorities and because they are learned early in life in the family and peer groups. But there are also other reasons for their persistence. One is that policymakers and reformers are usually not fully aware of and do not adequately address the expressive components of racial stratification. Another is that the minorities demanding changes do not themselves recognize their own expressive tendencies or the functions and consequences of such tendencies. In fact, minority spokespersons are likely to resist analysis pointing to their expressive behaviors and attitudes. Still another reason is the persistence of some vestiges of instrumental discrimination against the minorities; furthermore, some new forms of instrumental barriers may emerge, such as a *secondary job ceiling* that black Americans and similar minorities now seem to experience once they gain a foothold in traditional white middle-class jobs in the corporate economy and white-controlled institutions.

Racial Stratification and Minority Status

For the purpose of this chapter, we may distinguish two types of racial minorities by the initial terms of their incorporation: immigrant or voluntary minorities and castelike or involuntary minorities.

Immigrant minorities are people who came to the United States more or less voluntarily because they believed that this would lead to increased economic well-being, better overall opportunities, or greater political freedom. These expectations continue to influence the way the immigrants perceive and respond to their treatment by white Americans and the societal institutions controlled by the latter. The Chinese in Stockton, California (Ogbu 1974), and the Punjabi Indians in Valleyside, California (Gibson 1988), are examples of immigrant racial minorities.

Involuntary minorities are those who were initially brought into the United States society against their will, through slavery or conquest. Such minorities resent the loss of their former freedom, their displacement from power, and deprivation of their property. Examples of involuntary minorities include black Americans who were brought as slaves from Africa; American Indians, the original owners of the land who were conquered and shoved into "reservations"; and Hispanic Americans in the Southwestern United States who were also conquered and displaced from power.

I have described elsewhere how immigrant and involuntary minorities differ in their perceptions and interpretations of as well as responses to white treatment, and the effects of these perceptions, interpretations, and responses on their school adjustment and performance (Ogbu 1988, 1987, 1983; Ogbu and Matute-Bianchi 1986). Suffice it to say here that the immigrants come to the United States with expectations that greatly influence their responses to the barriers they encounter in society at large and in the schools. Like the involuntary minorities, the immigrants are confronted with economic, social, and political barriers; they may be given inferior and segregated education; they often suffer personal, intellectual, and cultural derogation; and they are often denied true assimilation into the mainstream of American life. Confronted with these *collective problems*, the immigrants tend to interpret them as more or less *temporary problems* they will overcome or can overcome eventually with hard work and education. One thing that helps the immigrants maintain this optimistic view is that they compare their present situation with that of their former selves or with that of their peers "back home." Such a comparison yields much evidence to support the belief that they have more and better opportunities in the United States for themselves or for their children. Even if they are allowed only marginal jobs, they think they are better off in the United States than they would be in their homeland. Furthermore, they tend to believe they are excluded from better jobs because of their status as "foreigners" or because they do not speak English well enough or because they were not educated in the United States. On the whole, the immigrants tend to accept the folk theory of the white middle class that anyone can get ahead in the United States through hard work and good education, even when the immigrants are experiencing barriers in opportunity structure (Suarez-Orozco 1986; Gibson 1988).

Other factors that help the immigrants adjust are their nonoppositional social identity and nonoppositional cultural frame of reference. The immigrants, at least during the first generation, bring with them a sense of who they are which they had *before* emigrating to the United States. They perceive this social identity as *different but not oppositional or ambivalent vis-à-vis white American social identity.* The immigrants also are characterized by *primary cultural or language differences or both*, differences that existed *prior* to their emigration to the United States. That is, their cultural and language differences did not develop in opposition to white American culture and language or as a part of boundary-maintaining mechanisms between them and white Americans. Thus the immigrants generally interpret such differences *as barriers they have to overcome* to achieve the goals of their emigration, but they do not fear or think that they must give up their own culture, language, or identity in the process. Finally, the immigrants tend to trust or acquiesce to white people more than the involuntary minorities do. Even when the immigrants encounter prejudice and discrimination, they tend to rationalize such treatments by saying that as "strangers" in a foreign country they have no choice but to tolerate prejudice and discrimination (Gibson 1988).

All the above factors lead the immigrants to adopt and maintain attitudes and behaviors that are conducive to school success. Immigrant parents impress on their children the fact that they themselves have *suffered* to come to the United States in order to give them "American education" so that they can get ahead in the United States or "back home." Immigrant parents not only stress the importance of education but also take steps to ensure that their children adopt appropriate academic attitudes and study hard—whether the children be Chinese, Koreans, Latinos from South and Central America, or Punjabi Indians (Gibson 1988; Kim-Young 1987; Suarez-Orozco 1987; Ong 1976). Another reason these minorities are academically successful is that *they do not equate school learning with linear acculturation or assimilation into white American culture or with a loss of their language and cultural identity.* Finally, the immigrants' school success is enhanced by their relatively positive and trusting attitudes toward the public schools and the school personnel, which the immigrants often consider to be superior to the schools and teachers of their homeland. Even when the immigrants meet with and resent prejudice and discrimination, they rationalize the experience in a manner that does not discourage their striving for school success (Gibson 1988).

The perceptions, interpretations, and responses of involuntary minorities are different. Not only do involuntary minorities not have "a homeland" situation with which to compare their present selves and future possibilities, but they also use white Americans as a basis for comparison and usually end up with negative conclusions and resentment. In their folk theory they "wish" they could get ahead through education and ability, but they know that they "can't" because of racial barriers which they interpret as part of their undeserved oppression. Some of their survival strategies compete with or detract from schooling as a way of getting ahead, and some produce role models that are counterproductive to school success. Their deep distrust of white Americans and the public schools makes acceptance of school rules of behavior problematic. And because of their oppositional social identity and cultural frame of reference, involuntary minorities do not interpret the cultural and language differences they encounter in school and society as barriers to be overcome, but rather *as symbols of identity to be maintained; they have a tendency to equate school learning with linear acculturation or assimilation into white American culture or with a loss of their language and cultural identity.* Consequently, there are both social and psychological pressures against crossing cultural or language boundaries, even in the school context. On the whole, the societal adjustment of involuntary minorities makes their school success more problematic than is the case for the immigrants. I use black Americans in the next section to show how the contrasting situation of involuntary minorities affects their school experience and school success.

Black Americans in U.S. Society

Instrumental Treatment: Economic Barriers

White instrumental discrimination against blacks has taken many forms, including economic, political, social, and educational barriers. I will use economic barriers as an example, since I have examined these historically in connection with black education. I will use "job ceiling" as a concept to explain how the economic barriers work against blacks. A job ceiling includes both formal statutes and informal practices employed by white Americans to limit the access of blacks to desirable occupations, to truncate their opportunities, and to narrowly channel the potential returns they could expect from their education and abilities (Mickelson 1984; Ogbu 1978). Whites have historically used the job ceiling to deny qualified blacks free and equal competition for jobs they desired, excluding them from certain highly desirable jobs requiring education and where education pays off. In this way whites have not permitted blacks to obtain their proportional share of high-status jobs, and a disproportionate segment of the black population has been confined to menial jobs below the job ceiling.

For many generations the job ceiling was very low. In fact, before the 1960s the segregated institutions and communities serving blacks were the major avenues for occupational differentiation on the basis of formal education and ability. It was in these segregated institutions that blacks gained the best access to professional and other jobs above the job ceiling (Henderson 1967; A. R. Ross 1973), although they were not usually admitted to the very top-level positions, which were filled by whites (Frazier 1957; Greene and Woodson 1930; Johnson 1943; Marshall 1968; A. M. Ross 1967).

Outside the segregated institutions and communities, some blacks were employed in the mainstream economy above the job ceiling, but their employment status there did not parallel their educational qualifications. In general, black advances in mainstream employment, especially above the job ceiling, occurred mainly in periods of national crises (Myrdal 1944; Ogbu 1978). And it can be argued that the increase in black employment opportunities above the job ceiling since the 1960s has also been due to similar national crises and unique events that Myrdal long ago spoke of.

The pattern of black employment began to change in the 1960s when employment opportunities above the job ceiling increased as a result of deliberate government policies under pressures from civil right groups. Executive orders, legislation, and special programs such as affirmative action were used to change hiring practices not only within the government bureaucracy but also in the private sector. Thus Wilson (1979: 34) reports that the average number of recruitment visits of representatives of corporations to predominantly black colleges rose from 4 in 1960 to 50 in 1965 to 297 in 1970. Furthermore, black colleges that had not been visited at all in 1960, such as Clark College, Atlanta University, and Southern University, received 350, 510, and 600 representatives of corporations, respectively, in 1970.

As a result, the number of blacks who entered high-level jobs above the job ceiling in the second half of the 1960s rose dramatically (Brimmer 1974; Ogbu 1978; A. R. Ross 1973). The employment of blacks above the job ceiling has continued to grow. On the other hand, some blacks who have gained entry into high-level positions in the corporate economy and other white-controlled institutions appear to be experiencing a secondary job ceiling: they complain that they are not climbing the professional ladder as fast as their white peers are (Smith 1987).

Analysts generally agree that the favorable changes in opportunity structure that began in the 1960s have affected mainly middle-class blacks,
especially blacks with college educations. No significant changes have taken
place in the employment status of blacks who have not gone to college. There
has been no comparable official policy to assist them. Of course, in the
1960s, when the pool of jobs increased owing to the Vietnam War and social
programs, black employment increased at all levels of the occupational
ladder. The decrease in the pool of jobs in the early 1970s not only slowed
down the employment of blacks lacking college educations but also resulted
in loss of jobs by those already employed, partly because they were the last
hired and therefore the first to be fired. The loss of jobs among blacks without
college educations has continued into the late 1980s; and under the economic
policy of the Reagan administration black unemployment sometimes reached
an astronomical level and remained consistently almost twice the national
level. Blacks who have not gone to college thus have remained in their
traditional marginal participation in which the linkage between schooling,
work experience, and earning is relatively weak (Newman et al. 1978; Newman 1979; Ogbu 1978, 1981; Willie 1979; Wilson 1979).

Expressive Treatment: Intellectual and Cultural Derogation

Whites initially based their derogation of blacks on biblical doctrines, according to Myrdal (1944). However, after the eighteenth century, when it
came to be accepted that man belonged to the biological universe, whites
began to assert that blacks were biologically inferior. Nowadays many whites
no longer openly admit that they think blacks are biologically inferior, but
Gallup polls indicate that the belief persists.

The derogatory beliefs are expressed in many forms, all of which serve
important emotional functions for white people. For example, until the end
of the 1950s it was customary for whites not to publicly acknowledge black
intellectual and other accomplishments. Thus Dick Gregory reports in his
autobiography that in the 84-year history of his college "the outstanding
athlete had never been a black." He himself helped to change this slight
when he *demanded* to be named and was named the best athlete of the year
(1965: 87).

Another form of expressive exploitation or barrier is for white Americans
to attribute to blacks undesirable personal traits. Guy Johnson (1944) presents
a detailed summary of negative stereotypes of blacks in books and articles
written by whites up to the late 1930s. Myrdal provides an even more
elaborate and incisive account of ordinary white people's beliefs about the
"in-born indelible inferiority of Blacks" (1944: 100). He notes that blacks
are thought to be "the opposite of the white race," to stand "for dirt, sin, and
the devil," "to be stupid, immoral, diseased, lazy, incompetent and dangerous
to the white man's virtue and social order." These projections become insti-

tutionalized in white people's behavior toward blacks, in their jokes, and in their oral and written tales about blacks. The aversion that these projections arouse accounts in part, according to Myrdal, for white people's belief that blacks are unassimilable, by which whites mean that it is undesirable to assimilate blacks (Myrdal 1944: 54). Thus the long history of social and physical segregation of blacks was an attempt to "quarantine what is evil, shameful and feared in society" (100).

Finally, throughout much of the history of black–white relations in the United States white people have used blacks as scapegoats. One common pattern is for whites to hold blacks collectively responsible for the offense of a single black person. For example, following Nat Turner's "insurrection" in Southampton, Virginia, in 1831, the geographical mobility of all blacks throughout the country was restricted (Haley 1976; Styron 1966). And in the Rosewood Massacre of January 1923 (CBS Television Network 1984), the allegation that a black man raped a white woman in Rosewood, Florida, resulted in some 1,500 white men from nearby towns marching into Rosewood and killing 40 innocent black men, women, and children. Whites have also used blacks as scapegoats in times of political and economic hardship. For example, during the economic recession of 1934, antiblack violence occurred throughout the United States; Wallace (1970: 84) gives a report of the violence in Columbia, Pennsylvania. Even as recently as the early 1980s, white violence against blacks and other minorities increased in California during the economic recession (State of California, *Governor's Task Force*, 1982).

To summarize, the debate about the inferiority of blacks has continued to date in one form or another. In the early 1940s Johnson (1943) interviewed white Americans in all regions of the country and found that the belief in the inferiority of blacks was widespread and used to justify the segregation of blacks in public institutions like the schools, to segregate them residentially, to limit their social contacts, to confine them to jobs below the job ceiling, and, most importantly, to prohibit interracial marriage. A poll conducted by *Newsweek* magazine in 1978 found that although white beliefs in the racial inferiority of blacks had been decreasing significantly since the 1960s, a significant portion of the whites interviewed still held such beliefs. For example, about one quarter of the whites, or 25 percent of those polled, said that blacks had less intelligence than whites, and about 15 percent thought that blacks were inferior to white people (*Newsweek*, February 26, 1979, 48).

Black American Adaptive/Coping Responses

Instrumental Responses. When black Americans compare their present situation regarding jobs and wages with that of their white peers, they usually conclude that they are worse off than they ought to be for no other reason than that they belong to a subordinate racial group. Generations of shared knowledge and experience of discrimination appear to have led them to believe that they cannot "make it" by merely following the rules of behavior or cultural practices that work for white Americans. Consequently, blacks have developed a folk theory of getting ahead that differs in some important respects from the folk theory of white Americans and that comprises the following survival strategies:

- Changing the rules. Because blacks do not really believe that the societal rules for self-advancement that work for white Americans work equally well for them, they try to change the rules. One example of this is the argument to abolish civil service tests on the basis of claims that they are designed to exclude blacks from jobs, not to enable them to get ahead (Ogbu 1977).

- Collective struggle. This strategy includes what white Americans legitimate as civil rights activities; but for blacks it also includes rioting and other forms of collective action that promise to increase opportunities or the pool of resources available to black communities (Newman et al. 1978).

- Clientship, or "Uncle Tomming." Black Americans have long known that one way to promote survival and self-betterment is through favoritism, not merit. They have also learned that favoritism can be solicited by being dependent, compliant, and easily manipulated: as a result, white Americans, both as individuals and in organizations, serve as patrons to individual blacks and to black groups and organizations. The federal government in particular has tended to assume the patron's role, serving as an employer, a sponsor of educational and other training programs, an adviser and protector of civil rights, and a distributor of subsistence assistance, or "welfare."

- Entertainment and sports. The strategy of entertainment includes activities of a wide range of performers, such as singers, musicians, preachers, comedians, disc jockeys, and writers (Keil 1977: 70). It satisfies people's need for entertainment and serves as a therapy to enable them to cope with the problem of subordination. In recent decades, entertainment and sports have become increasingly important in exploiting mainstream resources.

- Hustling and pimping. These are traditional strategies for exploiting nonconventional resources, or the street economy. Selling drugs is yet another kind of "hustle" (Foster 1975; Hammond 1965; McCord et al. 1969). And in the past "passing for white" was a strategy open to a limited number.

Over many generations the survival strategies became institutionalized and integrated into black culture. They have contributed to shaping the norms, values, and competencies of black Americans. However, with the raising of the job ceiling and other changes since the 1960s, some of the survival strategies have undergone changes. For example, mainstream employment has assumed a greater role, especially among the more educated blacks. Entertainment and sports are increasingly directed at tapping mainstream resources. And "passing for white" is probably not as common as it might once have been.

Expressive Responses. Black Americans have also responded expressively to white treatment. They have done so by forging a *collective, or social, identity that is oppositional vis-à-vis* white American identity and by forging *a cultural frame of reference that is also oppositional* to white American cultural frame of reference *from the point of view of blacks.*

Black Americans developed a new sense of peoplehood, or social identity, *after* their involuntary incorporation into U.S. society. This identity was created as a result of discriminatory treatment, including denial of true admission into mainstream society by the whites, which blacks perceived and experienced as collective and enduring. It seemed that blacks could not expect to be treated like white Americans regardless of their individual differences in ability, training, or education, regardless of differences in place of origin or residence or differences in economic status or physical appearance (Green 1981). Furthermore, blacks learned that they could not easily escape from their birth-ascribed membership in a subordinate and disparaged group by returning to "a homeland" and that most could not escape by "passing for white" (DeVos 1967; Ogbu 1984).

Historical and comparative studies suggest that minority populations that have become "persistent" or "enduring" within nation-states usually have developed boundary-maintaining mechanisms that are both cultural and oppositional (Castile and Kushner 1981; DeVos 1967; Spicer 1966, 1971). Black Americans are no exception.

As an aside, I want to make it clear that I do not consider the *totality* of black American culture to be the product of black–white stratification. I believe that there are some genuine differences in content between black and white American cultures and that several factors contribute to these differences. Some contents of black culture may be of African origin; the exclusion of generations of blacks from certain cultural, economic, and sociopolitical activities could have effectively denied them the opportunity to develop certain know-hows and values associated with such activities and characteristic of whites; and the survival strategies of blacks for coping with economic and other realities could have resulted in cultural content that is not necessarily found in white American culture (Ogbu 1978, 1981, 1986).

But more germane to my present argument is the expressive or qualitative aspect of black culture that derives from black American experience under racial stratification and which differentiates black culture from mainstream culture, that is, white American culture, even where the two cultures have similar contents.

Black Americans are characterized in part by *secondary cultural differences vis-à-vis* white American culture. Secondary cultural differences are those that emerge *after* a population has become an involuntary minority. Such a minority group tends to develop certain beliefs and practices, including particular ways of speaking or communicating as coping mechanisms under subordination, to protect their sense of self-worth or identity, and to maintain boundaries between them and their oppressors. These beliefs and practices may be new creations or simply reinterpretations of old ones. On the whole they constitute a new cultural frame of reference or ideal ways of believing and acting that affirm one as a *bonafide* member of the group.

A key device in the cultural frame of reference is *cultural inversion* (Holt 1972; Ogbu 1982b). In the present context this term has two meanings. Broadly speaking, it refers to the various culturally approved ways that black Americans express their opposition to white Americans. It also refers to specific forms of behavior, specific events, symbols, and meanings that blacks regard as inappropriate for themselves because they are characteristic of white Americans. At the same time blacks approve and emphasize other forms of behavior and other events, symbols, and meanings as more appropriate for themselves *because* these are not part of the white American way of life.

What I want to emphasize is that from the point of view of black Americans, cultural inversion results in the coexistence of two opposing cultural frames of reference guiding behavior *in selected areas of life.* One cultural frame of reference is viewed as appropriate for whites, but not for blacks; the other is accepted as appropriate for blacks but not necessarily for whites. Furthermore, the definition of what is or is not appropriate for blacks is emotionally charged because it is intimately bound up with their sense of collective identity, self-worth, and security. Therefore individuals who try to behave in the inappropriate way or who try to behave like whites, i.e., those who try to "cross cultural boundaries" *in forbidden domains,* may face opposition from other blacks. Their behaviors tend to be interpreted not only as "acting white" but also as betraying black people and their cause, as "trying to join the enemy."

The individuals trying to cross cultural boundaries or pass culturally may also experience, in the absence of peer pressure, what DeVos (1967) calls "affective dissonance." This is partly because their own sense of identity may lead them to feel that they are, indeed, abandoning or betraying black people and partly because they are not sure that whites will accept them.

Evidence of the oppositional cultural frame of reference or cultural inversion can be found in black speech, cultural beliefs and practices, notion of time, styles of thought or cognitive style, and in folklore, art, and literature.

With regard to speech, Holt (1972) suggests that inversion might have begun with black people's reaction to slavery. She says that black slaves recognized that for them to master white English was more or less to be subordinated by it because it would mean their acceptance of the white definition of the caste system. Black slaves, therefore, resorted to inversion as a defensive mechanism that allowed them to fight linguistic and psychological entrapment. The slaves gave words and phrases reverse meanings and thereby changed their functions. As Holt puts it,

> White interpretation of the communication events was quite different from that made by the other person in the interaction, enabling Blacks to deceive and manipulate whites without penalty. . . . This form of linguistic guerilla warfare protected the subordinated, permitted the masking and disguising of true feeling, allowed the subtle assertion of self and promoted group solidarity (1972: 154).

Boykin (1986: 58) notes that linguistic studies show black culture is almost in dialectical opposition to the culture of mainstream America, and this seems to be corroborated by findings of Folb in her study of contemporary inner-city youths. Folb found that these teenagers inverted the meanings whites give to many conventional English words. For example, for the teenagers "bad" means "good"; "nigger" is a term of endearment; "cock" refers to female genitalia, whereas whites use it to refer to male genitalia; "stallion" is an attractive or lusty female as opposed to a sexually attractive male in white speech; "ragged" stands for exceptionally well dressed; "wicked" and "mean" are used to signify outstanding, satisfying, formidable, and stylish (Folb 1980: 230–260).

In the realm of behavior Haskins (1976) reports that in the neighborhood where he grew up, the black males upheld norms that were in opposition to those of law enforcement officers who represented the wider society. The black males saw themselves as living in a hostile environment created by white Americans. Therefore they developed their own criteria for judging one another that were different from the criteria used by whites.

Oppositional cultural frame of reference today is not confined to inner-city people. It has also been reported in clinical studies of middle-class blacks, including black executives in white corporations and black officials in white-controlled institutions. For example, Fordham (1984) reports one researcher as saying that black professionals who "make it" in mainstream culture are people who have succeeded in adapting to basic contradictions arising from different demands of black and white norms. And according to Taylor (1973), black executives who "have made it" in predominantly white corporations have had to renounce the black cultural frame of reference. That is, they have had to stop behaving like blacks, discard symbols used by black peers, and behave like whites with white symbols or act in ways that are alien to other blacks.

Distrusting Whites and White Institutions. Unlike immigrant minorities, blacks have developed a deep distrust of whites. The two races have been engaged in a perennial conflict over education, jobs, crime and justice, political rights, and residential rights, or housing. This conflict has left black Americans with the sense that they cannot trust white Americans or the institutions that whites control, such as the public schools.

In the next section I take the four dimensions of racial stratification (instrumental and expressive barriers, instrumental and expressive responses) and apply them to the public-school experience of blacks. I show how these factors enter into and affect black children's adjustment to school and their academic performance.

School Adjustment and Performance among Blacks

American racial stratification affects black children's schooling in two ways: through the way "the system" treats blacks (i.e., societal policies and practices, and within-school treatment of blacks) *and* the perceptions of and responses of blacks themselves to schooling. The continuing influence of these complex sets of factors cannot be fully comprehended or appreciated without some historical perspective, a perspective which I adopt in the following analysis.

Societal Policies and Practices

Formal education in the United States, as in other urban industrial societies, has usually been structured and perceived in terms of training in marketable skills and credentialing for labor-force entry, remuneration, and advancement. Consequently, in studying minority education, one must consider this wider context and meaning of schooling. In a racially stratified society with a job ceiling, the type of schooling provided for racial minorities is often one that prepares them for their respective place in the job market.

In the case of black Americans, there are two ways in which white Americans have historically prepared them educationally for their place below the job ceiling. The first ensures that blacks do not achieve educational qualifications that would enable them to compete effectively with whites for typical jobs above the job ceiling. The second mechanism discourages blacks from making great efforts to succeed in school, a problem I will discuss in connection with the perceptions and responses of blacks themselves.

The Design of Black Education. Today there are public and private efforts to give black children the same quality education as that provided to white children, but *before the 1960s* there was no explicit policy or goal to educate blacks and whites equally for occupational and social positions. Prior to that time the type of education given to blacks depended on how white

Americans perceived black positions and treated them (Ogbu 1978). For example, before the 1930s blacks in the South were typically said to need "industrial education," by which whites usually meant training in low-grade manual skills. Most financial supports from the states and Northern philanthropists went into industrial education programs. However, during the 1930s, when industrial or vocational education courses became the target of state and federal financial supports in order to meet the needs of the mainstream economy for workers with upgraded industrial skills, the money failed to flow into black schools (Ogbu 1978: 118). Commenting on this development, Myrdal (1944) notes that southern whites believed that blacks should get industrial education so long as that did not mean preparing them to compete effectively with whites for jobs.

Again, consider the shift in the 1960s. Title VII of the 1964 Civil Rights Legislation and affirmative action programs gave blacks increasing access to higher-level jobs, jobs above the job ceiling that required more and better education than had been available to blacks. To ensure that blacks filling these new positions were "qualified," concerted efforts began to be made to "improve" their education, including active recruitment into predominantly white colleges and universities, so that within 10 years black college enrollment rose from 349,000 to 948,000 (Wilson 1979: 172).

I have described elsewhere (Ogbu 1978) the long history of inferior and segregated education of black Americans and how it complemented their inferior roles below the job ceiling. What needs to be said here by way of summary is that until recent decades, black education was different from white education; it was inferior to white education; and it was determined by white Americans' conceptions of the place of black Americans in the racially stratified order. The mechanisms by which the societal policies and practices kept black education different and inferior included segregation, exclusion from certain types of institutions and from certain types of education, inadequate funding and staffing, as well as different curriculum (Ogbu 1978).

Denial of Equal Rewards for Educational Accomplishments The second method by which white Americans have contributed to the twin problem of school adjustment and performance is by denying blacks access to jobs and wages commensurate with their educational credentials. Before the 1960s, blacks who had similar educational credentials to whites were often forced to take less desirable jobs, to receive lower wages, and to occupy lower social status. Nationwide, the more educated blacks, especially the college educated, suffered more discrimination in jobs and wages relative to whites (Ginzberg 1956; Kahn 1968: 12; Killingsworth 1967; Ogbu 1974, 1978).

Such treatment in the employment-opportunity structure affected black children's schooling in two ways. First, it caused some blacks to become disillusioned about the real value of schooling (Ogbu 1974), a point to which

I return later. Second, it was undoubtedly reflected in the way the schools socialized black children in their own reward system, which paralleled the reward system of the society at large. Black children were apparently not taught to get ahead or make higher grades through hard work and persevering academic effort. Furthermore, since local school officials were aware of the treatment of blacks in the adult labor market, they sometimes channeled black children into educational tracks that merely prepared them for their customary place in the employment structure, i.e., in jobs below the job ceiling.

I should point out that the problem of educational rewards has not totally disappeared. It is true that blacks are now hired and paid on the basis of school credentials, and it is also true that many have gained entry into jobs above the job ceiling. However, there is a widespread feeling among blacks in the corporate economy and mainstream institutions that they face a secondary job ceiling, i.e., that they are not given responsibility and not advancing in their jobs as their white peers are.

Treatment of Blacks within Schools

Gross mechanisms of discrimination like deliberate school segregation, differential staffing, funding, and the like, probably are no longer widespread because of legislative statutes or court rulings. But many schools continue to use subtle mechanisms to keep black schooling inferior to white schooling. Some findings from my own research in Stockton, California, from 1968 to 1970 show how minorities and whites may be in the same schools but do not necessarily receive the same education or learn similar rules of behavior for achievement. Take the case of 17 black and Chicano students whose records over a five-year period I examined. I found that all but one of them were given the same annual grade of C, regardless of how hard each child had worked and, strikingly, regardless of what teachers had to say in their written evaluations. There appeared to be little correspondence between the written assessment and the letter grades. On the whole, a child who received a C rating in first grade continued to receive the same rating in subsequent years, although the teacher at each subsequent grade level might write that he or she was "delighted" with the pupil's "progress." Since these children received the same average marks whether they worked hard or not, I have suggested that they were obviously not being taught to associate more effort or hard work with higher achievement (Ogbu 1974, 1977).

A typical example of lowered expectations of teachers and administrators was seen in one family where I was told the oldest son ceased to be "smart" because he was bored with courses that were too easy for him. When his parents approached his teacher and the principal to discuss the matter, the latter rejected their explanation and request for "extra work" for their son.

Their son's work continued to deteriorate and, at the time of my study, he was receiving mostly D's and F's in twelfth-grade courses.

Other researchers (Entwisle and Hayduk 1982; Berkeley and Entwisle 1979, cited in Jackson 1987) have uncovered additional school practices that may undermine the academic achievement efforts of black children: the assigning of report card marks on the basis of classroom "conduct expectations" rather than academic effort. Other subtle mechanisms include the use of biased textbooks and biased curriculum; testing, classification, and tracking; differential treatment of black children in the classroom and in disciplinary situations; prejudiced attitudes and expectations of white students and white school personnel; and lack of adequate understanding of and programs to deal with problems arising from cultural and language differences.

Perceptions and Responses of Black Americans

The extent to which black children, as a group and as individuals, succeed or fail in school depends not only on how white Americans and the schools controlled by the whites treat blacks but also on how blacks themselves perceive and respond to schooling. This section examines the adaptive or coping factors that affect black children's school adjustment and performance: status mobility frame of reference, folk theory of getting ahead in the United States, survival strategies, role models, collective or social identity, cultural frame of reference, and distrust of white Americans and the schools controlled by the whites. Because the coping responses have over time become an integral part of black cultural beliefs and practices, black students are not fully aware of how these factors affect their academic attitudes and behaviors, and they are often unaware of the nature of their own academic attitudes and behaviors. Nevertheless, such factors appear to have caused blacks to develop *a low-effort syndrome, or lack of serious, persevering academic effort as a norm* (Ogbu 1984).

Status Mobility Frame of Reference, Folk Theory, and Disillusionment. The fact that, under the job-ceiling phenomenon, blacks usually compare themselves with whites in terms of types of jobs they have, level of wages or educational payoffs, and related matters is problematic for their academic effort. When they make such a comparison, they usually conclude that they are worse off than they should be in spite of their education and ability because of the job ceiling operating against them. In the course of many generations of such an experience and comparison, blacks learn that they are not given the same chance to get the kinds of jobs and wages available to whites who have similar education. Eventually they come to see this treatment as part of an institutionalized discrimination against them which is not entirely eliminated by merely getting an education (Ogbu 1981b). Consequently, although their folk theory of getting ahead emphasizes the importance of education, they know that they "can't" get ahead because of racial barriers. One result has been disillusionment about the real value of schooling, which has led to a failure to develop "effort optimism" (Shack 1970). By this term, Shack means being serious, determined, and persevering in academic work, test taking, and the like. He notes that because white Americans have been able to receive adequate payoffs for their educational efforts, i.e., to get jobs and wages commensurate with their training and ability, they have been encouraged to develop effort optimism toward school and work, which is summed up in the white maxim "If at first you don't succeed, try, try again." On the other hand, because blacks have had to face the most sustained and extreme discrimination in American history—in particular a job ceiling—they seem to have learned that social and economic rewards are not proportionate to educational efforts; consequently, they have tended to develop a different maxim, "What's the use of trying?"

The disillusionment and its consequences for academic efforts are not of recent origin; nor are they unique to contemporary inner-city blacks. Indeed, early evidence of this comes from a speech made by John Rock, the first black to be admitted to practice before the U.S. Supreme Court. Published in *The Liberator* in 1862, Rock's speech addressed the discouragement that came from limited opportunity for blacks in Massachusetts to achieve a better future through education, employment, or business, in spite of the prevailing ideology of equality of opportunity (cited in Gabelko 1984: 265). In the early decades of the twentieth century, black writers expressed the dilemma of accepting the American Dream with its ethic of individual hard work, thrift, and discipline, because racial barriers made the dream meaningless and irrelevant to black Americans (Sochen 1971). Carl Rowan (1975) has suggested that the dilemma probably continued up to the 1960s. And for some blacks, it persists to this day.

Witness the academic attitudes and efforts of contemporary inner-city black adolescents as described in *Newsweek*'s "My Turn" column by a 15-year-old boy from Wilmington, Delaware (Hunter 1980). The article describes two types of black teenagers in the inner city. The "Rocks," who constitute the majority, have given up hopes of making it in mainstream economy through the white middle-class strategy of school credentials. They therefore stopped trying to do well in school or going to school at all. The "Ducks," or "Suckers," are the few, the "minority of the minority," who still hope to succeed through schooling. The "Ducks" are derided because they go to school every day and even want to go to college; they don't use drugs or alcohol. The "Ducks" are regarded as "wasting their time waiting for a dream that won't come true" because even their parents cannot find jobs.

I found similar disillusionment among blacks whom I studied in Stockton, California. When questioned directly, Stockton blacks would say that to get ahead, to get a good mainstream job, one should get a good education. But they did not seem to match their assertion with effort, even in guiding their children. Part of the reason is that they did not really believe that they had an equal chance with whites to be hired for a job or promoted on the job because of education and ability or that they would do well in an examination designed by white Americans. They believed, instead, that for a black to be hired or promoted when competing with a white person, the black must be "twice as good" or "twice as qualified" as the white.

Black youths in Stockton, like their parents, expressed interest in getting education for mainstream jobs. But at the same time they, too, did not match their wishes with effort. They did not put enough time, effort, and perseverance into their schoolwork. This was not because they did not know what to do in order to do well in school, because they explained during research interviews that the reason Chinese, Japanese, and some white students did well in school was partly because they expended more time and effort than blacks in doing their schoolwork.

Competing Survival Strategies and Role Models. Black folk theory of getting ahead in America stresses other means of getting ahead than schooling, namely, survival strategies within and outside mainstream technoeconomic systems. The survival strategies affect black youths' schooling in a number of ways. For instance, when survival strategies, such as collective struggle, succeed in increasing the pool of jobs and other resources for the black community, they may encourage black youths to work hard in school. But this success can also lead the youths to blame "the system" and to rationalize their lack of serious schoolwork efforts. Clientship, or Uncle Tomming, is not particularly conducive to academic success because it does not create good role models for school success through good study habits and hard work. Instead, clientship teaches black children the manipulative attitudes, knowledge, and skills used by their parents in dealing with white people and white-controlled institutions. As the children become familiar with other survival strategies like hustling, pimping, and drug dealing, their attitudes toward schooling suffer. This is partly because the norms that support survival strategies like hustling may reverse the mainstream work ethic by suggesting that one should "make it" without working, especially without "doing the white man's thing" (Bouie 1981; Ogbu 1974). Furthermore, students who hustle regard social interactions in the classroom as opportunities to gain prestige by putting the other person or persons down. This may lead to class disruption and suspensions (Ogbu 1985, 1987).

There is some evidence that many young blacks view sports and entertainment, rather than education, as the way to get ahead; and their perceptions are reinforced by the realities they observe in the communities and society at large and by the media. One can easily understand why this would be true: blacks are overrepresented in lucrative sports such as baseball, basketball, and football. The average annual salary in the NBA is over $300,000 and in the NFL it is over $90,000. Many of the superstars who earn between $1 million and $2 million a year are black, and these are people who may have had little formal education. Although the number of such highly paid athletes is few, the media make them and the entertainers more visible to black youths than they do black lawyers, doctors, engineers, and scientists (Wong 1987). As a result, young blacks tend to channel their time and efforts into nonacademic activities. There is some preliminary evidence, too, suggesting that black parents encourage their children's athletic activities in the belief that such efforts will lead to careers in professional sports (Wong 1987).

Identity and Cultural Frame of Reference. How do the oppositional identity and cultural frame of reference affect the school adjustment and performance of black children? First, the children take the cultural and language differences they encounter in school as symbols of identity to be maintained, rather than as barriers to be overcome. Black students perceive or interpret learning certain aspects of white American culture or behaving according to the white American cultural frame of reference as detrimental to their own culture, language, and identity. Consequently, they are less willing than immigrant minority students to make serious attempts to cross cultural and language boundaries. Second, also unlike the immigrants, black students tend to equate what is to be learned in school—the curriculum— the language of instruction, and the attitudes and behaviors that enhance academic success, with white American attitudes, culture, language, and behavior. Consciously or unconsciously, they do not appear to make a clear distinction *between* what they learn or do to enhance their school success, such as learning and using the standard English and the standard behavior practices of the school *and* linear acculturation or assimilation into a white American cultural frame of reference, i.e., the cultural frame of reference of their white "oppressors." The equation of standard English and standard practices of the school with a white American cultural frame of reference often results in conscious or unconscious opposition or ambivalence toward learning and using these essential elements at school.

We do not know at what age black children begin to feel the influence of the oppositional cultural frame of reference and identity, but the earliest evidence from research is among children approaching adolescence. The phenomenon is more commonly reported among high school and college students. Research among high school students shows that many tend to define academic tasks or behaviors as well as academic success itself as "white," "not black," i.e., not appropriate for blacks. In contrast, they define certain extracurricular activities traditionally open to blacks and where black students excel as appropriate for blacks. Black students who try to excel in academic work or who become involved in "white" extracurricular activities meet with strong peer pressure to give up such things. The students are criticized and called "Uncle Toms" (Petroni 1970), "crazy," and "brainiacs"

(Fordham 1985; Fordham and Ogbu 1986). But, as DeVos (1967, 1984) has pointed out with regard to involuntary minorities in Japan, even in the absence of peer pressure, some black students avoid adopting serious academic attitudes and perseverance at academic tasks partly because they have usually internalized the belief that such attitudes and behaviors are "white," and partly because they are not certain that they would be accepted by the whites even if they learned to "act white" and were rejected by their black peers. This state of affairs results in "affective dissonance" for such individual black students.

Take the case of black students in an almost all-black high school in Washington, D.C., reported by Fordham and Ogbu (1986). Here the students' peer culture strongly rejected striving for academic success because it was perceived as "acting white." The students regarded many behaviors associated with high achievement—speaking standard English, studying long hours, striving to get good grades—as "acting white." Students who were known to engage in such behaviors were labeled "brainiacs," ridiculed, and ostracized as people who had abandoned the group. The interviews with a number of bright students indicated that some had chosen to put "brakes" on their academic effort to avoid being labeled and harassed. Those who continued to try to do well in school felt compelled to engage in camouflage behaviors that discredited evidence of studying or working hard (e.g., verbally belittling the value of schooling, not speaking up in class, joining athletic teams or taking part in other peer group-approved extracurricular activities, or behaving like class clowns).

The pressure against "acting white" is not limited to lower-class or inner-city black students. It has been reported, though not systematically studied, for middle-class blacks in suburban and private schools (Abdul-Jabbar and Knobles 1983; Gray 1985). Self-reports verify that middle class and suburban black students face this problem and that it extends to black college students as well (Mitchell 1983; Gray 1985; Nemko 1988).

The twin phenomena of oppositional identity and cultural frame of reference present a dilemma for the black youth: he or she must choose between "acting white" (i.e., adopting attitudes and behaviors that are conducive to academic success but which other black students consider inappropriate for blacks) *and* "acting black" (i.e., adopting other attitudes and behaviors that black students approve as appropriate for blacks but which are not necessarily conducive to school success).

Distrust of Whites and the Schools, and Difficulty Conforming to School Norms. Blacks distrust white Americans and the public schools the latter control, as noted earlier. This adds to blacks' problem of school adjustment and performance. Blacks distrust the public schools more than the immigrants do because blacks do not have the advantage of a dual frame of reference to allow them to compare the public schools they attend with the schools they knew "back home." Instead, blacks compare their schools with white schools, especially with suburban white schools, and usually end up with a negative conclusion; namely, that they are provided with inferior education for no other reason than their minority status. Since they do not trust the public schools and white people who control them, blacks are skeptical that the schools can educate their children well. This skepticism is communicated to black youths through family and community discussions and gossip and through public debates over minority education in general or over specific issues like school desegregation. Distrust discourages academic effort in another way: sometimes black parents and children question school rules of behavior and standard practices rather than accept and follow them as the immigrants appear to do. Indeed, blacks sometimes interpret the schools rules and standard practices as impositions of a white cultural frame of reference which do not necessarily meet their "real educational needs."

My ethnographic research in Stockton provides several examples of situations in which blacks (and Mexican-Americans) questioned the value of what they were learning in school: How "relevant" was a high school history textbook, *The Land of the Free*, to the experience of various minority groups in the State of California? What was the value of a preschool curriculum stressing social development rather than academic learning? What was the "real purpose" of tests—both those given at school and civil service tests— weren't they designed to keep minorities down?

The problems associated with the distrustful relations become more complicated because of the tendency of schools to approach black education defensively. I have suggested elsewhere (Ogbu 1988a) that under this circumstance, black parents would have difficulty successfully teaching their children to accept and follow school rules of behavior and standard practices that lead to academic success, and that black children, particularly the older ones, would also have difficulty accepting and following the school rules and standard practices. During my research interviews in Stockton, both black and Mexican-American youths admitted that they did not listen to their parents' advice concerning their school behavior (Ogbu 1974, 1984, 1987).

Black youths' educational strategies. The kind of educational environment that I have described in this section does not encourage blacks to strive for academic success because (1) the treatment of blacks by "the system" discourages academic "effort optimism" and (2) the black coping responses to racial stratification have jointly produced a kind of low-effort syndrome. Under this circumstance, however, blacks have also developed what I call "secondary educational strategies" to enable them to achieve some measure of school success. The secondary strategies operate at the community level (e.g., collective struggle to eliminate segregated and inferior education), the family level (e.g., sending children to private schools), and at the individual student level (e.g., camouflaging academic striving). Because of lack of space, I will focus on students' strategies, summarizing what has been learned from research.

Among black students, especially older black youths, the collective orientation is *not* toward making good grades, even though they usually verbalize that good grades are a goal of theirs. There is little community pressure on them to strive toward academic success (e.g., there is no community gossip about or stigma on black youths who goof off and do not make good grades). Although families say that academic success is a goal for their children, their pressures for success are relatively weak. As for peer groups, their orientation is actually antiacademic success. Consequently, peer pressure is used to discourage striving for school success. Peers subject those who are trying to succeed to criticism and threat of isolation.

In this situation black youths who want to succeed academically more or less consciously choose from a variety of secondary strategies to shield them from peer pressure and other detracting forces. I have already touched on the secondary strategy of camouflage, by which a student conceals his or her real academic attitudes and efforts by pretending not to be serious about schoolwork and success. One technique of camouflaging is to become involved in athletics or other "team-oriented" and peer-approved activities. This appears to reassure peer-group members that one is not simply pursuing individual interests and goals or trying to get ahead of others. Another technique is to become a comedian or jester or class clown (Fordham 1985; Ogbu 1985). By acting foolishly, the youth satisfies the expectations of his or her peers of not being serious about school because the peers do not particularly condone academic success. The jester, however, takes schoolwork seriously when away from peers and does well in school. His or her academic success is usually excused on the ground that he or she may be "naturally smart." Academically successful males are the ones who more often play the class clowns.

A survey of ethnographic literature and related works suggests that academically successful black youths can be categorized according to the types of secondary strategies they use. The categories of successful black youths include the following: assimilators, emissaries, alternators, regulars, and ambivalents.

Assimilators are academically successful youths who *have chosen* to disassociate themselves from or repudiate black cultural frame of reference and identity in favor of white cultural frame of reference; their stance amounts to a kind of "cultural passing." These youths may have come to prefer white norms and values that are in conflict with the norms and values of their blacks peers (Fordham 1985). They tend to believe that to succeed in school and in other mainstream institutions they must give up their membership in the black peer group or even the black community. So the price of success is peer criticism and isolation.

Emissaries are youths who play down black identity and cultural frame of reference in order to succeed in school and in mainstream institutions by mainstream criteria, *but they do not reject black culture and identity.* As a black school counselor once explained this position to me, their motto is "Do your black thing but know the white man's thing." Emissaries approach school learning or participation in other mainstream institutions with the belief that their success by mainstream criteria and standards is a way of demonstrating that whites are not superior to blacks and that their success is a contribution to the advancement of their race. But some emissaries may deny that race is important in determining their school success. By deliberately choosing to follow school rules of behavior and standard practices, emissaries may remain marginal to black peer groups. That is, they may not become encapsulated in peer-approved activities (Haynes 1985; Fordham 1985).

Alternators more or less adopt the immigrant minority students' strategy of "accommodation without assimilation" (Gibson 1988). These students do not reject black cultural frame of reference or identity, but elect to play by the rules of "the system." Their stance seems to be "When in Rome, do as the Romans." They also adopt definite secondary strategies to cope with the conflicting demands of peer groups and those of the schools.

Regulars are somewhat like alternators. According to Perkins (1975: 41), these youths are accepted as regular members of the street culture but do not subscribe to all its norms. They know how to get along with everyone without compromising their own values and without being encapsulated. They are not fully committed to street or peer culture. Regulars tend to have a good knowledge of the street culture, though, and this enables them to engage mainly in relatively safe activities and to know how to handle "trouble" successfully and to ensure that it does not recur (Perkins 1975: 42). The values of the regulars are like those of the mainstream. At school they are considered good students who conform to most conventional rules. They tend to maintain close family ties. Their school success lies in their ability to camouflage.

Ambivalents achieve school success at a relatively high cost, and their academic success can be erratic. These are black youths who are caught between the desire to be with their peers and the desire to achieve by school or mainstream criteria. Some do not successfully resolve this conflict; some do (Mitchell 1983).

Other black youths who are academically successful do not fit neatly into categories. They employ a variety of secondary strategies, like getting involved in church activities and support groups, finding mentors, and engaging "bullies" as protectors in return for helping them with homework. Many other youths are, however, encapsulated in peer groups that are not committed to academic success, and as a consequence these youths do not strive for school success.

Recommendations

Racial barriers to equal access have been described in this chapter as coming from two sources. First and foremost are barriers from "the system," i.e., from the treatment of blacks by society at large and within the schools. This treatment adversely affects the quantity and quality of black education not only directly, but also indirectly by shaping black perceptions of and responses to schooling. The other source of barriers is the pattern of perceptions and coping responses of blacks themselves. The latter has produced a kind of low-effort syndrome in black academic striving. It follows from the analysis of the twin sources of the problem of blacks' school adjustment and performance that policies and programs to increase blacks' success in school must address the two sources of barriers to equal access.

Since the 1960s there have been major improvements in the black American opportunity structure as a result of civil rights pressures that had impacts on government policies and actions and on mainstream treatment of blacks. Since *Brown* v. *Board of Education* in 1954, substantial progress has also been made in reducing gross official and unofficial barriers to equal access such as school segregation. Furthermore, some efforts have been made to improve the school experience of blacks and their educational access within the schools through compensatory education and other special programs. In all these changes, blacks as a group and as individuals have played a major role. As a result, black Americans have made significant gains in educational attainment, in employment above the job ceiling, in closing the wage gap, and in politics; the gap in school performance or test scores has narrowed somewhat.

It is gratifying to see current concern about equal access and the strides taken in this direction. At the same time it is important to point out that the changes have not been evenly experienced among blacks and that for a large segment substantial barriers remain, especially in the lower segment of the black population. The problem of the lower half is not that they suddenly became *different* or pathological, but that they have never been reached or helped as middle-class blacks have.

One prerequisite for eliminating the racial barriers is to recognize that real change will come about through continued effort to open up decent futures for racial minorities and not just by attempting to patch up supposed past and present deficiencies. What middle-class blacks have achieved did not come about from rehabilitation but through changes in opportunity structures in education and jobs and related domains. From a comparative perspective, it is not common for dominant-group members of a society to give up discriminating against racial minorities voluntarily; consequently, it is important to continue vigorous civil rights activities to achieve these objectives.

The schools, for their part, must take steps to eliminate the barriers to equal access within them that were described earlier in this chapter. In addition, schools can and should establish programs to promote more trusting relations between them and minority students and communities. Trusting relations are likely to increase through open discussions of differences in the understanding of educational needs and process, areas of common interest and agreement, the responsibility of each side, and how the two sides can work together. Schools should also establish programs to enable black youths to increase their academic effort without experiencing negative social pressures from peers. Such programs should aim to make the youths aware of the reasons for, as well as the nature and consequences of, their low-effort syndrome. They should teach black youths how to adopt more pragmatic attitudes toward schooling, something like the stance of the alternators and the immigrants.

Black communities have a major role to play in turning things around, in changing attitudes, and in increasing the efforts of black youths toward schooling. Black youths will develop and manifest the norm of maximum academic effort and academic success when black communities assume greater responsibility for promoting such a norm. One step toward achieving this objective is to help children differentiate the attitudes and behaviors that enhance academic success from the attitudes and behaviors that result in loss of black culture and identity. Another important step is for black communities to help black children channel their time and efforts from nonacademic into academic activities. One suggestion for achieving this objective is for black communities to sanction, rather than merely verbalize, their wishes for appropriate academic attitudes and persevering effort as culturally rewarded phenomena. Black communities should provide their young people with concrete evidence that they approve, appreciate, and reward academic success in the same manner and to the same degree, at least, that they approve, appreciate, and reward success in fields such as athletics and entertainment.

Selected References

Abdul-Jabbar, K., and P. Knobles. 1983. *Giant Steps: The Autobiography of Kareem Abdul-Jabbar.* New York: Bantam Books.
Berkeley, M. V., and D. R. Entwisle. 1982. *Kindergarten Social Climate.* Report No. 284. Baltimore: Johns Hopkins University Center for Social Organization of Schools. (ERIC Document Reproduction No. ED1832 287.)
Bouie, A. 1981. *Student Perceptions of Behavior and Misbehavior in the School Setting: An Exploratory Study and Discussion.* San Francisco: Far West Laboratory for Educational Research and Development.

Boykin, A. W. 1986. "The Triple Quandary and the Schooling of Afro-American Children." In *The School Achievement of Minority Children: New Perspectives*, edited by U. Neisser, 57–92. Hillsdale, N.J.: Lawrence Erlbaum.

Brimmer, A. F. 1974. "Economic Development in the Black Community." In *The Great Society: Lessons for the Future*, edited by E. Ginzber and R. M. Solow, 146–173. New York: Basic Books.

Castile, G. P., and G. Kushner, eds. 1981. *Persistent Peoples: Cultural Enclaves in Perspective*. Tucson: University of Arizona Press.

CBS Television Network. 1984. "The Rosewood Massacre." *60 Minutes Magazine* 16–22. (Transcript.)

DeVos, G. A. 1967. "Essential Elements of Caste: Psychological Determinants in Structural Theory." In *Japan's Invisible Race: Caste in Culture and Personality*, edited by G. A. DeVos and H. Wagatsuma, 332–384. Berkeley: University of California Press.

DeVos, G. A. 1984. "Ethnic Persistence and Role Degradation: An Illustration from Japan." Paper presented at the American-Soviet Symposium on Contemporary Ethnic Processes in the USA and the USSR, New Orleans, April 14–16, 1984. (Unpublished manuscript.)

DeWare, H. 1978. "Affirmative Action Plan at AT&T Is Permitted." *The Washington Post*, July 4, 1978, A1, A7.

Entwisle, D. R., and L. A. Hayduk. 1982. *Early Schooling: Cognitive and Affective Outcomes*. Baltimore: Johns Hopkins University Press.

Folb, E. A. 1980. *Runnin' Down Some Lines: The Language and Culture of Black Teenagers*. Cambridge, Mass.: Harvard University Press.

Fordham, S. 1984. "Ethnography in a Black High School: Learning not to Be a Native." Paper presented at the eighty-third annual meeting of the American Anthropological Association, Denver, Colorado, November 14–18, 1984.

Fordham, S. 1985. *Black Student School Success as Related to Fictive Kinship*. Final Report to the National Institute of Education. Washington, D. C. (Unpublished manuscript.)

Fordham, S., and J. U. Ogbu. 1986. "Black Students' School Success: Coping with the Burden of 'Acting White.'" *The Urban Review* 18: 176–206.

Foster, H. L. 1974. *Ribbin', Jivin', and Playin' the Dozen: The Unrecognized Dilemma of Inner-City Schools*. Cambridge, Mass.: Ballinger.

Gabelko, N. H. 1984. "Identifying Discontinuities through Variations in Value Orientations: Applications to the Historiography of American Schooling." Ph.D. dissertation, School of Education, University of California, Berkeley.

Gibson, M. A. 1988. *Accommodation without Assimilation: Punjabi Sikh Immigrants in an American High School and Community*. Ithaca: Cornell University Press.

Ginzberg, E. 1956. *The Negro Potential*. New York: Columbia University Press.

Gray, J. 1985. "A Black American Princess: New Game, New Rules." *The Washington Post*, March 17, 1985, E1, E5.

Green, V. 1981. "Blacks in the United States: The Creation of an Enduring People?" In *Persistent Peoples: Cultural Enclaves in Perspective*, edited by G. P. Castile and G. Kushner, 69–77. Tucson: University of Arizona Press.

Greene, L., and C. G. Woodson. 1930. *The Negro Wage Earner*. Washington, D.C.: Association for the Study of Negro Life and History.

Gregory, D. 1965. *Nigger: An Autobiography*. New York: Pocket Books.

Haley, A. 1976. *Roots: The Saga of an American Family.* Garden City, New York: Doubleday.

Hammond, B. E. 1965. "The Contest System: A Survival Technique." Department of Sociology/Anthropology, Washington University, St. Louis, Mo. (Unpublished manuscript.)

Haskins, K. 1976. 'You Have No Right to Put a Kid Out of School.' In "Four Conversations: The Intersection of Private and Public," edited by A. Toblier, *The Urban Review* 8: 273–287.

Haynes, R. L. 1985. "Minority Strategies for Success." Special Project, Department of Anthropology, University of California, Berkeley. (Unpublished manuscript.)

Henderson, V. W. 1967. "Region, Race and Jobs." In *Employment, Race, and Poverty*, edited by A. M. Ross and H. Hill, 76–104. New York: Harcourt.

Holt, G. S. 1972. " 'Inversion' in Black Communication." In *Rappin' and Stylin' Out: Communication in Urban Black America*, edited by T. Kochman. Chicago: University of Chicago Press.

Hunter, D. 1980. "Ducks vs. Hard Rocks." *Newsweek*, August 18, 1980, 14–15.

Jackson, J. F. 1987. "Black Male Underachievement in the Elementary School Years: A Developmental Approach." (Unpublished manuscript.)

Johnson, C. S. 1938. *The Negro College Graduate.* College Park, Md.: McGrath.

Johnson, C. S. 1943. *Backgrounds to Patterns of Negro Segregation.* New York: Crowell.

Johnson, Guy B. [1944] 1969. "The Stereotype of the American Negro." In *Characteristics of the American Negro*, edited by Otto Klineberg. New York: Harper and Row, 3–22.

Kahn, T. 1968. "The Economics of Inequality." In *Negroes and Jobs*, edited by L. A. Ferman, J. L. Kornbluh, and J. A. Miller, 15–28. Ann Arbor: University of Michigan Press.

Keil, C. 1977. "The Expressive Black Male Role: The Bluesman." In *The Black Male in America Today: Perspectives on His Status in Contemporary Society*, edited by D. Y. Wilkinson and R. L. Taylor, 60–84. Chicago: Nelson-Hall.

Killingsworth, C. 1967. "Negroes in a Changing Labor Market." In *Employment, Race, and Poverty*, edited by A. M. Ross and H. Hill, 49–75. New York: Harcourt.

Kim, Eun-Young. 1987. "Folk Theory and Cultural Model among Korean Immigrants in the U.S.: Explanation for Immigrants' Economic Life and Children's Education/Schooling." Special Project, Department of Anthropology, University of California, Berkeley. (Unpublished manuscript.)

McCord, W., J. Howard, B. Friedberg, and E. Harwood. 1969. *Life Styles in the Black Ghetto.* New York: Norton.

Marshall, R. 1968. "Racial Practices of Unions." In *Negroes and Jobs*, edited by L. A. Ferman, J. L. Kornbluh, and J. A. Miller, 277–298. Ann Arbor: University of Michigan Press.

Mickelson, R. A. 1984. "Race, Class, and Gender Differences in Adolescent Academic Achievement Attitudes and Behaviors." Graduate Ed.D. dissertation, School of Education, University of California, Los Angeles.

Mitchell, J. 1982. "Reflections of a Black Social Scientist: Some Struggles, Some Doubts, Some Hopes." *Harvard Educational Review* 52: 27–44.

Mitchell, J. 1983. "Visible, Vulnerable, and Viable: Emerging Perspectives of a

Minority Professor." In *Teaching Minority Students*. 16: 17–28. San Francisco: Jossey-Bass.

Myrdal, G. 1944. *An American Dilemma: The Negro Problem and Modern Democracy*. New York: Harper.

Nemko, Martin. 1988. *How to Get an Ivy League Education at a State University*. New York: Avon.

Newman, D. K. 1979. "Underclass: An Appraisal." In *Caste and Class Controversy*, edited by C. V. Willie, 92–97. New York: General Hall.

Newman, D. K., B. K. Amidei, D. D. Carter, W. J. Kruvant, and J. S. Russell. 1978. *Protest, Politics, and Prosperity: Black Americans and White Institutions, 1945–1975*. New York: Pantheon.

Newsweek, 1979. A New Racial Poll: What Whites Think of Blacks. February 26: 48.

Ogbu, J. U. 1974. *The Next Generation: An Ethnography of Education in an Urban Neighborhood*. New York: Academic Press.

Ogbu, J. U. 1977. "Racial Stratification and Education: The Case of Stockton, California." *ICRD Bulletin* 12: 1–26.

Ogbu, J. U. 1978. *Minority Education and Caste: The American System in Cross-Cultural Perspective*. New York: Academic Press.

Ogbu, J. U. 1981a. "Origins of Human Competence: A Cultural-Ecological Perspective." *Child Development* 52: 413–429.

Ogbu, J. U. 1981b. "Societal Forces as a Context of Ghetto Children's School Failure." In *The Language of Children Reared in Poverty: Implications for Evaluation and Intervention*, edited by L. Feagans and D. C. Farran, 117–138. New York: Academic Press.

Ogbu, J. U. 1982a. "Cultural Discontinuities and Schooling." *Anthropology and Education Quarterly* 13: 290–307.

Ogbu, J. U. 1982b. "Cultural Inversion." Department of Anthropology, University of California, Berkeley. (Unpublished manuscript.)

Ogbu, J. U. 1983. "Minority Status and Schooling in Plural Societies." *Comparative Education Review* 27: 168–190.

Ogbu, J. U. 1984. "Understanding Community Forces Affecting Minority Students' Academic Effort." Oakland, Calif.: The Achievement Council. (Unpublished manuscript.)

Ogbu, J. U. 1985. *Schooling in the Ghetto: An Ecological Perspective on Community and Home Influences*. (ERIC Document Reproduction No. ED252270.)

Ogbu, J. U. 1986. "The Consequences of the American Caste System." In *The School Achievement of Minority Children: New Perspectives*, edited by U. Neisser, 19–56. Hillsdale, N.J.: Lawrence Erlbaum.

Ogbu, J. U. 1987. "Variability in Minority School Performance: A Problem in Search of an Explanation." *Anthropology and Education Quarterly* 18: 312–334.

Ogbu, J. U. 1988. "Equity and Diversity in Public Education: Community Forces and Minority School Adjustment and Performance." In *Policies for America's Public Schools: Teachers, Equity, and Indicators*, edited by R. Haskins and B. MaCrae, 127–170. Norwood, N.J.: ABLEX.

Ogbu, J. U., and M. E. Matute-Bianchi. 1986. "Understanding Sociocultural Factors: Knowledge, Identity and School Adjustment." In *Beyond Language: Social and*

Cultural Factors in Schooling Language Minority Students, 73–142. Sacramento, Calif.: Bilingual Education Office, California State Department of Education.

Ong, C. 1976. "The Educational Attainment of the Chinese in America." Special Project, Department of Anthropology, University of California, Berkeley. (Unpublished manuscript.)

Perkins, E. 1975. *Home Is a Dirty Street*. Chicago: Third World Press.

Petroni, F. A. 1970. "'Uncle Toms' White Stereotypes in the Black Movement." *Human Organization* 29: 260–266.

Ross, A. 1967. "The Negro in the American Economy." In *Employment, Race, and Poverty*, edited by A. M. Ross and H. Hill, 3–48. New York: Harcourt.

Ross, A. 1973. *Negro Employment in the South, Vol. 3: State and Local Government*. Washington, D.C.: U.S. Government Printing Office.

Rowan, C. T. 1975. "The Negro's Place in the American Dream.: In *The American Dream: Vision and Reality*, edited by J. D. Harrison and A. B. Shaw, 19–21. San Francisco: Canfield Press.

Shack, W. A. 1970. "On Black American Values in White America: Some Perspectives on the Cultural Aspects of Learning Behavior and Compensatory Education." Paper prepared for Social Science Research Council, Subcommittee on Value and Compensatory Education, 1970–71. (Unpublished manuscript.)

Smith, K. L. 1987. "An Exploration of the Beliefs, Values, and Attitudes of Black Students in Fairfax County." Ed.D. dissertation, College of Education, Virginia Polytechnic Institute, Blacksburg, Va.

Sochen, J., ed. 1971. *The Black Man and the American Dream: Negro Aspirations in America, 1900–1930*. Chicago: Quadrangle Books.

Spicer, E. H. 1966. "The Process of Cultural Enslavement in Middle America." *36th Congress of International de Americanistas, Seville* 3: 267–279.

Spicer, E. H. 1971. "Persistent Cultural Systems: A Comparative Study of Identity Systems That Can Adapt to Contrasting Environments." *Science* 174: 795–800.

Styron, W. 1966. *The Confessions of Nat Turner*. New York: Random House.

Suarez-Orozco, M. M. 1986. "In Pursuit of a Dream: New Hispanic Immigrants in American Schools. Ph.D. dissertation, Department of Anthropology, University of California, Berkeley.

Suarez-Orozco, M. M. 1987. "'Becoming Somebody': Central American Immigrants in U.S. Inner-City Schools." *Anthropology and Education Quarterly* 18: 287–299.

Taylor, S. A. 1973. "Some Funny Things Happened on the Way Up." *Contact* 5: 12–17.

Wallace, M. 1970. "The Uses of Violence in American History." *The American Scholar* 40:81–102.

Willie, C. V., ed. 1979. *Caste and Class Controversy*. Bayside, N.Y.: General Hall.

Wilson, W. J. 1978. *The Declining Significance of Race: Blacks and Changing American Institutions*. Chicago: University of Chicago Press.

Wilson, W. J. 1979. "The Declining Significance of Race: Revisited but not Revised." In *Caste and Class Controversy*, edited by C. V. Willie, 159–176. Bayside, N.Y.: General Hall.

Wong, M. L. 1987. "Education versus Sports." Special Project, University of California, Berkeley. (Unpublished manuscript.)

5.

Striving for Sex Equity in Schools

PAMELA KEATING

Précis

Overt sex bias in education and gross discrimination against women have been sources of concern and a focus of action for some time; but subtle instances of institutionalized sexism in schools remain largely unexamined. As long as these barriers remain, all students will be blocked from the kind of full and realistic participation in education that is fundamental to true opportunity. Pamela Keating identifies three areas that merit particular scrutiny: the organizational characteristics and corresponding power relationships in schools; gender expectations for achievement; and curricular issues of representation and the control of knowledge development.

Tests, textbooks, and academic counseling continue to foster sex role stereotyping. Textbooks can misrepresent or fail to address the variety of social roles men and women may perform, and test items may inadequately portray individual experience. Females are often steered away from careers in science and law; they are discouraged from mathematics and mechanical studies. Among the organizational characteristics of schools that favor male dominance are acceptance of coercion as the primary method of maintaining order and the bureaucratic top-down management structure. This environment is antithetical to nurturance and caring for individuals; the underlying values that must be adopted to be successful in this type of school organization are those of competition rather than cooperation or consensus building. These conditions help perpetuate the feminization of the teaching force, where the scarcity of male role models for elementary school boys is particularly unfair and where the sparseness of females in leadership ranks throughout the system misrepresents opportunities for all students.

But perhaps the most difficult and pernicious problem of sexism in schools is the influence of gender expectations in the larger society, To what extent do girls limit their options, unaware that their choices are shaped by social expectations? What are the schools' responsibilities to shape a new social order of fairness and genuine opportunity for all? Readers are challenged to consider the proposition that, to reduce limitations on later opportunities, we must instill in students a social ideal of fairness that is rooted in their current experience of schooling.

Pamela Keating is associate director of the Institute for the Study of Educational Policy at the University of Washington, where for four years she also directed the Northwest Center for Research on Women.

—The College Board

Political and Economic Equality: Women in School and Society

As a people, we have come to recognize the claims of women for equal citizenship. We have sought to assure social and civic fairness through specific legislation protecting equal educational opportunity for women and girls. Recognizing that schools both reflect and shape the society they serve, in schools we have responded to social change and simultaneously shaped public response to issues of fairness for females. Although the structural support for equity is firm, residual ambiguity remains in America regarding the changing roles of women. Schools show a concomitant sluggishness in realizing women's equitable access to educational benefits. Although considerable progress has been made in equalizing access to school programs and resources, some within-school conditions still limit access to knowledge for females and inhibit, in curriculum, instruction, and organization, the fullness of participation that is the essence of opportunity.

Ensuring equal opportunity to participate fully in the larger life of the country, through a citizen's right to vote, was the central effort of the women's suffrage movement at the beginning of this century. Seneca Falls, site of the 1848 convention calling for women's suffrage, and home of Elizabeth Cady Stanton, is still called the cradle of American feminism and could be termed the birthplace, as well, of our country's version of the worldwide phenomena of women's liberation.

The campaign for women's political equality in the United States developed during the nineteenth century following Enlightenment ideals of the natural equality of persons, and civic responsibility for giving free expression to individual interests. But it was not until the passage in 1920 of the Nineteenth Amendment to the U.S. Constitution—prohibiting the denial or abridgment of the right to vote on account of sex—that women's civil rights were safeguarded.

Although variously interpreted as an affirmation of full equality, judicial interpretation, however, unfortunately for women, was narrowly focused on the precise purpose and language of the Amendment. Differential treatment of men and women continued to be upheld in the courts through the middle of the twentieth century. Changes in women's work and control of childbearing have challenged prevailing conceptions of women's role, resulting now in greater activism by judges in equalizing legal protections.

As women's permanent participation increased following World War II, and as the civil rights movement focused national attention on equalizing opportunity, Congress acted to restrict employment discrimination. Title VII of the 1964 Civil Rights Act[1] prohibited discrimination in employment on the basis of race, national origin, religion, and sex. Although not specifically applicable to education, the content of the Act did cover employment broadly and, more significantly, served to codify our country's commitment to the rights of all citizens.

The Equal Protection and Due Process clauses of the post–Civil War Amendment (on which much hope had hung for early feminists committed to fuller civic participation) have since served to affirm women's social status as equal to that of men. The Fourteenth Amendment secures the Bill of Rights to citizens of each state and assures each citizen the full protection of the laws. Courts have come to treat "sex" like "race" and "national origin" as a "suspect classification." That is, where distinctions are made between men and women, a stricter standard of judicial review is required, and compelling state interests must be proved for the differentiation based on sex. Sex is not correlated with capacity to contribute to society; it is an immutable human characteristic. Imposing special restrictions or burdens on the members of a particular sex, solely on that basis, thus violates civic protections of persons under the law. The stigmatization and second-class citizenship associated with suspect classifications further compels the courts to equalize treatment of individuals.

States are prevented from acting differentially with regard to males and females in the educational programs they provide. As public institutions, schools have a duty to safeguard the rights of all students as citizens. Moreover, states' legal requirements for compelled attendance plus the documented effects of school success for subsequent opportunity means that special care is required in educational institutions and activities to assure equal opportunity for each student.

Educational institutions are obliged to conform to particular public provisions and guidelines in assuring equal treatment under the law. After satisfying standards of equal access to the school program, however, educators should seek an ideal of equal treatment for all students. Within the context of social accountability, they ought to examine internal practices and policies that differentially and adversely affect some students and develop equitable opportunities for learning. The schools' seriousness about educational equity forms the fundamental fairness of our people. Curricular and organizational commitment to fairness for all students—without regard to race, gender, or economic status—shapes social expectations and institutions. Reciprocally, significant alterations in social roles, especially the changing status and work of women, compel continued responsiveness from schools.

The most far-reaching mandate for sex equity in education is Title IX of the Education Amendments of 1972.[2] Antidiscrimination legislation, prior to its passage, did not cover discrimination in educational programs and policies specifically. Title IX originally was intended to amend the Civil Rights Act to prohibit sex discrimination in higher education, and eliminate another provision of that act that left employees vulnerable to this discrimination. A legislative compromise resulted in the coverage of all federally aided school programs. Provisions of the legislation were broadly applied to sex-segregated vocational education courses, interscholastic athletic programs that were less developed for girls than for boys, continuing school services to pregnant students, and class materials that reflected gender bias in the representation of women and men.

The landmark legislation was passed to ensure equal educational opportunities regardless of gender at every educational level—from kindergarten through graduate study including vocational and technical schools. "No person in the United States shall, on the basis of sex, be excluded from participation in, be denied the benefits of, or be subjected to discrimination under any educational program or activity receiving federal financial assistance." Under Title IX, federal departments and agencies providing funds to educational programs or activities are authorized to issue rules and regulations implementing its requirements. Federal funding for educational programs is contingent on compliance with its provisions. The powerful post-Depression strategy of tying allocations of federal money to institutional commitment to public purposes serves to ensure schools' cooperation in striving for gender equity in education.

Schools now offer girls and young women substantially more opportunity to participate in all sports programs. Since the passage of Title IX, five times the number of girls play high school sports as did previously. More than 10,000 young women currently attend college on athletic scholarships, including many who could not afford higher education without this assistance. School districts can no longer expel students or prevent them from participating in school activities because of pregnancy. School counselors have begun to test and score all students' performances using the same criteria and to advise both girls and boys to pursue careers and employment options that suit them, instead of suggesting sex-stereotyped choices.

In 1974, two years after Congress passed the Education Amendments which included the assurances of Title IX, it enacted the Women's Educational Equity Act[3] to help remedy discrimination against women and girls in education. WEEA is a funding program under which grants and contracts are awarded annually for the development, demonstration, and dissemination of model products and programs for achieving educational equity.

Two years later, Congress specifically directed that federally funded vocational education programs eliminate sex bias and stereotyping. Support has since been strengthened to encourage states in developing activities and strategies addressing issues of gender equity.

Assurances of equal access based on adequate educational preparation have enabled women to enter new job markets and experience heretofore unexplored opportunities for occupational and economic well-being. In the 15-year period from 1950 to 1974, the number of women in the work force doubled. By mid-1977, 41 percent of the country's labor force was female. Now more than half of all women over 16 are employed.[4] Women enter nontraditional jobs and careers with increasing frequency, and what was once unique in the public and professional lives of women is now usual, as women expand their involvement in various social roles.

Women have, nonetheless, experienced limitations on their earning power and opportunities for advancement that reflect society's slowness to change decades of social behavior and wariness to depart from past practice. Occupational and wage/rate stratification reveal a darker view of women's social opportunity. Despite some women's entry into nontraditional employment, women continue to be concentrated in low-paying, low-status occupations: secretaries, nurses, and elementary school teachers. For most women, opportunity is little more than an extension of the traditional care-giving responsibilities of mother and homemaker.

Barriers to women's full economic and social participation are embedded, obviously, in the larger society. Reducing limitations on women's later opportunity is nonetheless contingent on educating young adults who share a social ideal of genuine fairness. Educational equity is training for fairness in later life. Reducing and removing barriers to equal treatment in schools is an important investment in future social equitability. For all the fairness already achieved, however, more work still is needed in three areas that reflect a continuing gender imbalance in schools and society: the feminization of teaching; stereotyping by sex and role in educational materials and activities; and insufficient engagement in developing knowledge by and about women. In each instance, females' full participation within schools, as well as their opportunity for expanded involvement in the world of work and public life, is limited. Sex equity in the internal school dynamics of teaching and learning will be discussed separately.

The feminization of teaching, that is, the phenomenon of a predominantly female teaching corps in schools across the country, is an important dimension of American schooling. The issue is not that women are teachers. Indeed, historically, women have quite naturally enlarged their domestic responsibilities for the care and nurturance of their children to include keeping school. The preponderance of women in education may prove particularly valuable, in fact, as we come to understand and appreciate the nature of caring. A majority of women teachers is problematic, however, inasmuch as it means devalued work and role. Like most occupational clusters for women, teaching is characterized by low status and wages, presumably reflecting lower social valuation. This lower level of esteem for work traditionally performed by women means less remuneration, reduced economic mobility, and limited opportunities for personal and professional development. Women's movement in and out of the work force, frequently for care-giving responsibilities, in turn, interacts with market value.

The largely bureaucratic organization of American schools, often administered by men, exacerbates this devaluation of women teachers. Historically, teaching represented an important employment opportunity for women, as well as an extension of women's central social role. In the context of how schools operate, teaching as women's work remains underexamined for what it reveals to students about the appropriate roles and relationships of men and women in organizations. As schools communicate these patterns of institutional behavior to students, they develop boys' expectations for leadership and decision making, and suggest images of lesser status, even subservience, in girls. Moreover, schools are organized as highly structured environments where competition characterizes much of the motivational investment, and coercion is the primary method of maintaining order and stability. Some scholars speculate that females do not do as well in this kind of environment—either teaching or learning. In thus limiting full participation, the structured, hierarchical organization of schools appears to frustrate opportunities for females.

Men's and women's social roles continue to be inadequately addressed or misrepresented in educational materials and activities. For all the gender-fair examinations and adjustments that have occurred, sex stereotyping and sexism have not been eradicated from the curriculum and instruction of schools. The infrequency of school text adoptions and publishers' time lags in bringing new ideas into print limit the availability of up-to-date sex-equitable materials. Public attitudes, and expectations too, restrict the speed with which change can occur.

The ratio of males to females depicted in texts, tests, and instructional examples is severely skewed. Not only are males represented more frequently, they are engaged in more interesting activity. Females are portrayed in more limited fashion, for the most part, in traditional care-giving roles. In mathematics problems, stereotypic roles are often reinforced by picturing females cooking or sewing, whereas males are shown engaged in varied and interesting activities. Reading series and ancillary literature selections, as well as supplementary literature in other courses, do not reflect, really, women's actual opportunities and accomplishments. In tests, analogies and examples that draw on sex-typed male experience and depict stereotypic gender roles are inappropriate and insidious in modeling and measuring male and female behavior.[5]

Academic and career counseling continue to reflect traditional biases about women's expectations and achievements. Girls are still counseled away from additional math courses, frequently foreclosing further study in science and math. Reduced funding for counseling staff in many schools means that students are not being assisted in ascertaining real options for adult living and adequately preparing academically for alterations in social role. In reading selections and texts the portrayal of adult roles and relationships ought to reflect real life and the actual and potential opportunities available to both men and women.[6]

Developing and integrating knowledge by and about women in the curriculum is a final frontier for those seeking gender equity in access to knowledge. The issue is one of control. How is knowledge generated? How do we select the significant ideas that will represent a people or place or time? Who decides which ideas are included in the description of shared society; who tells the story of social experience? How are individual experiences valued? What do we know about women's experiences and how do we take this knowledge into account in shaping social expectations and public programs? What counts for inclusion in the cultural canon? Even the relatively sparse record of women's lives has not been integrated into the central study of our culture. In education the experience of women, as women, has been largely ignored.

Women have begun to write their stories, women's experience is being widely studied, and scholars are integrating knowledge about women into the curriculum—not as isolated instances, but as integral knowledge in human experience. The heretofore largely unexamined lives of women are being reconstructed from existing resources in efforts to report women's contributions to our cultural development and identify their experience for contemporary society. We have no full record of the experience and expression of women in our culture because of their essentially self-effacing social roles in our history. Representative accounts of women's actual activity that do exist—women's writing and artistic accomplishments—need to be identified and more fully incorporated into the history that we teach students in school. Students should be exposed to the distinctive perspectives of women's lives and afforded opportunities to recognize the implications of the differing experiences of men and women in the development of our society.[7]

Integrating newly developed knowledge about women and social roles has involved making teachers aware of the new scholarship on women, technical assistance with course revisions, and development of gender-fair materials for classroom use. Textbook editors have acknowledged social changes, and some have improved the accuracy and scope of their coverage of women and girls. But others continue to publish material that treats women in a token fashion, rather than blending the varieties of human experience for a fuller account of a people.

How, then, do schools create the conditions for full participation? How can educators develop opportunity for access in both schools and society?

Schools, seeking improvement or refinement of opportunities for females, will need to show sensitivity to women's roles within the school environment and investment in women in leadership positions; commitment to gender-fair counseling services and teacher training in academic advisement; and support for teachers' participation in curriculum-integration initiatives and course revision to include new scholarship on women. Patterns of unequal participation or representation in schools should be taken quite seriously. Administrators ought to actively recruit women to their ranks. District assignment practices should reflect an interest in providing a variety of role models to students. Inadequate materials ought not to be purchased, and stereotypic representations must be avoided altogether. Teachers should be offered opportunities to enrich their courses to reflect knowledge about women.

Schools have to improve their capacity for timely response to social change—organizationally and in curriculum and instruction—about gender and role. Already, sex-linked employment stratification has been observed in the relatively young computer industry, with job opportunities involving complex thinking (programming, marketing) being filled by men, while data-processing and other low-level, and low-paying, jobs are held predominantly by women.[8] While young girls appear equally enthusiastic about computer use initially, a marked decline in girls' participation has been noted during the middle school years. Reasons for adolescent females' low computer course enrollments vary—the onset of puberty; consciousness of sex-role socialization; sense of protected male "turf"; machine avoidance; math blockage; limited family expectation—but the pattern in itself is a problem. Simultaneous schooling responses to the disproportional participation of boys and girls could include the development of more sophisticated software, not based exclusively on math, but on other forms of logic; ensuring a "user-friendly" environment for computer work, to encourage use by a variety of people with very different interests in the technology; and extra math coaching for female students.

Similarly, just as schools should be staffed in part with women as administrators, men should be recruited for instruction in the primary grades—as models for young boys and to indicate to children men's capacity for child nurturance and support.

Recognizing and rectifying gender imbalance in educational participation is a political process. Given the role of education in American society, the fairest of schooling processes are required to maximize the opportunities for development—individual and social—of all students. In creating an equitable educational environment, the dynamics of the schools' response to, and contribution to, the social situation of women ought to be informed by principles of fairness in substance and process. Schools should be engaged in maximizing women's full participation by reviewing and exploring knowledge about women; modeling the desirable social environment for active civic participation; and raising professional and public awareness of sex-typing in words and images, options and activities.

Inside Schools: Different Expectations for Participation and Achievement

In the more particularized, personal interaction of teaching and learning in course work and classrooms, creating an equitable schooling environment is similarly, and more subtly, challenging. Recognition of individual differences and the development of distinctive capacities assume both an absence of gender bias in practice and an awareness of its influence in principle. To realize an ideal of social fairness, we first must acknowledge how unfair treatment and unequal results limit genuine equitability in school and later life. The interactions of males and females in school environments suggest that traditional male–female roles—social expectations as a function of gender—constrain all students' options and opportunities.

Two kinds of barriers limit students' full participation in, and benefit from, the schooling experience. One is the differential treatment accorded students as a function of their sex. Teachers, shaped by their own social experience, frequently play out past practices, and even prejudices, in their work with male and female students. The other concerns gender-related limitations on achievement. As a result of teachers' differential treatment of students and, presumably, the organization of the school itself, significant outcome differences in learning, achievement, and opportunity are found between males and females at the conclusion of the K-12 school progression.[9]

The problematic dimension of a predominantly female teacher corps, primarily in the elementary grades, is most evident in research findings relevant to teacher–student interactions. Since the early 1970s, researchers have documented the inequitable expectations, insensitive or inadequate teacher-approval behaviors, and unfair patterns of teacher–student interaction that seem to sustain a functional sex-role stereotyping in schools. These observations are not, however, merely data for those laying claim to fairer distribution of social rewards or the equalizing of opportunity in later (adult) life. Rather, they represent a documentation of inequitability and unfairness in the daily work of schools. They indicate the subtle and not so subtle consequences of sexism, and they describe the internal evidence of inequitability that limits learning for all students.

Studies show how girls' dependent behaviors are reinforced, and, hence, reproduced, in a reward structure where docility is valued, and females find reinforcement for quiet behavior, neat work, and conformity. Girls have been shown to hide their academic weaknesses and avoid intellectually challenging activity in order to maintain teacher approval. "Thus the young girl programmed into dependency on rewards will be more likely to avoid the academically challenging problem wherein lies the possibility of failure and loss of teacher approval but also the potential for academic growth and stimulation."[10] Unfortunately, the acquiescent attitudes females learn bear little relationship to the curious and analytical behaviors associated with increasing individual knowledge and competence.

Some research even suggests that the reinforcement of passive behaviors in schools actually diminishes ability and that declining IQ scores for some students are traceable to indications of shy, passive, dependent approaches to learning. Inasmuch as these attitudes differentiate boys' and girls' behaviors, schools effectively risk decreasing female students' ability by reinforcing acquiescent behavior in all students.[11]

Disproportionate teacher attention to male students has also been noted in several studies. In coeducational classrooms, boys appear to receive a greater share of teachers' notice and time.[12] Boys initiate more contact with teachers, and teachers initiate more contact with boys; and on "many days, teachers do not interact with their female students."[13] Teachers more frequently accept incorrect or poor answers from boys and respond more frequently to their requests for help. Boys are given attention regardless of their proximity to the teacher and are generally more visible in the classroom. Although there have been far fewer examinations of teacher–student interactions in junior and senior high school, more frequent teacher interactions with male students are reported.[14]

This heightened class presence of male students is not necessarily a positive experience, however; boys receive a majority of negative classroom communications. Although girls may be largely ignored, boys are frequently reprimanded. Boys' dominance in the daily student–teacher interactions may be as negative an experience as the reinforcement of passivity in girls.[15] The finding that some young boys do not change their behavior in response to teachers' suggestions as readily as do girls[16] suggests that the independent learning we may wish to foster for all students is, in fact, at variance with predisposing and externally reinforced behaviors of both boys and girls. Experimental studies indicating that changing teachers' classroom behaviors can change gender-typical student behaviors[17] should guide research and staff development activity in equalizing access to knowledge for all students.

Differences in the treatment of male and female learners is also evident in the courses students select and the kinds of learning made available to them. Students are still sorted into certain sex-linked course choices. Inadequate academic advisement often means that students are locked into stereotypic expectations, interests, and abilities that perpetuate the gender stratification inside schools and beyond. Even within supposedly neutral subjects of study, girls are often taught differently than boys with concomitantly different expectations for behavior.[18]

The consequences of disproportionate treatment of boys and girls, presuming essentially comparable cognitive capacities, seem most apparent in the variability of schooling outcomes experienced by males and females. In a recent review of research on sex differences and education, Elizabeth Fennema explores a fascinating hypothesis. Presuming that the goals of American education are the same for both boys and girls, one would note that they are taught in the same classes, seemingly equally free to select their course work, and continuing with postsecondary education at about the same rate. If, in addition to the goals, the educational opportunity is equal, then, she argues, the outcomes of schooling should be the same for females and males. But, of course, the outcomes are not equal for both. "Males do not develop their verbal skills to the same level as females, and females achieve at lower levels than males in mathematics and science. Perhaps more important, fewer females than males develop leadership skills, but more demonstrate lowered self-esteem in their ability to learn, negative attributional styles, and habits of dependency. Such inequities in educational outcomes hinder many females from participating fully and contributing significantly in adulthood."[19] Although girls have long been believed to have superior verbal ability and boys supposedly possess greater capacity for mathematical reasoning and scientific study, the differences between them in both aptitude and achievement actually seem small. Paradoxically, "psychological research finds small, persistent gender differences in only a few areas of performance, notably mathematical problem-solving at later grades, yet larger and more persistent differences are found in educational outcomes linked to occupational choice and life patterns."[20]

In the affective domain, more dramatic differences are found. Boys, for example, enter school evidencing independent learning behaviors and emerge, for the most part, as able, confident, motivated students. Girls exhibit dependent behaviors at both entry and exit. Dependency is described as more frequently requesting directions, passively waiting for help, maintaining proximity to the teachers, and apparent helplessness in the face of challenges. These behaviors are thought to be developed in the process of socialization. Sex-typed social reinforcement of dependency develops in early childhood, and schools seem to reinforce, rather than rectify, these differences.[21]

Citing the literature on achievement motivation, Fennema asserts the importance of independence in order to have strong achievement strivings and success. Dismissing the myth of differential self-esteem between males and females, she nonetheless identifies gender-linked lack of confidence in specific subject areas. "In mathematics, starting at least by grade 6 and persisting through high school, even when females achieve at the same level as males, females report significantly less confidence in their ability to perform mathematical tasks or to learn new mathematics. How confident one feels about succeeding at a task appears to be related to the stereotyped appropriateness of that task to one's sex."[22] Since children appear to select subject matters and tasks that are socially sex-appropriate, and apply themselves more diligently to work that they perceive to be of higher value, a reinforcement of sex-linked behavior occurs.

Even as females achieve at lower levels in mathematics and science, males do not develop their verbal skills to the same level as that of females. More males develop leadership skills. More females "demonstrate lowered self-esteem in their ability to learn, negative attributional styles, and habits of dependency."[23]

The internal response of female students to conceptions of their own ability is a more subtle effect of differential treatment. Because girls tend to exhibit the behaviors of good students, teachers seem to assume that they are well-behaved and working hard. Hence, when they fail to achieve as expected, girls and their teachers often assume a failure of ability, since application and industry were apparent. Boys, by contrast, tend to attribute failure to lack of effort; thus their perception of their own ability is intact and unquestioned.

A promising place to begin to alter expectations and attitudes of differential treatment is in teacher preparation programs. Teachers need to be taught how to develop a range of student abilities, respond to various capacities and interests, integrate learning experiences to help students make meaning in life, and nurture students' critical capacities for personal and social development.

The enculturating role of American education implies preparation for continuing change and development, as well as initiation into social customs, traditions, and the varied experiences of a diverse people. Schools have a dual responsibility: to conserve the best of our cultural past and anticipate our future, preparing free and independent people sharing the values of political democracy.

Schools serve the overt political purpose of socializing a nation. Pressing social concerns are vindicated in and through the schools; education, in turn, influences the country's social agenda. Schools are expected to contribute to the development of society by shaping students' knowledge and appreciations. The understanding and sensitivity developed with teachers and texts in schools will inform the opinions of our future citizens.

Equalizing Opportunity

Removing barriers to each person's full participation in school and society requires a commitment to gender-free education that enhances individual differences and captures personal contribution. To the extent that we agree that gender is socially constructed, we must acknowledge the importance of education in creating sex-equitable opportunity—that is, the options for social and economic mobility available to persons on the basis of talent, skill, or some similar aptitude or quality. Those schooling materials and experiences— texts, tests, projects, and activities—that limit the option of full participation for some students, because of bias or prejudice, are inappropriate in contemporary American schooling. If we are interested in nurturing talent and developing opportunities for growth for each child, regardless of gender, we need to pay particular attention to the organizational arrangements of schools inasmuch as they represent unequal sex-role relationships; assess the adequacy of the curriculum to integrate human experience; and, perhaps more important, carefully craft the interaction of teaching and learning as a personal exchange.

Fair treatment of all persons, males or females, regardless of race or economic status, is a responsibility of the democratic institution of the school. Striving for social equality must be a central educational commitment, developing full participation, its driving force.

In Lois Gould's "Fabulous Child's Story," a newborn is named "X" so no one can tell its gender.[24] Under a secret government experiment, Baby X is given to a couple to raise, on condition that the child's sex not be revealed and that activities agreeable to both boys and girls be made available to the

child. Considerable consternation greets this child among relatives, the parents of playmates, and, eventually, the administrators, teachers, and parents
in school. When professionally examined, X is deemed the least mixed-up
child ever. X's sex will be apparent when it matters, but X's opportunities
for participation in the activities and full life of the school are unhindered
by any restraints due to expectations of gender. Presumably, X has more
opportunity to develop distinctive capacities than if the sex of X is known.
The story concludes with the gathering of X's classmates around X, all dressed
in the neutral garb of children's overalls, witness to the mutual interest in
individual participation.

Equalizing educational opportunity means creating the conditions for
personal participation without regard to the social constructs of gender. It
also requires a reconstruction of social roles through the enculturating programs of the schools.

Notes

1. Public Law 92-261, Title VII, Sec. 701, March 24, 1972.
2. Public Law 92-318, Title IX, Sec. 901, June 23, 1972.
3. Public Law 95–561, Title XX, Sec. 3341, August 21, 1974.
4. Population Profile of the United States: 1983/84, *Current Population Reports* 145:
P23. Washington, D.C.: U.S. Department of Commerce, Bureau of the Census,
1985, 30.
5. For a review of equity issues in texts, tests, and classroom practices, see Esther
E. Diamond and Carol Kehr Tittle, "Sex Equity in Testing," 167–188; Marlaine E.
Lockheed with Susan S. Klein, "Sex Equity in Classroom Organization and Climate,"
189–217; and Kathryn P. Scott and Candace Garrett Schau, "Sex Equity and Sex
Bias in Instructional Materials," 218-232 in *Handbook for Achieving Sex Equity
through Education*, ed. Susan S. Klein (Baltimore: Johns Hopkins University Press,
1985).
6. For a summary of research on the female experience and science and mathematics,
see Elizabeth Stage, Nancy Kreinberg, Jacquelynne Eccles (Parsons), and Joanne
Rossi Becker, "Increasing the Participation and Achievement of Girls and Women
in Mathematics, Science, and Engineering," in Klein, *Handbook*, 237–268. For a
discussion of the prevailing myths about female students and mathematics, see also
Elizabeth Fennema, "Sex-Related Differences in Education: Myths, Realities, and
Interventions," in *Educators' Handbook: A Research Perspective*, ed. Virginia Richardson-Koehler (New York: Longman, 1987), 329–347.
7. For a discussion of "The New Scholarship on Women," see the chapter of the
same name by Sari Knopp Biklen and Charol Shakeshaft, in Klein, *Handbook*,
44–52. For a more specific description of the development of knowledge by and
about women, see Renate Duelli Klein, "Women's Studies: The Challenge to Man-
Made Education," in *Women and Education*, ed. Sandra Acker et al. (London: Kogan
Page, 1984), 292–306. The philosophical argument for equalizing women's access
to knowledge development is discussed by Maxine Greene in "Sex Equity as a
Philosophical Problem," in Klein, *Handbook*, 29–43.

8. See Myra H. Strober and C. L. Arnold. "Integrated Circuits/Segregated Labor: Women in Three Computer-Related Occupations" (Stanford, Calif.: Institute for Research on Educational Finance and Government, 1984), as discussed in Carol Kehr Tittle, "Gender Research and Education," *American Psychologist* 41 (1986): 1161–1168.

9. David Sadker and Myra Sadker, "The Treatment of Sex Equity in Teacher Education," in Klein, *Handbook*, 145–161. See also Chapter 5, "Sex Bias: The Hidden Curriculum in the Elementary School," in Nancy Frazier and Myra Sadker, *Sexism in School and Society* (New York: Harper and Row, 1973), 76–113. For a brief review of inconsistencies in the research on teacher–student interactions, see Tittle, "Gender Research and Education," 1162–1163.

10. Frazier and Sadker, *Sexism in School and Society*, 95.

11. Ibid., 96.

12. Sandra Acker, "Sociology, Gender, and Education," in Acker et al., *Women and Education*, 71.

13. Fennema, "Sex Related Differences in Education," 342.

14. Tittle, "Gender Research and Education," 1162.

15. Elizabeth Stage, et al., "Increasing the Participation and Achievement of Girls and Women in Mathematics, Science, and Engineering," in Klein, *Handbook*, 262–263.

16. Tittle, "Gender Research and Education," 1162.

17. See David Sadker and Myra Sadker, "Interventions that Promote Equity and Effectiveness in Student–Teacher Interaction." Paper presented at the annual meeting of the American Educational Research Association, 1985, as discussed in Tittle, "Gender Research and Education," 1162.

18. Susan S. Klein, Lillian N. Russo, Carol Kehr Tittle, Patricia A. Schmuck, Patricia B. Campbell, Peggy J. Blackwell, Saudra Rice Murray, Carol Anne Dwyer, Marlaine E. Lockheed, Barb Landers, and Joy R. Simonson, "Summary and Recommendation for the Continued Achievement of Sex Equity in and through Education," in Klein, *Handbook*, 492–496.

19. Fennema, "Sex Related Differences in Education." 335–336.

20. Tittle, "Gender Research and Education," 1166.

21. Fennema, "Sex Related Differences in Education," 333–334.

22. Ibid., 334.

23. Ibid., 334–335.

24. Lois Gould, "X: A Fabulous Child's Story," *Ms. Magazine*, December 1972, 74–76.

Selected References

Acker, Sandra, Jacquetta Megarry, Stanley Nisbet, and Eric Hoyle, editors. *Women and Education (World Yearbook of Education)*. London: Kogan Page, 1984.

"The Classroom Climate: A Chilly One for Women?" Project on the Status and Education of Women. Washington, D.C.: Association of American Colleges, 1982.

Deaux, Kay. "Sex and Gender." *Annual Review of Psychology* 36 (1985): 49–81.

Dewey, John, and James H. Tufts. *Ethics*. New York: Holt, 1932.

Eagley, Alice H. "Gender and Social Influence: A Sociopsychological Analysis." *American Psychologist* 38 (1983): 971–981.

Eagley, Alice H., and Valerie J. Steffen. "Gender Stereotypes Stem from the Distribution of Women and Men into Social Roles." *Journal of Personality and Social Psychology* 46 (1984): 735–754.

Fennema, Elizabeth. "Sex-Related Differences in Education: Myths, Realities, and Interventions." In *Educators' Handbook: A Research Perspective*, edited by Virginia Richardson-Koehler, 329–347. New York: Longman, 1987.

Frazier, Nancy, and Myra Sadker. *Sexism in School and Society*. New York: Harper and Row, 1973.

Gould, Lois. "X: A Fabulous Child's Story." *Ms. Magazine*, December 1972, 74–76.

Grant, Carl A., and Christine E. Sleeter. "Race, Class, and Gender in Education Research: An Argument for Integrative Analysis." *Review of Educational Research* 56: (Summer 1986): 195–211.

Kay, Herma H. *Sex-Based Discrimination (Text, Cases and Materials)*. 2nd ed. St. Paul: West Publishing, 1981.

Klein, Susan S. "Sex Equity and Education." *Theory into Practice* 25 (Autumn 1986): 219–299.

Klein, Susan S. "Closing the Gender Gap in Academic Achievement by Changing the Outcome Measures and the Classroom Environment." Paper presented at the annual meeting of the National Council for Research on Women, 1987.

Klein, Susan S., ed. *Handbook for Achieving Sex Equity through Education*. Baltimore: Johns Hopkins University Press, 1985.

Noddings, Nel. "In Search of the Feminine." *Philosophy of Education* (1985): 349–358.

Population Profile of the United States: 1984/85. *Current Population Reports* 150: P23. Washington, D.C.: U.S. Department of Commerce, Bureau of the Census, April 1987.

Public Law 92-261, Title VII, Sec. 701, March 24, 1972.

Public Law 92-318, Title IX, Sec. 901, June 23, 1972.

Public Law 95-561, Title XX, Sec. 3341, August 21, 1974.

Sarason, Seymour B., and M. Klaber. "The School as a Social Situation." *Annual Review of Psychology* 36 (1985): 115–140.

Tetreault, Mary Kay, and Patricia Schmuck. "Equity, Educational Reform, and Gender." *Issues in Education* 3 (Summer 1985): 45–67.

Tittle, Carol Kehr. "Gender Research and Education." *American Psychologist* 41 (1986): 1161–1168.

Tyack, David, and Elisabeth Hansot. *Managers of Virtue: Public School Leadership in America, 1820–1980*. New York: Basic Books, 1983.

6.

Being At-Risk in School

VIRGINIA RICHARDSON AND
PATRICIA COLFER

Précis

Students can be prevented from school failure and dropping out if school personnel shift their focus from programs based on categories of problem students to creation of a repertoire of teaching styles and strategies that take into account social and individual variables. That is, important events and relationships in the lives of students at school and elsewhere may enhance or hinder learning in school. It is life experience that causes a child to be "at-risk," a condition that varies, sometimes changing rapidly.

Virginia Richardson and Patricia Colfer believe that "at-riskness" should not be just another faddish term for troubled students or a descriptor that predicts the likelihood of a student's school failure and operates as a mechanism for blaming the victim. They express concern about the popular use of the term in newspapers, journals, speeches, and "even in the policy literature," implying that the definition and the condition are absolute. On the contrary, they say, in school practice the condition is "quite fluid"; a student can be "at-risk" at one time and not at another, and in one class but not in another.

Two case studies, one from an elementary school and one from a middle school, are used to illustrate the authors' perspectives on being at-risk in school. They focus on individual children and indicate techniques useful for dealing with their specific situations. The authors found some differences between these two levels of schools, and their recommendations vary somewhat accordingly. For better results at the elementary level, they advise that teachers need to understand that labeling a student as one who does not "fit in" has a serious impact on the student, despite the fact that the label has a fluid meaning and is shaped by what activities and academic goals teachers happen to select as important. The authors also urge that help for students with learning problems be provided by aiding regular classroom teachers in offering and managing in-class instructional alternatives. At the junior high or middle school levels, reorganization is needed to provide a more caring environment. Records maintained for each child should be up-to-date and informative, and someone in addition to the home-room teacher should be responsible for monitoring and supporting an individual child's life in school.

Virginia Richardson is associate professor of education at the University of Arizona in Tucson for whom research on teaching has been a long-standing interest and research focus. This paper utilizes in part an ethnographic study of 12 "at-risk" students of which she was co-director under an Exxon Education Fund research grant, reported in the book, *School Children At-Risk*.

Patricia Colfer is a graduate student associated with the research of Professor Richardson at the University of Arizona.

—*The College Board*

I do my homework and then I see TV and I stay up until around 9:00 or 9:30. My dad, I hardly ever see him, cause he works with horses at my brother's house and he trains them to race. He leaves at 5:00 AM and he doesn't come home until 9:00 PM, but he's always drunk and comes home drunk, and sometimes, it's a miracle, but he doesn't come drunk. Sometimes when he doesn't come real drunk he's real violent. Oh, I can't stand it when he's drunk. I always tell him, "You shouldn't drink, my mom has enough problems, she doesn't need more." But he doesn't listen to me. I told him once in front of his friends and his friends are always drinking and he got mad and he told my mom, "Tell your daughter not to be yelling at me in front of my friends." "I was telling you the truth that you shouldn't do that." He still does it. When my sister that is 20 and my brother that is 15, when they were little, my dad used to hit them a lot because he was real jealous if any man would come around here. He would look for footsteps all around the yard. He was real mean and would never let her go out when she was young. He wants me to go and be a nun.[1]

Daria, who is quoted here, is 14 years old and an eighth grader. Her words give partial understanding to how Daria views life at leisure, at home, at school. For Daria, school is a haven, a place where she can socialize, forget about her home environment, and ignore the father who dictates repressive restrictions she finds almost unbearable. Daria is not a happy girl; she was identified by school personnel as at-risk.

This chapter investigates two quite different but related questions:

- What does "at-risk" mean?
- What does it mean to be "at-risk"?

The term "at-risk" is appearing with increasing frequency in newspapers, journals, magazines, and speeches. In a recent issue of *Education Week* (1987), for example, the term was used many different times, in five different articles. It was used as a *predictive concept*—students who have certain kinds of conditions such as living with only one parent are at-risk because they might drop out or fail; and as a *descriptive concept*—students who are failing are at-risk. Failing school, then, can be an outcome of being at-risk or an identifier of an at-risk condition. Other outcomes that are mentioned are unhappiness in life and being unsuccessful as adults. The next section of this chapter explores these various definitions of "at-risk."

The third section examines what it means to be a student labeled at-risk, using the words of students, and their parents, teachers, and other school specialists, and observations of what happens to them in the classroom. Two students will be described: a lower elementary student and a middle school student. Names will be changed in order to protect the identity of these students and the adults surrounding them.[2]

The last section expands on an ecological view of at-riskness that was both framed and further developed while these studies were being conducted. The concept of at-riskness is viewed as a combination of personal and background characteristics of a child and the social and academic context of the school. The particular academic and social organization of a school and classroom, the norms of its teachers, the academic expectations held for its students, and the academic tasks encountered by the students may affect the students' at-risk status. The responsibility for the at-risk status of a child, therefore, does not reside in one individual—be it child, mother, or teacher— or in one institution—the school. Society creates schools in certain ways to meet its goals and expectations, thus creating environments in which certain children are at-risk. The solution to the at-riskness of children and youth, then, lies with all of us.

What Does "At-Risk" Mean?

In American society of the 1980s the term "at-risk" is used in many different ways for many different purposes. To be a youth at-risk could mean that a young person is chemically dependent, a school dropout, suicidal, either pregnant or potentially pregnant in teen years, or an alcoholic (Tugent 1986). The comparative patterns of recent decades cause alarm as we note how the number of at-risk children has increased. In a recent article, Rexford Brown summarized the data:

1. Children in poverty: up from 16 percent in 1970 to 22 percent today; 45 percent of black school-age children live in poverty; 36 percent of Hispanic children live in poverty.

2. Drug and alcohol abuse: up 60-fold since 1960.

3. Teenage pregnancy: up 109 percent for whites, 10 percent for non-whites since 1960.

4. Teenage homicide: up more than 200 percent since 1950.

5. Arrests of 18 to 24-year olds: up from 18 percent in 1960 to 34 percent in 1980.

6. Teenage unemployment: up steadily since 1961.

7. Students entering ninth grade but not graduating four years later: up from 24 percent in 1972 to 30 percent today. Dropout rates for disadvantaged black, white, and Hispanic males are 23 percent, 39 percent, and 44 percent, respectively. In some cities the dropout rate exceeds 50 percent (Brown 1986).

In the same article, Brown expands the at-risk categories to include chronic truants, underachievers, troublemakers, economically disadvantaged or poor, minority young people, runaways, delinquents, unemployed teens, and young people who lack motivation to do well in school or work. These categories identify the large group of young people who live marginally outside the socially accepted code for children and youth.

When the term "at-risk" is applied to students rather than to children, two types of definitions are used. The first employs certain background, social, and emotional characteristics to identify students who are at-risk of becoming at-risk youths as defined above. The second identifies students on the basis of problematic behaviors exhibited in school: low grades, skipping classes, or disruptive behavior in class.

The first approach attempts to identify problems before they occur in school. The indicators could be social: low socioeconomic status (SES) of the students' family, living with a single parent, a decaying or unstable neighborhood, or dropout models within the family. There could also be individual predispositions such as being handicapped, non-English speaking, or a member of a cultural minority in the school.

The second approach waits until school-related problems occur and then identifies the student exhibiting such behaviors as at-risk. These behaviors include excessive absences, deficiencies in reading and math, or retention in grade. The cause for these behaviors may be identified as the social and emotional predispositions described above; but the at-risk label is reserved for those students exhibiting unsatisfactory academic or social behavior in school.

Both types of definitions are used by schools, school districts, and researchers alike. Nearly 20 years ago, programs such as Head Start were created for at-risk (or disadvantaged) students who were identified on the basis of their families' income level. More recently, programs have been developed in schools and school districts for students identified as at-risk using both types of definitions. For example, one junior high school in the Southwest compiles lists of at-risk students on the basis of numbers of absences and detentions, and low or failing grades. Another high school district uses a list of eight characteristics that include both background predisposition and behavioral indicators to identify at-risk students. The behavioral indicators, for example, are 10 or more absences in any course, below the twenty-third percentile on state or competency tests, and more than one failure in a semester. Background indicators include living in a single-parent home and having a mother who did not finish high school. The policy states: "existence of three or more of these factors designates a student as being at risk of dropping out of school. Monthly lists are generated by school of all newly identified at-risk students" (Phoenix High School District, no date).

In the educational literature, the term "at-risk student" is relatively new. In the thesaurus of ERIC descriptors, for example, "high-risk students" has been used only since 1980. However, related terms such as "low achievement," "underachievement," and "disadvantaged" have been in use since the

ERIC data base was created in 1966. The 1987 ERIC categories of at-risk are: school and academic failure, potential dropouts, educationally disadvantaged, and underachievement.

The research literature contains primarily quantitative studies and, by and large, follows a model that identifies students as at-risk on the basis of counterproductive behaviors in school, relates these to possible social, emotional, academic or schooling causes and, at times, suggests and/or tests possible intervention strategies. Eventual outcomes of being at-risk are suggested or investigated.

The behaviors that identify students as at-risk include those not related to a particular school or setting such as inconsistent class behaviors, maladaptive interpersonal and social behavior, immaturity, lack of self-confidence, difficulty in taking action without adult support, and socially disruptive behaviors (Cross 1984; Pheasant 1985; Blechman, Taylor, and Schrader 1981). The specific at-risk school behaviors are the inability to keep up with the pace of instruction, lack of proficiency, inability to make a successful transition from grade to grade or topic to topic, poor academic ability, and disabled reader behavior (Fletcher and Satz 1984).

These behaviors or conditions comprise the framework for being at-risk. In later life these children can fail to conform socially, or they may have conflicts with authority (Spivack et al. 1986). They may be left out of the educational process, have learning problems, fail academically, fail specifically in reading mastery, need remedial instruction, perhaps be retained in some grade, or become delinquent (Litcher and Roberge 1979).

In identifying causes for these at-risk behaviors, researchers sometimes look at the social conditions of the home. Spivack, Marcuso, and Swift (1986), for example, suggest that these behavior patterns are established as a result of minority living conditions and low socioeconomic status, which are in conflict with school success. Vellutino and colleagues (1977) talk about the relationship between the sociocultural factors and primary verbal deficits that lead to problems in school. Divorce or other family disruption was shown to affect male children particularly (Hoffman 1979). Mothers' physical and perinatal problems were identified by Broman, Bien, and Shaughnessy (1985).

Some researchers also pay heed to the school as a possible cause of at-riskness. Buchanan, Schulz, and Milazzo (1983) note that inflexibility in altering the pace of instruction makes achievement difficult for some children. In addition, they suggest, some students receive little or no help in making transitions from grade to grade, topic to topic. The teachers themselves can contribute to student at-riskness by anger and lack of sympathy (Graham 1984) as well as by not accurately identifying which students may have trouble later on. Last, Campbell (1985) concluded that teachers may misjudge the maturity level of children entering kindergarten, thereby causing children to be placed in an environment for which they are not academically ready.

These researchers suggest interventions ranging from helping children

make the transition from one school state to the next, identifying risk areas
in the curriculum scope and sequence patterns, analyzing the flow of instruction and adjusting the environment to provide more time for academic engagement and direct instruction (Lentz 1983).

This prevailing model of addressing at-risk students' needs is similar to
the medical diagnosis and remediation model. If we can isolate the factors
leading to the student's at-riskness, we can work on changing those factors
and thus lessen the child's vulnerability in the school setting. However, many
of the factors isolated in these studies are related to background, such as the
child's racial minority status, and are thus not remediable directly by the
school. The remediation plan, then, fits into a deficit model, a problem
repeatedly described during the period when educators have focused on the
"disadvantaged" student. The blame is placed on the student and his or her
parents, and the responsibility for making up for the deficit becomes solely
the school's.

Major questions exist concerning the use of predisposing indicators. What
are the effects of labeling children for remediation of conditions over which
they have no control? And are there not students who have these predisposing
characteristics who succeed in school? Further, if we don't identify students
as at-risk on the basis of predisposing indicators and wait until the students
exhibit nonproductive behaviors in school, is that not too late? And what can
we offer those students once they are identified as at-risk?

These questions suggest a different type of inquiry: one that asks whether
teachers now think of any of their students as at-risk, and, if so, what happens
to these students. This thrust looks intently at the student at-risk within the
context of a specific school and community, and attempts to determine the
meaning of school from the child's viewpoint. Few of these studies have been
conducted in the United States. The tradition is somewhat stronger in Brit-
ain—for example, Birksted 1976; Ball 1981; and Davies 1983—and for
special populations of students in the United States, such as learning disabled, special education (Mehan, Hertweck, and Meihls 1986), and those
with limited English proficiency (Goldenberg 1984).

Several case studies of "problem students" were conducted by Erickson
and his colleagues as they attempted to develop a theory of student status as
socially constructed (Erickson 1985; Boersema 1985; Lazarus 1985; Pelissier
1985). Although none of these studies used the concept "at-risk," they
focused on students who would, today, be identified as such. These case
studies indicated how each student's problem status was socially constructed
within the particular classroom. They examined the child in relation to the
social context of the specific school and classroom.

What Does It Mean to Be At-Risk?

We will discuss brief case descriptions of two at-risk students drawn from
studies of at-risk students in an effective elementary school and in a middle

school, both with high populations of students with predisposing at-risk characteristics. These students are not "typical." No at-risk student is typical, nor should he or she be treated as such; each has a particular set of characteristics and circumstances that interact in a unique way with the particular school setting. We can gather meaning from those who are at-risk, those who define "at-riskness" in the schools, and those who interact with students at-risk.

Jerry

Jerry was a third grader in a desegregated elementary school with 266 students. He was in a large (51 student) classroom that combined grades 2 and 3 and that had two team teachers and a classroom aide. He was identified as at-risk in the beginning of the school year in separate interviews with the school principal, the counselor, and two teachers.

Jerry, and his first- and fifth-grade sisters (also identified as at-risk), were new to the school that year. They did not bring previous school records with them, but it was ascertained that they had attended school in Kentucky the previous year. Prior to that, they had lived in Germany where Jerry had attended kindergarten. Their father had been in the armed services, and their mother was Vietnamese. They had been near relatives in Kentucky; here they were alone. Initially, both parents were unemployed; later, Jerry's father obtained a job in which he worked very long hours.

Jerry was functioning academically at first-grade or beginning second-grade level. But his social problems compounded his academic problems and concerned his teachers and the counselor. His counselor described him as "a very incapacitated boy." He often came to school dirty and in old clothes that he had outgrown. He was ostracized and made fun of by the other children. Older students harassed him and his two sisters on the way home from school—primarily, said the counselor, because of his extremely aggressive older sister.

Jerry had difficulty communicating verbally. He took a long time to begin to talk and appeared very uncertain when he did. In class he was quite passive. He did not participate voluntarily. So, although he did not have behavioral problems, his nonparticipation in activities drew considerable attention from his teachers.

Jerry's classroom was, in fact, two classrooms, one with art centers, a library, a science demonstration table, a piano, a reading rug, a reading loft, and the other with grouped desks and chairs, blackboards, and additional study centers. Students could stay with the same teachers for three years. His teachers espoused a developmental philosophy for learning. As one teacher claimed, student problems were not academic; they were social and related to low self-concept. "Some kids take longer than others to learn how to read and write. What we do is make sure they don't begin to feel bad about themselves while they are learning." They did not like the idea of testing the students every year; they felt that if they could have the students for the full three years, most of them would be at or above grade level by the end of the third year. In order to promote positive self-concept and social skills, the teachers relied on group activities and deemphasized competitiveness. With the school, as a whole, they promoted in-class alternatives for students with special problems rather than pull-out programs with specialists. Jerry's teachers believed that they treated all students the same: they had a small number of rules and were extremely consistent and firm in applying them.

For Jerry's teachers and others in the elementary school in our study sample, the concept of at-risk was fluid. A number of students had been identified as at-risk at the beginning of the year who were no longer on the list at the end. Jerry still was. He had improved somewhat in both academic and social skills, but his teachers still viewed him as a problem. Like all the elementary teachers in the sample, they felt deeply responsible for their students, and as one pointed out, "if they fail, we fail." At-risk students, even those with handicaps or designated as learning disabled, were no longer considered as such if they began to fit into the rhythm of the classroom, gave the appearance of working hard at the academic tasks, and appeared reasonably happy.

The teachers' disappointment with Jerry's lack of responsiveness and their own failure was palpable in the interviews. Although they were ambivalent about the efficacy of labeling a student as learning disabled, they still had Jerry tested for LD identification on the basis of his academic verbal communication problems. The one-on-one work would be helpful to Jerry's self-concept, they felt. They were disappointed when the LD specialist asserted that Jerry was working up to his ability and therefore did not need LD services. They worked with Jerry on his social skills and with the other students on dealing fairly and respectfully with him. One teacher made it a point to tell him every other day what a wonderful person she thought he was.

All the adults in the school who were questioned about Jerry agreed that his problems stemmed from his home. The teachers, the counselor, the nurse, and the social workers all tried to contact Jerry's parents several times. His mother came to school once, his father not at all. The teachers sensed that his mother could not understand all that was being said, and she spoke very little during the conferences. But his father insisted that she could understand and that she was the appropriate person to participate in these discussions. The social worker and a parent-community representative visited Jerry's home. His parents never responded to notes or requests. The counselor concluded that the family was "not verbal," because when asked in what language the children spoke to their mother, Jerry responded, "We don't really talk much, we just do things."

In the second semester, Jerry came to school several times with gashes and bruises and passed out one day. The counselor talked to him and his sister about what was happening, and decided to call the Child Protective Services (CPS). Jerry's family moved soon after CPS started its investigation. As she usually does, the counselor called the new school and talked with them about Jerry. However, before the researcher could follow Jerry into his new school, his family had moved once again and could not be located.

Daria

Daria, the subject of our second case study, is an articulate, attractive, 14-year-old. She attended a Southwestern middle school with a large racial minority student population. In September the principal selected Daria as a candidate for a research project on eighth-grade girls at risk because Daria's final grades from both semesters in seventh grade were one A, one B, and seven D's. However, her problems had apparently not been seen as serious enough for her to be placed on the official school list of at-risk students at the beginning of the school year. The principal had developed this list in order to focus faculty attention on students at-risk for poor attendance, poor academic performance, and poor attitude.

School records indicated that Daria repeated first grade, attended eight elementary schools, and was frequently absent in all grades. She claimed that her asthma condition caused these absences. Daria also spoke about the cause for so much moving—"We hardly had any money to pay the rent"— and about how difficult it was to move away from her friends so frequently. She reminisced about causing trouble in kindergarten and first grade. Her kindergarten teacher had noted on Daria's adaptive education screening form: "She is constantly pinching or hitting someone." In later grades, however, three teachers wrote about Daria's cooperation in class.

Report cards in elementary school indicate that Daria was an average student in all subjects, all S's and C's, and only one D. Her scores on standardized tests, however, presented a different picture. Beginning in second grade, Daria's scores were below grade level. During each succeeding year, more of the tested competency areas indicated she fell below grade level. No comments were available from teachers about these California Achievement Test scores.

Daria remembers significant events from those early years through elementary school. She lived with nine people in a one-bedroom house, spoke only Spanish until she began school, and then was not allowed to speak English at home. She was kept in diapers until four at her father's insistence, learned about sex from her brothers who talked "nasty," witnessed physical fights between her father and sister, was beaten with a belt, and knew of her sister's attempted suicide. She also remembers one award she received in school for reading a book in second grade.

These memories are significant in Daria's case study. Her recollections were not filled with incidents from school, but stories of family members and her relationship to each person. Now, as an eighth grader, Daria expressed anger and resentment toward family members. Conversations with her designed to elicit ideas and feelings about school inevitably focused on her place in what she saw as a repressive family environment. Her present family experience dominated her thinking and conversations. School was a minor concern.

The focal person in Daria's family was her father, whom she characterized as "always drunk," "jealous," called "diablo" by her mother, prejudiced against "gringos," and a man who frequents "hookers' bars." He imposed strict rules for Daria: no friends at the house, no after-school clubs, no school dances, and no boyfriend until Daria was 16. Daria's mother was young, sickly, and would get a divorce; but, as Daria said, "If she does, all of us are gonna be out in the streets." Her mother was pregnant at 14 and currently had four children living at home, as well as two grandchildren spending considerable time in their house. Daria's mother and father frequently argued.

Daria's situation reflects a dysfunctional family. She spoke of running away now that she was getting older, of going crazy, of possibly hurting herself at those times when she became so angry at what people were doing to her. She also said that she might become pregnant whenever her father finally allowed her some freedom to go out. Daria escaped from these worries when she attended school.

Daria wanted to be at Milton Middle School. She found some of the classes boring, some teachers boring, but while there she could be with people who became her friends during schooltime. There was no class in which she was really interested. She believed that the middle school gave students more responsibility than elementary school, like buying your own lunches, being able to join clubs, and having more people from whom to choose friends. She liked school.

Daria was quiet in class and had no detentions or suspensions during eighth grade. Teachers said Daria was "sweet," did not cause problems, but sometimes didn't do her assignments. Daria's counselor for two years made this comment when asked about her: "I know of Daria but I haven't worked with her directly. I've talked to her as far as grades and things like that." Daria said she would go to two of her teachers for help; she never has. One other teacher once came to her and asked, "What's wrong with you?" She didn't answer. Daria told the stories of her homelife for the first time to the researcher. She thought that the teachers neither knew her nor paid attention to her.

Daria saw herself as sometimes lazy, forgetting to do her homework. But, she said, at other times she studied but just didn't understand. Daria was a participant in the school's special program aimed at helping students at-risk. But Daria failed eighth grade; there was no opportunity to attend summer school. She will return to the same "risk-conscious" school, having the same family, the same personal history, the same academic preparation as in the past. Possibly her words after the summer vacation will be the same as these words voiced during her eighth-grade year: "I don't really like holidays. They're boring. I have to stay home and I hate being home. I wish I could just have a different family cause I don't like mine. I wish I could run away and go to some place. I always dream about this, go to some place and somebody would adopt me."

Analysis

Recent literature and policy discussions of at-risk students assume that the definition is absolute—that is, a student is identified as at-risk on the basis of easily measured traits, behaviors, or background conditions such that everyone would agree on the identity of at-risk students. In school practice, the concept is quite fluid and situation-specific. In both the elementary school and the middle school that were studied, students could be at-risk in one class but not in another, and school personnel were aware of this fluidity. In fact, within the same classroom, students could be at-risk at one point and not at another. For the elementary teachers, at-risk students were those who exhibited interpersonal and/or academic difficulties in the class: those who were not responsive to the teachers' particular approach to instruction and community building.

For the middle school teachers, at-risk students were designated almost exclusively as those receiving low grades and therefore likely to drop out or be retained. Just as the degree of personal interchange differs dramatically between elementary and middle schools, so do the criteria for labeling students as at-risk.

In all cases, the designation of at-riskness relied very much on the nature of the student body within a particular school or classroom, and the goals, aspirations, and instructional programs of the teachers. At-risk students did not conform on dimensions judged by their teachers to be important. One has to look outside the classroom and school to determine, in part, why those dimensions are identified as important (see Oakes and Lipton's paper in this volume).

There were several significant differences between elementary and middle school teachers. One was the degree to which they took responsibility for the students labeled at-risk in their classrooms. The elementary teachers intensely believed that they should succeed with their students; the middle school teachers, responsible for more than 150 students a day, did not have such strong convictions. They spoke of always being available to help students with the subject or making up work, and of referring students to counselors. Another difference was that elementary teachers were aware of the degree to which the classroom was a social environment, and at-risk students were those who had difficulty fitting in. The middle school teachers ignored the social nature of their classrooms and schools, and focused on academic content and grades.

In both the elementary and middle school situations, the home lives of students played a large role in the explanation of at-risk behavior and potential solutions as identified by school personnel. For the school personnel, home lives became a problem, in fact a primary cause, when the students themselves exhibited behavior at school that indicated they were at-risk. The teachers expected parental help when their children were having problems. Sympathy for single working parents who were not able easily to come to the school was not expressed (see also Lightfoot 1978). Nor was any sympathy expressed for racial minority parents who might not understand or be comfortable with the dominant culture of the school organization. The concern about Jerry's homelife appeared justified. However, the solution of calling the Child Protective Services probably drove him from the school. Given the developmental nature of the school, Jerry probably would have gained a great deal from that school had he been able to stay longer.

By the time students like Daria reach middle school, they have had at least six years of experience in school. All the girls in our study of at-risk students remembered both positive and negative experiences. The positive experiences involved teachers who were fair and caring. In this middle school, as in most, there is an assumption that students should assume total responsibility for their academic progress. The intimate relationship between student and teacher that often occurs in elementary school rarely exists at this level. Several factors appeared to contribute to this lack of individual caring. The first is that in many of the middle school teachers' minds, academic emphasis is demanded: the sense that a detached treatment of students as young adults prepares them at this stage for the lives in front of them. The sheer numbers of students might make it difficult for teachers to notice and question students about the indicators of stress and unhappiness observed by the researcher. In the interviews the teachers appeared to be oblivious of their own contributions to a student's discontent and poor performance. The middle school philosophy that advocates a nurturing, caring concern for the individual needs of students at this age was expressed in faculty descriptions of the school climate but was not experienced by the girls in this project labeled as at-risk. The organization and teacher outlook resembled that of a traditional junior high school.

The response to this environment by the at-risk students was to view school as a place for social activities. Attending class was an interruption in the important aspects of their lives. For some students, school was an escape from home. Academic success was of little interest to them; nor were they concerned about or prepared to predict their own dropping out of school. By middle school, these students were indeed at-risk.

Implications for Policy and Practice

Labeling Elementary Students as At-Risk

Teachers in the elementary school study resisted labeling students as at-risk on the basis of social and/or personal predispositions. They also were ambivalent about programs that pulled students out of the classroom into contact with specialists. Further, even the Learning Disabled teacher in one of the schools in this study worried about labeling the students. The teachers' instincts are supported by research. Keogh and Daley (1983) have questioned the early identification of "problem" students with measures that focus strictly on the child rather than on the environment of the classroom and school (see also Cummins 1986). As Smith (1973) pointed out about labeling students as having reading problems:

> there is a risk that children will be classified as [having] reading problems when the only problem that exists lies in the unreasonable expectations of a parent or teacher, or of the system in which the teacher and child interact. (p. 191)

Although the teachers understood the concept of at-risk as fluid and dependent upon the nature of a given classroom, they were not able to assess the nature of their own classroom from a broad social perspective and its effects on students who did not "fit in."

Programs should be developed to help teachers understand the nature of the social context of their school. Individual teachers should be helped to understand the degree to which their own goals, activity structures, and academic tasks contribute to the at-risk status of students.

Special Programs for Elementary At-Risk Students

In one of the schools investigated in the Richardson-Koehler study, students in grades 2 and 3 that were identified as at-risk saw up to five different teachers each day depending upon their special problems (Richardson-Koehler, et al. 1988; see also Soo Hoo's paper in this volume). As was documented, this was not an effective educational practice for these students.

What, then, should be done for students who are having learning problems in school? One possibility for the at-risk students with academic problems in elementary school is a system that provides support for the regular classroom teacher to explore in-class instructional alternatives. One such system, called Teacher Assistance Teams (TAT), has been developed and tested by Chalfont and Pysh (1981). This program is based on the assumption that if teachers work together in a problem-solving process, they can generate and test effective strategies to teach many students with learning and behavior problems within the context of the general classroom. This system could reduce the numbers of students labeled learning disabled and aid teachers in developing their own instructional skills in a collegial manner.

Another system is to bring specialists into the classroom to work with individual or groups of students who are having difficulty. Thus the coherence of the classroom program would be preserved, and students would not be labeled needlessly.

At-Risk Middle and Junior High School Students

The problems confronted by the at-risk students in middle school were quite different than those in the elementary school study. These problems were primarily social and personal. Academics, though a problem in the minds of school personnel, were not of paramount importance to the at-risk students. Clearly the students in the study could not take advantage of the academic instructional program because of their extremely unhappy and disruptive personal lives. Does the school have the obligation to deal with these social and personal realities?

In the district that administers the middle level school in this study, all junior high schools were renamed middle schools, with the intent that they would begin to put into practice the middle school philosophy as expressed, for example, in the work of Wiles, Wiles, and Bondi (1981). According to some authorities on schooling, the practice of this philosophy of middle-level organization and curriculum would create a more positive learning environment for students. The conversion to this practice, however, does not occur automatically with a name change. In this middle school several programs, such as the homeroom adviser-advisee program, were established but not working. After asking for teacher volunteers to form teams to work with students in hopes that the latter would develop a sense of community, the principal received the names of only four volunteers out of 45 teachers. This school also had incentive programs for attendance and initiated a special program wherein groups of 10 students would be in a self-contained class for three weeks working on their "classwork" and developing better study habits. All the girls in our study were participants in this program. By the end of the year, two-thirds had either dropped out or failed eighth grade.

If we answer "yes" to the question whether schools have an obligation to help students with those aspects of their social and personal lives that interfere with their cognitive development, we must rethink attitudes toward and the organization of middle and junior high schools. The school must do more than refer students to social services: it must bring these services into the school. Second, we need to reorganize the school so that it provides a caring environment for students, particularly at-risk students. This means that one person must be responsible for each child's life in school—someone in addition to the homeroom teacher. It also means that the quality of information maintained on each child should be quite different and be provided in a timely manner.

Some authors have pointed out that a school organization that emphasizes student-teacher relations may compete with one that focuses on academics through departmentalization (McPartland 1987). In this case, however, the departmentalized academic curriculum was not reaching these at-risk girls at all. They needed someone who cared and listened.

More important, teachers within schools, particularly multicultural schools, should be helped to examine their own beliefs about students, the goals of education, and their own role in educating. Case studies, such as those being developed by Colfer (in press), could be used for discussions. From such examination, perhaps very different options will be developed and implemented at the school site, options that will work with the individual students at-risk within each school. Above all, teachers and administrators should understand the harm they may be doing in working with students in whom they have no interest, little understanding, and no compassion.

As usual in education, the problems of at-risk students will not be solved with one or even several programs. Such programs with their inflexible mandates can only harm an already difficult situation. Solving these students' problems will require time, patience, compassion, and respect from those teachers who are willing to work with these students; processes that bring together those involved in the day-to-day activities of the at-risk students and those who have studied and thought about these problems from different viewpoints; and money to support school people in these endeavors. This effort is imperative. As suggested by the middle school social worker:

> I think I'm concerned with the kids who are sitting in the classrooms who are dealing with an alcoholic parent or two alcoholic parents who have had a lot of past experience with sexual or physical abuse, a host of other problems like that, who are sort of surviving in school and maybe getting C's and D's and sometimes B's but as people, are barely surviving, and I have a real concern about these kids getting into high school and things becoming increasingly more difficult and those are the kinds of kids that I think are going to end up committing suicide and actually going through with it. So, I think there's a group that we're talking about and trying to deal with specifically in the school system right now and there's another group of kids that we aren't even coming close to dealing with. (Colfer, in press)

Notes

1. This is a quote from a subject in a study in-progress of nine at-risk girls in a middle school. This study will become a dissertation by P. Colfer, in partial fulfillment of the requirements for the degree of Doctor of Philosophy in the College of Education, University of Arizona.
2. These descriptions will be extracted from two studies of at-risk students: P. Colfer (see note 1); and V. Richardson-Koehler, U. Casanova, P. Placier, and K. Guilfoyle, *School Children At-Risk*, London: Falmer Press, 1988.

Selected References

Ball, S. J. 1981. *Beachside Comprehensive: A Case Study of Schooling.* Cambridge, England: Cambridge University Press.

Birksted, I. 1976. "School Performance Viewed from the Boys." *Sociological Review* 24: 63–77.

Blechman, E. A., C. J. Taylor, and S. M. Schrader. 1981. "Family Problem Solving versus Home Notes as Early Intervention with High-Risk Children." *Journal of Consulting and Clinical Psychology* 49 (6): 919–926.

Boersema, D. B. 1985. *"Hey Teacher! Who Am I, Anyway?": Teacher Determination of Student Identity.* Paper presented at the annual meeting of the American Educational Research Association, Chicago.

Broman, S., E. Bien, and P. Shaughnessy. 1985. *Low Achieving Children: The First Seven Years.* Hillsdale, N.J.: Lawrence Erlbaum.

Brown, R. 1986. "State Responsibility for At-Risk Youth." *Metropolitan Education* 2: 5–12.

Buchanan, A., R. Schulz, and P. Milazzo. 1983. *Instructional Risk Reduction: An Alternative to Instructional Remediation.* Washington, D.C.: National Institute of Education. (ERIC Document Reproduction Service No. ED 251 419.)

Campbell, S. M. 1985. *Kindergarten Entry Age as a Factor in Academic Failure.* Paper presented at the annual meeting of the American Association of School Administrators. (ERIC Document Reproduction Service No. ED 251 495.)

Chalfont, J., and M. V. Pysh. 1981. "Teacher Assistance Teams: A Model for Within-Building Problem Solving." *Counterpoint,* Council for Exceptional Children, 1–10.

Colfer, P. In press. *The Meaning of School to Hispanic, Yaqui and Anglo Eighth Grade Girls at Risk.* Tucson: College of Education, University of Arizona.

Cross, R. 1984. *Teacher Decision-Making in Student Retention.* Paper presented at the annual meeting of the American Educational Research Association, New Orleans. (ERIC Document Reproduction Service No. ED 252 930.)

Cummins, J. 1986. *Bilingualism and Special Education.* San Diego: College-Hill Press.

Davies, L. 1983. "Gender, Resistance and Power." In *Gender, Class, and Education,* edited by S. Walker and L. Barton, 15–30. London: Falmer Press.

Erickson, F. 1985. *Toward a Theory of Student Status as Socially Constructed.* Paper presented at the annual meeting of the American Educational Research Association, Chicago.

Fletcher, J. M., and P. Satz. 1984. "Test-Based versus Teacher-Predictions of Academic Achievement: A Three-Year Longitudinal Follow-up." *Journal of Pediatric Psychology* 9: 193–203.

Goldenberg, C. N. 1984. Roads to Reading: Studies of Hispanic First Graders at Risk for Reading Failure. Ph.D. dissertation, University of California, Los Angeles.

Graham, S. 1984. "Teacher Feeling and Student Thoughts: An Attributional Approach to Affect in the Classroom." *Elementary School Journal* 85: 91–104.

Hoffman, L. W. 1979. "Maternal Employment: 1979." *American Psychologist* 34: 859–865.

Keogh, B., and S. Daley. 1983. "Early Identification: One Important Component of

Comprehensive Services for At-Risk Children." *Topics in Early Childhood Special Education* 3: 7–16.

Lazarus, B. 1985. *Getting a Special Education Identity: How an Experienced Teacher Decides.* Paper presented at the annual meeting of the American Educational Research Association, Chicago.

Lentz, F. E. 1983. *Behavioral Approaches to the Assessment and Remediation of Academic Problems.* Paper presented at the annual convention of the American Psychological Association. Anaheim, Calif. (ERIC Document Reproduction Service No. ED 244 183.)

Lightfoot, S. L. 1978. *Worlds Apart.* New York: Basic Books.

Litcher, J., and L. P. Roberge. 1979. First Grade Intervention for Reading Achievement of High Risk Children. *Bulletin of the Orton Society* 29: 238–244.

McPartland, J. 1987. *Balancing High-Quality Subject-Matter Instruction with Positive Teacher-Student Relations in the Middle Grades.* Report No. 15. Baltimore: Center for Research on Elementary and Middle Schools, The Johns Hopkins University.

Mehan, H., A. Hertweck, and J. L. Meihls. 1986. *Handicapping the Handicapped.* Palo Alto: Stanford University Press.

Pelissier, C. 1985. *On Becoming a Pariah: A Case Study in the Social Construction of Student Status.* Paper presented at the American Educational Research Association, Chicago.

Pheasant, M. 1985. "Aumsville School District's Readiness Program: Helping First Graders Succeed." *Oregon School Study Council Bulletin* 28: 6. (ERIC Document Reproduction Service No. ED 252 967.)

Phoenix High School District. Unpublished, no date. *At-Risk Factors.* Phoenix.

Richardson-Koehler, V., U. Casanova, P. Placier, and K. Guilfoyle. 1988. *School Children At-Risk.* London: Falmer.

Smith, F. 1973. *Psycholinguistics and Reading.* New York: Holt, Rinehart, & Winston.

Smith, F. 1975. "Twelve Easy Ways to Make Learning to Read Difficult, and One Way to Make it Easy." In *Psycholinquistics and Reading,* edited by F. Smith, 183–196. New York: Holt, Rinehart, and Winston.

Spivack, G., J. Marcuso, and J. Swift. 1986. "Early Classroom Behaviors and Later Misconduct." *Development Psychology,* 22: 124–131.

Tugent, A. 1986. "Youth Issues in Prominence on National Agenda." *Education Week* 6: 9 and 13.

Vellutino, F. R., B. M. Steger, S. C. Moyer, C. J. Harding, and J. A. Niles. 1977. "Has the Perceptual Deficit Hypothesis Led Us Astray?" *Journal of Learning Disabilities* 10: 375–385.

Wiles, D., J. Wiles, and J. Bondi. 1981. *Practical Politics for School Administration.* Boston: Allyn & Bacon.

7.

Last Things First: Realizing Equality by Improving Conditions for Marginal Students

ROBERT L. SINCLAIR AND WARD J. GHORY

Précis

Dropping out of school is not a single event but a process. A student may start out well-anchored in the center of school activities; as strains develop in school relationships, the student may drift toward the edges or margins of academic and social activities in school. Robert Sinclair and Ward Ghory have proposed the umbrella term "marginality" for the sense of distance, disconnection, and estrangement a student may develop as he or she experiences strained and difficult relationships in the school or classroom environment.

One aspect of this marginality is the problematic interaction between the student and the school environment that creates a strained relationship. The other is the movement along a continuum that begins with an early, fairly shallow version of estrangement and progresses to a deeper, more serious stage of disconnection or alienation.

Explaining the first, the authors emphasize the "sheer variety" of its origins. They want us to realize that problematic relations result from a two-sided interaction between an individual and an environment at school. Students can become marginal in as many ways as they can experience inappropriate interaction with an educational environment. (One pair of examples is the gifted but bored mathematics student who does not benefit from extended practice at simple problems and the ill-prepared student who is also not benefiting from the same practice because he or she keeps making the same error without teacher intervention.)

To make their idea of degrees of marginality more useful for school teachers and administrators, the authors describe a four-stage progression starting with the initial deviations from or testing of school rules to a final stage when a young person has become alienated and openly rebels against regulations and behavioral norms. Teachers and administrators must find the appropriate way to deal with the student at each stage. Sinclair and Ghory believe there is a tendency for school officials to underreact in the early stages, when very firm responses to self-removal behaviors might bring the student back to the fold, and to overreact in the later stages, when harsh measures seem to drive the student even further toward the margins of the school.

School faculties should examine the stages through which marginality becomes more aggravated and develop strategies likely to re-engage students in productive school activities. Schools will become better places for all students when both students and teachers realize that problematic behaviors have two sides. They are not manifestations of an individual's fixed personality but involve responses to how that person is being treated in social interactions.

Robert L. Sinclair is a professor of education and the executive director of the Coalition for School Improvement at the University of Massachusetts in Amherst, Massachusetts.

Ward J. Ghory is head of the Upper School, Buckingham, Browne, and Nichols, in Cambridge, Massachusetts.

They are coauthors of *Reaching Marginal Students: A Primary Concern for School Renewal.*

—The College Board

The fundamental mission of public schools in the United States is to provide quality, integrated education for all young people through age 16 and for any interested youth through grade 12. Not only are schools expected to develop a comprehensive program of studies and activities related to successful accomplishment of academic, vocational, social, and personal goals, but citizens and courts also expect affirmative action to reduce barriers for access to higher education or success in society that arise from economic, racial, gender, or cultural differences among students.[1]

These far-reaching expectations expose a troubling contradiction between the responsibility of public schools to educate all students and the current inability of school personnel (as well as educators in other institutions) to reach and teach the (growing) population of youngsters on the margins of school and society. Our educational ideals dramatize the differences between the few who graduate from secondary schools fully prepared for ongoing development in college or leadership opportunities in the workplace and the many who leave high school, both before and after graduation, relatively limited in their prospects for meaningful employment or continuing education. Stark patterns of differential achievement—by race, class, and gender—belie the American vision of equality of opportunity. The values expressed and the responsibilities outlined in the democratic mission of the public school remain a dominant force sustaining continuing progress in American education, although the distance traveled toward our educational ideals may seem disappointing at times. It is this mission that stimulates and guides the current reform movement in American education.

Attending to students for whom schools are not satisfying and productive places is a largely unheeded but absolutely central starting place for creating meaningful and lasting school reform that will make our schools more responsive to all children and youth. Today, because skills taught in high schools are the bare minimum prerequisites for meaningful participation in society, reaching previously unsuccessful students must become a first priority. Further, we think that little long-term improvement in equality and quality will be gained by simply intensifying the features of the school environment that are often problematic to the very people we must assist—that increasing population of students who are marginal. Well-meaning attempts to ease disconnected and uninspired learners into compliance with a more "demanding" version of the conditions that drove them to the edge and contributed to their unproductive status will not be enough. Increasing what currently exists may force a larger portion of students to the margins of the school. The challenge is to create effective conditions for learning for every young person, particularly for those who are not experiencing success in school. Now is the time to make the problems of youngsters who are last in school first on the agenda for reform.

Evidence of the extent of marginality—that is, disconnection between students and the conditions designed for learning—is abundant and distressing. Nationwide, one in four students drops out of high school before graduation, and nearly one in two students does not graduate in certain locations and among certain ethnic groups.[2] Despite a decade of gains, the achievement of minority students still lags significantly behind that of white students, a class gap widens, and a racial schism persists.[3] Up to 40 percent of all junior high students and 60 percent of senior high students have trouble reading academic materials.[4] As many as two-thirds of the 17-year-olds still in school run the risk of becoming marginal because of inadequate writing skills.[5] Over one-third of all pupils achieve below grade level.[6] One in 10 secondary students gets suspended from school.[7] Nearly all high school students experiment with alcohol, more than half with marijuana, and about 40 percent with other drugs.[8] No doubt, these varied groups and different categories overlap in many ways. Nevertheless, this discouraging, unrelenting refrain of student difficulties emphasizes the necessity to learn more about how young people reach the point of rupture with institutions designed for their learning.

We advance the concept of marginality as a way to understand and address seemingly intractable problems of school learning that result when the relationship between the individual and the school environment becomes problematic. Starting where the strains first appear in a student's interactions at school, we consider the patterns and steps by which young people either become increasingly alienated or return to productive involvement in school. Finally, we propose a collaborative approach among educators to reduce marginality and increase equality and quality in school learning for those students who are not doing well.

The Meaning of Marginality

To be marginal is to experience a strained, difficult relationship with the school environment.[9] Students can be marginal in as many ways as they can experience unproductive dimensions of an educational environment. A young person, for example, can experience the physical dimensions of an environment as limiting conditions, as when an easily distractable student who needs private space for effective learning is assigned to an open-space classroom equipped with tables for groups of children, or when a student who needs new glasses is expected to work from a computer screen. Social conditions can also contribute to marginality when a student is distracted from academic tasks because his or her teacher, who is not effective as a classroom manager, must continually struggle to maintain control of a boisterous group. Intellectual conditions for learning can be alienating—both for the gifted mathematics student who does not benefit from extended practice on simple problems assigned as independent seatwork and for the ill-prepared student in the next row who repeatedly practices the same procedural error without teacher intervention. As these examples suggest, marginality can be specific to a single situation or can be generalized to many aspects of an educational environment.

Various types of students become marginal: the learner not working up to potential, the understimulated exceptional learner, the child with a long history of academic failure or substandard achievement, and the one student suddenly performing poorly despite previous success. Students can become marginal regardless of sex, race, family structure, or economic background, although these variables do seem to influence the likelihood of problems with school. Marginal learners can include children from low-income or minority homes as well as youth from well-to-do families who face less-than-constructive circumstances in the school setting. Gifted students become marginal, as did Lewis Terman's "less-successful" students who made up fully one quarter of his talented sample.[10] For some, the experience of disconnection or marginality will be short-lived. Yet for many, the disconnection and resulting deficiencies will be a critical step in forming attitudes and habits making marginality a way of life.

It is sobering to realize that anyone is at risk of becoming at least temporarily disconnected from full and productive involvement in classrooms and schools: the well-adjusted cheerleader whose parent dies, the merit scholar whose first romance ends, the legions of young people whose family life is strained, the children who become seriously ill or injured. Anyone can be quickly knocked out of a pattern of productivity and go unattended at school for long periods. Experiencing even greater odds against success are those learners whose ways of handling information and developing skills are not favored by relatively monolithic school environments: the learners who like to work with their hands, for example, the extroverts who prefer to work in groups and have to verbalize continually to stay on task, or the intuitive thinkers impatient with step-by-step processes. Precious little is done to draw the quick minds with special aptitudes, the linguistically different, the learning disabled, the culturally distinct into exciting school learning.

The sheer variety of ways and reasons for having troubles in school make us realize that problematic relationships result from two-sided interactions between an individual and an environment at school. To solve the problems of our schools, we need concepts that help us hold both ends of the individual–school equation in balance. We are advancing the term "marginal" to move away from the potentially negative and divisive connotations connected with most labels used to describe young people who have difficult relations with school. Use of the term "marginal" to explain student learning shifts the perspective from deeply seated problems rooted in the individual to problematic relationships between individuals and school environments. After all, differences among students are not the problem! Rather, the crucial issue is the extent to which the school environment can respond productively to the variations among students.

From this perspective, it is important to use care with terms, like "at-risk students," that may work against what we hope to accomplish with the sizable portion of young people who are troubled in school. Embedded in each description of a problem is an implied intervention approach. The "at-risk" language focuses on a population of students considered unlikely to succeed—those who are black or Hispanic and from low-income households. The term "at-risk" tends to isolate and stereotype these youngsters. Too often, one implication of such labeling is for educators and politicians to cluster these students in special groups for intensive treatment of their academic and social ills. The terminology easily lends itself to an overemphasis on identifying those students considered "at-risk," with an accompanying fascination with the quantification of variables that will predict or sort out who fits the "at-risk" label. The first and main problem becomes determining who these students are, rather than creating conditions that correct their difficulties. The identification–quantification mentality sometimes may lead to fallacious reasoning that increasing scores on tests and rising numbers of students taking advanced courses are evidence that the school is making progress with disconnected students. The tendency is to accept and protect the school conditions that can work well for those in the top academic tracks, by segregating some students, forcing them into the very settings that make them at-risk.

In contrast, when students are seen moving to the margins of a classroom or school, it is necessary to question what conditions in the school-student relationship are not working. Rather than providing a means to separate individuals and their behavior neatly into two categories—normal and "at-risk"—the marginal perspective highlights the fact that any individual's action is always relative and changeable, a matter of degree. The degree of school marginality depends not only on the characteristics of the student actor or action, but even more on the way in which the person or the behavior is interpreted and treated by educators.

As John Dewey emphasized, teachers and other educators inherit a perpetual responsibility to shape and reshape environments to promote constructive behavior. Problematic behaviors are not an individual's total personality and behavioral repertoire; in part, they are responses to how a person is being treated. Marginal learners can change even deep-seated, unproductive habits, just as constructive adjustments can be made in relatively static educational environments. There is no single point at which an individual becomes marginal or nonmarginal once and for all. It is necessary, therefore, to understand the path to becoming marginal and the ways in which educators can collaborate to reintegrate individuals with an improved and responsive school environment.

Becoming Marginal

The strained relationship that marginal students develop with the educational environment may lead others to view them as deviant individuals, either temporarily on the fringes or perhaps permanently out of mainstream. Too often educators identify lack of personal effort and weak academic potential as the reasons that marginal status persists and is seldom overcome. In fact, we cannot always attribute the reasons to the learner. By looking closely at the interaction between the learner and the environment, it is possible to gain an understanding of why so many students are becoming marginal. This understanding is a necessary beginning for action that may increase learning for all youth, including those who have not been successful in the past. Let us consider the sequence of events typically leading to students becoming marginal and identify the levels of seriousness of marginal students' behavior.

Sequence of Events

From our observations of schools and discussions with marginal learners and their parents, we have identified a general sequence of events experienced by students who disconnect from productive life in school.[11] The events are all too familiar to teachers and parents who are working to form a productive bond between students and learning conditions in school. We are not suggesting here that all students who become marginal follow the exact same sequence of activities. Nevertheless, there is a pattern to how students come into conflict with the learning environment and become marginal to it.

First Deviations. Students break or bend rules, usually in a minor fashion, as a way of obtaining what they want accomplished in school. For example, a student feigns illness to miss a test for which he or she is unprepared or "borrows" a book on reserve at the library to complete an assignment at home.

Consequences/Assuming Improvement. When a minor infraction is brought to their attention, administrators and teachers tend to downplay or even ignore the problem. At most, light penalties such as admonishments, make-up work, detentions, or apologies are applied. The assumption is that the student will return to compliance with school norms. Most do.

Repeated Deviations. The student attempts acts similar to the initial deviations, perhaps repeatedly, until caught again.

Consequences/Questioning Likelihood of Improvement. Stronger penalties are applied. Irritation with the student is expressed. The likelihood of improvement is privately or publicly questioned. Sterner warnings are issued. Privileges are withdrawn by parents. Teachers regularly question the student's behavior.

Stalemate. The student seeks support from peers or concerned adults and usually expresses resentment and hostility toward the punishers or perceived controllers. For the short term, the student becomes more careful and avoids trouble. But the opportunity to repeat or extend the problem behavior eventually presents itself and is taken. The student becomes known informally as a troublemaker or a poor student and is invited by other students with a similar status to be an accomplice. Often, wary relations between the school and the individual stabilize in a counterproductive stalemate at this stage. It is still possible for tension either to mount or to dissipate.

Crisis/Formal Stigma. An incident occurs in which the student's problem behavior can be clearly documented as extreme. A crisis is reached. Formal action is taken to stigmatize the difficult student, usually accomplished in a "degradation ceremony."[12] For example, during an angry scene a teacher may shame the pupil in front of the class. An administrator may suspend the student for a period so it is obvious to others that punishment has occurred. The shock value of this treatment, and the alarmed or disappointed reactions of parents and guardians, can often help the student to redirect behavior in an effort to shed the stigma.

Trying on the Marginal Role. Sometimes the problem intensifies. Rather than fight the stigma, the marginal learner accepts it, seeking support from similarly labeled peers. Simultaneously, the student takes steps to avoid the painful source of his or her stigma. Avoidance behavior (tardiness, class cutting, leaving school grounds) is common. A few students drop out or transfer. Substance abuse often increases. But many students turn to a teacher or the principal to complain about the way they have been treated (possibly their way of seeking help). Parents may call the school to do the same.

Confirming Experiences. At worst, the school, the family, the peer group, and the individual accept the student's marginal social status within the learning environment. The student adjusts to a new role, striving to fulfill expectations for deviance. Parental and school incentives to help tend to decrease because of repeated rejection and lack of progress. Failing grades or continuing behavior problems become expected and tolerated. Rebellious behavior can be the student's final attempt to draw attention to an extreme position or to punish the people and places that have rejected him or her. These incidents "radicalize" the student, who feels a surge of power from temporary "successes" or hardens his or her attitude from the rejection that results. Expulsion from either home or school may be a culminating event that confirms for the student and others the fact that a serious problem exists.

If actions are taken to compel the student to "fit in," the conflict between the learner and the school will likely mount. Sometimes, as the school responds with increasing severity to deviant behavior, the student becomes less willing to meet demands for compliance. In these cases it is easier for the student to connect with life on the margins, where there is acceptance of the behaviors the school cannot condone. The distance between the learner and the school widens as positions harden. The way to close the gap is unclear, especially if the school focuses on minimum expectations and does not explore ways to create or to extend possibilities for productive connections.

In forward-looking schools, principals, teachers, and parents bend over backward to find ways to short-circuit this sequence of events. Students who are becoming marginal receive a great deal of attention and account for a large proportion of the administrators' and counselors' workloads.[13] These professionals "let go" only after the failure of many attempts to foster improvement. Yet the dynamics of these interactions suggest that successful intervention must be geared to the level of seriousness of the marginal behavior in order to alter the student's path as he or she progresses from minor disconnection to serious alienation.

Levels of Seriousness

The marginal behavior of students occurs in four levels of increasing intensity: testing, coasting, retreating, and rebelling. Table 1 outlines the links between these levels and the sequence of events involved in becoming marginal. The associations proposed here show the typical match between the events and the severity of disconnection.[14] As students move from the initial stages of marginality toward more severe alienation, it becomes more difficult to bring them back into the life of the school. Those who observe a student's behavior at various levels can determine the degree of marginality and the form of intervention necessary to reestablish a constructive relationship between the learner and the educational conditions in the school.

Testing. It is not uncommon for a student to experience temporary disconnection. The desire to do well often prompts students to take a shortcut and then worry about being caught. This is testing behavior, which is the least serious level of temporary marginality but still a cause for concern.

Table 1. Becoming Marginal: Levels of Seriousness and Events

Levels of Seriousness	Events
Testing	First deviations
	Consequences/assuming improvement
	Repeated deviations
Coasting	Consequences/questioning likelihood of improvement
	Stalemate
Retreating	Crisis/formal stigma
	Trying on the marginal role
Rebelling	Confirming experiences

Testers desire to accomplish goals valued in the school environment, but they see their path blocked by legitimate means. In response, they test the limits of allowed behavior by stretching the truth, searching for exceptions to justify their approach, or interpreting closely the letter of the law to provide a thin cover for what they have done. Actually, a certain degree of brinksmanship is considered an appropriate way to test limits. For this reason, students who employ parental pressure to have special privileges granted, or who "brown-nose" to gain favor can be viewed as negotiating limits to create conditions more favorable to their success.

Testing behavior is more serious when individuals temporarily use illegitimate means, arguing that their end justifies these means. For example, students who cheat for a grade, copy homework, forge a note from home, purchase term papers, or deliberately plagiarize are expressing doubts about their ability to succeed in sanctioned ways. They represent as their own something that is not. This is the first split in adjusted identity, the first indication of a potentially serious conflict between individual and environment. This testing behavior may occur more and more frequently. Those who clearly and repeatedly break rather than bend the accepted norms are considered to have a bigger problem. Their action cannot be dismissed as a normal outgrowth of the independence-seeking behavior typical during adolescence, nor can it be summarily squelched.

Some positive value is placed on testing behavior because it can be creative; in such cases marginal people can actually improve institutions. Yet testing can also be the level where students develop tendencies that become reflected in unethical practices in their later life. At this level a fine line separates productive from destructive approaches to correcting marginal behavior. Still, the opportunity exists to teach principled action and to encourage testers to practice it.

Coasting. Coasting behavior is adopted by those who do not see school goals as realistically attainable or as meaningful to them, but who elect nonetheless to accept and follow the prescribed means because they are paths of least resistance. These are the students who simply go through the motions with little expectation of success. They sit for tests but do not finish them; they regularly appear in class but do not participate; they go to the teacher for help when forced to but seldom ask questions.

Coasters maintain a false front of appropriate behavior because the cost of authentic behavior seems prohibitive. Coasting behavior can be superficial or deep. Since their overt behavior is institutionally permitted, their implicit doubting or rejection of school goals is accepted as an internal decision. Usually little intervention occurs to assist in connecting the pupil's real interests with school. Labeled underachieving or alienated, these learners are often treated with a casual indifference or "benign neglect," which confirms their attitude of passive endurance or their sense of the absurdity of the educational enterprise. Their satisfaction with middling grades is reinforced by friends' expectations and performance. They annoy their parents because they do not aspire for more and cannot say what they desire to study or how they intend to be employed. Indeed, because their deeper interests are not expressed and explained, they really do not know what they want for the future.

Many adolescents must work through this reluctance to engage. It takes time to develop confidence in one's competence to accomplish in the "accepted way." Those who look upon themselves as nonconformists shun the skill-oriented, group-regulated school environment that seems to allow only conventional opportunities for connecting surface and depth behavior. Yet these adolescents find the best way to be left alone is to conform by going along to the minimum degree permitted as acceptable.

Coasters are at a turning point. Prompted by the need to consider college or work plans after high school, they may concentrate and improve in school— these students are the so-called late bloomers. Sometimes, they endure until graduation and perform tolerably. Others invest their attention in outside interests. For them, school is almost a cover they maintain while pursuing other interests. Finally, some react against their own inauthenticity, embrace as valid the way in which they feel different, then act to change or avoid the circumstances that are thwarting them. Once engaged, these can be thoughtful and penetrating students; if not engaged, they are likely to enter the next level of marginality.

Retreating. Retreating students are reluctant to maintain a charade of acceptable behavior. When they can, they reject not only the school's goals but also the available means for learning. The truant, the selective class cutter, the chronically tardy student, the pupils caught smoking in bathrooms or hanging out behind the stairs—these are the young people who withdraw to the margins of situations they see as increasingly absurd or hopeless. Their perceptions are generally confirmed when parents or school officials stigmatize and punish them without providing avenues for productive participation. They hold fiercely to their peers as their support in a turbulent, threatening environment.

Parents and educators must concern themselves with students in retreat. At this level students are taking on a new public identity and, more dangerous, a new internal one. Gradually, these individuals are reorganizing their personal identities around the behaviors that led them to become marginal. As this reorganization proceeds, the likelihood of permanent marginality grows. These students are taking their marginal position and worth in school to the core of themselves. In doing so they lose sight of the constructive elements of their own past behaviors and achievements: they reinterpret the past in light of their present position on the margins.[15] Thus the problem of marginality developed in school has a contaminating effect on the student's whole personality.[16] Unfortunately, the student's new public identity causes reactions from others that tend to intensify the internal reorganization. For students in retreat, the way they feel themselves to be different becomes the most important element of their public identity, a kind of "master status" around which all other social expectations revolve.[17] The symbols of this new status and identity, such as clothes, speech, posture, and mannerisms, serve to heighten social visibility and to attract further behavior-confirming treatment by peers and by the school. These symbols of their "difference" are likely to lead to labeling and stigmatizing by the larger school community, a response that tells these students that they are indeed who they think they are. When these students are labeled and stigmatized by the school, they are further cut off from constructive aspects of their past and from positive, potential abilities they may have. In this aggressive, defensive, self-protective, negative cycle, the assertive trappings of marginal status lead to the students being dealt with as if they were, and had always been, only their current public identities. Thus this treatment helps individuals internalize more and more of their public identity as the core of their own personal identity. The conflict between student and school has moved inward and becomes inaccessible to those involved in institutional, as opposed to personal, relationships with the student. It is critical, then, that steps be taken to create a more personalized setting if students in retreat are to learn effectively.

Rebelling. Whereas spontaneous acts of defiance can briefly erupt and quickly subside among discontented adolescents, rebelling as a level of marginality refers to situations in which students not only reject existing goals and means but create opposing goals and means. These sustained or planned efforts to strike back are often expressed in school-directed violence (vandalism), interpersonal violence (assaults), and repeated outbursts in the classroom. Since it involves considerable risk to challenge the school deliberately and flagrantly, rarely do rebelling students act without a small support group of co-conspirators.[18] Acts such as using or selling drugs and alcohol on school property, committing arson or damaging school property, and assaulting teachers and students can usually be understood in the context of rebelling.

Most marginal individuals need group encouragement to overcome personal fears or feelings of revulsion and guilt as they become involved in these acts. When avenues of participation in conventional activities are subtly or officially closed to marginal learners, subgroups tend to develop their own rigid code and standards of behavior. Group members feel pressured to repeat or extend the antisocial behavior that drew them together on the fringes. The danger is that an individual's behavior, self-view, peer relations, and formal treatment will all contribute to a mutually acknowledged, terribly constrained relationship with the school.[19]

Schools that strive to ensure equality and quality education for all individuals are often judged by their ability to respond to deviations of students. In this sense effectiveness is directly related to the ability of the school to intervene constructively with marginal learners. Understanding how and why students become marginal provides a base for action for principals, teachers, parents, and the learners who are disconnected. That students are in the process of becoming marginal does not imply that they are always going to be locked into an unproductive life in school. An awareness of what it is like to become marginal is the starting point for those who want to reverse the cycle leading to many students' permanent estrangement from the institution intended for their learning.

Collaboration for Increased Learning

The students on the margins, then, are a crucial problem that must be addressed in the next phase of the educational reform movement. We think they are the source for reconstructing schools and for renewing the commitment for equal and quality education. Simply put, if American public schools are to become even more effective, it is necessary to reach and teach those young people who are not realizing their potential. Too often national attention to reform is directed to structural changes in how schools operate or in how they are organized. By starting first with the problems of marginal students, it may be possible to move in a deliberate manner to redefine roles and responsibilities educators have toward all students.

Leaders of past reform efforts were too easily satisfied with proposing adjustments in school structure—from self-contained classrooms to team teaching, from set class schedules to flexible scheduling, from A, B, C report cards to checklists of skills, and so on. However, the well-intentioned changes in school structure did not result in changes in how educators thought about or acted toward students who were struggling with their learning. In the past reforms also focused on "tightening" the standards for scholarship. Attempts to establish higher standards translated into new textbooks, more homework, more required courses, strict attendance policies, stringent discipline policies, competency tests for graduation, more advanced classes, and so on. The impact here was a tendency to intensify the school conditions that already existed.

By starting with the problems of students who are not successful in school, it may be possible to link reform initiatives to creating necessary roles and responsibilities for educators in order to help marginal students increase their learning. Indeed, there should be complementary changes in structures and standards, but they must be anchored in the actual problems students are experiencing. Hence the starting point for reform should be stressing equality and quality for students who need and deserve help in increasing their learning.

Roles and Responsibilities

The effective school in a democracy is a self-renewing school—one that continually monitors its own progress, identifying and solving problems that interfere with the learning of students. Such schools are permeated by a "can-do" attitude based on confidence that the school community can steadily improve by reexamining its assumptions and modifying its practices. Concern for students who are not successfully taking advantage of the school environment is at the heart of a self-renewing school, for the desire to diagnose and the determination to solve student difficulties provide the impetus for ongoing improvement.

Despite understandable desires for overnight cures that would be accomplished by installing a new organizational model in a school, both educators and the general public must realize that improvement of the school environment for marginal learners comes through solving problems that are unique to each school. In addition to their many responsibilities for normal school functions, principals, teachers, parents, and students have special roles to play and specific responsibilities to uphold in the process of reducing marginality and increasing learning for all youngsters.

The major role of the principal is to lead teams of teachers, parents, and students through instructional and environmental problem solving.[20] Many generic problem-solving models are available for principals with varying leadership styles. A straightforward example, proposed by Ralph Tyler, includes the following six steps.[21] The beauty of this approach is that it centers on solving problems related to learning, making this the touchstone for school improvement.

1. Focus on significant problems interfering with student learning: Teachers themselves should identify priority problems, with input from parents and students.

2. Problem analysis: Teams of teachers, students, and parents look for further information about the problem and its context.

3. Conditions for effective learning: The analysis is aided by probing to see that all the conditions for effective learning are present: (a) student motivation; (b) clear learning objectives; (c) appropriate learning tasks; (d) confidence; (e) rewards and feedback; (f) sequential practice; and (g) provisions for transfer of learning.

4. Search for solutions: The team needs to search for all the possible solutions, then to examine each one to decide which appear to be the most effective and feasible.

5. Develop the plan: Teams should plan to change, as needed, present school policies, the curriculum, teaching practices, learning materials, daily and weekly schedules, administrative practices, parent involvement.

6. Plan implementation: Significant change in schools is estimated to require five to seven years.

As symbolic and cultural leader of the school, the principal has the responsibility of articulating the public school mission of quality, integrated education for all. Practically speaking, this involves encouraging teachers and school staff to believe in the capability of their learners and in their abilities to create vigorous ways for all students to learn. Schools that are consistently unsuccessful with some learners tend to be mired in a slough of restraining attitudes and counterproductive practices that defy efforts by students, parents, and educators to break the cycle of defeat and discouragement. It is the principal's responsibility to confront such defeatism in a tactful, supportive, but direct manner. Specifically, the successful principal finds ways to help teachers, parents, and students personally reconsider their ways of thinking about and their ways of interacting with marginal students.[22] Prior to problem solving in any school, but especially in schools that have a sizable population of marginal students, it is the responsibility of the principal to build a platform of shared concerns, positive attitudes, and common goals.[23]

In addition to serving in a problem-solving capacity on schoolwide teams, the special role of the teacher is to intervene when students are starting to show signs of becoming marginal. We consider two general approaches to be most visible: improving the student's coping skills and reorganizing the classroom environment.[24]

Educators have an obligation to help students become more powerful learners by teaching them the identifiable learning skills related to success within prevailing classroom conditions. We propose that every learner, especially the marginal one, needs coping skills of four types: learning to learn skills, content thinking skills, basic reasoning skills, and communication skills.[25] Of course, as learning environments and instruction vary, so will the specific coping skills needed by different students. Nevertheless, when teachers place a greater emphasis than is usual on teaching students strategies to process information covered in class, both marginal and more successful students stand to benefit. Giving attention to marginal students does not mean that more successful students will suffer.

When students consistently have difficulty relating successfully to classroom conditions for learning, the individual teacher has to adjust curriculum and instruction to connect more productively with the characteristics of these marginal students. Genuine concern for marginal students will inevitably produce constructive changes in classrooms, despite real and perceived school, district, and community constraints. Again, it is the thinking and commitment of teachers that must be stimulated before technical issues of implementation can be considered. Teachers can best approach the difficult task of changing habitual practices that are not working with marginal stu-

dents by communicating regularly with other teachers, parents, and counselors. For most teachers, time must be allowed and support provided before
hesitant attempts to try new approaches become more accomplished and sure.
Some of the aspects of a learning environment that can be adjusted to
encourage fuller participation and more successful learning by marginal
students include instructional grouping, curriculum organization, curriculum
evaluation, teacher expectations, and the use of nonschool settings like the
home.[26] As with other strategies for reaching marginal students, adjustments
in classroom conditions are likely to benefit all learners, including those
already progressing at average or above average rates.

Teachers and parents share a responsibility to communicate when signs
of marginality develop. The major role for those who act as guardians for
children and youth is primarily to "parent well." All children and adolescents
need the best base of consistent physical, emotional, and spiritual security
their parents or guardians can provide. Marginal learners especially need
advocates who can call a halt when school practices are not favorable, but
they also need advocates who can consider and interpret for students the
wise advice school professionals provide. It is a full-time role to build a
parental relationship that holds through adolescence. Marginal learners, like
all youth, need special relationships with adults (often in addition to their
parents), with whom they can confide, express developing values, and develop
more decisive control of their own actions. For many marginal learners, this
supportive role has regrettably been usurped by peer groups, who often lack
the experience to do more than console troubled friends while confirming
current behavior. Parents and teachers together may be able to get the power
of the peer group to work in productive ways for the marginal student by
initiating student tutoring, student cooperative learning, and teams for community service.

Parents have the responsibility to work with teachers without concealing
problems and without automatically assuming critical and adversarial viewpoints. Teachers have the responsibility to alert parents to signs of trouble
and to demonstrate concern, extra effort, and individual attention when it is
needed with marginal learners. Many strains confounding school environments can be traced to failures by the adults closest to children to assume
these obligations. The key to turning around learning problems is often a
team approach. Parents and teachers can work together to identify how a
person learns best, to diagnose skill and content needed, to set attainable
and optimistic expectations, to reinforce consistently desired behavior, and
to encourage young people to learn well. Although teachers primarily interact
with groups whereas parents concentrate on individuals, we think, with
marginal learners, only the personalized touch within the group setting can
make the difference.

Ultimately, the fate of marginal learners remains in their own hands.
Very little substantial progress will occur until they become aware in a

realistic way of how they are performing and use this awareness to begin to channel what they are doing in constructive directions. The special role of the marginal learner is to make a substantial commitment to perform better at school.

Coming back from the margins into a more productive relationship with the school environment is a process of personal growth involving greater knowledge and control of one's self and one's learning process. Marginal students have the responsibility to monitor and at times adjust their own attitudes, realizing that attitudes affect behavior and that attitudes can be changed. Educators and parents respond to attitudes. Positive ones—like "effort pays off," "this task is possible to perform," "be persistent," and "learn from failure"—create their own momentum. Marginal students also have the responsibility to become more aware of their learning needs and strengths. They have to see school less as a place where outside forces manipulate them, and more as a job they approach with personal strategies and goals. They need to develop and maintain more effective forms of deliberate action while accomplishing a task, by assessing their current knowledge state, by selecting strategies to fulfill specific goals, and by keeping a watchful eye on their own effort and progress. Perhaps the most challenging aspect of renewing schools for marginal students, as well as other learners, is creating this kind of consciousness and commitment among maturing and initially resistant students. It is a dimension of school reform that is almost completely overlooked except by practitioners working to help students establish a positive cultural identity. Although these powers can be developed by coaching, and by families and peer groups with effective direction, little will happen with serious marginal learners until they themselves start trying to gain control of their lives and learning.[27]

For marginal behavior to decline, the student's relationship with the learning environment has to improve. Conversely, for learning environments to become more responsive and successful at reaching all learners, educators' roles and responsibilities with marginal learners have to be reconsidered. As in any relationship, positive change comes through honest evaluation of behavior and grows from a commitment to act on new ways of thinking about the relationship. Structural educational reforms that are implemented without building these fundamental commitments ring hollow and soon fade. Focus on the learners who are not successful in school can be our best rallying point for collaborative efforts to create schools consistent with the perennial ideals and the ambitious mission of American public education.

John F. Kennedy was sensitive to the crucial role of public education in this country when he said, "I am certain that after the dust of centuries has passed over our cities, we too will be remembered not for victories or defeats in battle or politics, but for our contribution to the human spirit." The persistent problems that are so much with those who are not succeeding must catch the imagination and capture the commitment of leaders who will act to ensure that the soaring of the human spirit also will be experienced by students who now are forced to the margins of our public schools. To this end, we suggest that the last and first priority for each single school, as it mirrors the democratic society it serves, is to take the lead in providing equal opportunity for learning so that all young people may realize the promise of their potential.

Notes

1. For amplification of the mission of public schools, see John I. Goodlad, *What Schools Are For* (Bloomington, Ind.: Phi Delta Kappa Educational Foundation, 1979); and *A Place Called School: Prospects for the Future* (New York: McGraw-Hill, 1984), 45.

2. Ernest L. Boyer, *High School: A Report on Secondary Education in America* (New York: Harper and Row, 1983), 235–240.

3. Linda Darling-Hammond, *Equality and Excellence: The Educational Status of Black Americans* (New York: College Entrance Examination Board, 1985).

4. *Reading Performance Trends, 1981–1984: Their Significance* (Princeton, N.J.: National Assessment of Educational Progress, 1984). See also Lois E. Burrill, "How Well *Should* a High School Graduate Read?" *NASSP Bulletin*, March 1987, 61–72.

5. Ina Mullis, "Writing Achievement and Instruction Results from the 1983–84 NAEP Writing Assessment," paper presented at the annual meeting of the National Council of Teachers of English, Philadelphia, 1985. See also Archie LaPointe, "Test Results Provide Data Useful to Educators Planning to Improve Schools," *NASSP Bulletin*, March 1987, 73–78.

6. See the analysis of low achievement and underachievement in Robert L. Sinclair and Ward J. Ghory, *Reaching Marginal Students: A Primary Concern for School Renewal* (Berkeley, Calif.: McCutchan, 1987), 19–27.

7. Ibid., 27–29.

8. Lloyd D. Johnston, et al., *Highlights from Drugs and American High School Students, 1975–1983* (Rockville, Md.: National Institute on Drug Abuse, 1984).

9. The technical term "marginal" was coined by an anthropologist to describe the dilemma of individuals whose parents belonged to two different tribes. Although involved intimately in the life of both groups, these "marginal men" were devalued by group authorities and were visibly uncomfortable in many group settings. See Robert E. Park, "Human Migration and the Marginal Man," *American Journal of Sociology* 33 (May 1928): 892.

10. Lewis M. Terman, *The Early Mental Traits of Three Hundred Geniuses* (Stanford, Calif.: Stanford University Press, 1926).

11. For an analysis of the sequence of interactions leading to marginality by a sociologist concerned with deviance, see Edwin W. Lemert, *Social Pathology: A Systematic Approach to the Theory of Sociopathic Behavior* (New York: McGraw-Hill, 1951), 77.

12. Harold Garfinkel, "Conditions of Successful Degradation Ceremonies, *American Journal of Sociology* 61 (January 1956): 420–424.

13. Paul A. Gulyas, "Improving the Behavior of Habitually Disruptive High School Students," unpublished paper, Nova University, 1979. In Gulyas's study, 80 percent

of those detained received detention more than once; 27 percent of those suspended were suspended more than once, accounting for 40 percent of the cumulative days out owing to suspension; and about 2 percent of the student body were habitual disrupters, yet they accounted for more than half of the admnistrative case load.

14. This proposition derives from Robert K. Merton's seminal study of deviance in social systems, "Social Structure and Anomie," *American Sociological Review* 3 (October 1938): 672–682.

15. Edwin M. Schur, *Labeling Deviant Behavior* (New York: Harper and Row, 1971), 52–56.

16. Erving Goffman, *Stigma: Notes on the Management of Spoiled Identity* (Englewood Cliffs, N.J.: Prentice-Hall, 1963), 2–9.

17. Howard S. Becker, *The Outsiders* (New York: Free Press, 1963), 31–35.

18. The "sliding partner" relationship, especially characteristic of youth classified as having behavior disorders, contributes to the difficulty of helping marginal students take responsibility for their actions. Sliding partners encourage or at least passively support deviant behavior, then help each other escape consequences through mutual protection. See Dewey Carducci, *The Caring Classroom* (New York: Kampmann, 1984), 34–38.

19. Schur, *Labeling Deviant Behavior*, 69–71.

20. The crucial role of the principal in the local school is carefully and creatively discussed in Goodlad, *A Place Called School*, Chapter 9; and in Boyer, *High School*.

21. Ralph W. Tyler, "The Role of the Principal in Promoting Student Learning," paper presented at the Massachusetts School Administrators Conference, Sturbridge, Massachusetts, 1986; available from the Center for Curriculum Studies, School of Education, University of Massachusetts, Amherst.

22. For an analysis of how changing ways of thinking and how redefining roles serve as powerful interventions for increasing student learning, see Jim Cummins, "Empowering Minority Students: A Framework for Intervention," *Harvard Educational Review* 56 (February 1986): 18–36.

23. It is possible to overstate the leadership function of the principal to make it appear that the principal is acting alone in school renewal leadership. Frequently, a second change facilitator (an assistant principal, special teacher, or district supervisor) is nearly as active, and in some cases more active, than the principal. See Shirley Hord, Suzanne Stiegelbauer, and Gene Hall, "How Principals Work with Other Change Facilitators," *Education and Urban Society* 17 (November 1984): 89–109.

24. When students are having difficulty learning, a total of four categories of responses are possible at the classroom level: (1) use benign neglect; (2) empower students with the skills necessary to be successful; (3) change the environment; (4) remove the student.

25. For an elaboration of these skills and of skills instruction, see Sinclair and Ghory, *Reaching Marginal Students*, 99–107.

26. See ibid., 107–116, for elaboration of how these dimensions of a classroom can be adjusted for marginal learners.

27. A persuasive analysis of the complex of attitudes and skills needed to take command of one's own learning is presented in the chapter on metacognition in Robert J. Marzano et al., *Dimensions of Thinking: A Framework for Curriculum and Instruction* (Alexandria, Va.: Association for Supervision and Curriculum Development, 1988, 13–32.

Selected References

Becker, Howard S. *The Outsiders*. New York: Free Press, 1963.

Boyer, Ernest L. *High School: A Report on Secondary Education in America*. New York: Harper and Row, 1983.

Carducci, Dewey. *The Caring Classroom*. New York: Kampmann, 1984.

Cummins, Jim. "Empowering Minority Students: A Framework for Intervention." *Harvard Educational Review* 56 (February 1986): 18–36.

Darling-Hammond, Linda. *Equality and Excellence: The Educational Status of Black Americans*. New York: College Entrance Examination Board, 1985.

Garfinkel, Harold. "Conditions of Successful Degradation Ceremonies." *American Journal of Sociology* 61 (January 1956): 420–24.

Goffman, Erving. *Stigma: Notes on the Management of Spoiled Identity*. Englewood Cliffs, N.J.: Prentice-Hall, 1963.

Goodlad, John I. *What Schools Are For*. Bloomington, Ind.: Phi Delta Kappa Educational Foundation, 1979.

Hord, Shirley, Suzanne Stiegelbauer, and Gene Hall. "How Principals Work with Other Change Facilitators." *Education and Urban Society* 17 (November 1984): 89–109.

Johnston, Lloyd D. *Highlights from Drugs and American High School Students, 1975–1983*. Rockville, Md.: National Institute on Drug Abuse, 1984.

Lemert, Edwin W. *Social Pathology: A Systematic Approach to the Theory of Sociopathic Behavior*. New York: McGraw-Hill, 1951.

Marzano, Robert J. *Dimensions of Thinking: A Framework for Curriculum and Instruction*. Alexandria, Va.: Association for Supervision and Curriculum Development, 1988.

Merton, Robert K. "Social Structure and Anomie." *American Sociological Review* 3 (October 1938): 672–682.

Mullis, Ina. "Writing Achievement and Instruction Results From the 1983–84 NAEP Writing Assessment." Paper presented at the annual meeting of the National Council of Teachers of English, Philadelphia, 1985.

Park, Robert E. "Human Migration and the Marginal Man." *American Journal of Sociology* 33 (May 1928): 881–93.

Schur, Edwin M. *Labeling Deviant Behavior*. New York: Harper and Row, 1971.

Sinclair, Robert L., and Ward J. Ghory. *Reaching Marginal Students: A Primary Concern for School Renewal*. Berkeley, Calif.: McCutchan, 1987.

Sinclair, Robert L., and Sonia M. Nieto. *Renewing School Curriculum: Concerns for Equal and Quality Education*. Amherst, Mass.: Coalition for School Improvement, 1988.

Terman, Lewis M. *The Early Mental Traits of Three Hundred Geniuses*. Stanford, Calif.: Stanford University Press, 1926.

Tyler, Ralph W. "The Role of the Principal in Promoting Student Learning." Paper presented at the Massachusetts School Administrators Conference, Sturbridge, Massachusetts, 1986.

8.

Misunderstanding and Testing Intelligence

ASA G. HILLIARD III

Précis

The widely held view of intelligence as a fixed, immutable quality measurable by a test that provides a unitary rating of that measure called IQ is used for sorting people into categories, but the process of education is not aided by such a concept. Educators should put aside this static view and understand intelligence in terms of mental structures, processes, and operations—a rational basis for intellectual development in education.

According to Asa Hilliard, researchers using this approach will be able to identify a series of mental skills or abilities and develop instruments to test for them. This kind of information can help educators know what to do to aid development of a student's mind and foster the further unfolding of individual human potential. Tests should identify abilities that can be measured and improved through instruction; then instructional strategies should be developed to remedy specific deficiencies revealed by diagnostic instruments.

Hilliard cites Reuven Feuerstein and his colleagues, who have been building on the developmental perspectives of the Swiss psychologist Jean Piaget. The systems developed by Feuerstein and his co-workers, the Learning Potential Assessment Device for testing and Instrumental Enrichment for guiding remedial instruction, have grown out of a set of questions such as the following: How does the mind work? Can it be shaped? Can this shaping improve academic, social, and emotional performance? According to Hilliard, educators should insist that testing be related to this type of inquiry and be thought of as useful only as a means for bringing about improvement in individual students.

Asa G. Hilliard III is an educational psychologist and Fuller E. Callaway Professor of Education at Georgia State University. He has been involved in studying psychological test validity in cross-cultural usage for a number of years.

—*The College Board*

Many of the chapters written by my colleagues for this volume address specific school practices that serve both overtly and covertly to deny some students equal access to the knowledge schools are supposed to provide for all. Those inequitable practices discriminate most severely against boys and girls who are poor. And those poor boys and girls are, in turn, disproportionately from several of the nation's minority groups.

Some of the practices do a disservice even to those students who appear to benefit most from them. For example, the more affluent students are disproportionately sorted into high tracks and special classes designated for the gifted. True giftedness is rare, diverse, and often concentrated in one area of a child's development. But a student with a high score on a so-called intelligence test is classified as gifted, nonetheless, and usually sorted into classes with other "gifted" students. This is done without consideration of whether there are also in the school students who are, indeed, gifted in music or even abstract reasoning in mathematics in a way not measured by the "intelligence" test. Simultaneously, of course, students who are gifted in some area or whose true intellectual ability falls through the net of the test are grouped with their "slow-learning" peers.

Much of this injustice and malpractice grows out of prevailing, long-standing misconceptions about the nature of intelligence and the use and interpretations of measures employed in these classifications of students in schools. It is to the misunderstanding and improved understanding of intelligence and what stems from whatever conceptions dominate that this chapter is addressed. Of particular significance in what follows are the uses and abuses of so-called intelligence tests.

As far back as we can go in human history, people have been fascinated with the workings of the human mind. There is no end to attempts to develop schemes to represent the structure, operations, and functions of thought.

In the past philosophers and theologians thought most about thinking and its role in human behavior, both social and individual. But now the idea of "intelligence" has become the preoccupation of many psychologists and educators, some of whom have attempted to approach its understanding in a scientific fashion.

The study of intelligence has led to development of *instruments* that purport to measure it. We have *practices* in education that make use of the results of attempts to measure "intelligence." We have *beliefs* about the meaning of the results. And we have *public policies and institutional structures* growing directly out of beliefs about intelligence and tests purporting to measure it.

In the United States the idea of intelligence plays a central role in education and in psychology. The measurement of intelligence looms so large that few school psychologists or educational psychologists can conceive of operating without the essential instrument of their profession, the "intelligence" test. Moreover, psychologists find willing clients for such tests among educators and public officials. Yet there is no precise correspondence between the standardized tests called intelligence tests and some mental activity we called intelligence. (I refer here to IQ tests rather than to intelligence tests since, in my opinion, all commonly used IQ tests are really achievement tests.) Intelligence can and should be thought of independently of IQ or achievement tests.

Although the instruments and techniques for measuring intelligence have their detractors, it is safe to say that the general population is overwhelmingly receptive to such. At the very least, there is widespread tolerance for such instruments and practices, and for the purposes that they have served. There is not now, nor has there been in recent years, any significant resistance to general practices in IQ assessment from professional organizations or from institutions that serve their clients through psychological services. Resistance has been raised, through litigation, legislation, or regulation spurred by small interest groups, or even by dissatisfied individuals.

In spite of the apparent widespread acceptance of, or at least the absence of widespread resistance to, the use of conventional intelligence constructs and IQ instruments in education, the issues surrounding such use remain largely unexamined, obscure, and often confounded. As a result, laypeople, as well as professionals in both education and psychology, appear to possess few meaningful or valid criteria for determining the instructional utility of the continued widespread use of such thinking, instruments, and practice.

The Use of IQ Testing: An Impediment to the Intelligent Use of "Intelligence"

The time has come when we must raise fundamental questions about venerable beliefs and practices in education and in psychology. As long as ideas about intelligence and the use of IQ testing are confined primarily to the area of research and theoretical speculation, there is less urgency to approach these questions. However, when we observe the almost universal incorporation of concepts and beliefs about intelligence and IQ into educational practice, professionalism dictates that they be validated and justified.

Several years ago the National Academy of Sciences Panel on Placing Children in Special Education (Heller, Holtzman, and Messick 1982) was presented with a question by the Office of Civil Rights. The question was stimulated by the fact that large numbers of African American male children, disproportionate to their numbers in the general population, were placed in classes for the educable mentally retarded. The Office of Civil Rights questioned the scientific basis for such an outcome. Responding to the query from the Office of Civil Rights, the National Academy of Sciences Panel was appointed to address a much more fundamental research question than the original one posed by the Office. Eventually, the Academy of Sciences Panel raised the fundamental question of the educational utility of testing, labeling, and special placement in education. The resulting report of the Panel began with a simple and direct proposition: "It is the purpose of testing assessment and associated processes in education to improve the quality of instruction for children."

Profound consequences flow from the adoption of this statement of purpose. Perhaps for the first time in the history of school psychology, a truly rigorous justification is necessary for the use of testing instruments and concepts associated with such instruments as general practice in the schools. In the past any "misuse of intelligence" could be asserted merely by pointing out that someone had not followed the rules of standard test administration scoring or interpreting standardized tests as commonly accepted in the field. However, with the adoption of this child-benefit principle by the National Academy of Sciences Panel and with its gradual acceptance by wider audiences, we have entered a new period for testing and placing students. Now, not only must procedures be followed adequately, but *children must benefit from the use of testing, labeling, and placement.* The data to show these benefits do not exist (Gartner and Lipsky 1987). We can no longer be casual in the use of instruments for assessing intelligence, nor can we be casual about our understanding of the nature of intelligence itself.

At present, users accept on faith the idea that a single standardized IQ test gives a reasonably clear portrait of the manifestation of "intelligence." The primary piece of empirical data used to support the validity of IQ tests is their reasonably strong correlation with academic grades received a year or so after the IQ test is given. However, even a perfect association between IQ scores and school grades does not ensure that IQ tests measure "intelligence," however it may be defined at present. For example, if IQ tests are "achievement" tests, a strong relationship between them and other measures of achievement is to be expected. The contribution of prior experience or practice and of cultural knowledge to both IQ tests and to achievement tests must be differentiated and accounted for in order to give a meaningful explanation of the relationship of IQ test scores to school grades. The most obvious of many strategies that would help clarify this matter is to conduct experimental validity studies. Matched samples of experimental and control groups are needed, for example, where the groups are equated on prior exposure to the types of content and skills that are required on the IQ tests. Even then, to be really useful, the testing strategy should reveal fine-grained information about mental *processes*, not merely about mental *status*. The IQ testing literature is almost silent on these matters.

Intelligence Testing: A 70-Year-Old Money-Making Tool

When educational psychologists and educators use the idea of IQ as a placeholder for intelligence and use instruments for its measurement, without going beyond the conventional thinking discussed above, they can be char-

acterized as conceptually incarcerated. Becoming unbound conceptually requires that they engage in critical analyses regarding the intelligence construct, the instruments for the measure of intelligence, and the utility of
activities associated with both. The legitimation of certain teaching methods
and organizational arrangements in the schools is tied to the use of IQ testing.
There are also major vested interests involved in IQ test use that promote
their continued use (Narin 1980; Weiss 1987). There are, for example,
educators and psychologists who depend heavily on the testing industry for
their own financial gain. For others, the vested interest has more to do with
professional self-interest. Many professionals have invested years of training
to become proficient in the use of instruments to measure intelligence.
Indeed, for some, the testing function is tantamount to the totality of their
job definition.

Because of these vested interests, some educators and psychologists find
it difficult to consider problems and issues critically. For example, over the
years, a major argument surrounding intelligence testing has centered on the
cultural or other forms of bias in the instruments (Jensen 1980; Reynolds
1982). Such arguments are appropriate and have led to some limited changes
in tests. The fundamental argument, as indicated above, must always address
the thinking going into the making and use of tests. What benefits for the
clients will accrue because of the use of these tests? How can these benefits
be demonstrated? If the benefits cannot be shown, the vested interests are
challenged.

Ideas about intelligence have been linked almost exclusively to instruments that have been used for the measurement of intelligence. The consequences are unfortunate. For example, the accompanying conventional wisdom treats intelligence as global in nature. Therefore, it can be represented
adequately by a single score. Can such test scores be manipulated statistically
to reveal underlying "factors" that reflect actual mental processes in clients?
Does the present level of intellectual functioning of a client reflect adequately
his or her future potential? Most of the common answers that have been given
to such questions are tied to the type of testing instruments that have been
in use in the United States.

Over the full course of their history, intelligence tests have been used
almost exclusively to rank test takers. The ranking is considered to be in
terms of global ability of an individual within a hypothetical distribution of
ability indicators (IQ scores) in the general population. Occasionally, test
users speak about the "diagnostic" value of tests. However, there is little
widespread agreement on or evidence for the validity of such diagnoses or
their meaning and utility. And teachers are not urged to look carefully into
comparisons between students' scores and their own professional judgments
regarding students' abilities.

We need to know if testing instruments are useful or beneficial in schools
when used to help teachers implement a successful instructional program. A

closely related question is whether the conventional concept of intelligence itself is either useful or beneficial in school practice.

The Criterion of Pedagogical Utility

When speaking of the instructional utility of the test, we mean that there should be empirical evidence to show that the use of testing and the IQ in educational settings is associated with at least some of the types of student growth considered important to us, be that intellectual, social, or emotional. When we have a clear commitment to the notion of pedagogical utility— meaning that significant benefits are expected from test use in professional practice—we can proceed to the task of unraveling past misunderstandings about intelligence and intelligence testing. We can become unfettered from the incarceration of restricted thinking.

Criteria for Understanding Intelligence

It may not be possible to get agreement among psychologists and educators regarding a definition of intelligence. In fact, it is this lack of ability to get agreement on an operational definition that places research and practice in this area in such a poor light (Peckham 1981). Ideally, we should have a widely accepted operational definition: some general agreement as to the nature of intelligence, its origin, its pattern of dynamics, and so forth.

For the purpose of this discussion, we may place the psychologists who have been interested in intelligence and its application in education into two groups. In one group are those psychologists who believe that mental ability is basically stable and unchanging. In the other category are those who believe that mental ability is dynamic and malleable (Feuerstein 1979; Lidz 1987). We recognize in the history of psychology such leaders as Alfred Binet, who believed in the latter position, even to the extent that he developed a concept of "mental therapeutics," suggesting that low-performing clients could be taught in such a way that their performance level could be raised. Binet went even further and actually developed such instructional strategies and applied them successfully, demonstrating that change is possible. Unfortunately, this point of view and approach never became popular in the United States. When Lewis Terman adapted the Binet-Simon Test, he modified its structure and meaning. Most of the American psychologists who followed Terman in the testing field appeared to make a commitment to the concept of intelligence as fixed and to the goal of intelligence measurement through IQ tests as one of ranking subjects for placement into categories of capacity, such as gifted, average, and retarded.

During the past several decades, the work of Jean Piaget and other cognitive psychologists has provided the basis for a fundamental challenge to the tradition of mental measurement and test use. It is the cognitive psychologists who have given us a better map of the mind, a model of its dynamics. Perhaps none has given us a clearer cognitive map than has Piaget. What is important about the cognitive maps generated by these psychologists is that they do not appear to be reconcilable with intelligence testing, which is not intended to give a picture of the mind (Feuerstein 1979). Indeed, it is hard to know what to do with IQ tests if one has a deep understanding of cognitive psychology.

I propose that educational users' attention be focused less on the products of intellectual activity and more on the processes. Advocates of IQ tests generally ask the question: how much intelligence does the individual have? The cognitive psychologists have been more likely to ask the question: how does intelligence function?

Cognitive psychologists have helped us focus on comprehending mental functions, which leads to understanding of mental structures. If the functions, operations, and structures can be articulated in detail, we will have a more meaningful basis for the discussion of the idea of intelligence than the static notion of IQ. It is an empirical question as to whether such mapping is possible. Pursuing it, however, will speed development of the operational definitions that we need and upon which professional practice may proceed more productively.

Intelligence Is Understood by Educators When It Works for Them

"Intelligence" as an applied concept can have meaning only when it is useful for practitioners and clients. Can something be learned from the application of mental mapping that can help to affect and improve the validity of instructional strategies? If not, the continuation of professional efforts that do not have such a yield is a waste of time.

Mention must be made here of a diagnostic and remedial model that is beginning to receive widespread attention. Over a period of 30 years, Reuven Feuerstein and his associates perfected, through research and practice based on the work of Piaget, a clinically derived diagnostic and remedial system that is rooted in a carefully conceived construct of intelligence. Through thousands of hours of empirical observation, a cognitive map was generated that permits a clearer picture of mental functions. Specific deficiencies in mental functions are identified. Twenty-seven of these mental functions are described that appear to be prerequisites for successful problem solving. Through building testing instruments that provide clients the opportunity to demonstrate capacity or incapacity to perform such functions, a diagnostic process is created.

These mental functions are what Feuerstein and his associates say are prerequisites to successful performance on tests of cognitive operations. They are the prerequisites to successful development of cognitive structures. Feuerstein's Learning Potential Assessment Device therefore deserves to be termed a diagnostic instrument. If, in addition to a more sophisticated and precise diagnosis, appropriate instructional strategies are developed to target specific deficiencies, and the application of these remedial strategies results in fundamental changes in the capacity of students to perform mental functions, to perform mental operations, and to develop new mental structures, then a holistic system, utilizing an empirically derived operational definition of "intelligence," can be said to be in place.

The usual questions that traditional test givers and theoreticians have asked about intelligence are: How much intelligence is there? How do people compare on various measures of intelligence? Is intelligence fixed? Can it be measured reliably? However, when we come to a system such as that developed by Feuerstein—the Learning Potential Assessment Device (testing) and Instrumental Enrichment (remedial instruction)—another set of questions becomes important. First, how does the mind work? Second, can it be shaped? Third, can this shaping improve academic, social, and emotional performance? It should not need to be said that we do not measure "the mind" directly; we can observe the products of deliberation.

In fact, we may not even need a concept of intelligence as much as we need a meaningful and useful operational definition of it. We need a concept of intelligence only to the extent that it is requisite to the design of successful instruction.

To Accommodate or to Intervene: Two Ways of Responding

Some cognitive psychologists, such as Piaget, appear to be primarily interested in describing intellectual functions and the stages through which they develop. The logical implication of such an approach is that instruction should be designed to accommodate mental development as it is best understood. Feuerstein, on the other hand, a student of Piaget, reached back to H. Froebel, who gave us the concept of the "kindergarten." This metaphor causes us to think of growth and especially of nurturance. It is precisely at this point that the work of Feuerstein and certain other cognitive psychologists becomes seminal. These psychologists believe that it is possible to nurture mental growth to produce radical departures from predicted intellectual development within the learner. The evidence that this can be done is now overwhelming. Their work calls into question whether we should attempt to understand intelligence in order to assist the learner or merely to accommodate what we believe to be the limits of learners.

The Role of Culture

All mental functions are manifest through specific cultures, which include specific languages (Cohen 1969; Cole et al. 1971; Hilliard 1976; Donaldson

1978; Hilliard 1984). No language or culture is universal. Therefore, mental functions, operations, and structures are manifest in culturally specific forms for given individuals. It is the failure to understand this simple observation that has led to much pain in the application of mental measurement to educational practices. At the deep structural level, we find commonalities among all the world's people. However, at the surface structural level, which is defined most clearly in relationship to a *particular cultural context*, we find vast diversity. This diversity is not necessarily related to differences in mental power. Measurement psychologists in particular have demonstrated a persistent indifference to understanding the tools and findings of cultural linguists and cultural anthropologists and have not ceased inappropriate extensions of testing. The results as revealed in school practices are discriminatory and inequitable.

The Role of Politics

When Binet was asked by the French education authorities to help them, they had already decided that certain children should be segregated from the general population for purposes of instruction. Therefore, their question to Binet was whether it was possible to develop a scientific instrument to identify those children who required special education. In a way this was the first widespread attempt by educators to sort the "educable" from the "uneducable" population. It was the children of the poor, by and large, who were identified as in the need of special help. Since its adaptation in the United States, the intelligence test has been implicated in another kind of sorting. This is sorting the "educables" from the rest of the population. By this we mean the identification of students as gifted in order that they may be placed in special classes. The history of this practice over the years has resulted in an inflation in the gifted category. Large numbers of children are placed in these categories who exhibit no special talents during or after their identification as gifted. Sorting practices of this kind have led to inflated expectations of parents for their children and, frequently, intense pressure to perform.

We must be alert to the fact that there has been little neutrality in approaching discussion of intellectual functions (Chase 1977; Kamin 1979; Gould 1981). Not only has there been little neutrality, psychologists have joined others as activists in the use of ideas about intelligence in ways that are harmful to disenfranchised groups. Such activities have been amply documented by researchers such as Leon Kamin (1979), Alexander Thomas and Samuel Sillen (1968), and Stephen Gould (1981). There is little likelihood that the controversy surrounding the discussion of intelligence will be diminished significantly in the near future. For professionals, it is important to recognize at the outset that these controversies exist, that there is a history of politics mixed with science, and that sensitivities and politics together have contributed to a confounding of meaning with respect to the matter of intelligence.

The Consequences of Misunderstanding

The use of IQ testing and unvalidated ideas about intelligence in education has led to many abuses. Invidious distinctions are made between and among racial, economic, ethnic, and other groups. In addition, able students are misclassified, labeled, and misdirected into inappropriate classes. Perhaps, worst of all, the continued use of IQ testing and invalid constructs negatively affects the way that we think about the teaching-learning process. All teachers and learners should be involved in a dynamic, critical, reflective, growing process. An appropriate understanding of intelligence can help educators shift from goals of classification of students to goals of remediating students' learning difficulties. We must not permit the use of any instrument, belief, or practice that contributes to the failures of students.

Our views about intelligence, about how it is distributed within the general population, and about our ability to enhance its growth determine our choice of educational strategies. These choices ultimately determine children's access to knowledge and achievement. Forecasting failure for children results in severely limited opportunity for exposure to challenging, high-quality education. For example, if educators believe that children cannot do arithmetic, it is highly unlikely that they will be offered instruction in algebra. Yet it can be shown that many low-performing students come to life academically because of the opportunity to be challenged in a well-taught algebra lesson.

The negative effects of present practice fall heavily upon minority racial or cultural groups and upon poor children in general. These children are found disproportionately in low academic tracks and in special education classes for the mentally or emotionally impaired. The gross injustice here is that the number of children so classified is large. Most of those classified as learning-impaired are fully capable of meeting the regular academic requirements of school. However, many perform at a low level merely because they have not been exposed to high-quality instruction and are not expected to do well.

Conclusion

Not all misunderstandings about the nature of intelligence derive from difficulties in theoretical speculation or from technical problems in the field of mental measurement. Political and economic forces, more than scientific issues, mislead and confound professional discussion. Introduction of a utility criterion poses a measure of clarification. It is my view that thinking about intelligence can and ought to lead to beneficial services for students. Some professionals already have shown that this can be accomplished. We must observe the practices of these professionals across the nation and draw conclusions accordingly. When we seriously engage in observation and examination of good and effective instruction for all students, we will begin to demonstrate our commitment to all the children of the nation. We will then be problem solvers and not merely certifiers of the status quo. From a problem-solving orientation, enlightened by the data of successful practice, we can move to elimination of all those practices operating against the right to learn.

Selected References and Bibliography

American Psychological Association. 1985. *Standards for Educational and Psychological Testing*. Washington, D.C.: Author.

Block, N., and G. Dworkin, eds. 1976. *The IQ Controversy*. New York: Pantheon.

Chase, Allan. 1977. *The Legacy of Malthus: The Social Cost of Scientific Racism*. New York: Knopf.

Cohen, Rosalie. 1969. Conceptual Styles, Culture Conflict, and Nonverbal Tests of Intelligence. *American Anthropologist* 71 (5): 828–857.

Cole, Michael, et al. 1971. *The Cultural Context of Learning and Thinking: An Exploration in Experimental Anthropology*. New York: Basic Books.

Donaldson, Margaret. 1978. *Children's Minds*. New York: Norton.

Feuerstein, Reuven. 1979. *The Dynamic Assessment of Retarded Performers: The Learning Potential Assessment Device*. Baltimore, Md.: University Park Press.

Fuller, R. 1977. *In Search of the IQ Correlation: A Scientific Whodunit*. Stonybrook, NY: Ball-Stick-Bird, Inc.

Gartner, Alan, and Dorothy Kerzner Lipsky. 1987. "Beyond Special Education: Toward a Quality System for All Students." *Harvard Educational Review* 57:4.

Ginsburg, Herbert. 1972. *The Myth of the Deprived Child: Poor Children's Intellect*. Englewood Cliffs, N.J.: Prentice-Hall.

Gould, S. 1981. *The Mismeasure of Man*. New York: Norton.

Guthrie, Robert V. 1976. Even the Rat was White. New York: Harper and Row.

Heller, K. A, W. H. Holtzman, and S. Messick, eds. 1982. *Placing Children in Special Education: A Strategy for Equity*. Washington, D.C.: National Academy Press.

Hilliard, Asa G., III. 1976. *Alternatives to IQ Testing: An Approach to the Identification of "Gifted" Minority Children*. Final report to the California State Department of Education, Special Education Support Unit. ERIC ED 146-009.

Hilliard, Asa G., III. 1983. "I.Q. and the Courts: Larry P. v. Wilson Riles and PASE v. Hannon." *The Journal of Black Psychology:* 10, no. 1: 1–18.

Hilliard, Asa G., III. 1984. "IQ Thinking as the Emperor's New Clothes." In *Perspectives on Bias in Mental Testing*, edited by Cecil Reynolds and Robert T. Brown. New York: Plenum Press.

Hilliard, Asa G., III. 1982. *The Learning Potential Assessment Device and Instrumental Enrichment as a Paradigm Shift*. Paper presented at the annual meeting of the American Educational Research Association in New York, March 1982. ERIC ED 223-674.

Hilliard, Asa G., III., ed. 1987. "Special Issues on Testing African American Students" *Negro Educational Review* 38: 2–3.

Jensen, Arthur. 1980. *Bias in Mental Testing.* New York: Free Press.

Karmin, Leon. 1979. *The Politics and Science of I.Q.* Potomac, Maryland: Lawrence Erlbaum.

Lidz, Carol. *Dynamic Assessment.* New York: Gilford, 1987.

Narin, A. 1980. The Reign of ETS: The Corporation that Makes Up Minds. Washington, D.C.: Ralph Nader.

Owen, David. 1985. *None of the Above: Behind the Myth of Scholastic Aptitude.* Boston: Houghton-Mifflin.

Reynolds, C., ed. 1982. *Perspectives on Bias in Mental Testing.* New York: Plenum.

Shuy, Roger W. 1977. "Quantitative Linguistic Analysis: A Case For and Some Warning Against." *Anthropology and Education Quarterly* 1 (2): 78–82.

Thomas, A., and S. Sillen. 1968. *Racism in Psychiatry.* New York: Brunner Mazel.

Tyler, R., and S. White, eds. 1978. *Testing, Teaching and Learning.* Washington, D.C.: National Institute of Education, Department of Health, Education, and Welfare.

Weiss, John G. 1987. "Its Time to Examine the Examiners." *Negro Education Review* 38, 2–3.

Wigdor, A. K., and W. K. Garner, eds. 1982. *Ability Testing: Uses, Consequences, and Controversy.* Washington, D.C.: National Academy Press.

9.

Equal Access to Quality in Public Schooling: Issues in the Assessment of Equity and Excellence

KENNETH A. SIROTNIK

Précis

Educational measurement has typically been associated with concerns about excellence, but some of the widely accepted concepts and practices in this field, according to Kenneth Sirotnik, have actually blocked progress toward excellence and to an even greater degree have limited people's vision of how to employ data in the service of concerns for equity. All the measurements of "goodness" in our schools—standardized test score averages, for example—have serious shortcomings because a single indicator of success or effectiveness cannot capture a complicated qualitative judgment.

Sirotnik suggests that by using different principles for the collection, management, and application of data, schools and school districts can link their efforts toward excellence and equity, and develop reliable ways of overseeing their progress. Specific assumptions and working definitions of "equity" and "excellence" yield a notion of equity as a necessary—but not sufficient—condition for excellence. That is, *excellence* is indicated by conditions, practices, and outcomes in schools that are associated with high levels of learning for most students in all valued goal areas of the common curriculum. *Equity* is indicated when there are no systematic differences in the distribution of these conditions, practices, and outcomes based upon race, ethnicity, sex, economic status, or any other irrelevant grouping characteristic.

Educators generally should abandon the view of intelligence as a global, immutable quality. They should learn to look askance at categorical programs based on group labels. Sirotnik condemns such programs as symptomatic of a troublesome phenomenon in society he calls "groupism"—the inclination to account for human variability in terms of characteristics like race, ethnicity, and economic status that can be turned into descriptions of group behavior. Better and more comprehensive information on schooling practices and outcomes, Sirotnik believes, can provide school districts with information on progress in realizing educational equity and excellence. Only with such information can schools develop, correct, and improve programs. Specific proposals about what data might be collected and how they might be aggregated are set forth in detail in an appendix to this paper.

Kenneth A. Sirotnik is the chair of Policy Governance and Administration at the University of Washington. His research interests are educational measurement, evaluation, and school improvement and change.

—The College Board

W e are a society preoccupied with counting, sorting, selecting, and labeling human beings—with "attaching numbers to entities, like people and schools, in accord with certain rules."[1] The slogan "If you can't measure it, it ain't it" captures our numbers fetish, especially in the context of organizational accountability.[2] We have quantified "quality" control indexes for everything from industrial products to the education of our children.

On its surface this obsession with indicating quality quantitatively is relatively benign. It can be argued, in fact, that there are many econometric and psychometric applications in the political and social sciences that have produced useful results. In this paper, however, I wish to express a deep concern about two malignancies that either have derived from or, in some cases, have directed this obsession: reification and "groupism" (racism, ethnocentrism, sexism, and the like). After briefly discussing what I mean by these two concerns, especially in the context of educational assessment, I attempt to perform a little bit of surgery. I wish to remove these cancerous features from our methodological leanings and still leave the idea of educational assessment—both quantitative and qualitative—relatively intact and functional. I concentrate the bulk of this discussion around the fundamental concerns of this paper, *equity* and *excellence*, first by developing a set of working assumptions and definitions and then by deriving some implications for assessment.

Reification

> The tendency has always been strong to believe that whatever received a name must be an entity or being, having an independent existence of its own.
>
> —*John Stuart Mill*[3]

"Reify: To regard or treat (an abstraction) as if it had concrete or material existence."[4] This is exactly what happens in much of the interpretive work that has been done in the behavioral and social sciences, using the various and sundry psychometric techniques for quantifying and measuring behavioral and social *constructs*. Achievement, overachievement, underachievement, scholastic aptitude, alienation, anxiety, authoritarianism, creativity, leadership, level of aspiration, life satisfaction, organizational climate, self-concept—this is just the beginning of an extensive list of cognitive attributes and belief, attitude, value, interest, need, and personality attributes that have been "measured" at one time or another.

Measurement proceeds through *operational definition*, a marvelous process by which researchers and psychometricians hook up their attributions regarding human thought and emotion to the "real world." An operational definition is a specified set of procedures through which numbers are generated with all the nice properties (magnitude, ordinality, etc.) that are ascribed to what it means to measure. "Intelligence" is the classic example, and "Intelligence is what intelligence tests measure" is the classic operational definition. Just as a person's "height" gets hooked up to the numerical calibrations on a linear measurement device (e.g., a yardstick), a person's "intelligence" gets hooked up to the number of questions answered correctly on a test.

Unlike the case of measuring a person's height, however, the measurement *validity* of the numerous constructs in the behavioral and social sciences is usually open to question. After discussing the rather pleasant situation of validity in the physical sciences, Warren Torgerson discusses the situation in the social and behavioral sciences thusly:

> The situation in these less well-developed sciences is not nearly as neat, even though here, too, we have a wealth of observables and certainly no lack of constructs. There is, however, a rather serious shortage of important connections.[5]

The "connections" being referred to by Torgerson are those between attributes or constructs and their operational definitions. This gives rise to fundamental problems concerning validity, especially construct validity: "Are we measuring, in fact, what we think we are measuring?"

To be sure, invalidity does not necessarily render measurement totally dysfunctional, so long as interpretations and applications are appropriate, given reasonable levels of invalidity. The problem occurs, of course, when people begin to overinterpret what it is that they really have. Researchers operationally define "intelligence," "achievement," "self-concept," and the like in various ways and conduct various research studies using measures of these constructs. Much of this research finds its way into journals and then textbooks in educational psychology, sociology, and so forth; it pervades the curriculum of the preparation programs of educators; and "readers digest" versions of this research—particularly the construct labels, become part of the conventional wisdom and parlance of policymakers and the public at large. Pretty soon, people talk about and make decisions about other people's *intelligence, achievement,* and *self-concept* as if these attributes really existed in the same sense as, for example, people's height and weight.

Consider, for example, the fundamental decisions made about students by educators in districts and schools using students' scores on intelligence or achievement tests or both. Based on these scores, many students in many schools are labeled and sorted into "slow," "average," or "fast" educational tracks—designations that often stay with them over much of their K-12 schooling experience. And the quality of education they receive is tailored to these designations: watered-down, basic skills for the "slow learners" and enriched curriculum for the "fast learners."[6] The point is that a whole host of educational assumptions and self-fulfilling prophecies get set into motion once students are labeled on the basis of nothing more than an operational definition of an abstract, human construct. Johnny's or Mary's IQ score becomes a fundamental part of their beings, and prescriptions derive therefrom, just as surely as would a long-term diet be prescribed if they were 30 pounds overweight.

Recently the critique of the idea of *an* intelligence and intelligence testing has gained a wider audience and more popular acceptance. We are finally taking seriously the notion that it's not how smart you are, but how you are smart, that has the most useful implications for education and schooling. Some test publishers have discarded the term "intelligence" and replaced it with the phrase "scholastic aptitude." Their tests, however, are in many respects the same; except now, instead of an IQ, students get an SAI (scholastic ability index). More significant has been Robert Sternberg's examination of the mutability and complexity of intelligence as a more global construct, and Howard Gardner's work that challenges directly the idea of a single "mental ability" with the idea of a multidimensional view of intelligence.[7]

Among the most important of the recent critiques, in my view, is Israel Scheffler's reconceptualization and reconstruction of the whole root idea of human *potential*.[8] He argues against "potential" as a unitary and fixed human characteristic and, in effect, destroys the common notion of reaching one's "full potential," as if potential were a cup that could hold only so much liquid. Instead, potential represents the concept of *becoming:* the possibility, probability, and ability to *become*, conditioned on human and contextual circumstances. The implication for educators and education is clear: When it comes to intelligence, scholastic ability, learning potential, or whatever terminology you like, rather than worrying about *how much* of "it" students have, we need to be worrying about nurturing and developing students' potentials in any number of positive and useful ways.

Consider, as another example, how the goodness of schools has become reified in the form of score averages on standardized achievement tests. Politicians make judgments of the educational at-riskness of the entire nation based on cyclical downturns and upswings of these average tests scores. States get all excited and pass various and sundry educational reform legislation. At the height of the educational reform in the early 1980s, for example, at least one state passed legislation that included dollar rewards for schools in proportion to their average daily attendance and their increases in test score averages from one year to the next. Local communities and news media judge the quality of their schools, usually in comparison to one another, on the basis of these scores. Parents often make housing decisions involving thousands (sometimes hundreds of thousands) of dollars based on the relative standing of a particular school's test score average—parents, that is, who can afford such decisions.

At best, the idea that the scores students get on a bunch of multiple-choice test items somehow indicate the quality of their schooling is silly.[9] At worst, it is an insult to those educators who work in schools. Certainly these scores indicate, albeit imperfectly, some level of achievement in specific skill areas *as defined (often narrowly) by the test publishers*. But much of the variance in these scores can be accounted for by the economic status of the families or community. More important, what goes on in schools and what schools are presumably for is poorly represented in test scores alone. A compilation of goals from across the nation has revealed educational constituencies with a multiplicity of desires including, but extending well beyond, basic skills education.[10] Interpersonal understandings and human relations, citizenship and civic responsibility, enculturation, intellectual development in the disciplines, critical and independent thinking, emotional and physical well-being, creativity and aesthetic expression, self-realization, moral and ethical character development, and career, vocational, and life preparation are the additional categories of the many expressed goals for American public schools.

To begin to understand the quality of schooling, one must begin to understand the social context of the school, the conditions in the school, the curriculum and curricular planning and decision-making processes, the day-to-day activities of teaching and learning, the work environment for teachers and administrators, the classroom learning environments for teachers and students, and so forth. In her exploration of the quality of several high schools, Sara Lightfoot notes that

> goodness . . . is not a static or absolute quality that can be quickly measured by a single indicator of success or effectiveness. . . . "Goodness" is a much more complicated notion. . . . It refers to the mixture of parts that produce a whole. The whole includes people, structures, relationships, ideology, goals, intellectual substance, motivation, and will. It includes measurable indices such as attendance records, truancy rates, vandalism to property, percentages going on to college. But it also encompasses less tangible, more elusive qualities that can only be discerned through close, vivid description, through subtle nuances, through detailed narratives that reveal the sustaining values of an institution.[11]

A test score average provides very little basis for this kind of understanding.

Groupism

Now, the Star-Belly Sneetches
Had bellies with stars.
The Plain-Belly Sneetches
Had none upon thars.

Those stars weren't so big. They were really so small
You might think such a thing wouldn't matter at all.

But, because they had stars, all the Star-Belly Sneetches

> Would brag, "We're the best kind of Sneetch on the beaches."
> With their snoots in the air, they would sniff and they'd snort
> "We'll have nothing to do with the Plain-Belly sort!"
> —*Dr. Seuss*[12]

It can be argued, I think, that at the core of our need to measure this and that attribute of human beings is a reverence for individual differences—an irresistible need to compare ourselves to others and a penchant for trying to account for human variability in terms of other human characteristics, like race, ethnicity, sex, and economic status. The whole of behavioral psychology was founded on the science of individual differences and the attempt to measure them. This may all be very innocent until the process is confounded with conscious or unconscious "groupist"—racist, sexist, classist, chauvinist—ideologies.

The classic example, once again, is "intelligence," and the seminal critique, in this case, is Gould's *The Mismeasure of Man*.[13] Many, I find, are still surprised when they learn of our explicitly "groupist" legacy from the very beginnings of this "science" of individual differences. From the shenanigans of the early polygenesists and craniometrists, to the strictly hereditarian biases of the architects of IQ tests, the operant prejudices against non-whites, females, and the poor have been well documented by Gould.

Ironically, the father of mental testing, Alfred Binet, was among the few who recognized the profound dangers inherent in labeling and sorting based on crude indicators of an abstraction, i.e., "intelligence." His warnings, however, went unheeded by Lewis Terman, who revised and extended Binet's procedures into what became known as the Stanford-Binet Intelligence Test. This set into motion myriad individual and group, short-form and long-form, "IQ" tests. Binet deserved the credit for the testing procedures, but not for their advocated uses. Instead of a device geared primarily for identifying and helping learning-disabled children as intended by Binet, Terman perpetuated and popularized both the reification and discrimination of intelligence and intelligence testing:

> Preliminary investigations indicate that an I.Q. below 70 rarely permits anything better than unskilled labor; that the range of 70-80 is pre-eminently that of semi-skilled labor; from 80-100 that of the skilled or ordinary clerical labor; from 100-110 or 115 that of the semi-professional pursuits; and that above all these are the grades of intelligence which permit one to enter the professions or the large fields of business. Intelligence tests can tell us whether a child's native brightness corresponds more nearly to the median [of one or another of these classes]. This information will be of great value in planning the education of a particular child and also in planning the differentiated curriculum here recommended.[14]

Reification and groupism combine to produce a particularly pernicious and insidious set of circumstances. And the abuses of intelligence testing hold no special claim on this duo. Standardized achievement test scores not only are grossly attenuated indicators of educational quality for individuals and schools, but also suffer from much the same sources of discrimination as their close cousins, IQ scores. As I already noted, the testing community has finally become sensitized to the label "intelligence" and the fact that rather than inherited capacity, "intelligence" is more of a test of performance based on previous educational experiences—hence the change of terminology to "scholastic aptitude" or "scholastic ability."[15]

We have known for some time, however, how little difference there is between intelligence tests and tests of general achievement, such as those used commonly by states and districts to evaluate and hold their schools accountable. It has been estimated that over three quarters of the variance in intelligence test scores and the verbal portions of standardized achievement batteries are predictable, one from the other. In other words, the linear correlation between these constructs—"intelligence" and "achievement"—is upward of .85 or more.[16] By circumstance or design or both, the primary way in which this nation has judged its educational delivery system and in which states and districts tend to make these judgments on their own—standardized achievement testing—is riddled with the problems of reification and groupism.

The fact of the matter is that the normal distribution, the bell curve—beautifully symmetric and statistically pleasing as it may be—is a picture neither of quality or equality nor of the reality of human potential. Half our children below average is not an image of educational excellence. Disproportionate numbers of specific groups of children at one or the other end of this distribution is not an image of educational equity. And human potential is not a single, fixed attribute of human beings that can be carved into the image of a bell-shaped curve.

Equity and Excellence: Some Working Assumptions

> We will not know what is impossible of achievement, except by the achievement of what is possible. And that effort is, in any case, a moral commitment.
>
> —*David Hawkins*[17]

In delivering the sixteenth John Dewey Lecture nearly 15 years ago, Hawkins made clear the moral and ethical dimensions of a serious commitment to educational quality and equality. Perhaps the first commitment is to make clear and unmistakable the values and assumptions that are implicit in all human inquiry and activity. As a prelude to the above concluding statements, Hawkins noted "that the most significant single correlate of educational success in our schools, or by any more adequate measure, is the educational background from which children come." Schools, therefore, have "not evolved, by the measure of need, very far beyond [their] earlier function of extending an education *already* well begun and well supported along the way."[18] Nothing short of a commitment to *all* our children learning in the context of a quality educational experience will suffice if we truly expect schooling to evolve anywhere near close to a state of both equity and excellence. Dewey's vision, still visionary, must guide us forward:

> What the best and wisest parent wants for his own child, that must the community want for all its children. Any other ideal for our schools is narrow and unlovely; acted upon, it destroys our democracy.[19]

With this vision in mind, how can we rescue assessment—and measurement in particular—from the clutches of a history of misuse and abuse? Quite simply, we must preach what we practice as well as practice what we preach. And what we preach must be a set of values and beliefs—call them working assumptions, if you prefer—that are action-oriented and that serve as criteria against which the acts of all "responsible parties" to public education must be held accountable.[20] In what follows I will share with readers a set of assumptions that has helped frame discussions of equity and excellence among educators in both universities and schools with an eye toward developing some reasonable principles and procedures of assessment.[21]

WORKING ASSUMPTION 1.
There are no systematic differences in human learning potential other than those attributable to individual variation itself.

In other words, suppose, for the sake of argument, human learning potential could be measured in perfectly reliable and valid ways.[22] Then, if students were sorted into groups based on variables such as race, ethnicity, sex, economic status, eye color, or any other such irrelevant variable, there would be *no differences* in the distributions of human learning potential between groups.

WORKING ASSUMPTION 2.
Schooling environments can be created within which most students can achieve high levels of learning with respect to a valued, common curriculum.

In other words, schools can and do make a difference; that is, there is a variety of curricular and instructional processes, of adult working and student learning conditions, that can promote high levels of learning for most students.[23]

   Given assumptions 1 and 2, it should be clear that *with respect to high mastery levels of a quality common curriculum (see below), it is being assumed that most of our students—regardless of race, ethnicity, sex, economic status, or any other irrelevant characteristic—can achieve excellence in an appropriate schooling environment.*

With these working assumptions in mind, we come up with two working definitions:

1. *Excellence* is indicated by conditions, practices, and outcomes in schools that are associated with high levels of learning for most students in all valued goal areas of the common curriculum.

2. *Equity* is indicated when there are no systematic differences in the distributions of these conditions, practices, and outcomes based upon race, ethnicity, sex, economic status, or any other irrelevant grouping characteristic.

One caveat to keep in mind with respect to these ideal definitions is that the allocation of *more* resources to disadvantaged groups may well be necessary as schools reach toward equitable education. This is consistent with the deep and abiding commitment to social justice (as reflected in the quote from Dewey cited earlier in this section) that underlies these concepts of equity and excellence.[24]

From the assumptions and definitions thus far, it follows that equity is a necessary but not a sufficient condition for excellence. In other words, *there can be no educational excellence without educational equity.* Moreover, *without careful attention to quality education, we can all have equal access to educational mediocrity.* I have preferred, therefore, to stick with the perhaps shopworn notions of "excellence" and "equity" in contrast with the "students-at-risk" or "students-at-the-margins" terminology. The latter terminology risks the problems of labeling and reification noted earlier. All students, to some extent, are "at-risk" or at the periphery of a quality schooling experience. To be sure, some students—those from broken families, those suffering from battered child syndrome, those who are learning disabled—are clearly at more risk than others and need to be cared for accordingly. But, by and large, "at-riskness" is simply a proxy for the economic and educational disadvantages and the color of students. At the bottom the quality and equality of schooling are the fundamental issues of concern.

The above assumptions and definitions represent, of course, the *ideal* conditions of equity and excellence. The operational task is to approximate these conditions as closely as possible. Operationally speaking, then, relevant evidence on the progress of the march toward equity and excellence is twofold:

1. increasingly favorable information (see below) on the conditions, practices, and outcomes of schooling with a particular focus on student affective and cognitive development; and

2. decreasing differences (based on this information) between groups formed on the basis of such variables as sex, race, ethnicity, and economic status.

Finally, two additional working assumptions are necessary to begin the process of operationalizing these concepts of equity and excellence in the day-to-day working and learning environments of schools.

WORKING ASSUMPTION 3.
A working consensus can be obtained on the specifications of a "quality common curriculum" that is not overly detailed so as to severely limit creative implementation at local levels but that is sufficiently prescriptive so as to leave no question of educational commitment from the state to building levels.

In other words, we can "agree to agree" on (1) the intellectual/academic, personal, social, and career functions of schooling and the broad goals within these categories to be attained by *all* students, and (2) the variety of instructional processes to go with these curricular expectations.[25]

WORKING ASSUMPTION 4.
Information on the quality of schooling may include, but must not be limited to, scores on standardized achievement tests; educational conditions, practices, and outcomes all must be evaluated in order to assess the quality of schooling; and information pertaining to excellence must include both qualitative and quantitative approaches to explaining and understanding what goes on in schools.

In other words, information on student achievement can include scores on basic skills tests, grades, attendance, course-taking patterns *as well as* assessments of creative and expository writing, critical thinking and discourse, interpersonal relationships, self-esteem, transitions from schooling to work and higher education. Information on conditions and practices can include assessments of instructional resources, staff turnover rates, time for staff inquiry and planning, student-grouping practices, teachers' perceptions of school as a work environment, students' perceptions of classes as learning environments, observer perceptions of class- and school-level organizational dynamics, content analyses of curriculum materials, parent satisfaction, and so forth.

Equity and Excellence: A Design for Assessment

It is not the science which is sinful, but the use to which it is put. That knowledge is power does not give the victims of power a stake in ignorance. . . . What we must do is not to resist the growth of knowledge of human behavior, but to use what we know so as to preserve and to enhance our precious humanity.

—Abraham Kaplan[26]

In light of my opening critique of method and measurement in the social and behavioral sciences, how can I advocate their further uses? Obviously, evil lies not in the numbers, but in the intent of their derivation and use. Simply put, educators must take responsibility for the ways in which they choose to study and remedy educational problems.

I have outlined a set of working principles of equity and excellence that can help guide the efforts of educators as they attempt to improve the practice of schooling. Of course, as the term "working" implies, these will be evolving, exploratory efforts, particularly with respect to developing the operational implications of assumptions 3 and 4. Nonetheless, a bit of reflection can suggest some possible directions. Given the primary focus of this paper, I will outline some implications for the assessment of equity and excellence.[27]

Methodological and Analytical Prerequisites

It follows from the above discussion that a *relational, longitudinal, school-level* data base is necessary to conduct and interpret the requisite analyses for the assessment of equity and excellence. Moreover, for many of the most important analyses, *student-level* information (*within* schools) must be collected and updated as necessary.

The requirement for relational data bases should be clear: Whatever information is identified to reflect educational *excellence*, it must be cross-analyzed (cross-tabulations, cross-breaks, correlations, etc.) with at least three primary criteria to get at the issue of *equity*. These criterion variables are, of course, race/ethnicity, sex, and economic status. Student information would need to be disaggregated at the building level so that it could be analyzed in terms of these demographic variables. For example, attendance rates for School X might be compared for males and females; but such comparisons might be further explored for differences between grade levels, course-taking patterns, and so forth. The most efficient and flexible way of ensuring easy access to these kinds of analyses is to maintain relational data bases for all possible units of analysis (students, teachers, classrooms, schools).

Equally clear from the assumptions and definitions is the need for *longitudinal* study. It is clearly impossible to determine the extent of school *improvement* without some notion of where the school has been. For example, *excellence* will be reflected in increasingly favorable information from one period to the next, such as higher test scores, lower dropout rates, more favorable attitudes toward school. In addition, *equity* will be reflected in decreasing differentials between groups formed on the basis of the above demographic variables; for example, less difference between higher and lower economic status groups on test score performance, dropout rates, and attitudes as these data are analyzed from one period to the next. Although these examples have used only information collected on or from students, the same basic principles of analysis and interpretation would apply to information collected from faculty, on classrooms, and from parents.

Given the resources ordinarily available at the building level, districts must take an active role in supporting, nurturing, and sustaining the collection of information in schools. (I will return to some aspects of this support in the last section.) Statistical software and programming capability must be supported in order to select and merge files, cases, and variables and conduct the appropriate analyses. A related requirement is easy access and quick turnaround of the data analytic system. Quick access to statistical packages such as SPSS, SAS, or the equivalent should be sufficient to generate the minimal set of tables required to inform discussions pertaining to equity and excellence.

Creative use of resources and talent is the ticket here. It is not difficult to imagine, for example, districts setting schools up with their own capacity for doing the basic analyses on microcomputers with downloaded data files from the main data bases. Moreover, doing these analyses would be excellent educational experiences for secondary students learning about data processing and computer applications.

A Beginning Set of Information

No one set of information can possibly communicate all there is to know about the operating dynamics of equity and excellence in today's schools. Nonetheless, we have to begin somewhere. I have chosen to begin with information that is most readily available as well as indicative of conditions thought to relate to excellence and equity in schooling.[28] In other words, I have selected this set of information "for openers"—for opening an *informed* dialogue on the conditions in schools and the distribution of *quality* education to *all* students.

I must emphasize that although this information may describe something, it does not explicate anything. If we see disproportionality between economic status groups in the number of courses taken in advanced mathematics and science, we may infer inequity but little else. To infer more, we need to know more about what goes on in schools and classrooms: how time is spent, how learning is organized, what curriculum materials are in use, what attitudes are being reinforced, how evaluations are utilized, what beliefs and values are operant, how supportive are the conditions for teaching and learning. Collecting additional information pertaining to questions such as these is clearly essential for a more comprehensive understanding of the equity–excellence issue. Equally clear is that this kind of additional information gathering is more difficult, more time consuming, and more resource consuming in all phases of data collection, analysis, and interpretation. Districts and schools must make a serious commitment if they are to pursue this depth of understanding of the issues in question.

With these considerations in mind, then, consider the following list of *student* information *at the building level* that, when cross-analyzed and tabulated by race/ethnicity, sex, and economic status, can help inform initial discussions about equity and excellence in any given school and school system:

Student Information

1. Sex
2. Race/ethnicity
3. Economic status
4. Attendance
5. Dropout
6. Suspension
7. Expulsion
8. Grade-point average
9. Tracking placement
10. Course-enrollment patterns
11. Special class placements
12. Standardized achievement tests
13. Criterion-referenced competency tests
14. Assessments of higher-order thinking skills
15. Assessments of communication skills
16. Assessments of citizenship/effort

In addition to student data, there are several sources of information for any given school and school system that can be seen to pertain to equity and excellence and that should be relatively easy to compile into tables that can be compared from one year to the next.

First, there are several pieces of data that can be obtained for teachers without requiring them to respond to surveys. Consider the following list of variables:

Teacher Information

1. Sex
2. Race/ethnicity
3. Years of teaching experience
4. Area(s) of expertise
5. Area(s) of current teaching assignment
6. Hours of paid, school-based, planning and development time
   a. Alone
   b. With other educators

With these data, it is suggested that disproportionalities by sex, race/ethnicity, teaching experience, and areas of expertise relative to the types of courses taught (e.g., basic vs. advanced) be investigated. The results of these investigations can then be juxtaposed against tables generated from the above student data, thus shedding light on such questions as: Is there a tendency for the less experienced faculty to teach courses taken by relatively larger numbers of minority students? Are minority students more often in classes taught by faculty teaching outside their areas of expertise? Do teachers in schools with larger minority populations spend less time in professional development activities?

Second, it would be useful to compute the number of instructional full-time equivalents (FTEs) allocated to subject or department areas within schools. These data provide rough indices of the emphasis given to the various schooling areas (academic versus vocational, for example). When these indices of relative emphases are compared school by school, taking into account the minority- and economic-status composition of each school, issues concerning equity and excellence may become manifest. (These analyses can be fine-grained by computing FTEs by course type, e.g., college-required vs. noncollege-required.)

Third, if classes are tracked in the school, even though students may not have explicit track identifications (for example, college-bound vs. noncollege-bound classes), tables showing the average class sizes and the student composition of "high"- and "low"-tracked classes in terms of sex, race/ethnicity, and economic status would provide useful information in tracking the issues of equity and excellence.

I should note that these several categories of additional information and analyses are conceived largely from the standpoint of the secondary school. Corresponding analyses might be conceived for elementary school, but they would require more work than just reviewing school records. For example, grouping patterns in elementary classrooms would have to be carefully observed and analyzed to determine whether they are: mostly static and unchanging (and for which children?), thereby labeling students and creating self-fulfilling prophecies for their academic futures; or usually dynamic and fluid for all children to provide for individual and group instructional needs on an as-needed basis.

Information Writ Large

The working assumptions and definitions make clear that a small set of information or information on students alone is insufficient to describe equity and excellence. Contextual information on instructional delivery, the work environment of the school, and the learning environment of the classroom is also required to more completely explain and understand the process and progress of student learning. Suppose, for example, that heterogeneous grouping and cooperative learning strategies were employed by a school to provide more excellent and equitable education. Suppose further that assessments of student learning and attitudes were less than expected. Would we interpret this information as indicating the failure of cooperative learning and heterogeneous grouping? Not necessarily. To what extent were the principles and practices of these innovative learning techniques implemented, and implemented effectively? To what extent were administrators, teachers, parents, and students engaged in appropriate discussions about the rationale for, and acceptance of, alternative instructional practices? To what extent were teachers involved in planning and developing alternative curricula, in reflective practice and self-study? Clearly, conditions, circumstances, programs, and people all interact in the school setting, making it impossible to use only one kind of information for drawing evaluative conclusions.

The above set of initial information will represent a significant step for many districts and schools toward gaining some purchase on the quality and equality of education for all students. This information functions as a sign or a signal that can help monitor the "health" of a school, much like a thermometer can signal something about the health of a patient. But, as with the thermometer, that is all this information can do—that is, all it can do is signal; it cannot explain or tell *why*. For example, a fever reading on a thermometer cannot diagnose the patient's illness; the doctor must seek out additional information. Likewise, low test scores in a school do not, in themselves, immediately suggest the array of problems to be rectified. However, a patient with cancer can have a normal temperature; likewise, a school with high test scores may be well advised to still monitor the health of its educational delivery system through the use of more in-depth information.

One area of particular importance in understanding equity and excellence concerns *what goes on in classrooms*. How is time utilized by the teacher? How much of the time are students academically engaged? What is the affective nature of teacher–student and student–student interactions? Are critical-thinking activities included in the operational curriculum? Are students actively or passively involved as learners? Which students are more or less involved in learning activities? Information on these and many other questions might be gathered and then analyzed in terms of other classroom demographics such as class size and composition by race and ethnic group, sex, and economic status. A high-priority area for research and development, therefore, is *classroom observation*, namely, the design and implementation of a feasible and efficient means whereby such information can be obtained periodically on adequate samples of classrooms within schools.

A second area of importance, related to the first, is the content analysis of various features of the curriculum, particularly goals and objectives, materials such as textbooks, workbooks, and kits, and assessment devices such as tests, papers, and projects. For example, what are the implicit and explicit curricular expectations? And how do these expectations change, depending on which students and/or which classes (e.g., vocational vs. college-track) the curriculum is for?

Finally, a good deal more information can be suggested that could prove relevant to the understanding of equity and excellence in schooling. I have not begun to exhaust the fund of information that could be collected from students, teachers, parents, administrators, school records, and other sources. By way of summarizing the foregoing and indicating the extent of possible information yet to be considered, I supply a broader outline of information in the Appendix (p. 177).

Assessment: Uses and Abuses

> Accountability emphasizes looking back in order to assign praise or blame; evaluation is better used to understand events and processes for the sake of guiding future activities.
>
> —*Lee J. Cronbach and Associates*[29]

If information systems of the type I have been describing are mandated from "the top" for typical accountability purposes by states or districts or both, such systems will likely suffer the typical fate of such mandates: superficial and token compliance, bad feelings, and subversion behind the doors of schools and classrooms. Analyses of the nature of knowledge and the use of information suggest that the very people for whom the knowledge is useful must be intimately involved in the whys, wheres, whens, and hows of generating it. Analyses of the nature of organizations and organizational life suggest that the people who work in them must be provided genuine opportunities for dialogue, decision making, action taking, and evaluation. Analyses of the successes and, mostly, the failures of major attempts to make substantial changes in public schooling suggest that educators in schools must come to identify what may be problematic in their practice—and they must become intimately involved in inquiry and action toward the improvement of their practice. In short, the proposition that schools are, indeed, *the centers* of educational change will need to be taken seriously if serious efforts are to be made to assess and address excellence and equity.[30]

Educators in schools therefore will need to become actively involved in experimenting with alternative practices designed to promote more equitable and excellent schooling experiences. In an appropriate climate of playful but serious inquiry and reflective practice, the need for information and assessment becomes obvious and welcomed. Nonetheless, the potential for misuses and abuses of comprehensive bodies of information, especially in politically loaded situations, is ever present.

Elsewhere, my colleagues and I uncovered a number of issues and concerns involving the use of information and information systems that might be expected to occur even in relatively nonthreatening school situations:

overinterpreting information (especially test scores), difficulty in using aggregated information for groups, treating information as prescriptive rather than suggestive, betraying confidentiality and using information punitively, and so on.[31]

There is no point in ignoring the politically loaded nature of inquiry and action around the issues of equity and excellence, especially in communities and school systems that are racially and economically heterogeneous. In a climate short on trust and long on ideological conflict, the issues and problems regarding the use and abuse of information increase exponentially in importance and concern. However, given our commitment to excellence and equity, the *responsible* use of information would seem to be indispensable. This reinforces, therefore, the necessity for involving educators in the design and use of assessment procedures; for taking a very self-conscious and reflective stance with regard to the uses and abuses of information; and, particularly, for recognizing and acting on the explicit moral and ethical commitments that are being made with respect to the collection and use of information.

Conclusion

This paper may have appeared to some readers as a rather unusual mixture of ideas presented by someone trained in the principles and procedures of measurement and evaluation. After all, we psychometricians and evaluators are supposed to be objective, value-free methodologists who seek nothing but the truth in our empirical world. That inquiry of any sort is value-free, however, is patently absurd, as has been recognized by numerous thinkers far more thoughtful than I. This, of course, has particular import for those who attempt to implement educational policy. Even in a rather traditional treatise on "scientific method," Dewey tells us that

> the evils in current social judgments of ends and policies arise . . . from importations of judgments of values outside of inquiry. The evils spring from the fact that the values employed are not determined in and by the process of inquiry. . . . Social inquiry . . . must judge certain objective consequences to be the end which is *worth* attaining under the given conditions.[32]

I have thus tried to share with readers what I believe to be an informed critique of some troubling aspects of past and current assessment concepts and practices, within an explicit context of expressed commitment to equity and excellence and their simultaneous achievement in public schooling. My deep hope is that in an appropriate climate of increasing trust and working consensus on the kinds of fundamental assumptions noted herein, reasonable assessment practices can contribute to the realization of this achievement.

Appendix. Outline of Possible Information for Use in Assessing Equity and Excellence in Schools

I. Secondary-Student Information

A. Demographic data
   1. Age
   2. Sex
   3. Race/ethnicity
   4. Economic status (e.g., eligibility for free lunch)
   5. Special-ed. classification (re: physical problems) if any

B. Academic performance data
   1. Track placement/ability-level classification, etc. (if applicable)
   2. Special ed classification (re:learning problems) if any
   3. GPA overall and by subjects
      a. English
      b. Mathematics
      c. Science
      d. Social studies/History
      e. The arts
      f. Foreign language
   4. Number of courses (or credits) taken overall and by subject
      a. through f. (as above)
   5. Number of advanced courses (or credits) taken overall and by subject
      a. through d. (as above)
   6. Twelfth grade only:
      a. Graduated? (yes/no)
      b. Postsecondary follow-up (four-year college/university; two-year junior/community college; trade/vocational college; no further schooling)

C. Achievement assessment data
   1. Standardized test scores
   2. Criterion-referenced test scores
   3. Minimum-competency test scores
   4. Other routinely given tests, e.g., curriculum-related tests such as problem solving, critical thinking, state history/civics, etc.
   5. Other routinely conducted assessment
      a. Analysis of writing samples (creative and expository)
      b. Analysis of interpersonal-communication abilities
      c. Analysis of group-participation abilities
      d. Analysis of creative/divergent-thinking abilities

      e. Analysis of learning potential
   6. Quantity and quality of books read

D. Participation/behavior data
   1. Extracurricular activities
   2. Honors and awards
   3. Absenteeism
   4. Tardiness
   5. Dropout
   6. Suspensions
   7. Expulsion
   8. Other major disciplinary actions

E. Affective-additudinal data (survey questionnaire)
   1. Self-concept (general/academic/peer)
   2. Educational expectations (secondary/postsecondary)
   3. School-level climate and learning environment
   4. Class-level climate and learning environment
   5. General attitudes toward school

(*Note:* Selected items used in annual Gallup survey may be useful here.)

II. Elementary-Student Information

Same as above for secondary students with these exceptions:
—Reinterpret B.1 for static grouping configurations within classes enduring all semester.
—Eliminate B.3.f and B.4 through B.6
—Eliminate E.2
(*Note:* The number of survey questions in E. will need to be reduced and rewritten as appropriate.)

III. Parent Information

A. Demographic data
   1. Family income
   2. Race/ethnicity
   3. Number of years child (children) in this school

B. Home learning environment for students
   1. Availability of books/reading together/reading alone
   2. Hours of homework
   3. TV-viewing habits
   4. Frequency of help with child's schoolwork
   5. Academic expectations for child

C. School–family relations
  1. Frequency of telephone contact with school
  2. Frequency of visits to school
  3. Reception of school to initiated contacts
  4. Facilitators/inhibitors of general school involvement

D. School climate and learning environment
  1. Perceived problems
  2. Preferred functions of schooling
  3. Evaluation of school program
  4. Other general school issues

(*Note:* Selected items used in annual Gallup survey may be useful here.)

IV. Teacher Information

A. Demographic-biographic data
  1. Sex
  2. Race/ethnicity
  3. Years teaching
  4. Years teaching at this school
  5. Highest academic credential held

B. Professional activities/attitudes
  1. Frequency of in-service work
  2. Activities in educational organizations
  3. Familiarity with educational literature (journals, reports, etc.)
  4. Reason for entering teaching profession
  5. Satisfaction with teaching as a career

C. Work environment
  1. Adequacy of preparation for current teaching assignments
  2. Subjects currently teaching
  3. Subjects prepared to teach in
  4. Job satisfaction
  5. Perception of principal leadership
  6. Other perceptions of organizational climate

D. Curriculum and instruction
  1. Perceived functions of schooling
  2. Educational benefits
  3. Educational practices (re: goals, content, instructional materials, classroom activities, teaching strategies, assessment, use of time and space, grouping techniques, etc.)

E. Attitudes/opinions re: other school-related issues

    (*Note:* These can generally parallel those noted above for parents and students.)

V. Class-Level Information

A. Teacher information and aggregated student information on a per-class basis automatically becomes class-level data (in form of percentages, means, etc.).

    (See above lists for potential teacher data and aggregates of student data.)

B. Class characteristics
    1. Tracking designation (or the equivalent) if applicable
    2. Number of students (class size)
    3. Racial/ethnic composition
    4. Gender composition

C. Documents pertaining to curriculum and instruction
    1. List of topics taught or to be taught during the year (course)
    2. List of skills taught or to be taught during the year (course)
    3. List of textbooks, learning kits, commercial programs, and workbooks used or to be used during the year (course)
    4. Samples of assessment tools (including tests and quizzes) given or to be given during the year (course)
    5. Samples of in-class assignments, work sheets, homework assignments, etc., given or to be given during the year (course)

    (The contents of these documents can be analyzed with respect to such issues as goals, levels of knowledge, curriculum sequencing, articulation, integration, etc.)

D. Classroom observational data
    1. Teachers observing other teachers
    2. Principal's observations
    3. Perceptions of other observers (e.g., district staff)

    (*Note:* Observations might be structured around the usual curriculum commonplaces.)

E. Interview data
    1. Teachers
    2. Students
    3. Principal

    (*Note:* Interviews might be structured around the usual curriculum commonplaces as well as around organizational issues at the school level.)

VI. School-Level Information

A. Aggregated student, teacher, and class information on a per-school basis (overall or categorized by grade, department, team, demography, etc.) automatically becomes school-level data.

(See above lists for potential variables. Examples of variables under student participation would be: (1) attendance/absence rates, (2) transiency rates, (3) dropout rates, (4) suspension rates, and (5) expulsion rates.)

B. Human and material resources
1. Number of certificated staff by type
2. Total instructional FTE (overall and by class type)
3. Teacher–student ratios (overall and by class type)
4. Teacher turnover
5. Instructional dollars per pupil (overall and by class type)

C. Curriculum
1. Formal curriculum documents (as for class-level above)
2. Basic school curricular (graduation) requirements
3. Schedule of course offerings (secondary); typical daily structures (secondary)

Notes

1. This is a slight paraphrasing of Stevens's classic definition of measurement in S. S. Stevens, "Mathematics, Measurement, and Psychophysics," in *Handbook of Experimental Psychology*, ed. S. S. Stevens (New York: Wiley, 1951), 1–49.
2. See the discussion by Abraham Kaplan, *The Conduct of Inquiry: Methodology for Behavioral Science* (San Francisco: Chandler, 1964), 172–173.
3. As quoted by Stephen J. Gould, *The Mismeasure of Man* (New York: Norton, 1981), 320. As I reread Gould's work, I realize that much of my critique follows along the lines of his general analysis. But see also the arguments of Aaron V. Cicourel, *Method and Measurement in Sociology* (New York: Free Press, 1964), 7–38; and Kaplan, *The Conduct of Inquiry*, 60–61.
4. *The American Heritage Dictionary*, Second College Edition (Boston: Houghton Mifflin, 1985), 1042.
5. Warren Torgerson, *Theory and Methods of Scaling* (New York: Wiley, 1958), 5.
6. See the analyses by John I. Goodlad, *A Place Called School: Prospects for the Future* (New York: McGraw-Hill, 1984) and Jeannie Oakes, *Keeping Track: How Schools Structure Inequality* (New Haven: Yale University Press, 1985).
7. Robert J. Sternberg, *Intelligence Applied: Understanding and Increasing Your Intellectual Skills* (New York: Harcourt Brace Jovanovich, 1986); Howard Gardner, *Frames of Mind: The Theory of Multiple Intelligences* (New York: Basic Books, 1983).
8. Israel Scheffler, *Of Human Potential: An Essay in the Philosophy of Education* (Boston: Routledge and Kegan Paul, 1985).

9. Kenneth A. Sirotnik and John I. Goodlad, "The Quest for Reason amidst the Rhetoric of Reform: Improving instead of Testing Our Schools," in *Education on Trial: Strategies for the Future,* ed. William J. Johnston (San Francisco: Institute for Contemporary Studies Press, 1985), 277–298.

10. John I. Goodlad, *What Schools Are for* (Bloomington: Phi Delta Kappa Educational Foundation, 1979).

11. Sara L. Lightfoot, *The Good High School: Portraits of Character and Culture* (New York: Basic Books, 1983), 23.

12. Dr. Seuss, *The Sneetches and Other Stories* (New York: Random House, 1961).

13. See also *The IQ Controversy: Critical Readings,* ed. N. J. Block and Gerald Dworkin (New York: Pantheon, 1976); Philip Green, *The Pursuit of Inequality* (New York: Pantheon, 1981); and Clarence J. Karier, "Ideology and Evaluation: In Quest of Meritocracy," in *Educational Evaluation: Analysis and Responsibility,* ed. Michael W. Apple, Michael J. Subkoviak, and Henry S. Lufler, Jr. (Berkeley: McCutchan, 1974), 279–320.

14. Lewis M. Terman, *Intelligence Tests and School Reorganization* (New York: World Book, 1923), 27–28.

15. See, for example, the discussion in Norman E. Gronlund, *Measurement and Evaluation in Teaching* (New York: Macmillan, 1985), 295–296.

16. For nonverbal portions of achievement, the overlap in predictable variance is nearly 60 percent (i.e., correlations between intelligence and achievement are midway in the range of .75 to .80). See the discussion by Lee J. Cronbach, *Essentials of Psychological Testing* (New York: Harper and Row, 1970), 283–285.

17. David Hawkins, *The Science and Ethics of Equality* (New York: Basic Books, 1977), 119.

18. Ibid., 114.

19. John Dewey, *The School and Society* (Carbondale and Edwardsville: Southern Illinois University Press, 1976), 5. This work was first published in 1899.

20. These responsible parties are teachers, parents, administrators, legislators and other public officials, community representatives, and so forth. See the discussion in Bruce R. Joyce, Richard H. Hersh, and Michael McKibbin, *The Structure of School Improvement* (New York: Longman, 1983), 5.

21. This section of the paper is based, in part, on an unpublished manuscript by Kenneth A. Sirotnik and Richard W. Clark, "Framing the Concepts of Equity and Excellence for Discussion and Action." It profits also from ongoing discussions and work with members of the Equity and Excellence Task Force of the Puget Sound Educational Consortium, a school–university partnership of 14 school districts in the greater Puget Sound area and the College of Education, University of Washington.

22. I use the phrase "human potential" here in the sense of Scheffler's notion of the "capacity to become." See Scheffler, *Of Human Potential,* 46–51.

23. Assumption 2 pertains directly to Scheffler's notions of human potential as "propensity and capability to become." See Scheffler, *Of Human Potential,* 52–63. The assumption is that what goes on in schools and classrooms can and ought to substantially increase the probabilities and enhance the capabilities of all children for becoming well educated with respect to all the educational aims of our democratic society.

24. See also the conception of justice as *fairness* developed by John Rawls, *A Theory of Justice* (Cambridge, Mass.: Harvard University Press, 1971).

25. See Goodlad's analysis of responsibility in educational decision making in *A Place Called School*, 272–279.

26. Kaplan, *The Conduct of Inquiry*, 210.

27. Part of what follows is based on a task force report written for the Puget Sound Educational Consortium (see note 21).

28. I might have used the term "indicators" instead of "information" in this section were I inclined to follow the current trend toward "quality indicators" at the federal and state levels. However, the idea of "indicators," at least the way I perceive them being used, can fall prey to the reification problems already discussed. In fact, all we ever have at any point in time is some body of information that can contribute, it is hoped, in some useful way to understanding and improving our schools. A good discussion of the uses and abuses of educational indicators can be found in Jeannie Oakes, *Educational Indicators: A Guide for Policymakers* (Santa Monica, Calif.: Rand, 1986). A good set of guiding questions compatible with the information I am suggesting here can be found in the recent report by the Carnegie Foundation for the Advancement of Teaching, *An Imperiled Generation—Saving Urban Schools* (Lawrenceville, N.J.: Princeton University Press, 1988).

29. Lee J. Cronbach and Associates, *Toward Reform of Program Evaluation* (San Francisco: Jossey-Bass, 1980), 4.

30. I expanded considerably upon these themes and arguments in Kenneth A. Sirotnik, "Evaluation in the Ecology of Schooling: The Process of School Renewal," in *The Ecology of School Renewal*, 1987 Yearbook, Part 1, National Society for the Study of Education, ed. John I. Goodlad (Chicago: University of Chicago Press, 1987), 41–62; and Kenneth A. Sirotnik, "The School as the Center of Change," in *Schooling for Tomorrow: Directing Reforms to Issues that Count*, ed. Thomas J. Sergiovanni and John H. Moore (Boston: Allyn and Bacon, 1988).

31. Kenneth A. Sirotnik and Leigh Burstein, "Making Sense Out of Comprehensive School-Based Information Systems: An Exploratory Investigation," in *Information Systems and School Improvement: Inventing the Future*, ed. Adrianne Bank and Richard C. Williams (New York: Teachers College Press, 1987), 185–209.

32. John Dewey, *Logic: The Theory of Inquiry* (New York: Holt, Rinehart, and Winston, 1938), 503.

Bibliography

Block, N. J., and Gerald Dworkin, eds. *The IQ Controversy: Critical Readings.* New York: Pantheon, 1976.

Carnegie Foundation for the Advancement of Teaching. *An Imperiled Generation—Saving Urban Schools.* Lawrenceville, N.J.: Princeton University Press, 1988.

Cicourel, Aaron V. *Method and Measurement in Sociology.* New York: Free Press, 1964.

Cronbach, Lee J. *Essentials of Psychological Testing.* New York: Harper and Row, 1970.

Cronbach, Lee J., and Associates, *Toward Reform of Program Evaluation.* San Francisco: Jossey-Bass, 1980.

Dewey, John. *Logic: The Theory of Inquiry.* New York: Holt, Rinehart, and Winston, 1938.

Dewey, John. *The School and Society.* Carbondale and Edwardsville: Southern Illinois University Press, 1976 (first published in 1899).

Gardner, Howard. *Frames of Mind: The Theory of Multiple Intelligences.* New York: Basic Books, 1983.

Goodlad, John I. *What Schools Are For.* Bloomington: Phi Delta Kappa Educational Foundation, 1979.

Goodlad, John I. *A Place Called School: Prospects for the Future.* New York: McGraw-Hill, 1984.

Gould, Stephen J. *The Mismeasure of Man.* New York: Norton, 1981.

Green, Philip. *The Pursuit of Inequality.* New York: Pantheon, 1981.

Gronlund, Norman E. *Measurement and Evaluation in Teaching.* New York: Macmillan, 1985.

Hawkins, David. *The Science and Ethics of Equality.* New York: Basic Books, 1977.

Joyce, Bruce R., Richard H. Hersh, and Michael McKibbin. *The Structure of School Improvement.* New York: Longman, 1983.

Kaplan, Abraham. *The Conduct of Inquiry: Methodology for Behavioral Science.* San Francisco: Chandler, 1964.

Karier, Clarence J. "Ideology and Evaluation: In Quest of Meritocracy." In *Educational Evaluation: Analysis and Responsibility,* edited by Michael W. Apple, Michael J. Subkoviak, and Henry S. Lufler, Jr. 279–320. Berkeley: McCutchan, 1974.

Lightfoot, Sara L. *The Good High School: Portraits of Character and Culture.* New York: Basic Books, 1983.

Oakes, Jeannie. *Keeping Track: How Schools Structure Inequality.* New Haven: Yale University Press, 1985.

Oakes, Jeannie. *Educational Indicators: A Guide for Policymakers.* Center for Policy Research in Education, Rutgers University, The Rand Corporation and University of Wisconsin-Madison. Santa Monica, Calif.: Rand, 1986.

Rawls, John. *A Theory of Justice.* Cambridge, Mass.: Harvard University Press, 1971.

Scheffler, Israel. *Of Human Potential: An Essay in the Philosophy of Education.* Boston: Routledge and Kegan Paul, 1985.

Seuss, Dr. *The Sneetches and Other Stories.* New York: Random House, 1961.

Sirotnik, Kenneth A. "Evaluation in the Ecology of Schooling: The Process of School Renewal." In *The Ecology of School Renewal,* 1987 Yearbook, Part 1, National Society for the Study of Education, edited by John I. Goodlad, 41–62. Chicago: University of Chicago Press, 1987.

Sirotnik, Kenneth A. "The School as the Center of Change." In *Schooling for Tomorrow: Directing Reforms to Issues that Count,* edited by Thomas J. Sergiovanni and John H. Moore. Boston: Allyn and Bacon, 1988.

Sirotnik, Kenneth A., and Leigh Burstein. "Making Sense out of Comprehensive School-Based Information Systems: An Exploratory Investigation." In *Information Systems and School Improvement: Inventing the Future,* edited by Adrianne Bank and Richard C. Williams, 185–209. New York: Teachers College Press, 1987.

Sirotnik, Kenneth A., and John I. Goodlad. "The Quest for Reason amidst the Rhetoric of Reform: Improving instead of Testing Our Schools." In *Education on Trial: Strategies for the Future*, edited by William J. Johnston, 277–298. San Francisco: Institute for Contemporary Studies Press, 1985.

Sternberg, Robert J. *Intelligence Applied: Understanding and Increasing Your Intellectual Skills*. New York: Harcourt Brace Jovanovich, 1986.

Stevens, S. S. "Mathematics, Measurement, and Psychophysics." In *Handbook of Experimental Psychology*, edited by S. S. Stevens, 1–49. New York: Wiley, 1951.

Terman, Lewis M. *Intelligence Tests and School Reorganization*. New York: World Book, 1923.

Torgerson, Warren S. *Theory and Methods of Scaling*. New York: Wiley, 1958.

10.

Tracking and Ability Grouping: A Structural Barrier to Access and Achievement

JEANNIE OAKES AND MARTIN LIPTON

Précis

Why, in the light of all the research evidence that tracking is harmful to students in the lower tracks and that high achievers can function well in heterogeneous groups, is the practice so widespread and entrenched in our schools? Some related questions concern the forces that hold tracking in place. Is tracking in the way of certain school reforms? What are alternatives to tracking practices?

Jeannie Oakes and Martin Lipton raise these questions to assist school administrators, teachers, school boards, and others in examining the issue of tracking and grouping by ability. The authors review the literature on tracking; consider conventional arguments in its favor and responses that might be made to those arguments; and scrutinize the early twentieth-century beliefs, fears, and prejudices that helped spawn the practice.

Tracking originated at a time when schools were pressed to provide an emerging industrial society with a trained work force already sorted by ability levels. Since both the college and workplace now require a certain minimum level of competency and skill development, for all workers and students, many people are questioning the relevance of tracking practices. Poorly trained persons find no jobs in which they can earn a wage sufficient to accommodate their adult responsibilities; nor can they meet the demands of a more complex social system. Tracking contributes to differential school outcomes and unfairly sorts students for subsequent social and economic roles.

If tracking represented just an anachronistic organizational mechanism for channeling the stream of students through school, one might simply do away with it and reorganize. The broader issue framed here is not just how to reorganize a school and eliminate tracking, but how to deflect forces and change conditions that hold tracking in place.

The authors ask: Can people be stimulated to think beyond their immediate and apparent self-interests to consider whether tracking practices, which seem to serve particular individual interests, will in the long run contribute to the kind of social conditions in which people wish to live? In the chapter by Linda Darling-Hammond with Joslyn Green, it is suggested that tracking persists as a result of one of the few reward structures in teaching (good teachers as a scarce resource seek the reward of teaching in higher tracks) and because few teachers receive the training required to manage a heterogeneous classroom. Oakes and Lipton urge readers to consider tracking as a problem of democracy and to examine it in terms of local conditions such as school and district policies, beliefs about students' abilities and limitations, and other restrictive conditions that support tracking as a *structural* barrier to access and achievement in American schools and society.

Jeannie Oakes, formerly a researcher at the Rand Corporation, is a professor in the Graduate School of Education at the University of California, Los Angeles. She was a senior staff member working on John Goodlad's massive study of schools and is the author of *Keeping Track: How Schools Structure Inequality.*

Martin Lipton teaches English at Calabasas High School in Calabasas, California.

—The College Board

Since the 1920s American schools have organized curriculum and instruction by dividing students into ability-grouped classes and curriculum tracks. Since then educators have debated, off and on, whether these practices are necessary and effective, or harmful and discriminatory.

By now, empirical evidence, court decisions, and reform proposals suggest that tracking and rigid ability grouping are generally ineffective, and for many children, harmful. (Reviews by Good and Marshall 1984; Esposito 1973; Findlay and Bryan 1970; Noland 1985; Oakes 1987; Persell 1977; Rosenbaum 1980; Slavin 1986. For court decisions, see, for example *Hobson* v. *Hanson* 1967; *Pennsylvania Association of Retarded Children* v. *Commonwealth of Pennsylvania* 1971; *Mills* v. *Board of Education* 1972; *Dillon* v. *South Carolina Dept. of Education* 1986. For examples of reform proposals, see, for example, Adler 1981; Berman 1985; National Commission on Excellence in Education 1983; Achievement Council 1985; Powell, Farrar, and Cohen 1985; Goodlad 1984.) For younger children identified as "low" or "average" ability, and older ones who are not seen as college material, tracked curricula and ability-grouped classes often work against their high achievement. Moreover, though students of all races, classes, and genders are publicly identified as low- or average-ability, it is poor, black, and Hispanic children who are disproportionately assigned to these categories.

It is increasingly clear that children are consistently and systematically disadvantaged by a practice that is widely and firmly embedded in school traditions and culture. Consequently, the search for appropriate alternatives to tracking—just beginning to take place in many school districts—is, and will continue to be, fraught with difficulties. Altering tracking practices will not come quickly or easily.

In this paper we explore grouping and tracking from a contextual perspective, arguing that tracking is embedded in a schooling context and a societal context that together help us understand why tracking works to the disadvantage of most students, and why it persists in schools anyway. This contextual view holds that tracking is not as much a response to significant differences among children when they are very young as it is an ongoing contribution to differences as children grow older. (For a fuller explication of the contextual perspective, see Oakes 1987.) At the core of these two cultural contexts we find a fuller appreciation of what school reformers may be up against if they try, as more and more are doing, to change tracking practices without attending to the strongly held assumptions and firm traditions that underlie tracking.

The schooling context includes the day-to-day policies and practices within schools themselves that interact with tracking. The societal context includes the larger society surrounding American schools, that is, the beliefs, values, and circumstances that promoted tracking in the first place and that may continue to shape current practice. This societal context suggests why tracking, and not some other approach, was adopted and persists as the way we organize schools. Despite the intransigence of tracking that these contexts imply, we believe that schools can change, and we offer some suggestions about how constructive change can occur.

Practices, Arguments, Evidence: A Brief Review of Tracking

What Is Tracking?

Typically, when schools group students by their "ability," they divide them into separate classes for high, average, and low achievers, and, in high school, into classes for those who are headed for college or for jobs directly after high school. Elementary, middle, and senior high schools divide academic subjects (usually English, mathematics, science, and social studies) into classes at different ability "levels." Most often senior high students in the vocational or general (noncollege) tracks will be in one of the lower levels. Similar overlaps exist for college-bound students and high-ability tracks. But grouping also varies from school to school—in the number of subjects that are tracked, in the number of levels provided, and in the ways placement decisions about students are made.

Grouping practices also become confounded by "master schedules," which sometimes generate even more tracking than schools intend. Elective subjects, such as art and home economics, often become low-track classes because college preparatory students rarely have time to take them; non-tracked, required classes—health and drivers' education—sometimes become so when students' other classes keep them together for most or all of the day. For example, if students in the remedial reading class move en masse to the next (supposedly) untracked social studies class, social studies becomes a low-track class whether intended to be or not. For similar reasons, one drivers' education class we know of was filled largely with "gifted" students.

Four Conventional Arguments

Those who put forth the usual arguments about tracking admit to some inequity and some unintended administrative glitches associated with its practice. Typically, they are concerned educators, and they work hard to make tracking fairer. But they still contend that *most* children are served best by tracking. They frequently cite extreme cases—and fears—at the prospect of alternatives to tracking. Here, as an important backdrop to what follows, we would like to allay some of those fears. Nowhere will we suggest that calculus be taught to children regardless of their prior math experiences, or that *some* children shouldn't study calculus until all children are ready. Nor would we argue that all children who feel like it should be granted a place in the school's performance jazz band. And we would never suggest that children who need extra or special help should not receive it.

ARGUMENT 1.
Children learn best when they are with others who have similar abilities.

Response: Tracking does not promote achievement for average- and low-ability children. Students *not* in top tracks (a group that in the early 1980s included about 62 percent of senior high school students) and children in low-ability classes suffer clear and consistent disadvantages from tracking. Tracking often appears to retard the academic progress of children identified as average or slow (see reviews mentioned above). Moreover, high school students in vocational tracks often do not get better jobs as a result of their school placements. Some studies have found that graduates of vocational programs may do about as well in the job market as high school dropouts (Rubens 1975; Grasso and Shea 1979; Berg 1970; Berryman 1980; Stern et al. 1985).

Neither is tracking required to promote achievement for high-ability students. That tracking can and often does work well for the top students should be obvious. Certainly it is possible to create excellent classes in the midst of mediocre ones: Start by providing the best teachers, the most successful students, and, often, the smallest class size. Add special resources, a sense of superior academic "mission," perhaps a parent support group, and these top students will get the best education in town.

Might tracking yet be worthwhile even if advantages for the top 10 to 30 percent did result in a poorer education for all the rest? Some claim that top students need to be specially "groomed" to be our future scientists, business and government leaders. But what if we could have our cake and eat it too? What if, in addition to the considerable support found for the positive effects on the least-able students of membership in heterogeneous classrooms (Esposito 1973; Noland 1985; Persell 1977; Rosenbaum 1980; Slavin 1983; Slavin and Madden 1983), there was evidence to show that the top students do not necessarily need to learn less even when they are in mixed classes?

Such evidence exists. Many studies suggest that high-ability students progress just as well in mixed-ability classes (see reviews by Esposito 1973; Noland 1985; see also Dar and Resh 1986). Further, when advantages to students in the high-ability tracks do accrue, they do not seem to be primarily related to the fact that the students are similar, but to the special curricular and instructional advantages high-ability groups are given. For example, controlled studies of students taking similar subjects in heterogeneous and homogeneous groups show that high-ability students (like other students) rarely benefit from these tracked settings (Esposito 1973; Kulik and Kulik 1983; Noland 1985). Moreover, studies of students learning in small, heterogeneous, cooperative classroom groups provide additional evidence that the achievement of high-ability students actually can be enhanced in heterogeneous settings (Slavin 1983; Webb 1982).

ARGUMENT 2.
Slow or less capable children suffer emotional and educational damage when taught with brighter peers.

Response: Tracking does not enhance the feelings of slower children. Many times the opposite is true. Rather than helping children feel more comfortable about themselves, being in the low track can foster poor self-esteem, lowered aspirations, and negative attitudes toward school. Some studies conclude that tracking leads low-track children to school misbehavior and eventually to dropping out altogether (Rosenbaum 1980).

ARGUMENT 3.
Tracking greatly eases the teaching task and is the best way to manage student differences.

Response: This assumption pales in importance when we look at tracking's general ineffectiveness and disproportionate harm to poorer and racial minority students. Even if we could set aside these ethical concerns, and even if we could determine which of the subtle differences among children were truly important for assigning students to tracks, tracking would make sense only if it resulted in truly homogeneous groups. In fact, it doesn't (Oakes 1985).

Within tracks children's differences in learning speed, learning style, interest, effort, and aptitude for various tasks is always great. Often tracking simply makes the fact that instruction for any group of 20 to 35 people requires considerable variety in instructional strategies, tasks, materials, feedback and guidance, and multiple criteria for success and rewards. Unfortunately, tracking deflects attention from these instructional realities. When instruction fails, the problem is too often attributed to the child or perhaps to a "wrong placement." The fact that tracking may make teaching easier for some teachers who prefer to teach *as if* their students were very similar does not mean that any group of children—high, average, or low—will benefit most from that type of instruction.

ARGUMENT 4.
Tracking is fair and accurate.

Response: Tracking *prejudges* how much children will benefit and results in some children being denied the opportunity for academically and socially valued subjects. For example, nearly all children can learn from quality literature; nearly all can learn a second language; and nearly all can benefit from studying the important concepts of algebra. Some will learn more, some less. But tracking serves to exclude many children from ever being in classes where these "high-status" subjects are taught. Furthermore, when errors in judgment are made, they are more likely to underestimate what children can in fact do.

Fairness is also an issue when we consider well-established links between track placements and student-background characteristics. Poor and racial minority youngsters (principally black and Hispanic) are disproportionately placed in tracks for low-ability or noncollege-bound students; further, minority students are consistently left out of programs for the gifted and talented. Blacks and Hispanics are more frequently enrolled in vocational programs that train for the lowest-level occupations (e.g., building maintenance, commercial sewing, and institutional care). On the other hand, vocational opportunities for white children from wealthier families are more highly valued by society (e.g., accounting, computers, business, law).[1]

Track placements are often based on published, standardized tests. Fundamental concerns with measures of ability are discussed in detail in the chapters in this volume by Asa Hilliard and Kenneth Sirotnik. Here we simply point out the great potential for unfairness with these measures. Those differences that are easily tested and documented may not be the most important.

All the following and more may influence judgments about early track placements and even some in senior high school: social indicators of "maturity"; momentary concerns of "good and bad days"; month of birth that may determine if a child is the youngest or oldest in the group being tested; physical development influencing personal appearance, height, and handwriting; parental interest or influence; specific testing irrelevancies such as when a child's poor reading ability influences his or her math placement; changing schools and being "out of sync" with the new school's curriculum; and so on. However, differences among classes in the different tracks are far from subtle. Slight and irrelevant differences at the time of placement can have large consequences in the quality of education children receive.

Over the years of schooling, tracking can exaggerate earlier differences among students (Gamoran 1986). For example, younger children who are initially similar in background and achievement become *increasingly* different in achievement and hopes for the future when they are placed in different tracks. This effect seems to accumulate until, in high school, the differences between students are quite pronounced. One reason for this is that track placements tend to be fixed. Most students placed in low-ability groups in elementary school will continue in these tracks in middle schools and junior highs; in senior high these students are placed in noncollege-preparatory tracks. What is astonishing is how this near-guarantee that children will fall farther behind is so consistently thought of as an opportunity to "catch up."

Certainly there are notable exceptions. Many teachers know of children who catch on, get inspired, or, by sheer grit, pull themselves out of low-ability classes and succeed in higher classes. But, sadly, these exceptions may occur in spite of track placement, not because of it. For the most part, the evidence suggests that tracking's effects run counter to what school practitioners intend—helping all children learn. To better understand why this situation prevails and why it is so hard to change, we must examine both the school context in which tracking operates and the societal context that places powerful expectations on schools.

The Schooling Context of Tracking: Day-to-Day Practices

The schooling context of tracking includes conditions and events in schools and classrooms that interact with tracking, suggesting, first, how the tracking system influences the organization of curriculum and instruction generally, and, second, how membership in a particular track influences the experiences and accomplishments of students.

The schooling context of tracking is very complex,[2] including relationships among students' background characteristics, the particular tracking system the school employs, students' track placements, their school and classroom experiences, their responses to those experiences, their cognitive and affective outcomes, and their subsequent track placements. Essentially, tracking involves cycles of interacting policies, practices, and student responses.

The Structure of Opportunity and Accomplishments

School policies determine three structural qualities of the tracking system: *extensiveness* (the number of subjects tracked and the type of distinct curricula offered); *specificity* (the number of track levels offered); and *flexibility* (whether students move from one track to another). Policies also govern how students are classified and placed. Placement criteria (e.g., cut-off scores on standardized tests, prerequisite course requirements, and considerations of students' aspirations) may differ from place to place. Other placement policies determine whether students stay together at a particular level for classes in several subjects ("block scheduling") or are placed separately for each class.

All these policies work together to influence students' access to knowledge at both the school and classroom level. For example, at the school level, we need to look at what classes are available and what, generally, children are expected to learn. Schools that emphasize their vocational or general track are less likely to offer as many advanced courses in science, mathematics, and foreign language as schools with extensive college-preparatory programs. Teacher-assignment policies may influence the quality of instruction. Curriculum guidelines, textbook adoptions, formal decisions (subject departments) and informal decisions (expectations, socializing of new teachers), for example, help establish what knowledge and learning experiences are deemed suitable for particular children.

Depending on the class "level," students will have access to considerably different types of knowledge and have opportunities to develop quite different intellectual skills. Children in high-ability classes, for example, are more likely to be exposed to the topics and skills that will assist them in preparing for college. Critical-thinking and problem-solving skills emerge from the high quality of their course content.

Low-ability classes are taught different knowledge and are rarely expected to learn the same skills. Prominent in "low" English classes, for example, are basic reading skills, taught mostly by workbooks, kits, and easy-to-read stories. Learning tasks often require memorizing and repeating answers to the teacher. Critical thinking and problem solving, if they are considerations at all, are more likely taught from a "program" of problem sequences that are unconnected to high-interest, engaging, real-world problems. Since so much of importance is omitted from their curriculum, students placed in low-ability classes are usually denied the knowledge that would allow them to move into higher classes or be successful if they got there.

After considering what courses and knowledge are available, and to whom, we must continue with an equally critical examination of the quality of the teaching and class time different children receive. Teachers in high-ability classes more often encourage independent, questioning, and critical thinking. Children there tend to spend more time on learning activities, and less time on discipline, socializing, and class routines. Children are expected to spend more time doing homework. Their teachers tend to be more enthusiastic, and they make lessons clearer. Teachers in higher classes use strong criticism or ridicule less frequently than teachers of low-ability classes where teachers are often seen as less concerned and more punitive. In high-ability classrooms tasks are often better organized and the children are given a greater variety of things to do, whereas teachers in low-ability classes are more concerned about getting children to follow directions, be on time, and sit quietly.

These differences in learning opportunities portray significant schooling inequities, not to mention schooling's greatest irony: those children who need more time to learn appear to get less; those who have the most difficulty succeeding have fewer of the best teachers; those who could benefit from classrooms with the richest intellectual resources (successful classmates, enriched curricula, etc.) get the poorest.

Although directly influenced by policy, students' responses to schooling are important to the schooling context. These relationships are dynamic and interactive; that is, they are produced as teachers and students respond to one another and to other circumstances in their schools. Understanding tracking simply as a series of inputs, mediating variables, and outcomes is insufficient, and disentangling causes and effects over the long-term may prove impossible. Tracking as a contextual process is likely to spiral. At any point in time, a particular element (placement, student characteristics, class-

room experiences, effort, achievement) may be an input, mediator, or outcome; a cause or an effect.

Because track placements begin early (some suggest with assignments to
first-grade reading groups), it is likely that these interactive processes cycle
repeatedly during a student's schooling experience, not identically, but with
successive cycles building on the effects of the previous interactions and
effects. Small differences at any one point add up over time. The impact is
likely to be cumulative, in a particular direction, and, metaphorically, to
gather momentum. When the evidence about tracking effects is placed in
this cumulative contextual perspective, it becomes apparent how the schooling context structures tracking's long-term effects on student outcomes.

Initial (perhaps relatively small) aptitude differences among students are
exacerbated by elementary tracking policies, resulting student placements
and experiences, attendant attitudes, interests, and expectations, in elementary school. By middle school or junior high, track placement is more or less
crystallized. The process cycles throughout secondary school, with the differences between students growing dramatically wider.

The Societal Context: Goals, History, and Values

So far we have considered schools and their tracking systems in relative
isolation, as if they are untouched by a larger societal context. Tracking also
exists within a set of historical circumstances and values that provided the
basis for its institution in American secondary schools, and within a current
social milieu of norms and expectations about what schools ought to accomplish. If we are to understand why schools track, this context also requires
scrutiny. Here we offer additional background to the question of why, in the
face of negative effects, tracking continues to make sense to academics,
practitioners, parents, and even children themselves.

Tracking as a Means to Achieve Schooling Goals

Both in the past and today tracking policies have been inextricably linked
with the most fundamental goals of schooling. For example, the common
school probably best represented nineteenth-century curriculum policy. It
directed schools to provide universal, publicly supported, common primary
school education. This, of course, was intended to form the basis for a literate
citizenry—one that shared a set of values and was well-enough informed to
participate in democratic decision making.

With the complexity and expansion of universal education came two
fundamental interests of school policymakers: first, a child-centered concern
required schools to organize curricula to "educate" large, diverse groups of
students; and second, a society-centered concern required that schools provide society with politically socialized citizens and human capital. While

emphasis on these two goals has ebbed and flowed, policymakers have increasingly attempted to meet both by providing "appropriate" differentiated curricula and separate classes within a *comprehensive* (as distinct from *common*) school: curriculum tracks; ability-grouped classes within subject areas; special programs for the learning-disabled, educationally disadvantaged, language minorities, gifted and talented; and the development of courses directed toward having students pass standardized exams for special diplomas or college credit (e.g., New York's Regent's level classes, Advanced Placement, and, perhaps most recently, International Baccalaureate).

Tracking as a Solution to Turn-of-the-Century Problems

Turn-of-the-century problems were responded to with prevailing beliefs, fears, and prejudices, as well as a faith that technological answers could be found to most problems. Schools were no exception. The technology of testing, the factory model of efficiency, the reliance on grades for evaluation, the specialization of "subjects," and the nagging fear that there just weren't enough resources (really good education) to go around characterized the tenor of educational policy. This history helps clarify many of the schooling practices we see today and at least one very central belief that has guided schooling throughout this century: the belief that we best serve children and society when we identify *differences* between children and act on our theories of why the differences exist.

After a long debate about how to educate an increasingly diverse student population for diverse purposes, educators settled on a newly coined view of democracy that defined "opportunity" as the chance to prepare for largely predetermined and certainly different life outcomes. Facing problems they were ill-prepared to solve, schools settled on educational solutions that accommodated prevailing beliefs about racial and ethnic group differences, adopted emerging notions about intelligence, and embraced new theories about managing organizations efficiently. Concurrently, two phenomena supported different schooling for different children: standardized tests and scientific management.

The Influence of Testing. Standardized tests provided a seemingly scientific and meritocratic basis for the sorting process in schools. Standardized, psychological testing, founded on principles of individual differences, helped institutionalize beliefs about race and class differences in intellectual abilities. Early testing was designed to support the view that some children's intellectual, moral, and even biological differences were vast and immutable.

Scientific Management. The other development that made sense out of treating children differently was the philosophy of scientific management. Following the principles of scientific management, separating and exaggerating differences made more sense than valuing diversity for the contributions it could make. Time-and-motion studies, organizational centralization with authority concentrated at the top, prescriptions for preferred methods, and so on were touted as the only ways to bring order and efficiency to the apparent disarray of schools. Since the model for efficiency was the well-run factory, children were increasingly seen as "raw materials" out of which would be fashioned the "product"—productive adults. The apex of scientific management was manifest in the assembly line. One line might turn out Fords—to be sure, all running well and doing what Fords should do—and another line would turn out Lincolns—clearly a superior product.[3]

Today's Legacy

Many educators and parents still tend to think that differences in intellectual aptitude and prospects for school performance are profound and, for all practical purposes, unchangeable. Many, too, still link performance differences with biological or cultural influences, with race, or with social class. Most believe that children are so different in ability they cannot be educated within a common schooling experience. Also firmly entrenched is the view that separate school experiences are needed to prepare and certify students for their appropriate roles as adults in the workplace.

The process depicted here suggests that a school's student-body characteristics, assumptions about the educational implications of race and class differences, and prevailing beliefs about secondary schooling's purpose to prepare and certify students for their adult roles in the workplace interact to shape tracking at different types of schools. Schools thus seem to design tracking structures that make sense given the characteristics of student populations and prevailing beliefs about what programs are appropriate for those students.

This process is consistent with some recent evidence documenting systematic differences between schools serving different groups. For example, the greater the percentage of racial minority students, the larger the low-track program; the poorer the students, the less rigorous the college-preparatory program. (See, for example, California State Department of Education 1986.) Further, High School and Beyond data show that schools serving predominantly poor and minority populations offer fewer advanced and more remedial courses in academic subjects, and that they have smaller academic tracks and larger vocational programs (National Center for Educational Statistics 1985; Rock et al. 1985).

Of course, minority students and those of low socioeconomic status are, on the average, lower in achievement by the time they reach secondary school, and schools respond to those differences with programs they see as educationally appropriate. But "appropriate schooling" in this case—lower-track and vocational programs—is most often detrimental to these students.

Placement in these programs continues a cycle of restricted opportunities, diminished outcomes, and exacerbated differences between low-track students and their counterparts in higher tracks. These placements do not appear either to overcome students' academic deficiencies or to provide them access to high-quality learning opportunities.

Despite this evidence, tracking persists. Furthermore, the tradition of responding to student differences by separation rather than inclusion is so strong that it has followed schools out to the suburbs. There, largely homogeneous populations of white, middle-class children are also subjected to quite needless differences in the quality of their education.

Implications of a Contextual Perspective

We have noted so far that the schooling context of tracking consists of a complex set of relationships between structures and events within schools, and these relationships have long-term cognitive and affective consequences for students. We have also asserted that the societal context of tracking—the historically grounded assumptions and shared norms for responding to student diversity—shapes the content and processes of tracking.

The schooling and societal contexts also help explain why practitioners have an ambivalent response to empirical findings on tracking. First, practitioners almost universally recognize and lament the negative consequences of tracking for students in low-track classes; most teachers and administrators have had discouragingly unsuccessful experiences trying to make these programs work. Many suspect that when a group of the lowest-achieving and most poorly behaved students are together in classrooms, their performance is far below what it might be under other circumstances. But practitioners' concerns about protecting the educational opportunities of the top-track students are even more salient. Research conclusions that able students are likely to continue to do well even if they are placed in heterogeneous groups are dissonant with practitioners' experiences. The schooling context of tracking offers clear school advantages to students in the top tracks, and findings that high-achieving students can learn equally well in mixed classes simply don't account for the noticeable, concrete advantages that practitioners, students, and parents can see in high-track classes.

That the effects of tracking occur over many years may contribute to practitioners' and other school observers' "blindness" to those effects. Decisions at any one moment—especially in the early grades—may seem slight and even offer some short-range benefits or relief. The well-intended motives and some actual successes of remediation, for example, often obscure missed elements of mainstream course work. Not until the next school year will child, parent, and teacher have to come to grips with the even wider gulf between what the child and his or her classmates know. The answer is usually more remediation or, eventually, easier or different courses.

Moreover, the societal context also affects the degree to which practitioners can contemplate change. Definitions of "individual differences" and of what different students "need" are social as well as educational. Students who are identified as less able are more often those who are less advantaged socially and economically. What they need is not seen to be the same abstract knowledge and skills that are suited to their "more able" peers. What they need is more often thought to be functional literacy skills and good deportment that will provide them entry into the lower levels of the work force. Given these *socially influenced* definitions, practitioners are not easily persuaded that a largely common curriculum taught mostly in heterogeneous groups is a promising approach to educating diverse groups of students. Further, alterations in school practice must pass social as well as educational tests. Certifying some for entrance into colleges and universities and preparing others with functional skills and acceptable workplace behaviors are what society expects from its schools. Even if practitioners were convinced of the educational value of "detracking" schools, the tracked curriculum is well suited to certifying students for different futures.

Overcoming the Tracking Barrier

Disappointing findings about tracking (and even promising evidence about heterogeneous grouping) should not lead anyone to believe that simply mixing students together will solve the problems of tracking. Tracking is a response to school and social contexts, and because of its central position in the schooling structure, it helps perpetuate those contexts. Exploration of the contexts *and* the alternatives to tracking cannot be separated—so large must be the changes and so sustained the efforts. Schools without tracking will require curriculum and teaching strategies quite different from those now in many schools. In many cases the needed changes are revolutionary.

Mixed-Ability Schooling: A Promising Direction

Creating mixed-ability schools that work for all students is a radical proposition. To be effective these schools will demand fundamental changes in nearly every aspect of teaching and learning. It simply is not possible, for example, to teach diverse groups of students effectively when the curriculum is largely skill-based and rigidly sequential. Perhaps the most striking difference between students lies in the speed with which they master skills taught sequentially. Some students will race ahead; others will lag behind. Quicker students often must be kept busy with make-work; reteaching others becomes a chore; being retaught (and often retaught again) becomes a humiliation, particularly when others are waiting.

The curriculum well suited to mixed-ability schools is of a very different nature. It is organized around central concepts and themes—the "big ideas" of a subject area. Mastering these ideas is important, challenging, complex, related to real life, and, most of all, rich with meaning. Indeed it stretches the sense-making of *all* children. Students acquire skills as they become ready within a common conceptual framework. If, on the other hand, conceptual learning is crowded out by rote memorization of facts, trivial assignments, or concerns such as deportment or neatness, then those students who can do more challenging work won't, and those who can't, won't learn how.

In addition to a reconstructed curriculum, mixed-ability schooling requires dramatically altered instructional practice. In tracked schools, classroom teaching typically consists of children of the same age engaged in competitive, whole-group instruction: lecturing, common assignments, uniform due dates and tests, and a single set of standards of competence and criteria for grades. Students in mixed-ability schools, however, benefit by being clustered in small groups exchanging ideas, sometimes working on separate but interrelated tasks, and generally helping each other learn. Teacher talk cannot dominate here; neither can large sessions of question and answer. Teachers function more like orchestra conductors than lecturers: getting things started and keeping them moving along; providing information and pointing to resources; coordinating the diverse but harmonious buzz of activity taking place.[4]

These descriptions are not an attempt to outline a preconceived curriculum suitable for a nontracked, mixed-ability school. Rather, they represent a glimpse of what might be imagined and what occurs in rare and special school moments even today. But a reconstruction of school organization, curriculum, and classroom instruction that can nurture successful mixed-ability classes is a mind-boggling proposition.

More Gradual Approaches

Gradually altering tracking policies is no trivial matter either, regardless of how slowly change might take place. Gradual change may be directed at altering current practices, even while maintaining some tracking: for example, by using low-track classes (e.g., general mathematics) as "prep" courses for successful participation in high-track classes (e.g., algebra); by increasing the mainstreaming of both slow and gifted students; by reducing the number of track levels in academic subjects; by eliminating tracking in some subjects or grades; by team teaching; by ensuring racial and ethnic balances in classes at all track levels; or by blurring the distinction between vocational and academic programs of study. Even these changes require far more than simply tinkering or fine-tuning current practice; these changes require fundamental structural and behavioral changes.

Changing Assumptions: The Bottom Line

These suggested changes largely involve alterations in technological pedagogy. None is easy. Yet it is even more difficult to alter the assumptions about children, learning, and the purposes of schooling on which pedagogy is based. Successful mixed-ability schools require the belief that all students

can and will learn nearly all of what society truly values in an education.
There are no easy answers or packaged staff-development programs ready to
cure tracking problems, or, more accurately, the school and societal problems
reflected in tracking. Changing tracking will require more than the commonly
accepted strategies for improving schools, that is, conducting needs assessments, developing a one- or two-year-plan, or buying the services of a
respected staff-development consultant. Instead, these efforts must include
extensive school- and district-based data collection about tracking practices,
critical reflection on and extended dialogue about the values and assumptions
that underlie tracking and teaching, and generous experimentation with
school organization and teaching.

Practitioners and their communities, informed by research knowledge,
must themselves investigate how long-standing traditions, school and district
guidelines, standards of common practice, and beliefs about students' abilities and limitations are reflected in their school's tracking system. They must
take on the challenge of understanding the nature and power of their school
and social contexts. Such democratic, educational endeavors surely will be
worth the extraordinary effort they require.

Notes

1. The evidence of the variation between students within tracked classes has been
well documented for decades. See, for example, Goodlad, 1960.
2. The reader should note that this discussion does not represent a model in a strict
predictive or causal sense. Rather, it suggests frameworks for better understanding
logical and empirically supported interrelationships. Many of these links, moreover,
are supported by correlational research and qualitative studies of schools and classrooms. For a review of this research, see Oakes 1987.
3. Fortunately this history has been richly detailed in many fine studies. See, for
example, Callahan 1962; Cohen and Lazerson 1972; Gould 1981; Kliebard 1979;
Lazerson 1971.
4. See, for example, the vast literature on the effectiveness of cooperative small-
group learning strategies, e.g., Slavin 1983. Also note theoretical perspectives on
the importance of classroom organization for ability suggested by Cohen 1986; and
Rosenholtz and Simpson 1984.

Selected References

Achievement Council. 1985. *Excellence for Whom?* San Francisco: Achievement
Council.
Adler, M. 1981. *The Paiedia Proposal: An Educational Manifesto.* New York: Mac-
millan.
Alexander, K. A., M. Cook, and E. L. McDill. 1978. "Curriculum Tracking and
Educational Stratification: Some Further Evidence." *American Sociological Re-
view* 43: 47–66.

Berg, I. 1970. *Education and Jobs: The Great Training Robbery.* Boston: Beacon Press.

Berman, P. 1985. "The Next Step: The Minnesota Plan." *Phi Delta Kappan* 67: 188–193.

Berryman, S. E. 1980. *Vocational Education and the Work Establishment of Youth: Equity and Effectiveness.* Santa Monica, Calif.: The Rand Corporation.

California State Department of Education. 1986. *California High School Curriculum Study: Paths through High School.* Sacramento: California State Department of Education.

Callahan, R. E. 1962. *Education and the Cult of Efficiency.* Chicago: University of Chicago Press.

Cohen, D. A., and M. K. Lazerson. 1972. "Education and the Corporate Order." *Socialist Revolution* 2: 53.

Cohen, E. G. 1986. "On the Sociology of the Classroom." In J. Hannaway and M. E. Lockeed, eds., *The Contributions of the Social Sciences to Educational Policy and Practice: 1965–1985,* 127–152. Berkeley, Calif.: McCutchan.

Dar, Y., and N. Resh. 1986. "Classroom Intellectual Composition and Academic Achievement." *American Educational Research Journal* 23: 357–374.

Dillon v. South Carolina Dept. of Education, 1986.

Esposito, D. 1973. "Homogeneous and Heterogeneous Ability Grouping: Principal Findings and Implications for Evaluating and Designing More Effective Educational Environments." *Review of Educational Research* 43: 163–179.

Findlay, W. G., and M. M. Bryan. 1970. *Ability Grouping: 1970 Status, Impact, and Alternatives.* Athens, Ga.: University of Georgia, Center for Educational Improvement.

Gamoran, A. 1986. "The Stratification of High School Learning Opportunities." Paper presented at the annual meeting of the American Educational Research Association, San Francisco.

Goldman, E. 1952. *Rendezvous with Destiny.* New York: Random House.

Good, T. L., and S. Marshall. 1984. "Do Students Learn More in Heterogeneous or Homogeneous Groups?" In *The Social Context of Instruction,* edited by P. P. Peterson, L. C. Wilkinson, and M. T. Hallinan, 15–28. New York: Academic Press.

Goodlad, J. I. 1960. "Classroom Organization." In *Encyclopedia of Educational Research,* edited by C. Harris, 221–226. Third edition. New York: Macmillan.

Goodlad, J. I. 1984. *A Place Called School: Prospects for the Future.* New York: McGraw-Hill.

Gould, S. J. 1981. *The Mismeasure of Man.* New York: Norton.

Grasso, J., and J. Shea. 1979. *Vocational Education and Training: Impact on Youth.* Berkeley, Calif.: Carnegie Council on Policy Studies in Higher Education.

Hobson v. Hanson, 269 F. Supp. 401, 1967.

Kliebard, H. M. 1979. "The Drive for Curriculum Change in the United States, 1890–1958." *Curriculum Studies* 11: 191–202.

Kulik, C. C., and J. A. Kulik. 1982. "Effects of Ability Grouping on Secondary School Students: A Meta-Analysis of Evaluation Findings." *American Educational Research Journal* 19: 415–428.

Lazerson, M. 1971. *The Origins of the Urban School.* Cambridge, Mass.: Harvard University Press.

Mills v. *Board of Education*, 348 F. Supp. 866, 1972.

National Center for Educational Statistics. 1985. *Analysis of Course Offerings and Enrollments as Related to School Characteristics.* Washington, D.C.: U.S. Government Printing Office.

National Commission on Excellence in Education. 1983. *A Nation at Risk.* Washington, D.C.: U.S. Government Printing Office.

Noland, T. K. 1985. "The Effects of Ability Grouping: A Meta-Analysis of Research Findings." Ph.D. dissertation, University of Colorado, Boulder.

Oakes, J. 1985. *Keeping Track: How Schools Structure Inequality.* New Haven: Yale University Press.

Oakes, J. 1987. "Tracking in Secondary Schools: A Contextual Perspective." *Educational Psychologist* 22: 129–153.

Pennsylvania Association of Retarded Children (PARC) v. *Commonwealth of Pennsylvania*, 334 F. Supp. 1257 (1971) and 343 F. Supp. 279, 1972.

Persell, C. J. 1977. *Education and Inequality: The Roots and Results of Stratification in America's Schools.* New York: Free Press.

Pillsbury, W. B. 1921. "Selection—an Unnoticed Function of Education." *Scientific Monthly* 12: 71.

Powell, A. G., E. Farrar, and D. I. Cohen. 1985. *The Shopping Mall High School: Winners and Losers in the Educational Marketplace.* Boston: Houghton Mifflin.

Rock, D. A., et al. 1985. *Study of Excellence in High School Education: Longitudinal Study, 1980–82. Final Report.* Princeton, N.J.: Educational Testing Service.

Rosenbaum, J. E. 1980. "Social Implications of Educational Grouping." In *Review of Research in Education*, edited by D. C. Berliner, 8, 361–401. Washington, D.C.: American Educational Research Association.

Rosenholtz, S. J., and C. Simpson. 1984. "The Formation of Ability Conceptions: Developmental Trend or Social Construction." *Review of Educational Research* 54: 31–63.

Rubens, B. 1975. "Vocational Education for All in High School?" In *Work and the Quality of Life*, edited by J. O'Toole, 299–337. Cambridge, Mass.: MIT Press.

Slavin, R. E. 1983. *Cooperative Learning.* New York: Longman.

Slavin, R. E. 1986. *Ability Grouping and Student Achievement in Elementary Schools: A Best Evidence Synthesis.* Report of the National Center for Effective Elementary Schools. Baltimore: Johns Hopkins University.

Slavin, R. E., and N. Madden. 1983. "Mainstreaming Students with Mild Handicaps: Academic and Social Outcomes." *Review of Educational Research* 53: 519–569.

Stern, D., et al. 1985. *One Million Hours a Day: Vocational Education in California Public Secondary Schools.* Report to the California Policy Seminar. Berkeley: University of California School of Education.

Vanfossen, B. E., J. D. Jones, and J. Z. Spade. 1987. "Curriculum Tracking and Status Maintenance." *Sociology of Education* 60: 104–122.

Webb, N. M. 1982. "Group Composition and Group Interaction and Achievement in Small Groups." *Journal of Educational Psychology* 74: 475–484.

11.

School Renewal: Taking Responsibility for Providing an Education of Value

SUZANNE SOO HOO

Précis

The erosion of the curriculum means that only some students enjoy an integrated learning experience; many must fend for themselves, especially those students like Kelly, designated "high-risk" and evaluated as needing special help. Kelly and similar classmates, under procedures presumably designed to meet requirements of federal and state guidelines, are taken out of core curriculum classes like mathematics and English and are shuttled from place to place for special-assistance programs. Such pull-out programs destroy these students' social networks, waste time, and present information in discontinuous bits that the students are unable to integrate for themselves.

To improve learning opportunities for students at Kelly's elementary school, which qualifies for multiple federal programs, the school itself had to change. Suzanne Soo Hoo, the school principal, describes her successful struggle to develop a collegial leadership so school faculty members could become major decision makers devising new curricular, instructional, and organizational approaches tailored to benefit the particular students of their own school.

The transformation of both the school environment and students' learning situations might best be characterized in terms of reoriented school norms. Teachers, instead of being preoccupied with rules and regulations to control behavior, slowly developed a sense of being empowered as problem solvers, risk takers, and innovators. A sense that competence was valued over compliance began to spread throughout the school. Once teachers realized that they were free to engage their talents, they no longer remained isolated in individual classrooms and preoccupied with conformity. They began to collaborate on ways to help students by rearranging student schedules to provide more instructional time, changing the ways they worked to-

205

gether to share responsibility for a child's learning, and cooperating in other ways. One of the most difficult norms to develop and support, according to Soo Hoo, was a tolerance for ambiguity which was a necessary part of trying new arrangements without knowing whether they would work.

For Kelly, school became a better place. Working together, teachers generated a program for him that was no longer disjointed academically and in which he could develop long-term relationships with some teachers and classmates. Teachers rearranged how Kelly received the extra help provided by federal funds. They secured the approval of Kelly's parents and eventually the support of the district-level office that was responsible for compliance with federal guidelines. In fact, these teachers eventually proposed, implemented, and evaluated a restructuring effort that provided more social and academic continuity for almost all students in the school, where the majority of families could be described as poor and transient, with a discontinuous experience of education.

Suzanne Soo Hoo is the principal of Carver Elementary School in Cerritos, California.

—The College Board

As American schooling has developed in the twentieth century, the core curriculum that constitutes students' common learning has been badly eroded. The advent of vocational education and progressive tendencies toward relevance and linking education to life experience suggested alternatives to the core academic curriculum. Social and economic pressures to prepare citizens for productive lives pushed schools to provide training opportunities that competed with the context of the disciplines.[1] But the most significant influence in the increasing fragmentation of the academic experience has been the political and professional commitment to respond to individual differences in structuring the school curriculum, to make a valuable school experience available to all students.

In the name of equity we have endeavored to open schools to all children and youth, and to diverse educational learning needs. We have acknowledged historic patterns of systematic exclusion of some students from the common schooling program and sought to make schools uniformly accessible. The rationale for equalizing educational opportunity has been extended to include special educational services for students who require assistance in order to benefit from school.

In the past three decades, a growing number of federal and state categorical programs targeting aid to particular student populations have been imposed on public schools to respond to our concern for fairness. In well-intentioned attempts to provide all children the best learning opportunities, policymakers have proliferated special educational programs. As special programs are implemented at school sites, they combine to create an oppressive structure inflicting seriously disjointed schooling experiences on those students most in need of coherent education.

This paper discusses how these multiple programs act as a barrier to learning for high-risk students. By illustrating how a faculty examined its own school conditions and restructured its learning environment, the paper describes "school renewal" as the process of changing the school's culture, enabling teachers to develop alternative conditions.

Multiple Programs

The various special educational programs that schools offer are intended to provide students with special services to meet individual needs and ensure school success. Commonly, state and federal programs provide services for students with the following needs: speech and language problems; minimal to severe learning problems; physical motor problems; health problems (e.g., asthmatic, overweight); handicapped (e.g., severe hearing and visual loss); non–English speaking; and economically disadvantaged.

When a student qualifies for a special program, services are delivered according to government-prescribed specifications. Usually students who qualify for the services enroll in the programs; it is rare for parents to decline these opportunities.

Each special service requires approximately 20 to 60 minutes of daily instruction from a specialist trained to provide it. Almost all the programs are "pull outs," with students removed from their regular classroom settings for instruction someplace else. Consequently students miss parts of the basic program like reading, language, math, social studies, health, physical education, music, or art in order to receive speech, adaptive physical education, and Chapter I services.

Some programs are generally regarded as "over and above" services, which means that the intent is to supplement, not supplant, existing services. However, it has never been clear how a school could provide supplemental services, in addition to the regular program, without adding minutes to the school day or days to the school year.

Imagine what happens to a student who qualifies for more than one such special program. Visualize the hypothetical student who is asthmatic, overweight, speaks English poorly, comes from an economically disadvantaged home, has apparent learning, speech, and motor problems, and is also interested in joining the school band.

Presumably, this student should receive all those services addressed to any disadvantages he or she experiences, even if it means visiting six to eight specialists a day. In an attempt to respond to the needs of marginal students and reduce social inequalities, the state has created a situation that frustrates learning for students with multiple disadvantages.

School Observations—Kelly's Day

Although this example is an obvious exaggeration, there are students in schools who do participate in multiple programs and who endure the splintering of their school day into numerous classroom visitations with countless specialists.

One day a few years ago, two teachers and I "shadowed" a special education student in our school named Kelly who qualified for services from the Resource Specialist, Speech, Chapter I, and Adaptive P.E. programs. Notes were collected on the instruction Kelly was receiving, Kelly's response to instruction, use of time, and the children with whom he spoke. It soon became apparent that Kelly spent more time walking from room to room, getting out and putting away books and pencils, and talking at inappropriate times to classmates than he did concentrating on any specific learning activity.

In one day he was asked to respond to six different adults in six different classrooms with six different sets of classroom behavioral standards. In the Chapter I Learning Laboratory, he also visited various learning stations which compounded his number of satellite travels. To complicate this dizzy schedule, one teacher failed to notify Kelly of a room change that day, an omission requiring an additional stop in the office to obtain directions.

The Problems

The delivery of multiple services to needy students is plagued with problems. In my experience, academically and socially, the negative effects appear to outweigh any positive outcomes for students. Not only does the condition affect students, but there are questionable consequences for the teachers as well. An illusion is created that these services and programs make a beneficial impact on students.

Instruction

Instruction over the course of the kind of day described above is made up of discrete learning segments. One instructional period did not appear to have any relationship or relevancy to another period. The services experienced by Kelly, although carefully prescribed by the team of specialists, were not integrated. It simply is impossible to do so. Like shattered glass, Kelly's learning was broken up into mini-learnings that seldom related to each other. Is there any likelihood that the underachiever is capable of synthesizing these various learnings into reasonably coherent patterns?

One could assume that the silver lining in this rain cloud is the diverse teaching techniques and learning activities experienced by the student. Unfortunately, this was not the case with Kelly. Nor is it the case with most such students. In fact, what existed was a very narrow range of different instructional delivery systems. Students typically were passive. The team of specialists had not significantly increased the incidence of more varied modes of learning.

To further exacerbate the condition, Kelly is missing vital instruction back in his homeroom. He is, in fact, absent from the core curriculum. The very services intended to bring Kelly up to grade level create a shortfall in his learning while trying to ameliorate his learning weaknesses. Kelly runs a multiple-program treadmill.

Social Skills

Socially, Kelly tried to make friends every place he went. In some classrooms he tried to reestablish social relationships he had made with students on the playground. In most classrooms he was a social isolate.

Home circumstances resulted in our school being one of three Kelly attended in his five years of schooling. Given his family's high mobility and limited work opportunities, school might have been a place for possible emotional security and certainty. But there were few opportunities in his classrooms to interact socially.

Kelly had become, in a sense, a world traveler of special programs. He was asked to interact with six different teachers, and as many as 100 different students daily as he moved from homeroom, to speech, to resource specialist, to adaptive physical education, and finally to the Chapter I Laboratory. In each room he attempted to ground himself by establishing social relationships. But no one knew him very well. Often the specialists didn't remember his name. He was a phantom figure, moving in and out of the specialists' rooms.

The situation degenerated as he moved into secondary school, where there was yet another cadre of specialists to provide him with special services, as well as another group of four to six teachers to interact with in the different periods of the school day. How could a student possibly receive an integrated learning experience under these conditions?

Clearly the message sent to Kelly was that social relationships with peers and adults in that place called school are transient and unimportant. His chances for cumulative, integrated learning were slim indeed. All of this happens within a school organization with a pattern of annually forming and breaking relationships. At the end of each school year virtually all students are expected to sever relationships and start anew the following year.[2] For Kelly, the structure of schooling further compounded his already vulnerable social relationships.

Teachers' Changing Role

Current conditions at many schools reveal a collection of specialists providing multiple incongruent learning experiences and vying for prime spots on students' schedules. Valuable time and energy are devoted to the coordination of these specialists. These programs also compete with the schedules of the basic curriculum. Consequently the classroom teacher's emerging role is one of orchestrating multiple programs.

This change also influences teachers' perceptions of their job. In the past, classroom teachers sought to accommodate the diverse needs of students without question. In recent years, however, teachers have relied on so many specialists assuming various instructional responsibilities that they exhibit symptoms of an affliction that I call the "pampered poodle" syndrome.

This ailment is characterized by the teachers' declaration of their role as "regular ed" teachers and their resistance to teach, or be held accountable for, any student who has divergent needs. Further, when a "special need" student is enrolled in a "pampered poodle" classroom, he or she is usually shuttled out to a team of specialists. Teachers refer children out because they fail to fit the curriculum.[3] A familiar statement that could be made by a teacher with this ailment is "I'm teaching only the circles this year; please don't send me any triangles or squares. They're someone else's responsibility."

It seems that these teachers have lost the confidence to teach students with special needs. This situation parallels studies on teachers' attitudes toward integration and mainstreaming of disabled children which also cite teachers' lack of confidence in their instructional skills.[4] They doubt their ability as well as their responsibility. Could this feeling of impotence be one reason for teacher dropout?

More Is Less

The good news about the advent of multiple services is that schools receive financial assistance and personnel to support their responsibility to meet the special needs of students. The bad news is the unexpected impact and collision of multiple programs with the basic curriculum and repeated ill effects on teachers and children. One or two new services at a site are a privilege. Six or seven programs at a site are not.

We must ask ourselves whether the organizational patterns of multiple programs are dysfunctional, inadvertently providing pupils with uncommon, fragmented learning experiences. Do the added costs of special programs provide expected added returns? What and how much has really been gained from multiple services? In our zealous attempt to provide students with more, through special assistance, have we missed the target and given them less? What did policymakers have in mind?

Perhaps there is a dysfunction between goals and implementation. Perhaps as policy filtered through the bureaucracy, problems were born. In spite of all this, one school dealt with the resulting condition of multiple programs in a way that had some surprisingly valuable results. This school's program is described in the following section.

One Staff's Response

The Continuous Learning Program

Structurally bound by legislative and district mandates, schools experience great difficulty in overcoming the conditions of an overcrowded curriculum. There is an illusion of having too many candles on a birthday cake. More is not necessarily better.

A culture of renewal enabled the faculty involved to analyze the condition, question some traditional assumptions, and create a program designed to provide all students with a more educationally defensible school day. This program countered the negative side effects of the multiple program structure but did not displace it, since the staff was still accountable to outside directives and laws.

The Continuous Learning Program was initiated by two teachers who proposed that students be assigned to their classes for two consecutive years, rather than for one year, which is standard practice. The Program was aimed initially at providing more instructional time; it was hypothesized that students would benefit both academically and socially if they continued to stay together for this period of time. Youngsters would gain additional weeks of learning, we reasoned, by not having to adjust to a new teacher the next year. It would be an experiment to be evaluated by the staff and parents at the end of the second year. The teachers proposed to maintain a log documenting the merits and disadvantages of their plan.

As they developed their experiment, the teachers questioned some basic assumptions that the school and its staffs had made over the years. One illustration was their inquiry about the traditional "harvest mix," the school's annual ritual of assigning students to new classrooms and teachers each year. "Why do we do this?" they asked.

As they questioned tradition, the teachers analyzed existing conditions, expressed their philosophical positions, and contemplated options for the development of their class lists for this two-year experiment. In doing so, they expressed their deep concern for the socially isolated in our school, the student majority who come from low-socioeconomic, broken, and transient families. The school seemed to intensify the problems of some students by assigning them to new classes each year. Instead of dividing up students and shuffling them out to new teachers, we would work to keep students together.

After visiting a few alternative schools and reading some research papers, the teachers decided to form their class lists using "friendship clusters," whereby students were selected for classes using the criterion of established social groupings. With the help of kindergarten teacher colleagues, the two first-grade teachers observed kindergartners in the classrooms and on the playground in order to identify friendship clusters. The idea behind this was to further cultivate established social groupings by giving them the opportunity to stay together for a period of two years, rather than subject them to the annual harvest mix which divided them up.

On the first day of school, in the second year of the program, we saw some interesting student and parent behaviors. The second-grade students in the Continuous Learning Program arrived on campus with visible enthusiasm and confidence. They knew where their classrooms were, who their teachers were, and they were eager to see their classmates from the previous year. Within seconds of their arrival, students happily reunited with each other, enthusiastically shared summer experiences, and made a mad rush to hug their teachers. Parents exchanged warm hellos with teachers and seemingly left quickly and with confidence. The two teachers started their classes with an immediate rapport with students.

In contrast, the other second-grade students appeared anxious, cautious, and withdrawn. They sheepishly entered their classrooms to meet their new classmates and teachers. Parents lingered around the doors until the bells rang and hesitated leaving campus.

Other program merits as documented by teachers' logs, parent conferences, and test scores included the following:

- students developed strong peer relationships resulting in less alienation and fewer behavior problems;
- teachers found they had taught the children more because of the increased instructional time;

- teachers took more risks by experimenting with different kinds of instructional activities, attributed to better familiarity of teachers with students' needs;
- teachers experienced teaching a new grade level under the best conditions in that they already were acquainted with the students and parents and needed only to understand a new curriculum;
- parents expressed increased confidence in their children's teachers and made fewer complaints;
- test scores showed an all-time high (note that this was an unexpected windfall and that we do not see any correlation between our program and our scores).

At the end of the two years, the experiment was considered a success. Parent confidence as indicated in parent conferences had never been higher. Teacher satisfaction in the academic achievement and social development of their students was celebrated. Six other faculty members requested Continuous Learning Program the following years.

A Better Place for Kelly

The teachers accomplished a restructuring of the conditions for all students, and in doing so, they also made a significant improvement in the conditions for the special program youngsters as well. They generated a program that offset the disjointed learning experiences through furnishing a homeroom that publicly boasted social and academic continuity. The homeroom was the one place where the Kellys in the school could count on developing long-term relationships and could acquire a secure continuum of instructional expectations.

In addition, other changes were made by the staff to restructure Kelly's learning experiences. Kelly's Chapter I lab teachers initiated a meeting with his special education, speech, and adaptive P.E. teachers in order to prioritize the services he would receive. Realizing we risked being out of compliance by not serving him in specific areas, we contacted Kelly's parents, who agreed that Kelly would receive only one pullout a day; the Chapter I lab was chosen because it was the least restrictive and because we felt confident his needs could be met there.

A second change made by the group required Kelly's special education teacher to begin to give him assistance in his regular classroom rather than pulling him out of his class. This was designed to reduce his traveling through the building and to increase the chances of better articulation and exchange of instructional ideas with the regular classroom teacher. What ensued over time was a greater shift of control from the team of specialists to the classroom teacher as the primary agent in Kelly's schooling. A schoolwide practice of regular teachers becoming the first level of intervention for students with special needs was also proposed by the team and accepted by the staff. Interestingly, the school was commended for this particular practice by the district office, commended for restructuring conditions that shouldn't have been there to begin with.

Policy Issues

A review of all the effort expended to ameliorate the impact of multiple programs on a school site is warranted. Our school needed to review and analyze disjointed academic and social experiences, prioritize services (risking compliance issues), modify roles of regular and special education teachers, and develop comprehensive program options, like the Continuous Learning Program experiment. Singly, none of these tasks drains resources, but taken together they represent a loss of valuable time that the school could have focused on something else.

It is imperative that policymakers take an in-depth look at the conditions that exist in schools before they approve laws that may well veil the beneficial services that can be provided to needy students. Special attention should be given to the following issues:

1. Multiple programs impose a new structure on the school, particularly in the case of personnel. Kirst cites studies showing a personnel increase of 46.2 percent from 1961 to 1971 as a result of federal funding. The coordination and articulation of these teams of specialists mean a new layer of bureaucracy has been imposed on the school.[5]

2. There is a loose coupling between the intent and implementation of policy. Policymakers need a holistic perspective and should caution against fragmentation of academic and social learning when schools attempt to implement programs. Our school engaged in complex contortions to respond to the structure of multiple services.

3. Most programs emphasize services to a target population rather than a broader spectrum of instructional strategies. "Federal aid is seldom tied to teaching methods or curricular content."[6] Regular education teachers are largely untrained for these special programs and coexist with a division of labor in the form of curriculum specialists. They find little need to expand their repertoire of instructional skills.

Policymakers must address these issues and understand how multiple programs act as a barrier to access by imposing new conditions on the school. Pullout programs offer disjointed academic and social experiences for marginal students and cause them to miss regular classroom instruction. The National Institute of Education's 1977 study of Title I ESEA programs showed

75 percent of the students in compensatory reading programs were pulled out of their regular classrooms.[7] With teams of specialists at the school site, the regular education teachers tend to relieve themselves of the role of primary instructors to students enrolled in multiple programs, owing to the diffusion of ownership of the student's curriculum. Multiple pullout programs undermine the school's capacity for meeting the needs of marginal students. Surely this kind of separation of students and increased school structure was not intended in the name of equity!

Unfinished Business

Unfinished business includes reconciling Kelly's absence from the core curriculum when he attends his pullout program and what to do about marginal students we do not catch in our Continuous Learning Program. (Some of our students move in and stay only for six months.) And finally, more attention needs to be devoted to broadening our knowledge about learning and instruction. These are big issues that still confront one school.

The experiment also brought to light other examples in our school that fragmented the learning experiences of our students. Teachers questioned the function of such practices as ability grouping, departmentalized instruction, report cards, and the school calendar. We began to realize how the first three of these practices represented different forms of tracking that pushed children out to the margins of the classroom and school. And the traditional school calendar did not distribute learning evenly over the school year, causing significant summer fallout in achievement for our at-risk students, particularly those with limited English proficiency. It was like cracking open the door of a closet and watching all the junk fall out. Suddenly, spilling out of our school closet was an avalanche of calcified school practices that had gone unquestioned for years!

Renewal

How does a school begin to restructure its conditions? What is the nature of the school culture that encourages this kind of inquiry and experimentation? What are the underlying beliefs or the shared vision that enables a faculty to question given assumptions about schooling? A prevailing philosophy has characterized this campus for the past five years. It is a belief that the school is the unit of change and that teachers and administrators are empowered with the charge to determine the destiny of this school. It is a collaborative process whereby faculty members identify issues, reflect, and propose alternatives in an innovative and playful environment.[8] Its essence is trust, dialogue, and risk taking. We refer to this belief system and process as "renewal."

School Culture and Change

A number of conditions and circumstances limit the change that can occur in schools, stifling the kind of inquiry that should inform change. "The isolation of educators (both teachers and administrators) from one another, the lock step chopping up of the instructional day into isomorphic relationships with subject matters, the indiscriminate allocation of untenable student–teacher ratios, the almost nonexistent time for genuine reflective practice, and the lack of commensurate rewards given the nature of the job are among the worst of these conditions and circumstances."[9] If schools, individually, are to be altered significantly, educators must be released from regular instruction and routine duties, and provided opportunities for reflection. Unfortunately, seldom do educators engage in discussions about how to change classrooms and schools—about what conditions would be better for teaching and learning.[10]

Teacher Talk

For our faculty the spirit of renewal is teacher talk. Time provided during school hours several times a week for any configuration of teachers to meet, discuss, plan, reflect, exchange philosophies and values, and articulate curriculum, students' needs, and so on. We hold meetings while students attend assemblies, and we convene staff retreats a couple of times a year. This "quality time" is used to gain perspective and direction in our work.

In the beginning it took some time to build trust and to raise the level of the dialogue. Opportunities and encouragement for teachers to talk to each other about teaching and learning were limited.[11] Five years ago when we first started teacher talks, we weren't used to talking about schooling, and we did not discuss the conditions that acted as barriers to learning at our school. Instead our issues focused on whether there should be rolled or single-tissue toilet paper in the bathrooms, and whether we should allow children to use pencils with or without erasers. But, as a faculty, when we began to trust each other, and read together, and discuss our work, we began to ask real questions about learning and teaching.

A School Vision

In these dialogue sessions we share our beliefs, values, and philosophies. We express what is important to us, what our priorities are, how we see our roles, what we hope to receive from teaching, and the disappointments we suffer.

We have a vision of the ideal student at our school. Our students will think critically, communicate fluently, and interact well with others.

The teachers have also delineated the values we must embrace in order for teachers to maximize their full potential:

1. Teachers Are Professionals

Given the opportunities, teachers will thoughtfully reflect and discuss issues and solve the problems facing them, using all available data. Empowered teachers empower their students.

2. Teachers Are Innovators and Risk Takers

Teachers are encouraged to experiment and develop innovative curricular and instructional strategies in a supportive, fault-free environment. Teachers test the "given assumptions," examine outside resources, and reexamine their own past experiences.

3. Teacher Decision-Making Drives Curriculum

Teachers are in charge of their own destinies. Staff meetings and informal sessions serve as the vehicles to evoke critical reflection and evaluation. The curriculum acts as the catalyst for teachers and students to think critically together.

4. Collaboration Is Valued

Each teacher is a "star," in that each has distinct talents to contribute. These talents are shared on a regular basis as a celebration of human diversity. We also continually network with other schools, other districts, and universities. Research and careful examination of individual experiences provide ways to extend "our ways of knowing" and join theory and practice.

5. A Growing Tolerance for Ambiguity Is Developing

We are moving away from an evangelical position of teaching to a broader perspective, largely uncharted. Indicators of our progress are our growing tolerance for the unknown and a willingness to explore.

John Gardner encourages organizations and institutions to think about fashioning "a system that provides for its own continuous renewal," to develop skills, attitudes, and knowledge for continuous change and growth.[12] Indigenous to this system are the spirit of innovation and tolerance of ambiguity. People are inspired to try new ideas.

The process of systematic reflection helps establish the condition of transformation. Individuals think of multiple alternatives and challenge past practices. All these activities are signs of a dynamic organization and are not necessarily aimed at solving a particular problem. As Gardner phrases it: "I am less interested in inducing any particular change than I am in fostering and nourishing the conditions under which constructive change may occur."[13]

The Principal's Role

My leadership style as principal has changed dramatically in this school over the years. I restrained my inclination to implement quick fixes in order to provide my teachers with the opportunity to discover their own answers. I still am often uncomfortable with the ambiguity of this process, so I concentrate instead on listening and building a climate of trust. If teachers are willing to take a risk and think about alterations and possibilities, I know it needs to be in a highly supportive, encouraging environment.

As I look back, trusting and supporting teachers' decisions were both the hardest and most meaningful actions I experienced in my career. As my role was transformed from authority figure—the person who made decisions and imposed them on teachers—to teacher enabler—the person who facilitates teacher talks from which decisions are made—I learned to appreciate the benefits of shifting control to the teachers and becoming comfortable with the few knowns and the greater number of uncertainties that typify renewal. A large part of my job is to be the chief worrier about the culture of our school that fosters these teacher exchanges.

Over the years the faculty has become professionally empowered. They are given permission by me, but most important they have given themselves permission to critically evaluate, reconceptualize, and engage in multiple-option thinking. No one gives them the "right answers"; it is their responsibility to generate options appropriate for themselves and our school.

Our staff struggled with this process over the years. Ambiguity was terribly uncomfortable for those who demanded that the principal take the lead and tell them what to do. "After all, isn't that what principals are supposed to do?" they would ask. But it didn't take long for them to see that the lists we would generate as "some things we'd like to try" were far broader than one person's ideas.

In renewing schools, administrators encourage dynamic inquiry, collaboration, and self-discoveries. They support ideas, people, risk taking, collegiality, and experimental designs initiated by their faculties. Believing that schools should be sites of inquiry, these administrators raise the level of dialogue through thoughtful inquiry and research and act as the protectors and promoters of a transforming school culture.

The infrastructure that supports such principals is one that empowers the school and its staff. The superintendent and district office personnel are key resources for information and professional development and should buffer the school when it takes risks. As a result of prioritizing the services for needy students, for example, we often found ourselves out of compliance with guidelines for special programs; and compliance has become an important ongoing school responsibility since the advent of multiple programs. So much so that "many special education teachers and administrators have come to see themselves as compliance officers rather than as providers of educational services."[14] Our district superintendent and staff softened considerably the effect of bureaucratic policy regulations.

The superintendent also had the foresight to join a group of educators interested in developing a partnership made up of a university and several school districts. This partnership provided opportunities for administrators and teachers to engage in a special kind of dialogue about the conditions at the school, available research, and ways we could mutually support each others' efforts in dealing with important schooling issues. These partnership experiences were unlike the workshops, in-service experiences, and conferences we were used to. We began to think of schooling differently.

Change and Renewal

At our school renewal represents substantive change. It is unlike a series of workshops that come and then fade away. Renewal doesn't mean that "experts" from outside the school are invited to present and prescribe teaching strategies to a faculty, with a subsequent expectation of automatic implementation of new activities. It isn't a situation in which others tell us what to do and forget to ask us what we think. Rather, renewal means there is a school faculty that identifies its unique concerns and that collaborates in seeking alternative modes to current questionable practice. The faculty may occasionally bring in someone from outside the school to stretch their thinking, but not before they have grappled with the issues. Renewal means joint problem solving and exploration of new knowledge in specific response to the concerns of the school community.

Values, as well as behaviors, are shared and transformed as a result of teacher talks. Teachers share advice with each other beyond the "how to do" a new unit of study, to "what do I know about how students learn." They also express their expectations for students, their insecurities in pedagogy, ideas they would like to try, their responsibility to a greater society. This introspection and responsiveness characterize the dialogue that enabled teachers to restructure academic and social learnings for Kelly.

Renewal is rooted in the spirit and souls of good teachers, whereas change activities as a series of workshops are like blossoms on a tree that drop off as the season changes.

Renewing educators who believe in a process of reflection and self-examination, collaboration, and empowerment will eventually identify those conditions that frustrate learning. They can critically examine and confront the issues schools face. They are able to thoughtfully analyze their instructional delivery system and their curriculum. Their professional vision includes ongoing inquiry and reflection about what is known, as well as sensitive thinking for the future.

These educators, working thoughtfully, and in genuine collaboration, have enormous power for school transformation. Changing conventional practice is possible when educators can "consider, critique, modify, and adapt the best that research has to offer in the context of their day-to-day work and their personal and collective teaching experiences."[15]

Conclusion

Multiple programs, responding to individual needs, occasion a number of issues and problems in schools. These programs impose a new structure on public schools. Unanticipated adverse outcomes for both students and teachers require policymakers' review relative to the intention to provide special services to needy youngsters.

This paper has outlined some issues for policymakers and school leaders to address as they develop better ways to support students in schools. One school's process of renewal reveals some suggestions about assisting schools' capacity to engage in continual renewal. It suggests we need to empower schools by giving faculty quality time to reflect together and engage in productive dialogue, encourage risk taking and experimentation, and provide teachers with a supportive infrastructure to extend their knowledge and support their efforts to improve. Efforts to meet the needs of students who fail should be recast as creating conditions for restructuring schools for success.

Because schools are stable institutions with amazing capacity to maintain regularities, they sometimes inhibit their own ability to maximize excellence and, instead, create the conditions that induce failure. What can a single school do to thoughtfully restructure its learning conditions? How can a school faculty, living with the legacy of maintaining the status quo, begin to critically examine the assumptions made by their predecessors and realize their potential for making a meaningful contribution as educators?

I would assert that it is the renewing faculty that will find successful ways for students to gain access to knowledge. These faculties are thoughtful risk takers. Given a school culture of ongoing renewal and transformation, they will design new ways to educate effectively. I am confident that educators will discover the solutions to the conditions that impede access to learning, if they are given meaningful opportunities to identify and address the problems. To create this kind of inquiring faculty, we must make sure we provide school structures that encourage rather than inhibit reflection, that take account of the critical role of time in thinking of and testing ideas, and that provide the necessary resources to support continuing professional examination of current school practice.

Notes

1. John I. Goodlad, "Core Curriculum: What and for Whom?" unpublished paper presented at the International Seminar on Core Curriculum in Western Societies, Enschede, The Netherlands, November 13–15, 1985.
2. Robert Dreeben, *On What Is Learned in School* (Reading, Mass.: Addison-Wesley, 1968), 7–24.
3. John Elkins, "Education without Failure? Education for All?" *The Exceptional Child* 34 (1987): 7.
4. Yola Center and James Ward, "Teachers' Attitudes towards the Integration of Disabled Children into Regular Schools," *The Exceptional Child* 34 (1987): 41–55.
5. Michael Kirst, "Teaching Policy and Federal Categorical Programs," in *Handbook of Teaching and Policy* (New York: Longman, 1983), 436.

6. Ibid., 441.
7. Ibid., 437.
8. James G. March and Johan P. Olsen, *Ambiguity and Choice in Organizations* (Oslo: Universitetsforlaget, 1976), 75–81.
9. Kenneth A. Sirotnik, "The School as the Center of Change," Occasional Paper No. 5, Center for Educational Renewal, University of Washington, Seattle, July 1987, 5.
10. Seymour B. Sarason, *The Culture of the School and the Problem of Change* (Boston: Allyn and Bacon, 1971), 210–214.
11. Dan C. Lortie, *School Teacher* (Chicago: University of Chicago Press, 1975), 96–98, 232.
12. John W. Gardner, *Self Renewal* (New York: Colophon, 1965), 12.
13. John W. Gardner, *No Easy Victories* (New York: Colophon, 1968), 51.
14. J. M. Atkins, "Judges' Rulings Put Limits on Educational Reform," *Stanford Campus Report* (October 1980): 25.
15. Sirotnik, "The School as the Center of Change," 10–11.

Selected References

Atkins, J. M. "Judges' Rulings Put Limits on Educational Reform." *Stanford Campus Report* (October 1980): 25.

Center, Yola, and James Ward. "Teachers' Attitudes towards the Integration of Disabled Children into Regular Schools." *The Exceptional Child* 34 (1987): 41–55.

Dreeben, Robert. *On What Is Learned in School*. Reading, Mass.: Addison-Wesley, 1968.

Elkins, John. "Education without Failure? Education for All?" *The Exceptional Child* 34 (1987): 7.

Gardner, John W. *No Easy Victories*. New York: Colophon, 1968.

Gardner, John W. *Self Renewal*. New York: Colophon, 1965.

Goodlad, John I. "Core Curriculum: What and for Whom?" Unpublished paper presented at the International Seminar on Core Curriculum in Western Societies, Enschede, The Netherlands, November 13–15, 1985.

Kirst, Michael. "Teaching Policy and Federal Categorical Programs." In *Handbook of Teaching and Policy*. New York: Longman, 1983.

Lortie, Dan C. *School Teacher*. Chicago: University of Chicago Press, 1975.

March, James G., and Johan P. Olsen. *Ambiguity and Choice in Organizations*. Oslo: Universitetsforlaget, 1976.

Sarason, Seymour B. *The Culture of the School and the Problem of Change*. Boston: Allyn and Bacon, 1971.

Sirotnik, Kenneth A. "The School as the Center of Change." Occasional Paper No. 5, Center for Educational Renewal, University of Washington, Seattle, July 1987.

12.

Enhancing Access to Knowledge through School and District Organization

CAROL WILSON AND LANCE WRIGHT

Précis
Bureaucratic organization and values permeate school systems and pedagogy. As a result, students often are treated as cogs in a production machine without adequate regard for personal growth. Compliance is valued over competence, and teacher and student performance are judged in terms of checklists of behaviors instead of integrating information and experience. The bureaucratic ideal forstalls invention and limits response to individual need.

School business as usual does real damage. Two widespread practices supported by bureaucratic values are particularly harmful to poor and minority students. Sorting students into categories like so many factory parts, with those in the "nonstandard" category taught a different curriculum reflecting low expectations of these students, effectively limits their learning opportunities. Teaching basic subjects in very small units means that knowing is no longer seen as the ability to call up a reasoned view on some topic. Academic performance becomes equated with mastery of these disparate bits of knowledge, reflecting superficial assumptions about the learning process and what it means to be an educated person.

Carol Wilson and Lance Wright recommend refocusing attention on the experience of the child. All students should not be expected to learn the same skills in the same ways at the same ages—or else be shunted aside to "special classes." Schools could be transformed from places students experience as impersonal and rule-ridden to places where people are aware of their needs and adjust to their experiences without losing sight of academic goals.

To effect real structural changes, Wilson and Wright suggest that teachers and administrators first reflect on the broad issues of school organization. Depending on how schools choose to structure educational environments and address student variability, students' access and opportunities may be broadened or foreclosed. Alternative organizational arrangements ought to indicate responsiveness and academic excellence, and also satisfy the public need for accountability for effective school programs.

Carol Wilson is executive director of the Colorado Partnership for Educational Renewal.

Lance Wright is on the faculty of the School of Education at the University of Colorado in Denver, where he directs the Principals Academy.

—*The College Board*

This paper examines how school and school district organization and administration inhibit equitable access to knowledge for all students, especially for poor and racial minority children, those most "at-risk" for school frustration and failure.

The Corporate Model

The commitment to standardization and the cult of efficiency that characterized late nineteenth-century American industrialization mark American education to this day. Classifying students by grade, using programmed curricula and standardized examinations contributed to the development of systematic schooling in this country. The magnitude of immigration at the turn of the century forced schools to set standards in order to meet the level of need for a literate citizenry and competent labor force. The diversity of the population occasioned serious resocialization efforts inside schools to create a shared value system and homogeneous culture. The discipline of the factory—order and punctuality—and bureaucratic norms—adaptation and conformity—describe schools' development at the turn of the century. Efforts to centralize and control our decision making resulted in the American corporate boards, composed primarily of business and professional men, overseeing school activity. The large, urban systems we have today developed from the subsequent consolidation of small, relatively individualistic schools and districts, emulating the corporate organizational model.[1]

Schools in the United States are now customarily organized bureaucratically and distinguished by the following characteristics:

- Written policies and procedures
- Distinct division of labor
- A chain of command and control
- Power and authority based on rank, and
- Well-defined rules regulating behavior.[2]

The appeal of bureaucratic organization lies in its emphasis on efficiency and uniformity, as well as its consistency with corporate organizational arrangements in the larger society. Arguments for the use of this organizational pattern center on the large numbers of students and staff involved and the complexity of meeting students' many needs.

To address this diversity and complexity, the bureaucratic response most often entails attempts to standardize experiences and expectations for all students. All students, for example, could be expected to master some specific content and to demonstrate their mastery by performing well on an objective, multiple-choice or fill-in-the-blank test. This standardization is believed to provide equal educational opportunities for everyone. Attempts at such standardization can be found in the written policies and procedures of schools and school districts. They take the common form of a curriculum policy that refers to curriculum in terms of program goals, specific objectives, scope of subject matter, and sequence of learning activity. Objectives must be measurable, and a certain percentage of students must be able to master a certain percentage of the objectives.

Problems Associated with Uniform Performance

Although this is an apparently reasonable expectation, closer examination of some of the assumptions underlying such a behavioristic approach to school standardization reveals the problems associated with uniformity of performance. We can illustrate this point by using an actual objective from a reading program. In this particular district all second-grade students are expected to demonstrate mastery of a number of discrete objectives in the area of reading including the following:

> Given a word orally or an identified picture with a consonant sound in the medial position, the learner will identify the corresponding letter.

Several assumptions about the nature of learning and literacy inform this objective. One assumption is that testing students on this "skill" will reveal what students have learned relative to the objective. Another assumption is that a standardized objective ensures that all students learn the same skill in the same way. It is both efficient and, apparently, fair to expect uniformity of response. This assumption, in turn, is rooted in the bureaucratic notion of division of labor, not only by grade but by skill, in the interests of efficiency. Such a division of labor may well fit a production-line process of assembling or finishing, resulting in a particular product that will meet certain measurable standards. The problem with applying this concept to the development of literacy or, more broadly, learning can be seen in current ideas about teaching reading that run counter to these bureaucratic assumptions.

The idea that a learning task must be small, and part of a set of other discrete skills reduced from a larger skill, is obsolete in light of research-based knowledge about mental schema and cognitive processes.[3] Moreover, this notion of skill acquisition comes from a behaviorist perspective that construes learning as solely a perceived change in behavior.[4] This learning objective states the behavior that the students will exhibit to indicate understanding. In contrast, cognitive psychologists tell us that "learning" can be defined as the construction of meaning, with the focus on developing schema, not skills.[5] Schema are "meaning structures." We can think of them as mental files. Behavior alone does not reflect the development of mental capacity or the making of meaning.

Let us return to the original learning objective. If a student has no mental file for consonants in the medial position, this objective will not make sense and, consequently, learning will not occur. Even if students can demonstrate this behavior, any meaning they may construct about it is not likely to assist them in learning to read and comprehend what they read. Furthermore, just because we can see the behavior of a facile reader, we should not assume that this behavior necessarily reflects the mental schema of all literate persons, nor should we act on the notion that children will acquire literacy only by demonstrating sequences of such behaviors. Literacy, like language, develops very differently from the way in which it finally manifests itself. Children acquire literacy through language and through the whole act of reading, not by dividing the act into meaningless pieces.[6]

In a highly bureaucratic and tightly regulated environment all students are expected to master the same objectives, in a similar time frame, under ostensibly uniform conditions, regardless of individual interests or capacity, learning needs, personal circumstances or choice. The typical school strategy for coping with diverse groups of students is to segment and segregate their learnings, tracking their course work, according to perceptions of their ability.

As uniformity is promoted, the curriculum becomes mechanistic and lifeless because it does not develop in the interaction of teachers and students. As this example suggests, curriculum is thought of as something for students to "get," focused on narrow content-mastery, to the near exclusion of process and relationships. Students passively receive information. Little thought is given to what meaning students may develop from experiences with the content or anything related to it.

With an emphasis on efficiency, bureaucratic ideas encourage development of isolated and unrelated objectives that ignore the ways in which we know students learn. Typical measurement procedures, e.g., multiple-choice and fill-in-the-blank tests, exacerbate the problem of student passivity and accelerate the press for conformity. Little or no opportunity is provided for students to respond in an open-ended fashion about what they have learned about a topic or concept, and how this new knowledge or understanding fits with other information. Learnings that are not easily measured and quantified are given low priority. This approach does not encourage students to construct and accumulate meaning, but rather to "master" isolated facts and skills.

Describing the school curriculum solely in terms of a standard product subdivided into discrete activities and behaviors adversely affects the education of all students but is particularly unfortunate for low-achieving students who are considered at-risk of school failure. When these students in special need of successful school experiences, particularly in reading, encounter tasks like those described above, they often experience frustration and discouragement. The focus on behavioristic responses and discrete skill acquisition appears to be especially unproductive for these students. We have only to look at remedial classes made up of a disproportionate number of poor and racial minority students to observe the lack of success these students experience, given the dominant expectations of schools.[7] Even if these students produce the expected behaviors, the meanings they construct will vary greatly. They will interpret the particular behaviors in light of their own experience and the schema they have developed.

Teachers Head the Assembly Line

The problems associated with the behavioristic view of learning as promoted by most schools and school districts are sustained in part by expectations those higher in the organizational chain of command have for teachers. Teachers are held accountable for students' mastery of multiple objectives. Mastery is usually demonstrated by students' performance on standardized tests. Again, when learning is viewed in this way, with emphasis on "mastering" uniform objectives, little attention is accorded the individual needs of learners. Those who work most closely with students are precluded from making substantive instructional decisions that can address students' unique characteristics.

In the name of accountability teachers are expected to ensure student success in a narrow range of behaviors, in part because real learning and understanding are not easily compartmentalized or measured. The most typical form of classroom instruction springing from this desire for efficiency and uniformity is direct instruction, that is, the teacher telling students about a topic. This method may be appropriate in some situations, but it is used much too often, thereby teaching students to be passive receivers of information. Little real involvement of students in their own learning, what or how they will learn, is encouraged or rewarded. The curriculum has been prescribed beforehand, standardized, often by a district-level committee; the instruction is a function of the teacher's need for efficiency.

This behaviorist view translates to an efficient factory model in which principals can be seen as managers and teachers as assembly-line workers. Imagine teachers in their workplaces (classrooms), on the assembly lines (grade level, classrooms, departments, or teams), using certain production methods (a reading curriculum based on isolated skill development), with raw material (students) to create a product (students who can demonstrate mastery of these skills).

This factory metaphor for schooling fits the bureaucratic view discussed earlier. Unwittingly, fostering this view of education means erecting barriers to students' actual access to knowledge. Recall that the factory model assumes that teachers have very narrowly specified roles limited to the classroom, that curriculum and instruction should be the same for all students, that students are all alike, and that mastery of specific skills equals important and useful learning. In this paradigm principals supervise and evaluate teachers based on specific objectives in one-to-one relationships. Teachers are held accountable for student learning based on student mastery of isolated skills, a view which, as discussed earlier, derives from an obsolete notion about learning. The principal's job is to see that students and teachers stay on task and that the school runs smoothly.

The expectation for a smoothly operating school suggests another problem that arises from the contrast between the rapidly changing environment in which we live, and the relatively static and predictable environment resulting from bureaucratic impulses. Bureaucratic organization implicitly characterizes most district policies, procedures, and standard expectations for students. Since it is unlikely in such a setting that a sensing mechanism exists for detecting changes in the environment, there is little chance that the school or school district will be sufficiently sensitive or malleable to make corresponding changes in the way it operates. For example, current research on cognition and intelligence have not yet been integrated into systematic schooling. Most districts continue to conduct themselves as they have for decades, merely fine-tuning the factorylike functions. The tendency in a bureaucratic school organization, then, is to presume that the outside environment fits the school's or district's expectations for standardization, as evidenced by the example of discrete learning objectives. Outmoded organizational forms override understanding of well-researched principles of learning. To be truly educational organizations, schools must be organized and managed according to what we know about learning and learners.

A look at some data about our changing world as it applies to at-risk students might help clarify this central concern by demonstrating that students are not standard when they arrive at or leave school. In a paper presented to the Committee of Economic Development Task Force on the Educationally Disadvantaged, Scott Miller, of the Exxon Education Foundation, notes that in 1982 only 61.8 percent of the 18- to 19-year-old cohort had completed high school. For white students, the graduation rate (63.5 percent) was near average in 1982. For black students, the rate was 51.8 percent; for Hispanic students, 40.3 percent. Moreover, the National Assessment of Educational Progress reading test given to nine-year-olds showed great disparities between white, black, and Hispanic students. Whereas 1.2 percent of white students met the Adept level, none of the Hispanics and only 0.1 percent of the black students scored as well.[8]

Miller goes on to elaborate about how apparently similar educational circumstances often can be very dissimilar. His example is based on a contrast between two representative parents of two present-day learners. One parent is from the rural South and graduated from a school in an underfunded system during the 1950s. The other is a high school graduate from the North whose parents have good literacy skills. If the first parent had attended one of the more poorly funded colleges, many of which had mostly underprepared students, she or he probably could not have reached the same educational development level as the other student, even if the second student did not attend college.[9] The point here is that mastering objectives, accumulating credits, graduating from high school or college do not guarantee that students will attain standard educational development. These kinds of differences can contribute to great variability in contemporary learners' home environments, in terms of learning experiences provided and supported outside the school.

A district cannot change home environments, but it can establish conditions whereby schools within the district can structure settings that provide for equitable educational development for all students. All learners are shortchanged when learners exhibit only predetermined behaviors; students who are at-risk of failure suffer even more negative consequences. Conversely, when students develop significance and meaning, starting with their own experiences, and are allowed to build on these understandings, they can then use their knowledge in their subsequent educational development.

Barriers to Learning

Whether we view the bureaucratic tendencies in schools as an inappropriate emphasis on inflexible curriculum, on simplistic practices of testing, tracking, or grouping students, or as an overemphasis on direct teaching, a narrowly prescriptive curriculum policy can have far-reaching effects on the educational environment. Let's take a walk through a hypothetical school and see how standardized practices and administrative decisions become barriers to learning inside classrooms. Recall that the context for interpreting policy decisions is a specific chain of command in a relatively inflexible setting.

Our first stop is a first-grade classroom at High Creek Elementary School where the school day has just begun. The teacher has just taken attendance and lunch counts; the Pledge of Allegiance has been recited; and the pupils have settled into several work groups of varying sizes for reading and language arts instruction. Some of the students work in pairs, some in threes and fours, with books, papers, and hand puppets spread out on desks, chairs, and the floor; one group of six is seated at a listening center with headphones, and another group of seven is seated in a circle reading aloud to the teacher. The teacher aide gathers still another group near the door, gives each one a sheet of paper, and escorts them to the school library–media center. The teacher regularly looks up and scans the entire classroom, occasionally calling out words of encouragement, praise, or admonishment to pupils. Pupils appear to be intent on their work and interactions with one another. The classroom is humming with the sounds of lowered young voices, rustling paper, periodic laughter, and moving chairs. The morning progress is interrupted only by occasional changes of various group configurations.

Later that afternoon we visit a fifth-grade class while they are engaged in a round of debates about the American Revolution. We quickly learn how the four groupings of five students each are organized. Each of the four groups has selected an issue from their reading and research. Two students each have taken opposite stands on the issue, prepared written papers, and have come together with a moderator (the fifth student in each group) to share their papers and to debate the issue. The teacher explains that a sixth student is serving as recorder for each group in order to summarize main points for later large-group discussion. The teacher circulates among the groups, pauses to listen here and there, makes a comment or poses a question, then moves on.

Now consider the effect of district standardization of curriculum on these learning environments. Central office administrators, seeking high test scores with which to demonstrate to citizens the effectiveness of the school program, could choose to tighten up teaching and grade-level curricula. New requirements to publish specific learning goals, indicate instructional pacing for individual subjects (including documentation to explain failure to keep up the prescribed pace and written plans to catch up), and relegation of teacher aides to simple support activities and noninstructional duties force fundamental adjustments in classroom organization and activity.

In response to this regulation, our hypothetical first-grade classroom becomes more orderly and standardized, with pupils sitting at desks arranged in traditional rows. They either read aloud to the teacher or complete skill worksheets, everyone on the same page or completing the same worksheets, at the same time. The teacher aide enters grades in the teacher's gradebook, cuts out letters for bulletin boards, or checks skill sheets with answer keys.

The fifth-grade classroom we visited earlier no longer has the type of learning activity we witnessed. Social studies has become a routine of memorizing dates and events and writing answers to comprehension questions at the end of every chapter. These students, too, are seated at desks arranged in rows and regularly lectured to.

This rather typical district-level administrative response to community expectations of educational excellence indicates a number of assumptions about school standardization:

1. Test scores represent the single best indicator of educational accomplishment, regardless of the understandings, skills, and abilities pupils develop which achievement tests cannot capture.

2. A decline in scores reflects what is happening in district schools regardless of differences from school to school, from one subject area to the next, or from teacher to teacher.

3. Effectiveness is related to more stringent standards, district-design procedures, and rules that restrict or prohibit teacher decision making.

4. Instructional planning is a simple, clear-cut task best left to those who supervise teachers.

5. All teachers should teach to the same objectives.

6. All learning is linear; it can be broken into discrete units; relationships to the whole are unimportant.

7. The curriculum is something "given" to students.

8. Teachers should be directed and supervised by superiors in the system hierarchy.

9. There is one right answer.

If learning is viewed solely as a perceived change in behavior, and if fewer differences between students are acknowledged, bureaucratic organization and standardized expectations seem less problematic. Given current understandings of cognition and cultural difference, however, the problems with this organizational form become more apparent.

A Reformulation of Goals

The conditions that those at the district level can establish to promote educational development for all students center on allowing individual schools to focus on their own school communities with their attendant resources and issues. The goal of the district central office should not be to develop and enforce standards of behavior for students and staff. Rather, district administrators should provide support and resources for professionals to develop and collaborate professionally about the heart of their profession: students and how and what they learn.

Similarly, building principals can establish conditions within a school for teachers to work together in addressing the varied needs of students. In collaboration with each other, the principal, and district personnel, teachers can expand and deepen their knowledge base and reflect on their classroom practices. As they try different teaching practices, they should share the results of their work with each other and continue to explore alternatives that are consistent with current research and professional knowledge. Together they can transform their workplace into one characterized by ongoing inquiry into what it is they do and why they do it.

The principal becomes a permission giver, convener, alternative drummer, and the link to knowledge sources outside the school: e.g., the district office, professional literature and research, and outside experts. Whereas teachers may share some of these roles, the principal has the primary responsibility for providing information and scheduling time for professional staff development.

Given the nature of learning and learners, the principal and district personnel can best respond to students' individual needs and development by recognizing their variability as learners, and then by providing support for teachers to make the necessary decisions that promote nonstandard ways of addressing individual differences. In a local elementary classroom, for example, teachers work with students on language, that is, reading, writing, and speaking, by encouraging students to write their own stories, based on their personal experiences and using their natural language. When students have completed a first draft, they read their stories to other students who can ask the "authors" questions for the purpose of improving the writing. Students discuss their work, rewrite, and continue to share with one another. The teacher offers suggestions and assistance throughout, helping these students learn how to help each other to become both cooperative and independent learners.

Consider teachers who have become frustrated about the fragmentation of the curriculum into numerous discrete objectives based on specific skill mastery. In part the frustration is born of their concern about the numbers of students who are not mastering these objectives and not learning to read. A principal's activities could be significant in helping the teachers acknowledge these concerns and subsequently do something about them. The principal should spend time talking with teachers in small groups about what they did and why they did it. During these professional exchanges the principal should not hesitate to raise questions about what is occurring in the teaching of reading and simultaneously suggest that it is acceptable to think in alternative ways about reading and learning. Moreover, as teachers address these issues, the principal should suggest ways to bring knowledge to bear on the concerns of the school faculty. The district office, in turn, should provide resources to principals and their faculties, and link educators in schools, as well as district personnel, for sharing information and experience. Teachers should be encouraged to seek outside advice and assistance even as they work collaboratively inside schools and classrooms.

It is not a matter of individual teachers within a school or individual schools within a district attending to their own business in a vacuum. Rather, teachers and administrators within and among schools must work together to share their knowledge about students and learning, as well as to incorporate current research and professional understanding into what they already know and believe. The broad vision and goals that the school board has been empowered by the state to develop, and which presumably reflect the values and beliefs of the district, bind schools in a district organization. These directions and directives are the basis for curriculum development as a dynamic set of conditions that fosters individual growth and learning.

By articulating overarching goals, district administrators can provide direction for schools and, at the same time, acknowledge the need for flexibility between individual schools and classrooms. A goal, for example, might speak to students' gaining appreciation for artistic expression in society. Educators can ensure that all students have experiences that will enable them to achieve this goal, whether in literature, music, the visual arts, or dance.

It is important that, at the level of the school, teachers and administrators work together to meet these broader goals for all students, ensuring equitable opportunities to learn desired knowledge. Implicit in this approach is the need for curricular balance, the integration of information and substantive experiences for all students in the domains of knowledge and ways of knowing. That is, all students must learn about mathematics and science, literature and language, society and social studies, the arts, and the world of work.[10] To function effectively, they need to know how to analyze and discuss, how to question, collect information, and construct meaning from disparate knowledge and experience.

With an emphasis on the construction of meaning, students can be encouraged to learn through various activities. Teachers can build on students' actual experiences and interests through the use of manipulatives in math, experiments in science, reflection and role playing in literature, and so forth. They can assess student progress by asking students what they have learned, collecting writing samples and other student-developed work, and displaying student projects and products.

Teachers should be prepared to analyze and employ current knowledge about learners and learning. Then, working within the school and joining others in other schools, they can focus their professional attention on furthering their understanding of students and their cognitive processes, and the implications for instructional practices.

Principals must encourage teachers to examine their professional practices and engage in meaningful discourse with their colleagues. They should emphasize the importance of inquiry by actively engaging in these reflective, collegial activities with teachers and with other principals. Principals need to encourage teachers to be personally creative and to develop professionally by finding ways to relieve teachers of time-consuming, noninstructional duties, and principals must support teachers' initiatives and development opportunities. Principals should provide professional leadership and resources for classroom teachers and participate in developing dynamic learning environments.

District office personnel, in turn, can assist principals and teachers in building collaboration and gaining access to current research in and understanding of the subject fields, learning and cognition, and information about the students in the particular school and district. They can facilitate networks of teachers and administrators with similar interests across the district and provide opportunities for collegial interaction.

Professional educators, and the public, must disabuse themselves of the idea that school improvement results from greater standardization, increased measures of accountability, prescriptive solutions to complex problems, or administrative directives.

In *The Changemasters* Rosabeth Moss Kanter, Yale sociologist and Fortune 500 consultant, describes the management ethos of six cutting-edge companies, examined for what they can teach us about emerging organizational forms. Whether "tin cupping" for support for an idea or innovation, or working with others in planning and development processes, the people featured in the narrative for each company are creative and collegial. They consider themselves engaged in a common enterprise that enlists their commitment and supports their involvement. Successful innovators appear to avoid voting and directing in favor of discussion and developing consensus. They model an equity and accessibility in organization and professional function that may better represent our real concern for social democracy than current patterns of organization in education provide.

Inasmuch as bureaucratic organization constrains real learning and frustrates efforts to create, innovate, or change, we have an administrative structure that is incompatible with an Age of Information. The rapid speed of change in our society argues for adaptability in organizational forms and fluidity in structural response to social needs. Entrenched operating procedures and outmoded, inadequate practices hamper internal opportunities for full and equitable access to knowledge and information.

Notes

1. David B. Tyack, *The One Best System: A History of American Urban Education* (Cambridge, Mass.: Harvard University Press, 1974), 39–59, 126–176.
2. Talcott Parsons, *Max Weber: The Theory of Social and Economic Organization*, trans. A. Henderson and T. Parsons (New York: Free Press, 1947), 330–334.
3. John R. Anderson, *The Architecture of Cognition* (Cambridge, Mass.: Harvard University Press, 1983), 292.
4. Howard Gardner, "Cognition Comes of Age," *Language and Learning* (Cambridge, Mass.: Harvard University Press, 1980), xxiv.
5. Jerome Kagan, *The Nature of the Child* (New York: Basic Books, 1984), 206.
6. Anderson, *The Architecture of Cognition.*
7. Jeannie Oakes, *Keeping Track: How Schools Structure Inequality* (New Haven: Yale University Press, 1985), 13.
8. Scott Miller, "The Educationally At Risk: A Look at Some Data," a presentation to the Committee for Economic Development Task Force for the Educationally Disadvantaged, September 23, 1986, 3 and 12.
9. Ibid., 15.
10. John I. Goodlad, *A Place Called School: Prospects for the Future* (New York: McGraw-Hill, 1984), 286.

Selected References

Anderson, John R. *The Architecture of Cognition.* Cambridge, Mass.: Harvard University Press, 1983.
Gardner, Howard. "Cognition Comes of Age." In *Language and Learning.* Cambridge, Mass.: Harvard University Press, 1980, xxiv.
Goodlad, John I. *A Place Called School: Prospects for the Future.* New York: McGraw-Hill, 1984.

Kagan, Jerome. *The Nature of the Child.* New York: Basic Books, 1984.

Kanter, Rosabeth Moss. *The Changemasters.* New York: Simon and Schuster, 1983.

Miller, Scott. "The Educationally At Risk: A Look at Some Data." A presentation to the Committee for Economic Development Task Force for the Educationally Disadvantaged, September 23, 1986.

Oakes, Jeannie. *Keeping Track: How Schools Structure Inequality.* New Haven: Yale University Press, 1985.

Parsons, Talcott. *Max Weber: The Theory of Social and Economic Organization.* Translated by A. Henderson and T. Parsons. New York: Free Press, 1947.

Tyack, David B. *The One Best System: A History of American Urban Education.* Cambridge, Mass.: Harvard University Press, 1974.

13.

Teacher Quality and Equality

LINDA DARLING-HAMMOND, WITH JOSLYN GREEN

Précis

Real educational accountability is the insistence that every day in every classroom there is a teacher with an adequate knowledge base and a sense of how to use that knowledge in ways that are responsive to the capacities and needs of the children in that classroom. The scarcity of such teachers may be the most serious barrier to genuinely reforming schools and providing all students with the kind of equitable access to knowledge that is the particular concern of this book.

Linda Darling-Hammond, writing with Joslyn Green, reflects on extensive research in order to identify the conditions, practices, and personnel patterns related to teaching that seem to militate against improving the school experiences of some children.

Their data suggest that the children most in need of skillful and sensitive teaching are the least likely to receive it. Poor black and Hispanic students, for example, are concentrated in central cities, where teacher shortages tend to be at least three times greater than in rural areas or suburbs. Long-standing policies and incentive structures in education maintain inequity in the system. For example, easier teaching assignments are among the few real incentives to staying in the profession, fostering teachers' movement away from urban schools to easier suburban assignments, and, within schools, from the lower to higher tracks, where both students and teachers are provided with greater resources and more stimulating experiences.

Various steps, some quite innovative and others previously endorsed by educators but rarely considered at policy levels for wide adoption, should be tried to effect change. Differentiated staffing should be reconsidered; new ideas to help beginning teachers, like "induction schools" where they could train for a year, also warrant support.

A necessary starting point for reform, the authors argue, is consensus that teaching is a profession. That is, members agree that they have a knowledge base, that what they know is directly related to good practice, that being prepared is essential to being a responsible practitioner, and that unprepared people will not be permitted to practice.

Advocacy of professional standards is premised in part on the belief that when minimum standards are adopted by any group—doctors, lawyers, accountants—it is those most neglected or least well-served by members of the professional group who benefit the most. It follows, then, that supporting professional standards for teachers should be a priority for practitioners and others interested in improving the caliber of instruction for all students.

Linda Darling-Hammond, formerly a researcher with the Rand Corporation, is now professor of educational policy at Teachers College, Columbia University. She is the author of numerous research reports and analyses related to school reform trends in the teaching force and differences in educational attainments among minority students.

Joslyn Green is a writer who has worked with the Rand Corporation, the Education Commission of the States, and other education organizations.

—The College Board

A s matters now stand, the students in greatest need of the best teaching are the least likely to get it. Because the qualifications and abilities of American teachers are substantially unequal, not all students receive the same caliber of instruction. Because the distribution of teacher quality is skewed toward those students who attend affluent, well-endowed schools, poor and minority students are chronically and disproportionately exposed to teachers with less training and experience. Perhaps the single greatest source of educational inequity is this disparity in the availability and distribution of highly qualified teachers.

Providing equity in the distribution of teacher quality requires changing policies and long-standing incentive structures in education. Preparing teachers to teach the children who need them the most also requires improving the capacity of all teachers—their knowledge and their ability to use that knowledge—by professionalizing teaching. Because the poor and less educated are most at the mercy of quacks and charlatans in any occupation, they benefit the most when professional standards rise. So, too, disadvantaged students will benefit the most when teachers as a group are better prepared.

This paper takes a closer look at each of these propositions, examining the evidence that supports them and exploring how they interlock. Taken all together, the propositions argue against policies that indulge bureaucratic impulses to compartmentalize the problems that confront at-risk students or to prescribe procedures for teachers to follow in classrooms. More important, they argue for policies that strengthen learning by strengthening the preparation of teachers and improving their chances of performing effectively in the classroom. If, in fact, the interaction between teachers and students is the most important aspect of effective teaching, then reducing inequality in learning has to rely on policies that professionalize teaching and provide equal access to competent teachers.

Greatest Need, Least Help

Neither the distribution of students nor the distribution of teachers is random across schools and districts in the United States. Poor and minority children are increasingly concentrated in central-city schools, where teacher shortages are most acute and underqualified entrants to teaching are most numerous.

According to data gathered for a recent Rand report on urban education (Oakes 1987, 2):

- By 1980, 81 percent of all blacks and 88 percent of Hispanics resided in metropolitan areas; 71 and 50 percent, respectively, lived in the inner cities.

- In 1980, 80 percent of low-income blacks and Hispanics were concentrated in the poorest neighborhoods, an increase of 40 percent since 1970.

- By 1980, minority children comprised the majority of students in most large urban districts. By 1984, most Hispanic and black students attended schools with nonwhite majority enrollments.
- By 1988, only 7 of the nation's 25 largest city school systems maintained a white enrollment of more than 30 percent.

Meanwhile, as the supply of teachers has dwindled over the past 15 years, teacher shortages have begun to reemerge and, as has been the case over much of the past century, they have affected urban schools most severely.

- In 1983, the most recent year for which national information is available, shortages of teachers—as measured by unfilled vacancies—were three times greater in central cities than in rural areas or suburbs, and much greater in large school districts (which are most often urban) than in small districts (National Center for Education Statistics 1985a) (see Figure 1).
- More than 14 percent of all newly hired teachers in central-city school districts in 1983 were uncertified in their principal field of assignment, nearly twice the proportion experienced by other types of districts (see Figure 2).

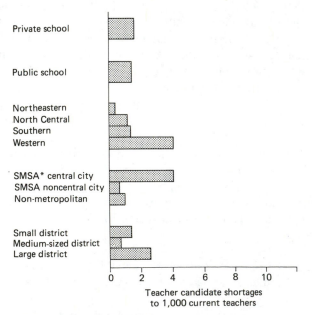

*Standard metropolitan statistical area.

Figure 1. Teacher candidate shortages. (*Source*: NCES 1985a.)

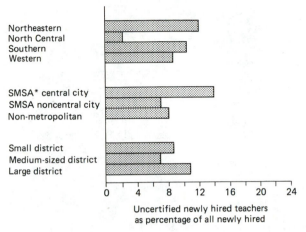

Figure 2. **Newly hired teachers uncertified in principal assignment field.** (*Source*: NCES 1985a.)

- The most severe shortages of teachers occurred in such fields as bilingual education and special education, fields that are in especially great demand in central cities; these fields are also among those with the highest proportions of uncertified teachers (see Figures 3 and 4).

- A survey of high school teachers in 1984 found that the schools where uncertified teachers were located were disproportionately central-city schools with higher-than-average percentages of disadvantaged and minority students (Pascal 1987: 24).

- In 1985, 5,000 teachers who did not meet the usual standards of training or preparation were hired on emergency certificates in New York, Los Angeles, and Houston alone. Many of these districts' vacancies were not filled when schools opened that fall (Darling-Hammond 1987a).

Teacher shortages subvert the quality of education in a number of ways. They make it difficult for districts to be selective in the quality of teachers they hire, and they often result in the hiring of teachers who have not completed (or sometimes even begun) their pedagogical training. In addition, when faced with shortages, districts must often hire short- and long-term substitutes, assign teachers outside their fields of qualification, expand class sizes, or cancel course offerings. No matter what strategies are adopted, the quality of instruction suffers.

Shortages of teachers are a serious problem wherever they occur; so are inadequately prepared teachers. But as we look at the types of students who are most likely to live in districts where shortages and poor preparation are

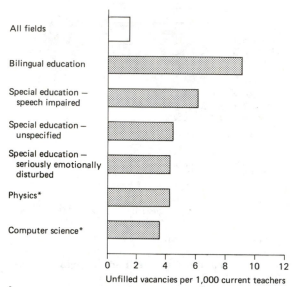

Figure 3. Fields with largest proportional teacher shortages. (*Source*: NCES 1985a.)

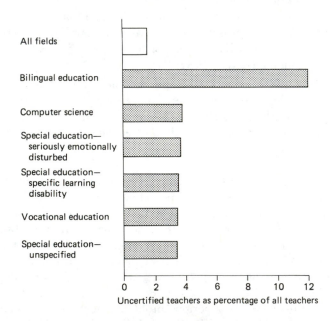

Figure 4. Fields with largest proportions of teachers uncertified. (*Source*: NCES 1985a.)

most common, we see that inequality of opportunity is, in general, not randomly distributed. It is, in general, the lot of the children who attend inner-city schools, and most of those children are black or Hispanic and poor.

As Watson and Traylor (1988: 26) put it:

> As the market model operates in education today, it is most often to the detriment of the poorer and predominantly minority districts and schools, where too many teachers teach in subject areas in which they are not certified or in subject areas where they have limited or no training. Working conditions, including salaries, are often less then optimum.

That description is a mild statement of the extent to which working conditions in urban schools are disincentives to teacher recruitment and retention. A recent study of urban schools by the Institute for Educational Leadership concluded that "Urban teachers . . . labor under conditions that would not be tolerated in other professional settings" (Corcoran, Walker, and White 1988). The study found substandard physical facilities; lack of space for storage and sometimes even classrooms; shortages of materials, supplies, and equipment; large classes; and inadequate support services. It's no wonder that many teachers try to teach elsewhere.

Why Teachers Are Distributed Unequally

As in most other occupations, the relative attractiveness of salaries, benefits, and other working conditions influences the availability of teaching talent to the occupation as a whole and to various employers within the occupational sector. Teachers are no exception, and the dramatic differences in salaries and working conditions across school districts explain much of the disparity in teacher supply between cities and their generally wealthier suburbs. However, teaching is somewhat unique in the paucity of rewards and incentives available during the course of a career. The flat salary and career structure in teaching provide little chance to "get ahead" financially or otherwise. School environments tend, as Phil Schlechty of the Greens Professional Development Academy in Louisville, Kentucky, often notes, to be among the few work settings in which "the only reward is the lack of punishment."

The Pecking Order

When well-prepared teachers are a scarce resource and the rewards for good teaching are few, teachers and principals come fairly quickly to the conclusion that easier teaching assignments are one of the few real incentives to staying in the profession. The result of an incentive structure that makes easier assignments virtually the only reward for seniority and skill is that beginning teachers pay their dues teaching the most challenging students in the tougher schools, then transfer out to schools (and, eventually, districts) where the working conditions are better and the students are easier to teach because they have been taught at home.

This informal system, which makes sense for experienced teachers, works out badly for the schools they leave behind and for the new teachers who replace them. For, in fact, most new teachers get hired into the most difficult schools, since those are the schools in which most vacancies occur.

Some schools hire almost no new teachers. Schools in advantaged suburban districts, for example, or in the outer ring of large urban districts tend to fill their vacancies from the list of experienced teachers who want to transfer. An alert principal finds out who are the good teachers on the list and recruits them. Once a teacher lands a good position in an advantaged school, he or she often does not leave until retirement. So the most advantaged schools tend to have both the most expert teachers and the fewest vacancies.

In the difficult schools, where the parade begins, the situation is reversed. In the inner-city schools that serve predominantly minority students and cannot offer competitive working conditions and salaries, turnover is high. The teachers sent to them either leave for other schools that seem to have more advantages or get so discouraged that they leave teaching entirely. Indeed, attrition rates for new teachers average between 40 and 50 percent over the first five years of teaching (Wise, Darling-Hammond, and Berry 1987; Grissmer and Kirby 1987).

Teacher shortages, like the one that is building now, exacerbate an already serious situation. When there is a teacher shortage, disadvantaged schools have to hire the new teachers that other schools would rather not take. Sometimes inner-city schools simply cannot fill vacancies with certified teachers. So they hire uncertified teachers, or they fill positions temporarily with short- or long-term substitute teachers. They expand classes and make do with fewer teachers. They cancel courses. They ask teachers to take on classes outside their fields of preparation.

Most schools do very little to structure support and training for beginning teachers, and what little they do is least sufficient in the schools that depend most on inexperienced teachers. In the best-case scenario some districts may have department chairs or resource teachers whom they can charge with responsibility for training beginning teachers. That system, whatever its other benefits or limitations, is woefully inadequate in a situation where, for example, a department chair has one period a day to supervise four beginning teachers and three teachers who are teaching out of their fields. Arrangements like this make successful induction least possible where it is most needed.

Why Tracking Persists

The same forces that produce the flow of good teachers to advantaged schools, and the ebb of good teachers from disadvantaged schools, are at work within schools wherever tracking persists. That good teachers are a scarce resource and that the rewards for good teaching are few are, in fact, among the reasons that tracking does persist, in the face of growing evidence that it does not particularly benefit high achievers and tends to put low achievers at a serious disadvantage. There are two major reasons for the persistence of this practice: one pertains to the kind and quality of preparation teachers receive generally; the other pertains to the allocation of teaching resources.

Managing a heterogeneous classroom requires training that relatively few teachers receive and skills that relatively few of them therefore acquire. It requires refined diagnostic ability. It requires a broad repertoire of teaching techniques and the ability to match techniques to varied learning styles and levels of knowledge. It requires skills in classroom management even more considerable than those required in a homogeneous classroom. Because relatively few teachers are prepared to manage heterogeneous classrooms effectively, tracking persists.

The second reason is that well-prepared, highly skilled teachers are a scarce resource, and scarce resources have to be allocated. Such resources tend to get allocated to the students whose parents, advocates, or representatives have the most political clout. This results, not entirely but disproportionately, in the best teachers teaching the best curricula to the most advantaged students. Evidence suggests that teachers themselves are tracked, with those judged to be the most competent and experienced assigned to the top tracks (Oakes 1986; Davis 1986; Findley 1984; Rosenbaum 1976).

The most vocal parents are successful in identifying and requesting the most reputable teachers for their children and in applying pressure for class changes or teacher transfers when teachers do not meet their expectations. Other children are assigned to novices or teachers who have not mastered the teaching techniques that would put them in high demand. As Oakes (1985) notes, students' assignments to tracks are fairly predictable:

> One finding about placements is undisputed. . . . Disproportionate percentages of poor and minority youngsters (principally black and Hispanic) are placed in tracks for low-ability or non-college-bound students (NCES 1985, Rosenbaum 1980); further, minority students are consistently underrepresented in programs for the gifted and talented (College Board 1985).

A more refined allocation of teaching resources is occurring now with the proliferation of gifted and talented programs across the country. Teachers who are among the most skilled are offering rich, challenging curricula to select groups of students, on the theory that only a few students can benefit from such curricula and teaching. Yet the distinguishing feature of programs for the gifted and talented frequently turns out to be not the difficulty of the work presented but the quality. Students in these programs are given opportunities to integrate ideas across fields of study. They are asked to think, write, create, develop projects. They are challenged to explore. Although, arguably, most students would benefit from being similarly challenged, the opportunity for this sort of schooling remains acutely restricted. In many instances the reason for the restriction is simply the scarcity of teachers who can teach in the fashion such curricula demand.

Meanwhile, as studies of classroom content have begun to discover, students placed in the lowest tracks or in remedial programs too often sit at their desks for long periods of time, matching the picture in column A to the word in column B, filling in the blanks, copying off the board. They work at a low cognitive level on boring tasks that are profoundly disconnected from the skills they need to learn. Rarely are they given the opportunity to talk about what they know, to read real books, to construct and solve problems in mathematics or science (Oakes 1985; Davis 1986; Metz 1978; Trimble and Sinclair 1986). If their teachers know no other ways to teach, and if their parents are not the highly educated and highly vocal sorts who loudly ask for transfers, what these students learn is quite different from what students learn in upper tracks.

Even within schools, then, good teaching is too often distributed unequally. The experienced teachers who are in great demand are rewarded with opportunities to teach the students who already know a lot. New teachers too often get assigned to the students and the classes that nobody else wants to teach, which leaves them practicing on the students who would benefit most from the skills of expert, experienced teachers.

How Teaching Expertise Matters

American school policy has often started from the assumption that teachers are conduits for policy or curricula rather than active agents in the production of learning. Consequently, many reform initiatives have emphasized improving schools by changing curricula, programs, tests, textbooks, and management processes rather than by improving the knowledge and capacity of teachers. Indeed, American policymakers seem to doubt whether there is anything that a teacher brings to the classroom other than the state's or school district's mandated materials, procedures, and regulations. They question whether teacher preparation is necessary and seem to believe that novice teachers are as safe and effective as experienced teachers. These beliefs support the myth that allows teaching expertise to be unequally distributed— the myth that all teachers and classrooms are equal.

Over the past 20 years, educational research has exploded the myths that any teaching is as effective as any other and that unequally trained and experienced teachers are equally advantageous to students. In a study documenting the positive effects of teaching experience on teaching effectiveness, Murnane and Phillips (1981: 453–454) note:

The question of whether teachers become more productive as they gain teaching experience has been of interest to policymakers for many years. One reason is that schools serving children from low-income families have typically been staffed with less experienced teachers than schools serving middle-class children. This has led to court tests of whether the uneven distribution of teaching experience constitutes discrimination against low-income children.

Having confirmed that teacher experience does make a difference, researchers are now identifying what it is that expert veterans do in the classroom that distinguishes their teaching from that of novices (see, e.g., Berliner 1986; Shulman 1987). Much of this research also demonstrates the importance of teacher education for the acquisition of knowledge and skills that, when used in the classroom, improve the caliber of instruction and the success of students learning (see, e.g., Berliner 1984).

In a striking illustration of how strongly preparation affects a teacher's style and presentation of content, Lee Shulman (1987) tells the story of "Colleen," an active and inventive teacher of literature, which she knew very thoroughly, but a petty tyrant when she had to teach grammar, which she felt she knew poorly. In her literature classes Colleen adopted a Socratic style that was rich, conceptual, wide-ranging, and responsive to the students. When she shifted to grammar lessons, she adopted a didactic, rote-oriented style of instruction to overcome her lack of self-confidence and her uncertainty about the content. In Admiral Farragut style ("damn the question, full speed ahead!"), her story illustrates how teaching style changes to become less effective pedagogically when teachers are less well prepared.

When the allocation of teachers who are certified or uncertified, prepared or unprepared, experienced or inexperienced is unequal, so is the opportunity for students to learn. The differences in style and content are not an abstract proposition; they are very real, and have clear consequences for children.

Fortunately, the incentive structure does not work completely. Fortunately, very talented people, motivated by their own commitment and desire to contribute, still choose to work with the students in greatest need of good teaching. But the odds are working against them, and the deck is stacked, for the most part, against their students.

Corollaries: Equity and Professionalism

A key corollary to this analysis of inequality is that improved opportunities for minority and low-income students will rest, in part, on the professionalization of teaching. There are two reasons for this assertion. First, the professionalization of an occupation raises the floor below which no entrants will be admitted to practice. It eliminates practices of substandard or irregular licensure that allow untrained entrants to practice disproportionately on underserved and poorly protected clients. Second, professionalization increases the overall knowledge base for the occupation, thus improving the quality of services for all clients, most especially those most in need of highly sophisticated teaching.

Analysts of the effects of professionalization in other occupations rightly observe that the imposition of new standards often initially restricts the supply of practitioners, boosts prices, and makes services to the poor more scarce (Watson and Traylor 1988; Larson 1977; Starr 1982). These effects are predictable in unregulated private markets and generally are overcome only by government action—such as federal programs over the last 20 years designed to induce physicians to settle in underserved areas, and government support for legal defense organizations that serve the poor. Over time, though, professionalization also increases the attractions of the occupation, producing, as we have seen more recently in law and medicine, an increase—even a surfeit—of willing *and* well-trained practitioners.

At the same time, less professionalized occupational structures do not ensure equality, and may, as in the case of teaching, exacerbate inequality in the long run. Poor and minority schools already experience the scarcity of teachers produced by low wages and poor working conditions. The current lack of meaningful standards in teaching only masks the shortages, it does not correct for them. The lack of investment in teacher knowledge detracts from the effectiveness and the satisfactions of teaching. The argument made here is that, on balance, a publicly regulated teaching profession can improve both the *quality* and *equality* of education by producing the knowledge base and the working conditions needed to ensure an adequate and steady supply of well-trained teachers to students whose life chances depend on them.

The students who currently have the poorest opportunities to learn will benefit the most from measures that raise the standards of practice of all teachers. The inner-city schools they attend are compelled by the current incentive structure to hire disproportionate numbers of substitute teachers, uncertified teachers, and inexperienced teachers, and they lack resources for mitigating the uneven distribution of good teaching. The student who lives with reasonably prosperous and well-educated parents in one of those suburbs justly famed for the excellence of its school system is for the most part insulated from the problems that plague teaching overall. Not so the black or Hispanic student placed on a low track in a beleaguered inner-city school. Least likely to benefit from present circumstances, that student is most likely to benefit from changed circumstances that improve the capacity of all teachers.

That, in general, the best teachers now teach students who need good teaching the least has another corollary, one that first affects teaching overall though it thereafter affects students: the standard of practice in a profession is most likely to rise when the structure of the profession encourages the people with the most energy, talent, and experience to tackle the toughest problems. For that structure tends to produce the new knowledge on which the progress of the entire profession depends. The most highly skilled surgeons do not generally perform routine tonsillectomies, for example, just as the ablest lawyers do not generally work on standard wills or contracts. They tend instead to work where the professional challenges are the greatest. For medicine and the law are structured so that working on the greatest challenges brings the greatest rewards. The results are not completely benign. In medicine, law, and other professions, services are not provided equally to all who need them. But good results extend beyond the experts' immediate clients to the profession at large, which is strengthened by each advance in knowledge.

In education, as we have seen, the incentive structure works in reverse. There are, however, signs of some change. Although disincentives to equality remain firmly in place in most school systems, some systems are experimenting with alternatives. In Charlotte-Mecklenberg, for example, and in Rochester, New York (both systems with career ladders), master teachers have agreed that teaching children in the schools that most need expert teaching is part of their privilege and their obligation. In such experiments, and in the policy changes they both incorporate and suggest, lies great hope for equalizing opportunities to learn.

The Case for Structural Change

In Charlotte-Mecklenberg, Rochester, Miami, Louisville, Cincinnati, and in a great many other places around the nation, new ideas for improving teaching have been initiated in recent years. For many reasons, this is a time of great ferment and of promising new beginnings in matters that affect the structure of teaching work and the transmission of teaching knowledge. Dissatisfaction with the status quo did not necessarily originate in concern for the special circumstances of minority students. Nonetheless, one of the most urgent reasons to change the status quo is that, as we have seen, current policies are not evenhanded. Were there no other reasons for making fundamental changes in teaching (though, of course, there are), that reason alone should be sufficient.

We would do well to remind ourselves of the inherently unequal effect of current policies whenever we consider the special circumstances of the students those policies put at greatest disadvantage. Current initiatives to create special labels and programs for "at-risk" children and youth are unlikely to succeed if they do not attend to the structural conditions of schools that place these children at-risk, not only from their home or community circumstances but from their school experiences as well. The pressures to respond to special circumstances with special programs are great, and the tradition of succumbing to those pressures is well established, in education as in other areas of national life. But special programs, with all their accoutrements of special rules, special procedures, special budgets, and special constituencies, will be insufficient in this instance as long as the status quo remains unchanged in more significant ways.

The changes that seem most likely to improve learning opportunities for disadvantaged students are those that restructure the way teachers prepare to teach, begin teaching, and are encouraged to teach well. It is important, especially for disadvantaged students, that changes in those areas build each teacher's capacity to acquire and use knowledge.

Improving Teacher Preparation

In the United States we have never supported teacher preparation very much or very well. In most universities, schools of education get the fewest resources. Even during those periods of intense interest in improving education that seem to occur about once a generation and in which we find ourselves at the moment, neither the federal government nor most states nor most school systems seem inclined to spend much money or attention on preparing teachers well. As Berliner (1984: 96) observes:

> It is time for creative thinking on how to revitalize teacher preparation programs. It is also time for budgetary allocations for such programs. Currently, we do not have much of either. At my own institution, the University of Arizona, we have found that it costs the state about $15,000 to educate a liberal arts undergraduate in, say, comparative literature, history, or psychology. To educate an individual for the vitally important profession of teaching, the state pays $2,000 less. . . . I am afraid that Arizona, like the 49 other states engaged in teacher preparation, gets precisely what it pays for.

One reason for this lack of support is a deeply felt ambivalence. Are there things to know about teaching that make teachers more effective? If so, teachers ought to learn those things. Or is teaching something that anyone can do without any special preparation? If so, anything that purports to be preparation is certainly not worth supporting. Clearly the tension between these two points of view, unresolved for the past 200 years, continues today. In some states, discussions of the importance of professionalizing teaching have led to new requirements for prospective teachers: take more courses, take different courses, pass tests. Meanwhile, though, 23 of the same states have reacted to potential shortages of teachers by setting up alternate routes to certification that bypass standard preparation. Furthermore, almost all states (46) have for many years allowed emergency credentialing.

The ambivalence would disappear if we were to conclude that teaching is, most accurately and appropriately, a profession rather than an occupation.

A profession is formed when members of an occupation agree that they have a knowledge base, that what they know relates directly to effective practice, that being prepared is essential to being a responsible practitioner, and that unprepared people will not be permitted to practice. This is not the place for a full-fledged discussion of why and how teaching should become a profession, a topic that has elsewhere begun to receive the attention it deserves (see, e.g., Darling-Hammond 1987b; Wise and Darling-Hammond 1987). But it is the place to acknowledge that professionalizing teaching would improve the preparation of teachers and also help change many of the other circumstances that now impede the progress of disadvantaged students.

As far as those students are concerned, ambivalence about whether teachers should be well prepared to teach is a luxury we can no longer afford. Improving education for minority students clearly requires policies that improve the preparation of teachers. The institutions that prepare teachers need the money it will take to produce knowledge about teaching and to create programs that effectively transmit that knowledge to the people who want to teach. Prospective teachers need money to support the cost of their education.

Interestingly, the federal government has used both these policy approaches to build medical education. The government has supported the efforts of medical schools to develop the capacity to produce and transmit knowledge. It has provided scholarships and loans for medical students. Now that the United States has perhaps the finest system of medical education in the world, the great debates of 80 or so years (see Starr 1982) have lost all but historical interest. But before medicine coalesced into a profession, back when people thought the doctor-to-be might as well learn just by following another doctor around, the debate raged. Was medical education necessary and desirable? Or should medical training be dispensed with in favor of the follow-me-around-in-the-buggy approach? The decision to formalize and strengthen medical education brought tremendous advances in knowledge. But perhaps the greatest benefit of setting standards of competence in medicine has been that the people who were least well served by doctors are now much better protected from quacks and charlatans and incompetents.

To general considerations of improving the preparation of teachers, we must add at least one consideration that relates directly, though not exclusively, to improving education for minority students. For many reasons, increasing the supply of well-prepared teachers who are themselves members of minority groups is vital. Teaching ought to reflect our population, as should all parts of our society, and the disinclination of nonminority teachers to work in inner-city schools makes the flow of minority teachers to those schools essential. Yet the schools of education in historically black colleges and universities, from which most black teachers have graduated, are facing great difficulties. Never well financed for the most part, these institutions are more poorly funded now than ever. Their education programs are in jeopardy in the several southern states that tie pass rates on tests of teacher competence to approval of teacher-education programs. (If at least 70 or 80 percent of the students in a program do not pass the state test, the state rescinds its approval of the program.) The irony is that very often the material tested is knowledge of subject matter or general knowledge taught outside the school of education, yet it is the school of education whose fate hinges on the test results.

A distinction needs to be drawn here that is often ignored. The distinction is that supporting the institutions that prepare teachers and supplying particular support for the ones that characteristically train most minority teachers is one policy, and testing teachers is another. For all the talk about the central importance of good teaching to good education, the first policy remains essentially untried. Supporting teacher education has simply not been a strategy that policymakers have yet been willing to adopt. Testing, on the other hand, has proved a popular policy; as currently practiced, it is a low-cost, easily mandated activity with immediate symbolic payoff to elected officials.

Blurring the distinction has some advantages, since testing teachers can thereby be seen as a vigorous attack on the problems of preparing teachers. Testing has other advantages. It costs states very little, especially since the people who take the tests pay for the privilege. A policy of testing teachers or applicants to education schools is also a highly visible policy, clear evidence of a willingness to act.

Testing could ultimately help to improve the preparation of teachers if the tests used measured what teachers actually need to know. Then the consequence might be to focus the efforts of schools of education and encourage them to do a more thorough job of preparation. But the tests that are currently available measure only basic skills and general knowledge. If they treat pedagogy at all, they treat it poorly. Tests like these do little to improve the education of teachers. They can only perform a screening function that is by and large unrelated to the potential effectiveness of the candidates who pass or fail them. In a wide-ranging review of the validity of currently used teacher tests, Haney, Madaus, and Kreitzer (1987: 227) conclude:

> These results indicate clearly that current teacher tests, and the manner in which cut-scores are being set on them, are differentiating among candidates far more strongly on the basis of race than they are on the basis of teaching quality. . . . This suggests to us a modest proposal: do not use such tests and cut-scores until it is clearly proven that these tests select among teacher candidates more on the basis of some independent measure of teacher quality than on the basis of race.

It's true that an all-out effort to improve the preparation of teachers would cost far more than simply testing teachers. But discussions of cost would more usefully be discussions of cost-effectiveness. We tend, in education, to see each suggestion for reform as discrete, as a program to add on here, a requirement to add on there, an allocation to add to the already-large sums of money being spent. But if we were instead to think strategically about reform, we would see that the money spent preparing teachers adequately is money that would not need to be spent thereafter to patch up the problems inadequate training creates.

Better Standards, More Often Met

As the preceding discussion begins to make apparent, improving teaching requires not only devoting more resources to the preparation of teachers but also developing meaningful standards for assessing preparation. It does no good, and potentially great harm, to assume that cut-off scores on multiple-choice tests of basic skills or of general knowledge set "standards" that measure teacher preparation in any meaningful way. Standards like that bear so little relationship to what teachers genuinely need to know that we might as well screen teachers on the basis of height.

Fortunately, many people are interested in finding more meaningful ways to test teachers and in developing the capacity of the teaching profession to establish meaningful standards for certification. Promising work is being done by the newly established National Teaching Standards Board, Lee Shulman and colleagues at Stanford, the Connecticut State Department of Education, and the Minnesota Board of Teaching in the development of more valid assessments of teaching.

Adding urgency to the search for better standards is the fact that current standards so clearly work against the interests of poorly served minority students. The standards we now have measure very little that relates to good teaching, and they screen out large proportions of the potential teachers who are likely to staff inner-city classrooms. The standards we need would force a more challenging and knowledge-based curriculum in teacher education and screen on more appropriate bases. The chances are good that standards that produced both those effects would also produce fewer disparities in test outcomes.

Setting standards is, of course, only half the battle. For whenever there are shortages of teachers, the temptation is to "solve" the shortage by filling classrooms with teachers who do not meet the standards. Too often unresisted in the past, that temptation is apparent today in the fact that 23 states have in the last few years set up alternative certification programs. If the myth were true—the myth that in public education all schools are equal, all classrooms are equal, all teachers are equal—then hiring teachers with substandard certification would indeed solve the shortage problem. But in fact the effect of lowering standards is to fill only some classrooms in some schools with less-qualified teachers.

We have here argued that substandard certification should be eliminated because it reduces the overall qualifications of the teaching corps. But what about the counterargument? What about shortages? If having too few teachers means canceling courses or increasing class sizes, won't that exacerbate problems in the inner-city schools where shortages will be the most acute?

To such very real problems, there are a variety of feasible solutions:

- *Financial strategies.* By improving school finance formulas so that resources are more evenly distributed, the schools that must now pay teachers lower salaries would be better able to compete for talent.

- *Incentives.* Among the incentives designed to make teaching in particular locations more attractive could be offers of special scholarships and loans to prospective teachers who agree to work in those locations.

- *Differentiated staffing.* Maintaining standards in the face of shortages would be possible if the additional staff for schools were not poorly prepared teachers hastily pressed into service but well-prepared instructors and aides whose responsibilities were more limited than a teacher's and who worked under direct teacher supervision. Instructors might be people who have a bachelor's degree but have not gone through a teacher-preparation program, for example; aides might, under the supervision of senior teachers, perform some of the more routine tasks of classroom management and record keeping. A senior teacher, like a registered nurse, would have more training and greater responsibilities than the educational equivalents of licensed practical nurses and hospital orderlies.

Differentiating staffing would require changes of other sorts. It would require breaking down the "egg-crate" classroom structure and changing the assumption that a single teacher must be solely responsible for teaching 30 children. It would require team teaching, so that senior teachers most competent to diagnose, assess, and decide could carry those heavy responsibilities for larger numbers of students, while being less directly involved with the more routine matters that occupy their assistants.

An entirely different, though complementary, approach to solving the problems that shortages present is only now becoming feasible. Consonant with the view that teachers were not all that important to schools, the federal government and state governments for many years collected so little data on the supply of teachers or the demand for them that predicting shortages was virtually impossible. As realization of the importance of having such data has grown, so has the possibility of predicting shortages with some accuracy. Prediction, of course, is a means, not an end. If a state can predict shortages of certain kinds of teachers, it should offer incentives to those kinds of teachers. It should strengthen the programs that prepare those kinds of teachers. It should increase the attractions of teaching in the places most likely to suffer shortages of those kinds of teachers.

Perhaps the biggest problem has been the failure to recognize that standards and shortages interrelate. Standards are simply not standards in any meaningful sense of the term if they are abrogated at the first signs of shortage; shortages remain shortages, of talent if not of warm bodies, when the people put in charge of classrooms cannot meet standards of good teaching. Once the problem is recognized, solutions can be created. Until it is recognized, the fact that classrooms have been inadequately staffed for some students for quite a long time is apt to remain education's dirty little secret.

More Help for New Teachers

On the first day of school, in the first week of school, throughout the first year of teaching at the very least, even a well-prepared and fully certified new teacher has a lot to learn. Although we all recognize the truth of this assertion—none of us more feelingly than new teachers themselves, and their students—there has been precious little organized help for beginning teachers. They have been left to sink or swim. As a result, well over a third of beginning teachers leave teaching within five years, most of them in the first year or two. Some beginners, through trial and error and luck and maybe a little help from their friends, learn to be effective teachers. The others learn how to get through the day. Needless to say, the results of this laissez-faire approach are least satisfactory to the students who most need teachers who know how to teach, not merely how to cope.

The good news is that help for beginning teachers may be on its way. Clinical experience is in some places becoming a more important part of training teachers in schools of education. Districts are also launching new teacher induction programs. One reason for setting up career ladders has been to make the expertise of master teachers available to less experienced teachers. An idea with great potential that is now moving from the discussion stage toward implementation is the notion of "professional development schools," schools in which beginning teachers would train for a year.

The state of Minnesota, for example, is about to require that all beginning teachers go through an internship very much like a residency in medicine. All new teachers will train their first year in professional development schools located in school districts but accredited by the State Board of Teaching, which is Minnesota's professional teaching standards board. The goal is to build a teaching force in which every single member has been explicitly taught how to base decisions on the best available knowledge and how to make decisions in the most responsible way. To give beginning teachers such an introduction to the profession, one that equips them with the tools they need thereafter, could cost about $10,000 per teacher (Wise and Darling-Hammond 1987). Over the course of the teacher's career and over the course of a child's education, that is a very small investment for a very substantial gain.

Less Turnover, Better Distribution

Although measures to improve the capacity of all students to acquire and use knowledge are central to improving education for disadvantaged minority students, reducing staff turnover in the schools that serve those students remains essential, as does attracting the best teachers to those schools.

One conceivable response, given the role that current transfer policies play in the flow of talented teachers to good schools and the ebb of talent from troubled schools, would be to disallow seniority-based transfers. Such a response alone would be counterproductive, however, since losing people from teaching altogether seems the likeliest result. But improving working conditions in the schools where they are now most dismal is a measure that would improve the retention of all teachers, while encouraging a more even distribution of good teaching. Having an office as well as an attractive, well-stocked classroom, being able to make a telephone call in privacy, and using a copying machine that works are accoutrements of work life that are as important to teachers as to anyone else. True, creating good working conditions comes at a cost. But so does failing to create them.

A Promising Prototype

In Rochester, New York, the school district in 1987 negotiated a contract with teachers that raises beginning salaries to $29,000 a year and top salaries to $70,000. Dramatic as those figures are, they are only part of the story, and perhaps not the most interesting part. For the heart of the matter in Rochester is the decision to combine the professionalization of teaching with an equalization of learning opportunities for students. Some of the money that supports the experiment has come from the state. But much of it is coming from the reallocation of resources within the district, on the grounds that money previously spent enforcing mandates is better spent attracting, developing, and retaining high-quality teachers.

The mechanisms interlock. A career ladder will allow expert veteran teachers to become master teachers, those who assume this title will be asked to use their energy and talent in the schools that now have the highest turnover and serve the least-advantaged students. Teachers have given up the limits on the working day and seniority transfer rights set in earlier contracts. (Transfers are still possible, but they will be granted on other grounds.) Meanwhile, teachers have gained concessions that professionalize their working conditions.

Some of the inner-city schools staffed by master teachers will also be professional development schools where incoming teachers are trained: the double goal is both to produce highly qualified teachers for schools throughout the system and to offer state-of-the-art education to children who have traditionally been the least well served. In theory, it is a privilege and an honor for the best teachers in Rochester to teach in these central-city schools. In practice, Rochester is recruiting teachers from suburban districts and even professors from the University of Rochester, not only because of the better salaries but also because of mounting enthusiasm to participate in this grand experiment.

The experiment suggests that the spiral of circumstances that usually leaves the students with greatest need least well served can be reversed in ways that benefit both teachers and students.

The Bottom Line

Until we can say that everyone who is teaching in a classroom has a base of knowledge and a sense of how to 'use that knowledge to make the decisions on which effective education depends, there is no real accountability in public education. Using test scores or credit hours or per-capita expenditures as measures of schooling does not get to the heart of the issue. The public education system ought to be able to guarantee that every child who is forced to go to school by public law—no matter how poor that child's parents are, or where that child lives, or how little or how much he or she has learned at home—is taught by someone who is prepared, knowledgeable, and competent. That is real accountability. When it comes to equalizing opportunities for students to learn, that is the bottom line.

References

Berliner, D. C. 1984. "Making the Right Changes in Preservice Teacher Education." *Phi Delta Kappan* 65: 94–96.

Berliner, D. C. 1986. "In Pursuit of the Expert Pedagogue." *Educational Researcher* 15: 5–13.

College Entrance Examination Board. 1985. *Equality and Excellence: The Educational Status of Black Americans.* New York.

Corcoran, Thomas B., Lisa J. Walker, and J. Lynne White. 1988. *Working in Urban Schools.* Washington, D.C.: Institute for Educational Leadership.

Darling-Hammond, Linda. 1984. *Beyond the Commission Reports: The Coming Crisis in Teaching.* Santa Monica, Calif.: Rand.

Darling-Hammond, Linda. 1987a. "What Constitutes a 'Real' Shortage of Teachers?" Commentary. *Education Week* 6: 29.

Darling-Hammond, Linda. 1987b. "Teacher Professionalism: Why and How." Paper prepared for the New York City Commission on Professionalizing Teaching.

Davis, Donna G. 1986. "A Pilot Study to Assess Equity in Selected Curricular Offerings across Three Diverse Schools in a Large Urban School District: A Search for Methodology." Paper presented at the Annual Meeting of the American Educational Research Association, San Francisco.

Dreeben, Robert. 1987. "Closing the Divide: What Teachers and Administrators Can Do to Help Black Students Reach Their Reading Potential." *American Education:* Winter: 28–35.

Findley, M. K. 1984. "Teachers and Tracking in a Comprehensive High School." *Sociology of Education* 57: 233–243.

Grissmer, D. W., and S. N. Kirby. 1987. *Teacher Attrition: The Uphill Climb to Staff the Nation's Schools.* Santa Monica, Calif.: Rand.

Haney, W., G. Madaus, and A. Kreitzer. 1987. "Charms Talismanic: Testing Teachers for the Improvement of American Education." In *Review of Research in Education*, 14. Washington, D.C.: American Educational Research Association.

Larson, Magali S. 1977. *The Rise of Professionalism: A Sociological Analysis.* Berkeley: University of California Press.

Metz, M. H. 1978. *Classrooms and Corridors: The Crisis of Authority in Desegregated Secondary Schools.* Berkeley, Calif.: University of California Press.

Murnane, R. J., and Barbara R. Phillips. 1981. "Learning by Doing, Vintage, and Selection: Three Pieces of the Puzzle Relating Teaching Experience and Teaching Performance." *Economics of Education Review* 1: 453–465.

National Center for Education Statistics. 1985a. *The Condition of Education.* Washington, D.C.: U.S. Department of Education.

National Center for Education Statistics. 1985b. *High School and Beyond: An Analysis of Course-Taking Patterns in Secondary Schools as Related to Student Characteristics.* Washington, D.C.: U.S. Government Printing Office.

Oakes, Jeannie. 1985. *Keeping Track: How Schools Structure Inequality.* New Haven: Yale University Press.

Oakes, Jeannie. 1987. "Tracking in Secondary Schools. A Contextual Perspective." *Educational Psychologist* 22:129–53.

Oakes, Jeannie. 1987. *Improving Inner-City Schools: Current Directions in Urban District Reform.* Center for Policy Research in Education Joint Note Series. Santa Monica, Calif.: Rand.

Pascal, Anthony. 1987. *The Qualifications of Teachers in American High Schools.* Santa Monica, Calif.: Rand.

Rosenbaum, J. E. 1976. *Making Inequality: The Hidden Curriculum of High School Tracking.* New York: Wiley.

Rosenbaum, J. E. 1980. "Social Implications of Educational Grouping." In *Review of Research in Education*, edited by D. C. Berliner, Vol. 8, 361–401. Washington, D.C.: American Educational Research Association.

Shulman, Lee S. 1987. "Knowledge and Teaching: Foundations of the New Reform." *Harvard Educational Review* 57: 1–22.

Snider, William. 1987. "Study Examines Forces Affecting Racial Tracking." *Education Week* 7: 1, 20.

Starr, Paul. 1982. *The Social Transformation of American Medicine.* New York: Basic Books.

Trimble, K., and R. L. Sinclair. 1986. "Ability Grouping and Differing Conditions for Learning: An Analysis of Content and Instruction in Ability-Grouped Classes." Paper presented at the annual meeting of the American Educational Research Association, San Francisco.

Watson, Bernard C., and Fasaha M. Traylor. 1988. "Tomorrow's Teachers: Who Will They Be, What Will They Know." In *The State of Black America.* N.Y.: National Urban League.

Wise, Arthur E., Linda Darling-Hammond, and Barnett Berry. 1987. *Effective Teacher Selection: from Recruitment to Retention.* Santa Monica, Calif.: Rand.

Wise, Arthur E., and Linda Darling-Hammond. 1987. *Licensing Teachers: Design for a Teaching Profession.* Santa Monica, Calif.: Rand.

14.

Educators for a Truly Democratic System of Schooling

CHARLES M. HODGE

Précis

The major shortcoming of teacher-training institutions today is their failure to devise a curriculum that produces teachers with the awareness, understanding, and skill necessary to deal successfully with students from diverse cultural backgrounds and students whose ways of learning differ. Teachers should have a broad and varied repertoire of instructional approaches with which they can respond appropriately to the needs of particular students.

Given the evident necessity for those connected with teacher education to join in an effort to advance equity in education, Charles Hodge claims it is time to move beyond the two conflicting views of teacher training. According to one view, the education of teachers should be weighted heavily toward the liberal arts disciplines, whereas the other emphasizes pedagogy provided in a school of education. Instead of remaining bogged down in old arguments about the mix of general education, pedagogy, and clinical practice, today's focus should be on how teachers can best learn about and become skillful in dealing with individual differences, the effects of cultural and socioeconomic circumstances, and other personal factors that affect the ways students learn. If there are to be enough teachers qualified to equalize opportunity in elementary and secondary schools in America, Hodge asserts, the curriculums of the schools of education must be shaped by the valuing of equity as a first priority—a vision of equity that requires teachers to understand and respond to students rather than requiring students to accommodate themselves to the patterns and prejudice of teachers. A new teacher-training process must be developed through collaborative effort between the schools and institutions of higher learning. Simply changing certification requirements is insufficient for educating equitably.

Charles Hodge is dean of the College of Education and Human Development at Lamar University in Texas. He was previously dean of the College of Education at the University of Central Arkansas, and assistant director for research and planning in the Arkansas Department of Education.

—*The College Board*

The need for better schools has arisen once again as a national priority. With parents now a minority group, many citizens are diffident when it comes to educational improvement. But political and business leaders have kept concern alive with slogans such as "Better schools mean better jobs."

The pattern of attention parallels that of the years immediately following the launching of Sputnik in 1957. First the spotlight focused on inadequate schools. Then it broadened to encompass teacher education. Most states either have passed legislation in recent years addressed to standards for teachers and teacher education or are in the process of doing so.

Teachers perform the pivotal role in eliminating significant barriers to access to knowledge. In accord with our democratic principles, access and equity that lead to acceptable student learning are central expectations of the schooling process. Although there exist unresolved societal circumstances that impinge on the ability of schooling to be successful in achieving desired goals, those barriers that exist within the domain of schooling must be removed by the profession associated with the educational enterprise. The barrier removal process should be supported by enabling policies established at the state and local levels. The education of the teacher in support of achieving educational access and equity for students is certainly a domain within the purview of the profession. The teacher who is unable to respond to the dynamic changes that continue to have an impact on the schooling process is, in fact, a significant barrier to students' access to knowledge.

The National Debate over Teacher Education

A central issue of educating the educator is revealed by the conflict between those who argue that a general education and knowledge of a discipline represent the exclusive preparation for a teaching position, and those who support a balance of general education and professional knowledge.[1] Most teacher educators take the latter position, and maintain the importance of a common body of knowledge representing the art and science of teaching that should be acquired by prospective teachers. Cruickshank distinguishes between the two positions:

> General education is one of several terms used to define the education that is purported to be of value to all persons. Professional education, on the other hand, is used to define the education needed to practice in a particular profession. In education it is referred to as pedagogy of the art and science of teaching.[2]

Efforts have been made to accommodate the differences between the two positions. Even though academicians have held steadfast to the general education–discipline position, current reform in teacher education, in fact, represents conciliatory efforts by teacher educators to rethink their position on the total teacher-education curriculum. The education reform movement has produced recommendations that would significantly reduce pedagogy and increase liberal arts content, lengthen the number of years required to complete a program, and revitalize the content of the professional knowledge component, to name a few. The findings of the National Commission on Excellence in Education[3] provided a new impetus for teacher educators, individually and collectively, to seize the opportunity to put forward a different agenda for the preparation of prospective teachers.

In the main this different agenda has focused on establishing purported higher standards for individuals entering and exiting teacher-preparation programs. The reform movement gives considerable attention to requiring prospective teachers to successfully complete various tests, maintain a recommended grade point average, and complete an increased number of courses in the liberal arts as prerequisites for admission to and the completion of teacher-education programs. Usually all of this is recommended to the exclusion of proposing a comprehensive approach for fundamentally changing the total environment of the schooling process.

A representative sampling of different approaches to preparing prospective teachers comes from a variety of sources. In 1982 the National Education Association recommended, "All teacher education programs should have three integrated components: liberal arts, at least one subject or teaching level speciality, and a professional curriculum."[4] While an identified balance between liberal arts and professional education is not recommended, the Association offers standards and requirements for the professional knowledge component.

The National Commission for Excellence in Teacher Education offered its recommendations in 1985. The Commission's report, *A Call for Change in Teacher Education*, takes a strong position on the importance of the inclusion of a liberal education in the teacher-education program. The Commission's position on academic concentration and liberal education created disagreement among Commission members as to whether such an emphasis could or should be achieved in the traditional four-year undergraduate program. On the issue of liberal education, the Commission sets forth a comprehensive approach:

> All teacher education students should continue to meet at least as extensive general or liberal education requirements as other students in the college or university they attend. Liberal education should be a cohesive, planned program—not merely an accumulation of courses scattered across a number of departments. Among the courses that should be included are sociology, anthropology, and psychology, which should foster an appreciation of different cultures and heritages. Teachers also need both knowledge and understanding of literature, history, language, and the arts. All teachers need to understand the context of their world; and they must profoundly value learning, ideas, and artistic expression.[5]

A report issued by the Task Force on Teaching as a Profession, Carnegie Forum on Education and the Economy, is equally supportive of a strong liberal arts component of the teacher-education program. The Task Force, in recommending a bachelor's degree in the arts and sciences as a prerequisite for the professional study of teaching, asserted:

> Four years of college education is not enough time to master the subjects to be taught and acquire the skills to teach them. The undergraduate years should be wholly devoted to a broad liberal education and a thorough grounding in the subjects to be taught. The professional education of teachers should therefore take place at the graduate level. An alternative might be to combine the undergraduate program and a graduate program, awarding both the bachelor's degree and the graduate degree. In either case, states and higher education institutions should abolish the bachelor's degree in education.[6]

The Holmes Group calls for "dramatic changes in education as a field of study."[7] Central to the Group's recommendations is the elimination of the undergraduate education major accompanied by a revision of the teaching subject content. Prospective teachers are to study with college instructors who model the best elements of good teaching and provide the structure for a thorough intellectual understanding of a discipline.

If all these proposals were put together in the programs of the 1,300 institutions in the United States now preparing teachers, they could together provide fundamental restructuring. To date, however, such reform is at the level of rhetoric; reality lags far behind.

The Traditional Approach to Teacher Education

Without doubt, the traditional approach to preparing prospective teachers has not reached the desired potential. John I. Goodlad surveyed the situation and observed, "Teacher education programs are disturbingly alike and almost uniformly inadequate."[8] James D. Koerner, a quarter of a century ago, charged that "education as an academic discipline has poor credentials. Relying on other fields, especially psychology, for its principal substance, it has not yet developed a corpus of knowledge and technique of sufficient scope and power to warrant the field's being given full academic status."[9] The traditional questions remain: To what extent is liberal education to be included in the curriculum? Are liberal-education requirements to be taught in arts and sciences departments by arts and sciences faculty? Is there a sufficiently established body of knowledge that legitimizes the professional education component?

By 1950 teacher-education programs had emerged in most of the country as four-year programs, and a multicomponent curriculum pattern had been established. The curriculum of the traditional teacher-education program has usually had three components: general education—courses in subject areas to be taught by prospective teachers; professional education—courses on foundations, teaching and learning theory; and clinical and field-based teaching experience. Generally, this teacher-education pattern remains intact today and continues to be a source of concern, investigation, and even ridicule.

Despite the efforts to include more provision for the liberal arts, the persistent criticism remained: "The trouble is that our teachers come out of the teachers colleges, where they spend all their time telling the students how to teach. We ought to be getting our teachers from the liberal arts colleges, where they get a broad general education and have good solid work in a major, so that they come out knowing something."[10] Education courses (the professional education component) have been described as puerile, repetitious, dull, and ambiguous, and as resulting in intellectual impoverishment.[11] In his analysis of the traditional teacher-education program, James B. Conant found considerable variation in the prospective teachers' exposure to general-education courses and, more important, a lack of consensus among teacher educators on the amount of professional-education courses needed. He observed:

> All the programs I have examined include a study of educational psychology, at least one course in methods, and one course that treats historically or philosophically the relation of the school to society. In every institution some practice teaching is specified. But here the uniformity ends.[12]

The traditional teacher-education program represents a kind of standoff between teacher educators and academicians. The unsigned truce has resulted in a degree of surrender, in form at least, to the clamor for an increased emphasis on general education in the teacher-education curriculum. Meanwhile, some teacher educators are rethinking the content of the professional body of knowledge associated with the art and science of teaching. The results to date have produced a scattered approach that has not silenced the critics or produced the teachers needed for today's classrooms.

The Equity Crisis

Teacher-education programs are seriously in need of positive change. Special attention should continue to be given to determining the role of general education and the identification and expansion of the body of knowledge identified as professional. In view of the large number of reports and miscellaneous recommendations tending to prolong the debate over pedagogy and general education, it is likely that an uneasy truce will continue. At present, however, the attack on education courses is as intense as it has ever been. The truce is, in fact, a surrender by those who prepare educators. The perpetuation of the current situation is to the detriment of equitable educational opportunities for America's youth.

The general debate overlooks and obscures the critical issues of educational equity discussed in preceding chapters. For example, teachers continue to be prepared without a serious focus on what is now known about intelligence and the effect culture and socioeconomic circumstances have on the learning styles and abilities of students. As a result, teachers are prepared for a mythical, culturally homogeneous, school setting. They are prepared to teach only in the more homogeneous school of the past.[13]

This miseducation of educators is a contributor to a major educational crisis of today: the absence of educational equity in the schooling process. Schooling that provides positive educational opportunities for all students should be at the center of the current teacher-education reform movement. A victory requires that the reform debate shift from a "more" to a "different" stance. The crisis demands that teacher-education preparation programs give more attention to different conceptualizations of liberal arts and pedagogy, not just to any general education. The debate and the reform must shift to the teaching and learning occurring in the classroom, the place where the crisis surfaces.

The manifestation of the absence of equity in the classroom is clear. The decline of diversity within the teaching profession and the failure of teacher-education programs to prepare teachers who understand the impact of cultural diversity on the teaching-learning process compound the crisis. The absence of equity precipitated by insensitive teaching strategies in the classroom has resulted in high dropout rates and low academic achievement among elements of a culturally diverse student population. There are not only at-risk students but at-risk schools which, in turn, are producing a nation of functional or marginal illiterates.

Beyond the general education–pedagogy debate, the forward thrust and ultimate victory of teacher-education reform will derive from preparing prospective teachers who have sensitive understanding of the extent to which students' cultural differences and varied learning styles have an impact on learning itself. Thus the first step toward achieving educational equity for all students must be taken by teacher educators.

And these teacher educators must include educators in the schools who deal on a daily basis with the problems and issues. The profession as a whole must promote and shape school–university partnerships. Access and equity are promoted through efforts at school renewal. Prospective teachers, as a part of their program of preparation, should understand that ongoing school renewal contributes to improving the schools' learning climate for students.

The limited attention given to equity and school renewal by the educational reform movement is both alarming and frustrating. Legal and policy mandates designed to ensure access and equity are, at best, only the preliminaries. In the final analysis the classroom teacher must be the facilitator so that the promise of equity results in tangibly improving the academic achievements of all students. The essential factor in the education experience for the future teacher remains the process and content of teaching and learning. This educational experience rests on the quality of the interactions between students, teachers, and subject matter. Attention to equity is too often missing from such interactions. A study by the Board of Inquiry Project, National Coalition of Advocates for Students, describes the need:

> Ultimately the curriculum and teaching practices of the school must be measured against the purposes of the instruction itself. If students are to become resourceful, independent, tolerant people, capable of living and working in a multicultural society, the curriculum and teaching practices of the school must reflect those aims.[14]

It is crucial to educate teachers who have an understanding of the diverse array of experiences represented by the school population. Within the past ten years, the number of minority students in the public schools has increased significantly. The increase will continue. Conversely, the representation of diversity within the teaching profession has decreased significantly. It is projected that by the year 2000 a third of the public school students will be black or Hispanic.[15] Representation of these minorities in the teaching force could be only 10 percent or less. Further, a fourth of the students from inner-city schools are products of homes where the income level is well below the poverty level. Further evidence of the crisis is provided:

> The largest numbers of illiterate adults are white, native-born Americans. In proportion to population, however, the figures are higher for blacks and Hispanics than for whites. Sixteen percent of white adults, 44 percent of blacks, and 56 percent of Hispanic citizens are functional or marginal illiterates. Figures for the younger generation of blacks are increasing. Forty-seven percent of all black seventeen-year-olds are functionally illiterate. That figure is expected to climb to 50 percent by 1990.[16]

Such students have high dropout rates and a high rate of school failure.[17] In the pursuit of equity, a conclusion of the College Board is significant:

> Of paramount importance is the content and substance of education received by black students. Although finances and broad program supports cannot be ignored, in the final analysis it is the interaction that goes on between students and teachers in individual schools and classrooms that defines educational quality and equality. Subtle and not-so-subtle differences in curriculum, course content and teaching methods, the qualifications and commitment of school personnel, and the opportunities for innovation and enrichment at the school site ultimately determine which students will receive a true education and which will merely be trained to assume a permanent role in the nation's underclasses.[18]

It is clear that the crisis in education today is centered on the absence of equity for the students purportedly served, but this absence of equity is only dimly perceived. As a step toward resolving this crisis, teacher educators must establish an agenda for victory. Teacher-education programs must prepare teachers who, by knowledge and skills, are committed to achieving equity for each student.

It is appropriate for the profession, as Asa Hilliard suggests, to address the achievement of equity in the school setting by using collective influence to ensure an ethnically diverse teaching corps, to redefine the liberal arts and pedagogy curricula so that they are devoid of ethnic bias, and to identify and use as models those teachers who, through appropriate strategies and behaviors, have been successful in working with at-risk students.[19] The Hilliard approach permits the profession to utilize a redesign of the teacher-education process to prepare teachers who are sensitive to the differences between students.

Teacher-education programs continue to prepare prospective teachers who tolerate discrimination and unequal treatment of students. Teacher-education programs fail to provide the various teaching strategies and behaviors that appropriately compensate for inherent cultural and ethnic bias in the teaching corps. As a part of the curricula, general education, and pedagogy, teacher-education programs must adopt the goal of preparing prospective teachers who accept a positive attitude toward students regardless of ethnic or socioeconomic background. The general-education component must support the achievement of this goal. That is to say, prospective teachers must know the extent to which cultural values and judgments have an impact on learning and be prepared to use appropriate teaching strategies. The teacher-education curriculum must have a theoretical and philosophical base relating to the impact of culture on learning development. The curriculum must give evidence of recognizing an understanding and appreciation of cultural diversity and richness. The prospective teacher must be prepared, then, to recognize and deal constructively with the ways schools structure inequality.

Facing up to Deficiencies in Teacher-Education Programs

Unfortunately, although there is useful research on elements of teacher education and teacher-education programs, there has not been a comprehensive nationwide study of institutional practices since those of Conant and Koerner, both in 1963. The answers to the questions posed below must come from institutional self-study designed to effect change. Currently, Goodlad and his associates are seeking answers to these and other questions in a study focused on a representative sample of colleges and universities selected from eight regions of the United States.[20] Until their data are available, it is necessary to respond in the light of personal experience, enlightened by the pieces of research evidence available.

To what extent do future teachers engage in serious reading, reflection, and discourse regarding the principles on which our democratic society is based and the role of schools in forwarding them? I doubt that their intellectual encounters are more than superficial, when one considers either their general- or professional-education program. Most institutions set forth an array of general-education choices; few specify a preteacher-education curriculum ensuring the implied studies. Ernest Boyer addresses the chronic problems of agreeing on a core, given the special interests that are brought to bear in defining such and the fragmentation of current undergraduate curricula.[21] Courses in the historical and philosophical foundations of education, once common to teacher education, where areas neglected in general education might be addressed, have disappeared or are optional today in many teacher-education programs. One grows uneasy about the answers to this question likely to be turned up through analyses of the college curriculum of future teachers.

To what extent do future teachers address in their professional curricula the issues of equity regarding access to knowledge? Again, one grows uneasy over the decline of education courses most likely to provide the implied intellectual encounters. And these issues are not likely to be the subject matter of their general-education courses.

To what extent do teacher-education curricula ensure the observation of and experience in several different settings where cultural diversity will be encountered? My experience suggests that one simply cannot assume the provision of such experiences either before or during student teaching. Few nonurban teacher-preparing institutions send their student teachers to observe and practice-teach in city schools.

Are urban colleges and universities attracting into their teacher-education programs a significant proportion of minority students—commensurate, let us say, with the proportion of minority children and youth in the surrounding schools? The answer here is a clear "no." Indeed it is not at all uncommon for schools and colleges of education to enroll a significantly smaller proportion of minority students than are enrolled in the institution as a whole.

To what extent are minority role models numbered among the faculty of schools and colleges of education attracting or potentially in a position to attract large numbers of minority students? Again, the answer is likely to be discouraging. For example, in teacher-preparing institutions that once were balanced in white and black enrollment but that are now mostly or all black, the faculty frequently is predominantly white. Our society simply has not made teaching attractive to those members of minority groups who have done well in the educational system. If they aspire to and ultimately attend colleges and universities, other occupations beckon. The sad story of seeking and failing to attract an adequate supply of able white students into teaching is now being reported with a vengeance in regard to minorities.

To what extent are universities and school districts, with strong encouragement and support from state legislatures and the business community, joined in addressing the inequities in schooling so that future teachers will be inducted into fully equitable school conditions? The concept of such partnerships currently is in vogue. But Goodlad and his associates, who have been seriously involved in promoting and developing school–university partnerships for the simultaneous improvement of schooling and the education of educators, speak at least as much to the difficulties as to the successes. In a book addressing fundamental principles of collaboration, which includes several case studies, Goodlad and Sirotnik conclude with some sobering comments on how difficult it is to get the diverse parties into a serious, rock-hard agenda.[22]

If questions such as these fail to produce strongly affirmative answers, institution by institution, we should not be surprised to learn that teacher-preparing institutions are not producing individuals who are sensitive to and knowledgeable about pervasive inequities in the conduct of schooling. Nor should we be surprised that our schools perpetuate practices that effectively bar some students from the knowledge and skills they need in order to be effective workers, parents, and citizens. We can be outraged, but shouldn't be surprised, at realizing that large segments of our society could not care less.

As stated earlier, the somewhat pedantic and polarized debate over the need for general and professional studies in the teacher-education curriculum goes on, as it has throughout this century.[23] It is time for each teacher-preparing institution to ask itself questions such as the foregoing and to keep asking them until strongly positive answers are forthcoming.

Conclusion

Reforms of teacher education have perpetuated the debate between the teacher educator and the academician. The conflict has centered on accommodating the belief that teacher education is singularly better served by the inclusion of more liberal arts courses in the curriculum. This debate and the process of improving teacher education have generally ignored the major crisis confronting education: the absence of equity, permitting the outcomes of schooling to be vastly different and unequal for students from various ethnic and cultural groups.

If schooling is to be a more equitable process enabling students to achieve to maximum capacity, a complete reconceptualization of the teacher-education program is required. The redesigned program should recognize the important role the teacher performs in achieving equity in the school setting. In fact the redesigned program must be predicated on the belief that the extent to which equity has not been achieved is due in large part to miseducation of the educator.

Member institutions of the Holmes Group should accept as a primary goal the design of a reconceptualized teacher-education program.[24] The resources of these institutions should be put to productive use by seeking realignment of the liberal-arts curriculum in support of a restructured content of professional pedagogy. The Holmes Group can best serve the reform movement by adding to the body of knowledge that enhances the profession's understanding of the dynamics of the schooling process.

Programs that educate educators must include strategies designed to effect school renewal. Such an approach requires collaborative agreements and the creation of university–school partnerships in support of simultaneously renewing schools and restructuring teacher education.

In the pursuit of equity, the responsibilities of other stakeholders in the educational enterprise must not be diminished or ignored. Officials of the national, state, and local governmental and policy-making structures must be held accountable for actions or omissions that impede the quest for equity in the schooling process. Public policy must enable teacher-education programs to evolve from research, collaboration, and the identified needs of the profession, rather than from state-licensing requirements.

To be sure, parents are not innocent, uninvolved observers in the development of a responsive education system. Parents and other stakeholders whose attitudes are reflected in the school and classroom environment must cooperate and work in tandem with the essential agents for change—teachers. It is obvious that a shared sense of purpose must exist in the interrelationships within the larger community. The pursuit of equity, then, must be viewed within the context of the social, political, economic, and professional pressures that can be brought to bear on formulating and implementing strategies for establishing public policy that fosters school renewal guided by our democratic ideals.

The reform victory will require the emergence of a new philosophy that gives structure and substance to preparing teachers to serve the diverse population of students who comprise the majority of America's schools now and into the next century. The future challenge to the profession does not rest on convincing detractors of the worthiness of professional pedagogy. The future of our social structure is dependent on the extent to which the education of educators results in teachers who promote and achieve equity in the teaching–learning environment of schools and classrooms.

Notes

1. For an overview of the issue in the historical context and a discussion of the call for a "truce among educators," see James B. Conant, *The Education of American Teachers* (New York: McGraw-Hill, 1963), 1–14.

2. Donald B. Cruickshank, *Models for the Preparation of America's Teachers* (Bloomington, Ind.: Phi Delta Kappa Educational Foundation, 1984), 4.

3. National Commission on Excellence in Education, *A Nation at Risk: The Imperative for Education Reform* (Washington, D.C.: Government Printing Office, 1983).

4. National Education Association, *Excellence in Our Schools, Teacher Education: An Action Plan* (Washington, D.C.: 1982), 10.

5. National Commission for Excellence in Teacher Education, *A Call for Change in Teacher Education* (Washington, D.C.: American Association of Colleges for Teacher Education, 1985), 11.

6. Task Force on Teaching as a Profession, *A Nation Prepared: Teachers for the 21st Century* (New York: Carnegie Forum on Education and the Economy, 1986), 3.

7. The Holmes Group, *Tomorrow's Teacher* (East Lansing, Mich.: Holmes Group, 1986), 14.

8. John I. Goodlad, *A Place Called School: Prospects for the Future* (New York: McGraw-Hill, 1984), 315.

9. James D. Koerner, *The Miseducation of American Teachers* (Boston: Houghton Mifflin, 1963), 17.

10. Conant, *The Education of American Teachers*, 73.

11. Koerner, *The Miseducation of American Teachers*, 18.

12. Conant, *The Education of American Teachers*, 125.

13. As compared to those of today, the schools of the 1950s and earlier were much different places. In the South schools were still racially segregated by law. Nationwide, student attendance zones were closely tied to the neighborhood pattern and schools were viewed as an extension of the value system of the community. With the advent of desegregation, the growth of schooling as big business, changing neighborhood patterns, the requirement for racially balanced schools, and cross-district busing, schooling in America became a complex bureaucracy. The effect has been to destroy the sense of racial, cultural, ethnic, and values compatibility that existed within the school and within the schooling process. Teacher-education programs did not keep pace in preparing teachers for this restructured school environment.

14. Board of Inquiry Project, *Barriers to Excellence: Our Children at Risk* (Boston: National Coalition of Advocates for Students, 1985), 49.

15. I. McNett, *Demographic Imperatives: Implications for Educational Policy*, 1983, as cited in Martha L. Bell and Catherine V. Morsink, "Quality and Equity in the Preparation of Black Teachers," *Journal of Teacher Education* 37 (March-April 1986): 16.

16. H. Levin, *The Educationally Disadvantaged: A National Crisis*, 1985, as cited in Bell and Morsink, "Quality and Equity," 16.

17. For an analysis of illiteracy in America, see Jonathan Kozol, *Illiterate America* (Garden City, N.Y.: Doubleday, 1985), 4.

18. The College Board, *Equality and Excellence: The Educational Status of Black Americans* (New York: College Entrance Examination Board, 1985), 4.

19. Asa Hilliard, "Education Equity: What Does the Future Hold?" Paper presented at the annual meeting of the American Association of Colleges for Teacher Education, Washington, D.C., 1987.

20. For an overview, see John I. Goodlad, "Studying the Education of Educators: Values-Driven Inquiry," *Phi Delta Kappan* 70 (no. 2): 104–11.

21. Ernest L. Boyer, *College: The Undergraduate Experience in America* (New York: Harper and Row, 1987). See in particular Chapter 6.

22. Kenneth A. Sirotnik and John I. Goodlad, eds., *School–University Partnerships in Action* (New York: Teachers College Press, 1988).

23. Zhixin Su, *Teacher Education Reform in the United States (1890–1986)*, Occasional Paper No. 3, Center for Educational Renewal, College of Education, University of Washington, Seattle, 1986.

24. Generally, the member institutions of the Holmes Group are minimally described as Land Grant research institutions.

15.

Political Limits to an Education of Value: The Role of the State

JOSE A. CARDENAS

Précis
The needs of students whose cultural and ethnic backgrounds tend to be outside the traditional mainstream are typically not met by what might be characterized as one-size-fits-all education. Although extension of services to special groups of middle class, English-speaking students—the gifted and the physically handicapped, for example—has proceeded now to the point of general acceptance, much less has been done in response to special conditions related to variables of race, culture, national origin, and gender. To the extent that equity concerns in these terms are going to be advanced in the next decade, state government will play a pivotal role, maintains Jose Cardenas. The states are the emergent power in education today, particularly state education agencies, public officials who shape state policies in education, and quasi-public groups that influence these policies. Only a few pioneering states have pushed for a shift from a traditional regulatory role (the length of the school year, required units of American and state history, for example) to a role of real leadership. Furthermore, an inverse relationship seems to exist between state attention to compliance with regulations and political and professional commitment to devise innovations that enhance all students' learning experiences.

It is obvious that a new pattern of state leadership must be developed, designed to enhance the educational opportunities of students who currently are not well served. State officials need to devote their energies to equitable tax policies and fair resource allocation, to the enlightened exercise of their regulatory functions, and, perhaps most important, to policy leadership.

Political and economic forces in each state should be brought to bear on concerns for children in such a way that positive opportunities will result. Only when all students can equitably access state resources, Cardenas claims, can there be a reversal of the current situation, in which (as the population deviates from the white Anglo-Saxon mainstream) the chances for appropriate educational program responses to special needs diminishes.

Jose Cardenas, former School Superintendent, is currently executive director of the Intercultural Development Research Association in San Antonio, Texas.

—The College Board

The absence of the topic of education from the U.S. Constitution and from the Reserve Clause of the Tenth Amendment has formed a strong legal basis for treating education as a function of the state. Although the federal government has had a historical concern with the responsibilities incurred by provisions for the general welfare as well as First Amendment guarantees,[1] the Equal Protection Clause of the Fourteenth Amendment, early local and state ordinances, educational practice, and an unbroken sequence of court findings have consistently confirmed the sovereignty of the state in the provision of educational programs to its citizenry.

Education is a function of the state. This unique feature of American education marks it apart from almost every other system of education throughout the world. Although the state may assign wide prerogatives to local school districts and accept information and resources that reflect the national interest and concern, it is the individual state that is responsible for the quantity and quality of education in that particular state.

This concept of state sovereignty in education was created during the historical development of education in this country. Education was a concern in each of the thirteen original colonies prior to the formation of the country, and this concern led to early legislation in each of the colonies that subsequently became states.

In the formative years of the country, the educational effort was as loose a confederation as was the first political attempt at unifying the newly independent country, and subsequent attempts to create a stronger union did not include education as one of the responsibilities granted to the central government under the new Constitution, thereby preserving the decentralized character of American education.

Legal Basis for the State Role in Education and Local Responsibility

Although legally education is a state function, the operation of educational programs traditionally has been a local responsibility. State constitutional provisions to establish an efficient system of education seldom led to more than cursory legislation for the establishment of schools at the local level, with little direction or resources for the townships to do so. And though romantic notions prevail about the high quality of schools in the absence of state regulation, the reality is that the local districts provided poor schools and managed them badly.[2] It wasn't until the beginning of the twentieth century that school districts in most states started to receive extensive state assistance for the operation of the public schools.

The extensive early delegation of responsibility to the local schools created two characteristics that have greatly diminished in recent times, extensive parental and community involvement and almost unlimited local control.

As late as 1930 the local school districts in the United States bore the brunt of the cost for the support of the schools, with 83 percent of the funds being generated at the local level. State interests in education, which led to the establishment of comprehensive state systems of school finance, also led to extensive legislation concerning the operation of the schools in order to protect the state investments.

State participation in the making of educational decisions in turn pre-empted parental and community involvement in the affairs of the school. Trends for the construction of large urban schools resulted in bureaucratic structures much more concerned with responding to mandates from the state capital than to the wishes of the school constituency.

Judging by the reams of new legislation being enacted by the state legislatures, erosion of local control and initiative not only will continue but will accelerate in future years. Although the continued existence of the local school district does not appear to be in jeopardy, it seems that direction for the operation of the schools will continue to shift from the local community to the state level.

The Federal Concern

Although the absence of a provision for education in the federal Constitution and in the Reserve Powers Clause of the Tenth Amendment makes education a function of the state, there is sufficient legal basis for the involvement of the federal government in education. Providing for the general welfare and defense, securing the freedoms of the First Amendment and ensuring the equal protections provided for in the Fourteenth Amendment serve as firm bases for federal concern and involvement.

Historically, federal involvement in education has been cyclic, with federal engagement intensifying during periods of national stress or crisis and diminishing after the crisis has subsided. In recent years federal crises leading to increased involvement in education have come about with more frequency and have lasted for a longer time. It appears that the last cycle of intervention has not subsided before a new crisis initiates a new cycle.

Economic recessions, the rise of technology, marketing competition, military and political commitments, and deficits in the balance of payments have combined to maintain a strong federal contribution to education. Although the style of federal involvement in educational activity has changed in the last decades, the federal commitment of financial resources has not. Federal funds for education have increased from $834 million in 1964 to $19.5 billion in 1986. This tremendous increase in absolute dollars may be attributed both to a federal commitment to education and to the growing realization that the federal government has the best financial structure with a broad tax base to support the rising costs of education.

Federal involvement in education has changed in the amount of aid provided, in the scope of intervention, and in the style of intervention. Percy Burrup and Vern Brimley cite five general categories of federal aid to schools: aid to promote the cause of education, aid to broaden the scope of education, aid to educate individuals for whom the federal government accepts responsibility, aid to improve the quality of education, and aid to compensate for deficiencies in the school tax base.[3] Michael Kirst adds four additional categories of federal action in education: regulation, discovering knowledge and making it available, providing technical assistance, and exerting moral suasion through use of the bully pulpit.[4] The following table summarizes Kirst's description, and adds the characteristics of pre-1964 federal advocacy for education.

Characteristics of the Federal Administration's Advocacy for Education Since 1964

Pre–1964	1964 to 1980	Post–1980
Small role	Large and influential role	Mitigated role
Little regulation	Detailed and prescriptive regulation	Deregulation
Faith in local and state systems	Mistrust	Renewed faith
State and local options	Equity concern	Efficiency with state and local options
Small, unrestricted grants	Large categorical grants	Large and unrestricted grants
Minimum support to private education	Minimum and indirect support	Significant support to private education

Limitations on the growing national interest and intervention in education were clearly established in *San Antonio Independent School District* v. *Rodriguez*, where the federal Supreme Court yielded jurisdiction to the state political process.[5] Legal constraint on federal intervention in education has been supplemented by the changing characteristics of federal intervention as depicted above, giving the individual states in recent years more responsibility in their control of educational activity.

The State Role in Education

The absence of education in the federal Constitution is more than made up for by its extensive coverage in state constitutions. Invariably the state government is charged with establishing a system of free public schools. Originally conceptualized as essential for participation in a democratic society, education has now become an economic imperative in each of the fifty states.

With education being a function of the state, it is expected that the role of the state in education would be very large. As stated previously, this was not true until the beginning of the twentieth century. Whereas the state contribution for the support of education in 1930 was only 16.9 percent of total costs, by the 1986–1987 school year the state share grew to an even 50 percent at a cost of $80.4 billion.

Much of the responsibility for the implementation of the educational program has been delegated to local school districts, quasi corporations especially created by the state for this function.

In spite of the delegation of responsibility for implementation of school programs, the state continues to increase its participation in education. State participation in education can be subdivided into three roles: the provision of fiscal and material resources, regulation, and leadership. The extent to which the emphasis is placed on any one or more of these roles is very much a matter of style in each of the individual 50 states, but the state plays a part in each.

Resources

Because the state is the entity charged with responsibility for the implementation of a public educational system, each state faces the responsibility for providing the necessary funds for implementation and operation. Although the relationship between the two appears to be obvious, the history of education in the various states indicates that the responsibility for creating a system of education was not always accompanied by the resources for doing so.

Although the responsibility for funding education has been dealt with much more seriously by the states in the second half of the twentieth century, existing systems of school finance in many of the states are less than ideal.

The responsibility for the operation of schools at the local level has frequently been granted to school districts with the accompanying responsibility for acquiring the necessary funds in support of the educational program. Since local school districts have no inherent taxing authority, it must be given by the state to the individual school districts.

The granting of taxing powers to school districts, usually as a tax levied on real and personal property within the boundaries of the district, may have seemed sufficient during periods of predominantly agricultural and industrial economies, but by the middle of the twentieth century it was apparent that local property taxes were insufficient to support a state system of education, requiring the commitment of large amounts of state funds in support of the schools. The large taxing base of the state and the various options for taxation at the state level made it feasible for states to increase their share of the cost of education to the present 50 percent level. Aside from the 6.2 percent contributed by the federal government, approximately half of the cost of education today is paid for by taxes collected at the state level and half by taxes the state authorizes the local districts to collect.

Extensive variations on the location of taxable property have led to wide variation in the amount of wealth available for local taxation. Simplistic systems of funding education have led to wide disparities in the amount of wealth accessible to local school districts, wide variations in the extent to which local districts can fund education, wide variations in the amount expended for education, and wide variations in the amount of tax effort necessary for the support of at least a minimum-quality educational program.

In 1971 a federal district court ruling in *Rodriguez* v. *San Antonio Independent School District* declared the Texas system of school finance unconstitutional, and by implication most of the systems of school finance in the other states.[6] Although this decision was subsequently reversed by the Supreme Court in 1973, individual state systems of school finance were found wanting by a succession of state courts.

The legal basis of school finance suits stems from a determination that the state constitutional provision for the establishment of a state system of education gives the state the role of distributing resources on an equitable basis. State funding of education, and by implication the quality of education afforded by the state, must give each school system access to the wealth of the state as a whole, rather than being highly dependent on the wealth of the individual local school system.

The provision of other resources by the state in an equitable manner is even more complicated than the distribution of funds. Whereas equity in the distribution of money involves only the concept of quantity, the distribution of other resources may involve the additional concept of quality. Such a dilemma is immediately obvious in states that have established and maintain a system for the distribution of textbooks and other instructional materials.

This argument surfaced at the local level in *Lau* v. *Nichols* in which the San Francisco Unified School District was found to be denying equal educational opportunities to Chinese children who had limited proficiency in English by affording them the same teachers, materials, and instruction given to English-proficient children.[7] In keeping with this unanimous decision by the United States Supreme Court, it can be inferred that the state distribution of educational resources would also have to be compatible with known characteristics of minority and other classes of children.

Regulation

The second role played by the state in the educational enterprise is the regulatory role. Much of this responsibility is vested in the central education agency, which acts as an agency of the state in regulating education. In this role the state education agency has the responsibility for the distribution of financial and material resources, the pre-service and in-service development of personnel resources, the monitoring of educational services, holding school systems accountable for the proper and efficient use of resources, and applying punitive measures through the processes of resource allocation and accreditation.

The capability to regulate education varies from state to state, but in general most states have extensive capability in monitoring input measures though they tend to be much less efficient in the regulation of teacher–learner interactions.

The historical concept of local control tends to become a buck-passing mechanism when it comes to the regulation of instructional activity. Although state departments of education can be bureaucratically meticulous in the enforcement of school laws, rules, and regulations dealing with teacher-certification requirements, subjects taught, days and hours of school operation, and even the number of minutes spent on each curricular area, this meticulousness seldom extends to the outcomes of education.

Recent national attempts at determining the number of school dropouts and research studies on the causes of such dropouts have been stymied to the point that the efforts were dropped in favor of determining the definition of school dropouts and methodologies for counting them.

Perhaps the biggest failure of the states in the regulation of education has been in meeting its responsibility for the implementation of equitable school programs. Just as financial equity provides for equal access to wealth, the concept of equity in educational programs provides for equal access to learning opportunities. School districts failing to provide an appropriate educational program should be held accountable by the state.

The concept of appropriateness of educational program has been readily understood if not adequately implemented by local school districts and the state during the latter part of this century. Concepts of special education for students with mental and physical handicaps have been generally accepted by educational systems.

The extent of a handicapping condition which must be responded to may still be in discussion and litigation, as is the case in determining the school's responsibility to multiple-handicapped children, children needing controlled environments such as air conditioning or a plastic bubble, or in recent cases, children who have been exposed to the dreaded AIDS disease.

When culture, race, national origin, or sex is the variable under consideration, the educational systems have been much more lax in accepting and implementing the concept of equity in educational programs. As a population deviates from majoritarian, white, Anglo-Saxon, Protestant culture characteristics, the chances for fair and appropriate programs are diminished considerably.

The growth of the American public school has paralleled the growth of the American middle class. Prior to the existence of an extensive middle class, there was no extensive American system of education. As in the European system which served as a model for early American education, private schools educated the children of the upper class, philanthropic institutions looked after the needs of the disadvantaged, and the church schools taught the basic skills as a prerequisite for religious instruction.

Although initially extremely limited in the ability to offer services to atypical children, as the need for education and for the development of salable skills has increased in the American economy, the ability of the American school to expand its offerings to atypical populations has increased similarly.

Still grounded in the fundamental concept of serving the middle class, schools started developing special programs to serve a wider range of people within the middle class. States developed and implemented special services for atypical middle-class populations not previously served. Classes for the mentally retarded, originally the educable mentally retarded and subsequently the trainable mentally retarded, were developed and implemented. Soon "special education" programs began to differentiate between mentally retarded, emotionally disturbed, learning disabled, dyslexic, slow learners, and a variety of other impediments for effective middle-class participation in the public schools. The growth of specialized educational services for the mentally atypical was paralleled by a similar growth in services for the physically handicapped. Original state-operated schools for the blind and the deaf led not only to mainstream services for this group but also to a bountiful number of special programs addressing other handicaps.

The amount and types of services offered to middle-class populations have been constrained only in the extremes, where the cost of the service or the amount of service has been deemed to exceed a reasonable cost–benefit ratio or has created a physical or moral risk to the rest of the middle-class school population. The education of children requiring elaborate environmental controls such as air conditioning or a plastic bubble are examples of handicapping conditions deemed too expensive or troublesome by the school. The education of children exposed to the AIDS virus is an example of concern for physical risk; the education of pregnant teenagers is an example of moral risk.

The extension of educational services to special cases of middle-class children has sometimes required legal intervention by the state or federal government or both, yet the implementation of such services has proceeded with general support, acceptance, and success. Unfortunately this has not been the situation in the development and implementation of educational responses for children not associated with the white, Anglo-Saxon, English-speaking middle class.

Almost one hundred years after the termination of slavery and the granting of full rights to blacks, most of the black children in the United States were attending segregated schools offering vastly inferior educational programs. Ten years after the U.S. Supreme Court order in *Brown* v. *Board of Education*, more than 90 percent of black children in the South were still attending segregated school facilities.[8] The Civil Rights Act of 1964 and the Elementary and Secondary Education Act of 1965 were a carrot-and-stick combination by the Congress of the United States to bring states into compliance with the *Brown* decision.[9]

Although there has been a certain amount of reluctance and even recalcitrance in accepting the concept of extending educational services to mentally and physically handicapped children, the negative response has been nothing compared to the reluctance, recalcitrance, and even defiance of the concept of extending educational opportunity to minorities, those with limited English proficiency, and the disadvantaged.

It took nine justices of the United States Supreme Court in *Lau* v. *Nichols* to inform the school authorities of the San Francisco Unified School District that having 1,800 Chinese children who spoke no English being taught by a proportionate number of teachers who spoke no Chinese constituted a serious educational problem. It was also necessary for the Supreme Court to determine that it was much more reasonable for the school to adapt its educational program to accommodate the Chinese language than for the Chinese children to adapt their language to accommodate the San Francisco schools.

In one state the state education agency issued a report some years ago on dropout rates for selected school districts. One district was reported as having a dropout rate of 90 percent with a 10 percent margin of error, making the true dropout rate somewhere between 80 and 100 percent. It was not surprising that the specific school district had a 90 percent dropout rate. The quality of its educational programs for Hispanic students, who formed the vast majority of the student population, had been the subject of extensive litigation in federal courts and in Office of Civil Rights administrative hearings. What was amazing was that the school district had been monitored, visited, reviewed, and *accredited* by the state education agency. Minority educators in the state at the time were heard to murmur that the accredited status of the school district was related to the fact that most of the students who dropped out were minority students. It is doubtful that a school district with a predominantly white, Anglo student population would stay accredited for long with a 90 percent dropout rate.

Neither the state, which has responsibility for education, nor the local school districts, which are delegated the responsibility for the operation of school programs, have been subjected to any rigorous demands for accountability in educational outcomes as a result of state regulation. Although school districts have experienced extensive failure in the education of large segments of the population, there have been few penalties associated with this failure. If anything, school systems have been rather successful in having the victim of the educational inadequacy held accountable for the crime, and in many cases they have even been extremely successful in having the victim agree to the culpability.

Leadership

Aside from the regulatory role, the state serves as the focal point for school leadership, which should lead to the improvement of educational opportunity. Ways in which this leadership is exercised include the provision of technical assistance for local school systems leading to an improvement in educational programs, the conducting of research and development activities, and the identification, acquisition, modification, and dissemination of innovative instructional practices.

There is an inverse relationship between state leadership and the state regulatory roles. In states where state leaders have clearly defined goal-oriented roles, the need for regulation diminishes. State default in its leadership role increases the pressure for responsiveness and leads to extensive and intensive regulation.

Unfortunately, central education agencies sometimes lack a sufficiently dynamic orientation to fulfill the leadership role. Central education agencies can be tractive institutions, much more aware and concerned with legislative and practical constraints to change than with innovative practice. Rather than visualizing ideal educational environments, the state education agencies can be the strongest defenders of the status quo, expending much of their energy in the defense of that which is, rather than in the conceptualizing of that which should be.

As with the state capacity for meeting its regulatory role, states vary in their capacity to meet their leadership role. The 50 states could be sorted into three groups that describe the quantity and quality of educational leadership provided by state education agencies, with a plentiful supply of cases for each of the three groups.

The first group would include states that provide extensive direction and leadership for education. These states function in the historical tradition of Horace Mann (Massachusetts), Henry Barnard (Connecticut and Rhode Island), Caleb Mills (Indiana), and Calvin Wiley (North Carolina), organizing, developing, and improving educational programs within the state.

The second group would consist of those states that seldom pioneer in educational innovation or reform, but eventually accept and internalize the no-longer-new innovation and reform.

The third group would be made up of those states whose central education agencies fight any attempts to alter the existing system of education. These education agencies resist all innovation and reform until forced to accept it, usually by legal enactment, at which time the state education agency immediately institutionalizes the new program and diligently protects it from removal or any further modification.

New Pressures for Educational Accountability

In recent years two new pressures have manifested themselves, demanding extensive changes and increased accountability in the educational system, thereby creating new demands on the states' educational leadership.

The first is the equity movement as described in the states' regulatory role; the second is the loud voice of the business and industrial community demanding nationally, as well as in each of the states, a better product from the educational system.

The change our country is undergoing as it moves from a manufacturing, mineral, and industrial economy to a service and technological economy has resulted in three altered characteristics of American labor that are extremely significant for education. First, business and industry can no longer absorb even a portion of the growing pool of unschooled, untrained, cheap, unskilled labor that formed the backbone of the American labor force in the past. Second, the failure of the schools to educate a large segment of the population has created a financial liability in terms of lost wages, lost taxes, incarceration, rehabilitation, welfare, and delinquency which costs many times more than the cost of education, and the private sector has become very aware of the burden of its share of the cost. The slogan "You pay me now, or you pay me later" is not lost on the private sector; after all, it was the private sector that coined the phrase. Third, the private sector is already experiencing problems in acquiring the skilled labor necessary for the competitiveness, and even the survival, of American technology-oriented business and industry. It is anticipated that this shortage of skilled labor will become much more extensive and critical in the years ahead.

It is surprising that this crisis in American labor needs has been relatively lost on the schools. Many educators are unable to interpret and understand the new demands that the private sector is making on them. In the past the schools have enjoyed a nice relationship with the private sector, easily meeting the demand for cheap, unskilled labor. (If the schools have not succeeded in anything else in the past, they have certainly been extremely successful in providing business and industry with an extensive supply of unskilled labor.) The new demand for skilled labor has been much more difficult for the schools to meet.

The problem of meeting the demand for skilled labor is further compounded by the shrinking of the white middle class and the rapid growth of minority populations, providing the schools with a higher number and a higher proportion of the type of student with which the schools have consistently experienced the most failure.

In states in which educational leaders have communicated with the private sector and joined hands in the struggle for educational reform, the results have been encouraging. Where state educational leadership has been lacking, the results have been disastrous.

State attempts to bring about educational reform in the absence of equitable allocations of resources and instructional fairness have proved counterproductive. A focus on outcome measures, particularly achievement-test requirements for promotion and graduation, rather than on input equity, has exacerbated rates of failure and school dropouts among minority and disadvantaged students.

Conclusion

As our country has grown, we have seen a change in the responsibility and support of education. Originally provided at local initiative, education has become a central responsibility of the states and a major federal interest. Although the interest and support of education at the federal level increased and decreased periodically, the interest and support of education at the state level has consistently increased over the years.

The extent to which the various states will flourish politically and economically is very much dependent on the extent to which the individual state meets its educational responsibilities. Vigorous commitment is required in discharging the three major educational responsibilities of the state: the furnishing of adequate and equitable resources for the support of education, the enlightened exercise of its regulatory role, and the provision of educational leadership resulting in further state growth and improvement.

Notes

1. The Constitution of the United States, Preamble: "We the people of the United States, in Order to form a more perfect Union, establish domestic Tranquility, provide for the common Defence, promote the general Welfare, and secure the Blessings of Liberty to ourselves and Our Posterity, do ordain and establish this Constitution for the United States of America."

The Constitution of the United States, Amendment I, December 15, 1791: "Congress shall make no law respecting an establishment of religion, or prohibiting the free exercise thereof; or abridging the freedom of speech, or of the press, or the right of the people peaceably to assemble, and to petition the Government for a redress of grievances."

2. Newton Edwards and Herman G. Richey, *The School in the American Social Order* (Boston: Houghton Mifflin, 1947), 248.

3. Percy E. Burrup and Vern Brimley, Jr., *Financing Education in a Climate of Change* (Boston: Allyn and Bacon, 1982), 160.

4. Michael W. Kirst, Jr., *The Federal Role and Chapter I: Rethinking Some Basic Assumptions* (Washington, D.C.: Research and Evaluation Associates, 1986), 4.

5. *San Antonio Independent School District* v. *Rodriguez*, 411 US 1 (1973).

6. *Rodriguez* v. *San Antonio Independent School District*, 337 F Supp 280 (WD Tex 1971).

7. *Lau* v. *Nichols*, 483 F2d 791 (9th Cir 1973), cert. granted, 412 US 938 (1973).

8. *Brown* v. *Board of Education*, 347 US 483 (1954); David L. Kirp and Mark G. Yudof, *Educational Policy and the Law* (Berkeley, Calif.: McCutchan, 1974), 307.
9. The Civil Rights Act of 1964, 42 USC, Sec. 2000c-2000d; The Elementary and Secondary Education Act of 1965, Title I, 20 USC, Sec. 241.

Selected References

Brown v. *Board of Education*. 347 US 483 (1954).
Burrup, Percy E., and Vern Brimley, Jr. *Financing Education in a Climate of Change.* Boston: Houghton Mifflin, 1947.
The Civil Rights Act of 1964. 42 USC. Sec. 2000c-2000d.
Edwards, Newton, and Herman G. Richey. *The School in the American Social Order.* Boston: Houghton Mifflin, 1947.
The Elementary and Secondary Education Act of 1965. Title I, 20 USC. Sec. 241.
Kirp, David L., and Mark G. Yudof. *Educational Policy and the Law.* Berkeley, Calif.: McCutchan, 1974.
Kirst, Michael W., Jr. *The Federal Role and Chapter I: Rethinking Some Basic Assumptions.* Washington, D.C.: Research and Evaluation Associates, 1986.
Lau v. *Nichols.* 412 US 938 (1973).
San Antonio Independent School District v. *Rodriguez.* 411 US 1 (1973).

The Continuing Agenda

Précis

La plus ça change. When it first appeared in 1990, *Access to Knowledge* introduced readers to a range of issues then defining the debate about the future of American education and, indeed, of our society. In the years that have elapsed since that initial publication, two of these—tracking and gender equity—have come even more to the forefront of the education debate. This final section includes four articles representing recent research and opinion on these vital issues. In "Ability Grouping: On the Wrong Track," Robert E. Slavin and Jomills H. Braddock examine the ramifications of tracking and ability grouping so aptly described by Jeannie Oakes and Martin Lipton in Chapter 10. Among the issues raised by Slavin and Braddock are the difficulty of "detracking" our nation's classrooms and the need for staff development to make this a reality. "Learning to Teach An Untracked Class," by Joan Kernan Cone, speaks precisely to these issues. Describing the eight years it took to detrack the curriculum at El Cerrito High School, Cone's article also drives home the enormous influence of teacher expectations on student performance.

If detracking at least offers the possibility of improved student performance, the second issue, gender equity, is perhaps less readily understood. Although in "Closing the Gender Gap," Susan Murphy does make the point that women's "lesser" performance on standardized tests is more apparent than real, the gap between men and women in other academic areas appears to be both real and irrefutable. Myra Sadker, David Sadker, Lynn Fox, and Melinda Salata examine some of the causalities in "Gender Equity: The Unfinished Agenda"—among them, the loss of self-esteem most girls suffer in early adolescence and inequity of instruction.

Robert E. Slavin is director, elementary school program, Center for Research on Effective Schooling for Disadvantaged Students, Johns Hopkins University. Jomills H. Braddock III is professor and chair, Department of Sociology, University of Miami, Coral Gables.

Joan Kernan Cone teaches English at El Cerrito High School in California. Susan H. Murphy is dean of admission and financial aid, Cornell University. Myra Sadker is dean and professor, David Sadker is professor, Lynn Fox is assistant professor, and Melinda Salata is a graduate research assistant, School of Education, American University.

—The College Board

reform movement and the issues it raises inhibit teachers' ability to advance access to knowledge. Participants divided on the central question of whether teachers are capable of changing in the major ways called for by reform reports. Some hold that teachers know exactly what reforms are required and will change if empowered to do so. Others found teachers so set in their ways, deficient in training and knowledge, that they are unlikely to change unless thoroughly reeducated.

Another topic that surfaced at the colloquium was the discrimination against students with limited English proficiency. Given the hundreds of thousands of children attending the nation's public schools whose English language skills are limited, and given the fact that the number of these children is increasing rapidly, ensuring equal access for language minority students must become a more prominent part of the school reform agenda.

At the conclusion of the colloquium most participants agreed that the papers and discussions had served at least one vital function. They had asked the "right" questions—questions that posed challenges applicable to the daily concerns of all educators. Many participants said they planned to share the papers with their colleagues and to discuss these ideas for reform in their local communities.

Everyone, it seemed, took heart from the initiative of the College Board to bring together scholars, policymakers, organization leaders, and school practitioners as a community of concern and as agents of educational reform. Real change is contingent on using the combined talents of such individuals, who need to be encouraged to think differently about educational problems, schools, and students.

The Berkeley colloquium ended on an optimistic note: that the papers collected in this volume, once they reach more readers, will stimulate even broader conversation about school reform among a still wider audience, one which, in turn, has the potential to bring about real change in our nation's schools. The papers contained in this volume were commissioned in the spirit of creating a dialogue and a conversation about an important set of issues in U.S. education. This book aspires to extend that conversation, especially as it concerns the students who are often least well served. We believe that further discussions of this kind can catalyze a new direction in educational reform. To the extent that insight and energy combine for change, we will further the College Board's commitment to ensuring educational excellence for all students and to extending their access to knowledge.

16.

Ability Grouping: On the Wrong Track

ROBERT H. SLAVIN AND
JOMILLS H. BRADDOCK III

"The only thing that matters in my life is school, and there they think I'm dumb and always will be. I'm starting to think they're right. Hell, I know they put all the black kids together in one group if they can, but that doesn't make any difference either. I'm still dumb. Even if I look around and know that I'm the smartest in my group, all that means is that I'm the smartest of the dumbest.

"Upper tracks? Man, when do you think I see those kids? I never see them. Why should I? Some of them don't even go to class in the same building with me. If I ever walked into one of their rooms, they'd throw me out before the teacher even came in. They'd say I'd only be holding them back from their learning."[1]

The quotation above is from a conversation with Ollie Taylor, an 11-year-old African American boy in Boston who had recently been assigned to the low track in his school. In this conversation, Ollie illustrates many of the problems and dilemmas of ability grouping, especially in integrated schools. First, and most obviously, Ollie reminds us of the shame of being assigned to the low track. At age 11, Ollie presumably has a great deal of information about his capabilities relative to other students'. He may know that he was keeping up with them, but also presumably knows that he is not one of the top achievers; however, assignment to the low track puts a stamp on him that is different from anything that he learned about himself in heterogeneous classes.

Second, Ollie reflects the belief that the low track is specially designed for black students like himself; he believes that race is one factor in assignment to tracks.

Third, Ollie discusses the profound division between students in high and low tracks. He describes his feeling that both students and teachers in the high track would "throw him out" if he dared to trespass on their area of the school.

Ollie Taylor's experiences are far from atypical. They are not unique to African American students, nor to other minority students. A recent longitudinal study by Jomills Braddock shows the pervasive negative effects of ability grouping on all students.[2] This study is an analysis of data from the National Longitudinal Study, which provides unusually rich information on ability grouping practices and student outcomes in a nationally representative sample of schools and students. Braddock followed eighth-grade students who attended schools in which ability grouping was or was not used, and examined many outcomes for these students in the tenth grade. He statistically controlled for prior grades and test scores and other factors; and compared high, average, and low achievers separately in the tracked schools to their counterparts in the untracked schools.

The results were striking. Students in the low track performed significantly less well on achievement tests (reading, mathematics, science, and social studies) than did similar low achievers in untracked schools. Yet there was no consistent corresponding benefit of ability grouping for high or average achievers. Put another way, Ollie Taylor's pain was no one's gain.

Test scores were not the only indicators of the negative effects of tracking. Low-track eighth graders were much less likely to end up in college preparatory programs in tenth grade than were untracked low achievers. This effect suggests that being placed in the low track in eighth grade slams the gate on any possibility that a student can take the courses leading to college. The gate remained open for equally low-achieving eighth graders who had the good fortune to attend untracked schools.

Like Ollie Taylor, low-track students in the study had lower self-esteem than did untracked low achievers, and had markedly less positive perceptions of intergroup relations in their schools. Again, these negative effects were not offset by positive effects on any outcomes for high or average achievers.

Braddock's data provides the largest, best-controlled multiyear study of ability grouping ever conducted. However, the effects of ability grouping have been studied for 70 years, and the results of scores of studies have been similar to those he found.

Opportunities to Learn

Students cannot learn what they have not been taught. One of the clearest outcomes of ability grouping at all instructional levels is that students in low-ability groups are exposed to substantially less material and to lower-quality instruction than are students in middle- or high-ability groups. The pace of instruction is slower in low-ability reading groups and in low-track classes in middle and high schools. Furthermore, students in low-ability groups are likely to be exposed to more low-level basic skills than are students in middle and high groups. Even more to the point, low achievers in tracked settings are exposed to far less context and to a lower level of content than are similarly low-achieving students in mixed-ability classes. In fact, a study by Jeannie Oakes found that the level and pace of instruction provided to heterogeneous middle school classes was like that given to the top track in tracked schools.[3–4] The presence of low achievers in heterogeneous classes does not cause teachers to slow down or "dumb down" their curriculum; instead, it appears to allow low achievers to benefit from the richer and more fast-paced curriculum traditionally offered to the top track (although this is not to say that the top-track curriculum is ideal for anyone, including those who have traditionally been in it).

Ability Grouping and Achievement

In the long history of research and debate on the effects of ability grouping, the same essential arguments have been advanced on both sides. Proponents of ability grouping have claimed that grouping is necessary to individualize instruction for students and to accommodate their diverse needs. In particular, they have been concerned about the possibility that including low achievers in heterogeneous classes would slow down the progress of high achievers, and have claimed that high achievers benefit from the challenge and example of other high achievers. In contrast, opponents of ability grouping have been concerned about the negative effects of the practice on low achievers, in particular denying them access to high-quality instruction. This group opposes the practice on principle as undermining social goals of equity and fairness in our society. There is an interesting lack of parallelism in these arguments. The pro-grouping argument is primarily concerned with *effectiveness*, and the anti-grouping argument is primarily concerned with *equity* and democratic values. Consequently, the burden of proof in terms of effectiveness must be on those who would track.

Clearly, ability grouping fails to meet this burden of proof. Reviews of research on ability grouping have failed to find any positive effects of between-class ability grouping for any subgroup of students.[5–6] These reviews consider studies done in all kinds of schools over many years. Not only were average achievement levels no better in ability-grouped classes but hardly any individual studies find educationally meaningful positive effects.

There is only one aspect of ability grouping research that engenders serious debate about achievement effects. This has to do with the effects of programs for the gifted. General agreement exists that acceleration programs are effective. For example, gifted seventh-grade students who take Algebra I (usually given to students in ninth grade) perform far better on algebra tests and little worse on Math 7 tests than equally bright students who take Math 7. There is, however, little reliable evidence to favor the far more common enrichment programs often provided to gifted students.[7]

Whatever the effects of programs for the gifted, it is important to keep in mind that such programs apply to only 3 to 5 percent of students. No serious reviewer suggests that there are educationally important positive effects of comprehensive ability grouping plans for a broader range of high achievers (for example, the top 33 percent of students). Even if there were evidence in favor of enrichment programs for the gifted, there would still be no evidence whatsoever to deny that such enrichment programs might be effective for all students, not just gifted ones.

Ability Grouping and Segregation

One of the most consistent effects of ability grouping is to create classes that have disproportionate numbers of students from the same racial or social groups. As Ollie Taylor put it, "I know they put all the black kids together in one group if they can." In high schools, black and Hispanic students are greatly overrepresented in the vocational track and underrepresented in academic programs. These groups are also overrepresented among the low tracks in junior high and middle schools, and in low-ability reading groups in elementary school. Furthermore, the U.S. Office of Civil Rights has estimated that more than half of U.S. elementary schools have at least one "racially identifiable" classroom in its highest or lowest grade. A racially identifiable classroom is one in which the proportion of students of a given race in that class is substantially different from that in the school as a whole. This is considered an indication of discriminatory ability grouping. Leaving aside race and ethnicity, students from low socioeconomic circumstances are also greatly overrepresented in the low tracks.

Ability Grouping, Self-Esteem, and Feelings of Inferiority

The most poignant aspect of the conversation with Ollie Taylor excerpted earlier is the degree to which placement in the low track made him feel inferior and worthless. A great deal of research shows that Ollie's feelings are not unique. Braddock's study found students in the low track to have significantly lower self-esteem than low achievers in mixed-ability classes; there were no differences for middle and high achievers. Earlier studies have also found that in comparison to others, students in low tracks are low in academic self-esteem, even controlling for their actual achievement, and more often report feelings of inferiority, shame, and anger. In addition, this study found that tracked low achievers more often felt that their fate was out of their hands (external locus of control) than did untracked low achievers.

Ability Grouping, Delinquency, and Dropout

The experience of being in the low track has many effects beyond low self-esteem and feelings of inferiority. When their achievement and other factors are controlled for, students in the low track are still more likely to be delinquent than are other students and are less likely to complete their education.

Alternatives to Ability Grouping

Arguments in favor of ability grouping depend entirely on the assertion that grouping is necessary to meet the differing needs of children of different performance levels, especially those of high achievers. Yet evidence from dozens of studies done over a 70-year period has consistently failed to find any benefits of between-class ability grouping for students at any performance level. Given the segregative impact of between-class ability grouping, the negative effects of grouping on such outcomes as self-esteem, delinquency, and dropout, and the antiegalitarian nature of the practice, there is little reason to maintain the between-class ability grouping practices so prevalent in American middle and high schools and not uncommon at the elementary level.

Although it is easy in concept to say that between-class ability grouping should be reduced or eliminated, it is much more difficult in practice to bring this about. An old Russian saying is appropriate: "It's easy to make an aquarium into fish soup, but hard to make fish soup back into an aquarium." American schools have used ability grouping for decades and know few alternatives to the practice. Strong political pressures, especially from parents of high achievers, inhibit change. Teachers need to learn about, witness, and experiment with new practical methods for teaching heterogeneous classes. Parents, teachers, and students themselves need to be satisfied that a change from homogeneous to heterogeneous grouping will meet the needs of all students, including those of high achievers.

A few general principles for ending tracking seem to be worth stating at the outset. First, untracking must be seen as a part of an overall improvement in instructional practices and curriculum for all students. Untracking must never be—or appear to be—taking from high achievers to give to low achievers. Instead, it must be seen as bringing into the school methods and materials that are better for all students. Second, the expectations for student performance in untracked schools must be similar to those formerly characteristic of the top track. As noted earlier, Jeannie Oakes' observational research in homogeneous and heterogeneous middle school classes found that the pace and quality of instruction in the untracked classes was like that in the high tracks; as schools end tracking they need to make certain that this is in fact the case and is perceived to be the case. For example, some schools that have successfully ended tracking have put teachers who formerly taught gifted classes in charge of helping all teachers make their (heterogeneous) classes into "gifted" classes, in the sense that all classes can experience activities typical of enrichment programs for the gifted.

The key goal of untracking should be to make the "top track" curriculum accessible to a broader range of students without watering it down. This may mean doing more active teaching and less seatwork; using more projects and hands-on curriculum and less passive lecture; using more cooperative learning; using more frequent curriculum-based assessments of student progress with adequate time allowed; providing low achievers with assistance (including adult and peer tutoring) closely linked to their classroom curriculum; and many other strategies. Note that with the exception of the last of these, all are generally considered effective strategies for all students, not just for low achievers.

One alternative to between-class ability grouping often proposed is the use of cooperative learning methods, which involve students working in small, heterogeneous learning groups. Research on cooperative learning at all grade levels consistently finds positive effects of these methods if they incorporate two major elements: group goals and individual accountability. That is, the cooperating groups must be rewarded or recognized based on the sum or average of individual learning performances. Cooperative learning methods have also had consistently positive effects on intergroup relations and on self-esteem, acceptance of mainstreamed academically handicapped students, and ability to work cooperatively.

In addition to cooperative learning, there are many other strategies known to be effective for students in general and likely to be particularly appropriate for teaching heterogeneous classes. One is the use of active teaching strategies. A much broader range of students can benefit from engaging, active, well-organized lessons than can learn from worksheets and textbooks. Another such strategy is an emphasis on "constructivist" teaching, in which students begin with large, "authentic" problems and work together to discover how to solve them and, along the way, learn the more basic skills underlying them. Well-researched programs using this approach are becoming widely used in creative writing and mathematics classes.

Extending learning time for low achievers can be a very effective means of helping them keep up with a demanding curriculum. Extra time embedded in the school day for preteaching, i.e., giving at-risk students information on a lesson they are about to receive, or for remedial work that is closely linked to the students' regular classroom work can help low achievers succeed in heterogeneous, high-expectation classes. Curriculum-based assessment and directed services to help at-risk children succeed can obviate the need for special education or separate remedial services for many children. The effective assistance for low achievers is extremely important in untracking efforts, not only for the benefit of low achievers but also to keep teachers from feeling as though they must slow down the curriculum. If untracking is to be effective for everyone and also perceived to be so, it must provide a fast-paced, high-expectations curriculum for all students, and assistance targeted to low achievers must be part of the plan. Targeted assistance can be provided by peer tutors, volunteer tutors, special education or Chapter I teachers, or even computers.

None of the instructional methods that have promise for teaching heterogeneous classes can be mandated schoolwide next Monday morning. All require top-quality staff development over an extended period of time. Staff development programs should make extensive use of peer coaching or other means of following up initial training sessions, along with in-class follow-up from fellow teachers, expert coaches, or outside trainers. In addition, it is important to involve teachers in making decisions about how staff development will take place and, more generally, how the school will change to increase its effectiveness for all students.

It is also important to see that teachers are able to make individual choices about whether to use particular teaching methods or curriculum materials. Untracking is fundamentally a school-level decision; teachers and others should participate in making the decision, but once it is made it will generally apply to the whole school or at least to whole grades within a school. However, it does not make sense to require all teachers to use cooperative learning or within-class grouping or process writing or other methods.

It would be a mistake to eliminate all forms of grouping. Flexible within-class grouping to provide additional assistance to students who need help has been found to be effective in upper-elementary mathematics, for example. There is also evidence to support use of the Joplin Plan, in which students are placed in mixed-ability classes for most of the day, but are regrouped according to reading performance across grade lines. Acceleration programs for extremely able students have been supported by research, and advanced placement and other advanced course work for high school students can be beneficial. However, they need to be accompanied by efforts to see that minority students and other underrepresented groups also have access to them. A comprehensive, reasonable, and practical strategy for restructuring schools might well include some forms of grouping. What must end, however, is the kind of ability grouping that sorts students into categories that have long-lasting consequences; that is the between-class grouping strategies often called tracking.

Why Tracking Must End

Tracking is ineffective. It is harmful to many students and inhibits the development of interracial respect, understanding, and friendship. It undermines democratic values and contributes to a stratified society. There are effective and practical alternatives. Tracking must end.

Academic tracking is an anachronism. There may have been a time when curriculum tracking in schools actually coincided with the needs of the society and the economy. That is, a designated number of academically proficient students were needed to pursue further education and careers that depended upon that education, and a number of nonacademically oriented students were needed to enter the work force directly and perform the important and occasionally well-paying jobs that required less education. That situation has changed dramatically. If the United States is to maintain its standard of living, it must develop a work force capable of thinking, learning, and making decisions. Writing off a substantial proportion of our students never made sense from a social standpoint, and is rapidly becoming suicidal from an economic standpoint. Yet, curriculum tracking still exists and is widely practiced in most American schools today. The effects of curriculum tracking and ability grouping on student learning opportunities are especially negative for students of color, who are overrepresented among the low groups. African American and Hispanic students constitute our largest—and fastest growing—student populations, and the future well-being of the country depends upon their access to high-quality education. Corporate leaders and educators have focused increased attention on the level and kinds of skills American youth bring to the work force, and to the content and quality of their high school courses and programs of study. As the population of the United States becomes ever more racially and culturally diverse, issues of intergroup tolerance and understanding take on greater significance for our national well-being. In this vein, business leaders' concern with the kinds of graduates produced by our public schools is not limited to cognitive and technical skills, but also includes social skills—especially the ability to relate to people of different backgrounds—and the ability to be good team players. Thus, the adverse effects of tracking on students' social skills and affective outcomes related to racial intolerance suggest the need for change. As a society, we cannot tolerate low skills in a major portion of our work force and expect to thrive; we cannot tolerate intolerance and expect to survive.

Notes

1. T.L. Cottle, "What Tracking Did to Ollie Taylor." *Social Policy* 5 (1974): 24.
2. J.H. Braddock and R.E. Slavin, *Life in the Slow Lane: A Longitudinal Study of Effects of Ability Grouping on Student Achievement, Attitudes, and Perceptions.* (Baltimore, Md.: Johns Hopkins University, Center for Research on Effective Schooling for Disadvantaged Students, 1993).
3. J. Oakes, *Keeping Track: How Schools Structure Inequality.* (New Haven, Conn.: Yale University Press, 1985).
4. J. Oakes, "Can Tracking Research Inform Practice? Technical, Normative, and Political Considerations," *Educational Researcher* 21 (1992): 12-21.
5. R.E. Slavin, "Ability Grouping and Student Achievement in Elementary Schools: A Best Evidence Synthesis," *Review of Educational Research* 52 (1987): 347-50.
6. R.E. Slavin, "Achievement Effects of Ability Grouping in Secondary Schools: A Best Evidence Synthesis," *Review of Educational Research* 60 (1990): 471-99.
7. R.E. Slavin, "Are Cooperative Learning and Untracking Harmful to the Gifted?" *Educational Leadership* 48 (1991): 68-71.

17.

Learning to Teach an Untracked Class

JOAN KERNAN CONE

66**W**hen it was snack time," wrote Soo-Jin, recalling her group placement in second grade, "the teacher let groups five and four get the Graham crackers and apple juice first. We would be stuck with the broken pieces—which she gave us two of—and juice that tasted like water." This year Soo-Jin is not in "group zero"; she is in my ninth-grade English class, a heterogeneously grouped college prep class for all but certified gifted students. In that class she has written a number of expository essays and narratives, read *The Odyssey, Jane Eyre,* and *China Boy* on her own in addition to the required literature texts, and earned all A's and one B the first semester in a schedule that includes biology, algebra, world history, PE, French, and English. For all (or perhaps because of) her success in the class, Soo-Jin again feels slighted academically. All evidence indicates that she is an honors student and yet she was not programmed into an honors English class. Why? The answer lies in the rigidity of ability tracking. Soo-Jin's placement in ninth-grade English was decided in second grade when she was not tested for "gifted" and again in eighth grade when she was not programmed into algebra and foreign language.

Next year there will be no Soo-Jin's in El Cerrito's ninth-grade English classes. Next year all ninth graders will be programmed into carefully balanced, heterogeneously grouped English classes, the last stage in an untracking effort that has taken eight years to accomplish.

Eight years ago students at El Cerrito High were rigidly tracked into four English class groups: low, average, high, gifted. Teachers referred to their classes by labels: "my third-period low class," "his average juniors," "their gifted ninth graders." For a small group of teachers in the department, however, the labels were as much a description of our expectations for students as a description of student ability, a description that nagged at our awareness of the connectedness of expectation and performance and the workings of self-fulfilling prophesy. In the spring of 1986 we enrolled in an inservice class taught by University of California, Berkeley, psychology professor Rhona Weinstein aimed at creating school success for at-risk students.

When the class ended, four English teachers signed on to do a collaborative research project with Ms. Weinstein and her research assistant.[1] That group, Promoting Achievement through Cooperative Teaching (PACT), as we came to call ourselves, spent the next year reading earlier research, arguing over its validity, relevance, and application in urban classrooms, and gradually created a model for teaching "ninth-grade low" students. Over that year we met every Thursday for an hour and a half after school to discuss more research articles, share teaching successes and failures, and encourage each other's commitment to breaking the cycle of failure for our students.

By the end of the next year, we had learned two important truths. First, classes limited to students testing at the stanine two and three level did not work: No amount of remediation, collaborative learning, parental contact, or shift of locus of responsibility was going to inspire students to succeed if they had no positive peer models of achievement and deportment. We took this concern to our principal and vice principal and got permission to broaden PACT classes to include stanines two through five. The second truth was more complicated: merging "average" and "low" classes was not enough: We needed to learn how to teach heterogeneously grouped classes.

For the next year, teaching strategies became the focus of our weekly meetings. What was the secret of teaching required texts and discourse modes to students with different skill levels? How could the high-achieving students be challenged without leaving the low-achieving students behind? How should discipline problems, absenteeism, and homework policies be worked out? As we developed our pedagogy for teaching at-risk ninth graders, we grew increasingly aware of the damages of ability tracking for all students, high-achieving as well as low-achieving, twelfth graders as well as ninth. That realization led to a bold move. Inspired by the work of Jaime Escalante and the film *Stand and Deliver*, we decided to untrack Advanced Placement English. Instead of admitting only students with top grades and high scores and glowing teacher recommendations, we invited into AP English Literature and AP English Language all students willing to complete a summer of rigorous writing and reading assignments.

That decision set into motion a commitment to untrack the entire department and led, over time, to the creation of a unique untracking model based solely on student choice. For the past three years all tenth-, eleventh-, and twelfth-grade students at El Cerrito High have self-selected their English class, college prep English or accelerated English (in twelfth grade, AP) on the basis of their willingness "to work hard or harder." The only exception to self-selection is, or was until recently, ninth-grade English. Despite the disapproval of some PACT teachers, ninth-grade honors English was maintained out of fear that parents of certified gifted eighth graders would abandon the public school system if their children were not programmed into an elite ninth-grade English class.

The results of a recent questionnaire alerted us to the effects of the ninth-grade honors class on our self-tracking model. When asked what influenced their choice of English class, a high percentage of sophomores and juniors and a significant number of seniors mentioned their ninth-grade placement. Typical responses: "I signed up for accelerated because I have been taking honors English classes since ninth grade." "I have always been in honors classes." "I was in honors last year so I just moved along." "I was in college prep last year so I just went with what they gave me." "Because I had [college prep English] all these years." It was clear that students' choice of English class was influenced by a perception of themselves as either accelerated or college prep, a perception established or reinforced by their placement in ninth-grade English.

Twelfth graders' responses indicated the most freedom from the control of that placement. A number of seniors were "crossing over." Scott, a student who had been in accelerated for three years, wrote, "I took college prep because I did not want to do all the work for AP." Joe, a certified gifted student, said: "The idea of reading books over the summer did not appeal to me." Megan, a National Merit Scholar, told us: "The main problem I had with being in AP was facing another year with the same 30 people I've had English with since ninth grade." Mica, new to accelerated classes, wrote, "One of the students in last year's AP class advised me to take this class. I really didn't know much about it. I thought it was only for the gifted." Le said: "I wanted to prove to myself I could do AP work."

After studying the data from the questionnaires, the department voted unanimously to do away with ninth-grade honors English in favor of an untracked, one-tiered class—to empower all students to make future English choices free of high school assigned labels.

Three days after our vote, we announced the change to parents and students at a meeting for incoming ninth graders. Unlike the parents of gifted students who a few years before had literally applauded our decision to open AP, many of these parents were not happy with our decision about untracking freshman English. While there was a smattering of applause, there were many questions, most of them tinted with anger. Why, they wanted to know, why now, why not the next year? And, "How will they [students who had not been in high track classes previously] compete with our children?" And, "How can you guarantee that the best students will be challenged?" Slowly and firmly we explained the why and the how: We don't see education as competition; we see it as working together to learn. Also, the what: Our curriculum will not change, we will continue to teach the curriculum that has challenged students for years. And we asked that they support us as senior parents had and to trust us and our past success. During the next few days our vice principal got calls from parents testing our resolve. We held firm on our position and he held firm with us. We all held our breath. The threats to enroll their children in private high schools did not materialize.

Teaching Untracked Classes

Over the years as PACT members have worked out the structure of our untracking model and our philosophy of untracking, we have learned how to teach untracked classes. In the beginning we did not know how important that was. I assumed, for instance, that when I opened AP English Language and Composition to all students willing to commit to a summer and year of academically challenging work, that was all I needed to do: students would rise to the level of the tasks I set. Within the first weeks of the class, however, I realized that creating an opportunity for all students to take AP English was not enough; I needed to create opportunity for success in AP English for all students. That realization led me to change dramatically the way I taught the class.[2]

Two years after that first successful year with an untracked AP class, I requested an untracked senior English college prep class. I assumed that what I had learned in my AP class about deadlines, attendance, use of effective talk, and small group instruction could be applied in a college prep class. I was right; but only after I had dealt honestly with the significant difference between the two classes.

To be blunt: I found that college prep students were not AP students. Whereas AP students had read and written essays on three books over the summer vacation, college prep students (with only two or three exceptions) had read none, even though they had been given a list of suggested summer readings. In addition, whereas in the AP classes there were no students with poor attendance records, no students on the verge of not graduating, no students who did not intend to go to college, there were many such students in college prep classes. While both classes had a broad spectrum of students in terms of grades and SAT scores, the range was considerably broader in the college prep classes. In AP, for example, there were 12 students who had a weighted GPA of over 4.0; in college prep there was one. In AP 13 percent of the students had under a 3.0 GPA; in college prep only 8 percent had over a 3.0—most significant, in college prep 20 percent of the students had less than a 1.99. Even more problematic, there were a number of students in college prep classes for whom school was a negative experience. To cope, they had invented strategies. Some cut class regularly, attending just often enough to pass. Some "created themselves as invisible," attending class, completing assignments, but making no or minimal connection with other students or the teacher. Some sabotaged classes through disruptive behavior.

The range in the college prep class in terms of attitudes about school, history of school success, and self-perception as learners and the effect those attitudes had on the class made learning to teach an untracked college prep class far more difficult than learning to teach an untracked AP class. It took only one year in AP to give me a sense of what worked and what didn't. It has taken three times that long in my college prep classes. Little wonder: The makeup of an untracked college prep class is far more complex than the makeup of an untracked AP class. More complex, more demanding, and more reflective of the damaging consequences of ability tracking.

Creating a Safe Environment for Learning

The last few years have taught me that the first task in an untracked class is the establishment of a safe environment. All students must be free to ask questions, share what they know and admit what they don't know, read their writing, make mistakes, take stands and change stands, grow as thinkers. All students must be expected to learn and must see that learning is expected of them. All students must know that rudeness and ridicule will not be tolerated.

The last few years have also taught me that the best way to get across appropriate classroom behavior is not a list of rules but a series of activities that require students to talk with each other and listen carefully. I begin the year with a seating chart lesson. On the second day of school, I hand out a blank seating chart to students and ask them to fill in as many of their classmates' names as they know, working silently and alone. After a few minutes, I introduce myself. "I am Joan Cone. J-O-A-N C-O-N-E." I ask students to raise their hands if they have any questions about the spelling or pronunciation of my name. I then point to the student sitting in the front seat of the first row and ask her to introduce herself, following the model, making sure that she speaks clearly and slowly enough for everyone to hear. During the activity I remind students to raise their hands if a name is not clear. After all students have introduced themselves, I say something like "I was born in Des Moines, Iowa, and my favorite movie is *Apocalypse Now.*" Then I call on a student by name and ask her place of birth and favorite film. Thus we make our way around the room a second time, students calling on students across the room tennis match style. Throughout this activity I am strict about politeness and attentiveness; if a student is disrespectful, interruptive, or rude, I stop the class to restate the rules of etiquette gently but firmly. For the next few days, we do variations on the seating chart activity, naming our most difficult classes, listing the first three things we would do if we won the lottery, revealing things about ourselves few people know so that by the end of the first week students feel relatively secure calling on each other and making their voices heard, safe in an orderly and respectful class in which everyone is expected to contribute, and clear about what I expect in terms of classroom etiquette. This activity also prepares students to assume control of class activities. Once students know each other's names, they—not I—call on each other to read literary passages and to share writing.

The Issue of Attendance and Missed Work

Attendance is not an issue in AP classes where it is rare that a student misses class. It *is* an issue in college prep where sometimes as much as one-fifth of the class is absent. One of the biggest problems with absenteeism is make-up work. In years past, I took responsibility for reviewing class work with absentees and making sure they understood missed assignments. I no longer do that. Now students are responsible for makeup work—their own and their classmates'. When absentees return to school, they do not ask me what they have missed; they check the student-written log book instead. If the log is unclear, they contact the log-writer, a student appointed for a week who records all class activities and assignments in an informative and entertaining way. Makeup work is due the day after the student returns from a one- or two-day absence, a week after a long-term absence.

Logs do not answer all problems related to absenteeism. They are particularly insufficient in assisting students with literature. It is not enough to say to returning students: "Read Act I of *Othello*." This is especially true of students for whom reading is not pleasurable. These students need to know more than the pages covered the day they missed; they need to be invited into the literary work in a way that involves them and makes them want to come back the next day. Years ago I did not know this. When students were absent while I was teaching a piece of literature, I sent them to the library or to an isolated area of the room to read on their own until they caught up with us. Few caught up. Now instead of sending students off to read on their own, I enlist the help of their classmates. Students review the story line and development of the characters so that the returning student understands well enough to participate in the class. The next day, I ask him to retell the plot to clear up any confusions or errors in his understanding. If he has problems, his classmates help him again. Reviewing in this way serves other students as well as absentees since it assists the whole class in recalling the previous day's reading and gets them focused on the next part of the play or novel.

Strict Deadlines: Showing Respect

It took me over a year to see that the strict rules about deadlines I was setting in AP could be applied in college prep. When it became clear to me that the most dedicated students were meeting the deadlines and the least dedicated were ignoring them, I realized that it was my expectations that were at fault. By allowing students to miss due dates for major papers and take important tests late, I was telling students that a deadline wasn't a deadline unless they wanted it to be. More important, I was telling them, "I don't expect you to get things in on time so I won't be too strict with you." Once I realized the disrespect behind my leniency, I tightened up. Now deadlines are deadlines. Missed homework gets a zero. Late major papers receive credit but no grade. Missed discussions cannot be made up. When discussions are on written papers, I attach a note to the essay to acknowledge the writing as well as the missed opportunity to share in class talk. "Good writing. I wish you could have been here to add your ideas to ours. You missed a great discussion." Admittedly, it is not easy to be strict about deadlines, but every time I fudge, I am sorry. I not only pay on the next assignment ("One more day, please, one more day"), I know that I have lowered my expectations with students who do not need kindness that weakens them.

Talk: the Secret to Success in an Untracked Class

To make my untracked AP class work, I restructured the curriculum so that all students would feel comfortable asking questions, sharing interpretations, reading their writing—joining the real as well as the metaphorical conversation of the class. When I tried to incorporate the same level of talk in college prep, I was unsuccessful. Some students refused to participate in class talk out of fear of being branded nerds or of not knowing the "right" answers. Other students dominated class discussions, seeing them as an opportunity to show off, control the class, or get the class off task to avoid continuing class work.

Before I started the second year of untracked college prep senior English, I analyzed what was going wrong. Most students were not used to "making meaning together"; to them a quiet class was an orderly class. They had been in classes where the teacher or the best readers dominated talk about literature, where little or no emphasis was placed on writing for an audience, where talk meant chaos. To teach them to use speech as a method of learning together, I chose a short but sophisticated work as our first piece of literature: *Sula* by Toni Morrison. From the very first day I stressed the need to ask questions and make meaning together. We had barely finished the first 10 pages of the book, when Melanie blurted out, "What's up with Shaddrack— are his fingers really growing or is he freaking out?" She asked what many students wanted to know and in asking set an example for them. From then on as we made our way through the book, students asked and answered questions constantly, clearing up confusions, defending interpretations, rethinking the text with each other, teaching each other how to read and analyze literature. "Did Shaddrack see Sula kill Chicken Little?" "What did he mean by 'Forever'?" "How could Sula have *hmm-hmm*-ed [laughter] her best friend's husband?" "Did Nel forgive Sula at the end?" "Are Sula and Nel really just two sides of one character—is that what the author is saying?"

From *Sula* we moved quickly to *Othello*, amid groans about Shakespeare. Here, instead of having students ask questions whenever they didn't understand, I had them write at the beginning of each day's class what they understood and did not understand about the previous day's reading. On the second day on the play, for example, I asked them to write everything they knew about the play so far. Phillipa was adamant. "I don't know any-thing," she said, "I hate this play and I hate Shakespeare."

"Okay," I said, "then write about that for five minutes."

And she did. "I know I hate Shakespeare. I know I don't understand this play. I know nothing about this stupid play." She called me over to show me what she had written.

"Push yourself," I suggested, "or just sit quietly until everyone else is finished."

She resumed writing. "Okay, so I know there's this guy named Othello who is a famous soldier and he fell in love with this young girl. Another guy's in love with her, too. I forgot his name. Her name is Desdemona and she eloped with Othello. And there's this other guy who is jealous of Othello and mad at him. He works for Othello setting out to destroy Othello. Who is black but Desdemona's dad, who is white, doesn't like him because he's black."

Once Phillipa settled down to write, she saw that in fact she did know something about the play—something that she could share with the class. They in turn could share what they knew with her and add to her understanding. Inviting Phillipa to read aloud what she had written was purposeful; I wanted to demonstrate to the class that writing helps us discover what we know. Over the course of our study of *Othello*, I made sure that all students participated in writing and reading what they knew about the play so that they all shared in making meaning of the play. Sometimes in these class openers I asked students to summarize the plot, sometimes to assume the personnae of various characters ("All the males write as if you are Desdemona, all the females in the voice of Othello—what is happening to you at this point in the play and how do you feel about that?"), sometimes to guess what would happen next in the play. But always it was writing begetting talk and talk begetting writing and both begetting understanding.

Along with our reading and talk of literature, we read our own writing to each other: first personal narratives, then reflective essays, then expository and argumentative essays—in small groups and to the whole class. When students wrote pieces too private for the whole class to hear, I asked them to come at lunch to read them aloud to me so that they could get a sense of performance about their work.

Thus academic talk came into our class—controlled by me in the beginning, controlled by students' growing sense of appropriate behavior as the year progressed.

Creating Students through Respectful Tasks

When we first began our untracking efforts years ago, we took as our guiding principle, "If it's good for gifted students, it's good for all students." As I gradually learned to teach untracked senior English, that sentence nagged me. I was increasingly pleased with the *how* of my teaching, but increasingly displeased with the *what*. Specifically, I was concerned that AP students' academic fare was superior to that of the college prep students. In literature, for example, AP students read Baldwin, Conrad, Woolf, and Hong Kingston while college prep students read a majority of texts listed as "adolescent lit," with only an occasional piece by a writer like Morrison. In the words of a college prep student, "They read hard books and we read short ones." I decided to take our motto to heart and to insert into the college prep curriculum works I had previously taught only in AP. The first such assignment was Shelby Steele's "Being Black and Feeling Blue," a provocative essay from his book *Content of Our Character: A New Vision of Race in America* that I had used the year before with AP students. To get students into the piece, I began reading it aloud. Before I had gone three paragraphs, August interrupted, "This sounds like me, I want to read." And he took over, reading as if he were giving a speech, looking up occasionally when students voiced agreement with his/Steele's points. When he had finished, students argued over the essay—some angry with Steele, others agreeing, all excited. At the end of the discussion, a young woman asked, "Why did we have to wait until senior year to read this kind of stuff?" While it was clear that she was talking about the subject matter of the essay, I took her question as permission to bring in more sophisticated pieces that pushed students to think deeply and to struggle with truths.

Since then the distinction between AP fare and college prep fare has faded. Now college prep students read Virginia Woolf, too: not all of *A Room of One's Own* unless they choose to, but all of the first chapter and all of the chapter on Shakespeare's sister. Now *Chronicle of a Death Foretold* is for AP and college prep students, as is *Go Tell It on the Mountain*, *The Autobiography of Malcolm X*, and *One Flew Over the Cuckoo's Nest*. As I began looking for quality works for college prep I grew excited and daring. From Bay Area newspapers I bring in essays by Ellen Goodman, Clarence Page, Stephanie Salter, and Cynthia Tucker. From the University of California, Berkeley, I have invited Troy Duster and Jabari Mahiri to discuss pieces of their research with us. From the local video store I rent films: *Jou Dou, American Me, House of Games, The Dead, The Meeting*. Every place I look I find new things to teach and new ways to teach old things. This year, after reading the Prologue and eight of the *Canterbury Tales*, my first period college prep class set up our own Chaucerian competition using newspaper stories that reflect today's culture and ethics as inspiration for poems, raps, or narratives. The winner received not "a supper at the expense of the Host" of the Tabard Inn, but a dollar from the 16 members of the class who signed up to vie for the title of best storyteller.

These sophisticated reading assignments led me to examine the kinds of writing tasks I was assigning college prep students. In AP I was asking students to write in a variety of discourse modes, to play with diction and tone, to employ sophisticated punctuation, to practice writing to AP prompts under a time constraint. In college prep classes I was assigning descriptions, personal narratives, and simple personal arguments. Once I saw how decidedly different my tasks and expectations were for the two classes, I upgraded the writing curriculum in college prep to include lessons on style and mechanics, argumentation, exposition, and reflection as well as practice in writing to prompts such as those used in college composition placement tests. I also began to assign AP literature-type prompts for final discussions and essays on books, to give students practice in writing analytical essays that reflected careful reading and serious thought. As writing from both classes appeared on the bulletin board, it became increasingly obvious that students' choice to take college prep English was a choice of less work, not less quality.

The Role of Choice

Last year as I was experimenting with bringing "non-canonical" writers into the college prep curriculum, a friend suggested that students should have some say in who and what they read. His comment made me think. What would happen if students were given an opportunity to choose their literature? That idea has developed into an important part of my college prep curriculum. In brief, on a designated day, students come to class with the title of a book they want to read and convince at least three other students in the class to read it and discuss it with them. A few days later the book groups meet during class time to begin reading their books (checked out from the library, borrowed from a friend, bought) and to decide on the number of pages they will read each day to finish by the deadline—usually two or three weeks away. While students read their books, class work is limited to activities that do not require homework: plays, mini-lessons on mechanics and grammar, writing and discussions of essays. Generally, I set aside at least one or two days a week during this time for groups to meet to discuss their books. The day the book is due, I ask students to write the whole period on a generic prompt such as, "If you could make a film of your book, which five scenes would you be sure to include? Describe each scene carefully and tell why it is significant. Make sure that your essay demonstrates that you have read the book thoroughly and thoughtfully." I read the papers that night and hand them back the next day for students to use in their discussions. The following two or three days, the groups present their books to the class as a whole and answer questions about them.

In the beginning, I set strict guidelines on the books students could choose: the book had to be at least 250 pages long, written in the last five years, with no film of it and no Cliff Notes written on it. Once I saw that students were taking the activity seriously, I dropped the restrictions: my only criterion now is that the book be a piece of literature appropriate for school reading. What do students read when they are given the freedom to choose? The books my students most recently chose were typical of the range of titles. In first period: *Invisible Man, Alive: The Story of the Andes Survivors, Waiting to Exhale, Mama, Disappearing Acts*, and *Beowulf*. In fourth period: *Alive, Bury My Heart at Wounded Knee, Disappearing Acts*, and *A Season on the Brink*. In both classes there were a few students who read no books, five students in first period and four in fourth.

At the end of last year I interviewed students about the role of student choice in high school literature programs. They were adamant about the importance of choice: "Having choice made me feel powerful." [Kandi] "Having choice gave me freedom. I could read the books I wanted to read with people who were interested in the books I was." [Tassie] They were just as adamant, however, that they not choose all their books. "I think it is a good idea [to have choice] but the teacher needs to choose books, too, otherwise we may not choose the books we're *supposed* to read and we'd feel cheated when we got to college." [Angel] Phillipa agreed, "Even if you don't want to read all the books teachers assign, you need to be exposed to them otherwise you feel left out like the teacher didn't think you were capable of reading a certain book so she didn't teach it to you."

This year again I see that giving students choice about their reading encourages them to read good books. When we finished the last book presentations recently, students said things like, "I think we should all read *Alive*—that sounds like a book we need to read as a class." [Becky] "I know what book I'm going to read next—*Waiting to Exhale*. I want to read another Terry McMillan." [Richard] "When do we choose our next book?" [Michael] "I heard *Jazz* is hard, but I want to read it next." [Kanika]

First You Need to Learn How

As an advocate of untracking, I often hear teachers and administrators say, "Untracking is fine but first we need to learn how to teach an untracked class." I know what is behind that statement. Fear of parent resistance, classroom chaos, personal failure, school failure. But I know, too, that continuing to stay in a state of not-knowing-how does little good. It is my experience that teachers learn how to teach untracked classes by teaching them, not by waiting to learn how to teach them. And we learn by working with other teachers who are learning: planning lessons together during shared conference hours; talking over successes and failures; encouraging each other to experiment and take chances and read research; seeking help from administrators, counselors, and parents; conducting classroom research on un-tracking efforts.

To teachers who say, "But first we need to learn how to teach untracked classes," I say: Remember when you learned to ride a bike? You learned not from watching your older brother ride his bike, not from your dad's expla-nation about the brakes and pedals and handlebars, not even from your mother's steadying the bike for a while. You learned from riding—from practicing every day until you could do it on your own. That's how it has been for PACT teachers in our continuing commitment to learn to teach untracked classes: We needed the support we got from research, university classes, school administrators, and each other. But more than anything, we needed to get in our untracked classes and teach. And as in the days when we were learning to ride our bikes, we sometimes still fall, sometimes get bruised (our egos now, not our shins), sometimes take a challenging road too fast. But for all we don't know yet, we are exhilarated by our new skill and our growing sense of confidence.

Notes

1. R. S. Weinstein, C. R. Soule, F. Collins, J. Cone, M. Mehlhorn, K. Simontacchi, "Expectations and High School Change: Teacher-Researcher Collaboration to Prevent School Failure," *American Journal of Community Psychology* 19 (1991): 333-402.
2. J. Cone, "Untracking Advanced Placement English: Creating Opportunity Is Not Enough," *Phi Delta Kappan* 73 (1992): 712-17.

Bibliography

Baldwin, J. *Go Tell It on the Mountain.* (New York: Laurel, 1952).
Bronte, C. *Jane Eyre.* (New York: Washington Square Press, 1972).
Brown, D. *Bury My Heart at Wounded Knee.* (New York: Washington Square Press, 1981).
Chaucer, G. [Lumiansky, R.M., Tr.] *The Canterbury Tales.* (New York: Pocket Books, 1948).
Ellison, R. *Invisible Man.* (New York: Random House, 1947).
Feinstein, J. *A Season on the Brink.* (New York: Simon & Schuster, 1986).
Haley, A. and Malcolm X. *The Autobiography of Malcolm X.* (New York: Ballantine, 1987).
Kesey, K. *One Flew Over the Cuckoo's Nest.* (New York: NAL/Dutton, 1963).
Lee, G. *China Boy.* (New York: Signet, 1991).
Marquez, G.G. *Chronicle of a Death Foretold.* (New York: Ballantine, 1984).
McMillan, T. *Disappearing Acts.* (New York: Viking, 1989).
McMillan, T. *Mama.* (New York: Pocket Books, 1989).
McMillan, T. *Waiting to Exhale.* (New York: Viking, 1992).
Morrison, T. *Jazz.* (New York: NAL/Dutton, 1993).
Morrison, T. *Sula.* (New York: NAL/Dutton, 1987).

Rebsamen, F. [Tr.] *Beowulf.* (New York: Harper Collins, 1991).
Reid, P.P. *Alive: The Story of the Andes Survivors.* (New York: Avon, 1979).
Rouse, W. [Tr.]. *The Odyssey.* (New York: Mentor, 1937).
Shakespeare, W. *Othello.* (New York: Washington Square Press, 1957).
Steele, S. *Content of Our Character: A New Vision of Race in America.* (New York: Harper Collins, 1990).
Woolf, V. *A Room of One's Own.* (New York: Harcourt Brace Jovanovich, 1929).

18.

Closing the Gender Gap: What's Behind the Differences in Test Scores, What Can Be Done About It

SUSAN H. MURPHY

The 1992 release of the American Association of University Women report, *How Schools Shortchange Girls*, brings to the fore many issues that have seemed dormant for a number of years.[1] The urgency of gender equity, once uppermost in many educators' minds, especially when Title IX antidiscrimination legislation passed in the early 1970s, seems to have abated for many professionals and many institutions. After all, more women than men are enrolling in higher education at the baccalaureate level, and the gap that once existed has virtually disappeared. Only a college that has been single-sex or ones with particular disciplines such as engineering or agriculture or nursing, once enclaves for only men or women, maintain a focus on gender issues. For others, the pressure has dissipated, or at least become subordinate to other more urgent campus concerns. The AAUW report reminds all of us in education that no matter how far we have come in addressing the issues of gender equity, we still have a great distance to go.

In this regard, those of us in the professions of admissions and financial aid have an essential role to play on our campuses. Not only must we convince our presidents and faculties of the reality of the demographics in the educational pipeline but we must also remind them of the needs for the future. By the year 2000, for the first time in history, a majority of all new jobs will require a postsecondary education; the best career opportunities will be in the professional and technical fields requiring the highest education and skill levels; and almost two-thirds of the new entrants into the American work force between now and 2000 will be women or minorities.[2] Thus, it is critical that we make sure that women are encouraged to pursue the widest range of curricular choices, that the opportunities for reward and recognition are as open for them as they are for men, and that our faculties in all disciplines are ready to educate both sexes. We must provide information that addresses adequately the differences that do exist between the sexes, and we must be facilitators of change, not only on our particular campuses but also in the education community at large.

Too often the discussion about women and college enrollment begins with a focus on their weaker performance on standardized tests, particularly in areas of mathematics and science. It is not unusual for the SAT and Achievement Tests to be used as examples of differential performance between men and women and cited as reasons why, perhaps, women are thought to be less capable of handling the rigors of certain challenging courses of study. Those who reach such conclusions ignore the many reasons behind the score differentials.

Almost since the SAT was first administered, men and women, as groups, have demonstrated different levels of performance. For many years, the differences followed the stereotypical, and perhaps expected, pattern of women scoring higher in the verbal area and men scoring higher in math. Because that seemed reasonable, given the educational patterns and career expectations of the country, it received little attention. However, starting in the early 1970s, women began to lose the advantage they once held on the verbal section of the SAT, while making little progress in math. The variance in recent times between the two groups has been as much as 13 points on the verbal and 52 points on the math sections (see Figures 1–2).[3] It also should be noted that similar score differences between men and women are exhibited in other nationally administered tests.

Who Takes the Test?

When examining these patterns, what most people forget is the composition of the test-taking population. The SAT seems so ubiquitous to those thinking about higher education that many overlook the fact that only those students who plan to attend colleges that require the test sit for the exam—and the pattern of men and women choosing that option is quite different. The differences between male and female SAT-takers in the most recent year for which data are available (1990–91) reflect a trend that began in the early 1970s.

Women represented 52 percent of SAT-takers, outnumbering men by more than 44,000. More women than men came from lower economic backgrounds, were the first in their families to aspire to higher education, and were from African American, Native American, or Latino backgrounds. Fewer women than men attended private schools or enrolled in higher levels of study, especially in math and science (see Figures 3–6).[4]

Simply put, the populations of men and women taking the SAT are significantly different; it should be no surprise, therefore, that their performance varies. More women than in the past are turning to higher education as a means for advancing their social and economic opportunities, and thus a broader spectrum of individuals sits for the test. While increasing numbers of women are entering the military after high school, they still represent less than 10 percent of those in the service.[5] They also are significantly underrepresented in the technical and vocational areas just out of high school—i.e., many of the skilled crafts. Thus, to compare directly the two populations taking the standardized tests and draw conclusions simply on the basis of aggregate test scores leads to questionable conclusions.

When studies have been done using more stable populations selected specifically for norming purposes, a different story emerges. The last PSAT/NMSQT norms study showed that gender differences on both verbal and mathematical sections of the test are disappearing. The mean verbal scores went from 34.8 for women and 33.6 for men (1.2 points in women's favor) in 1960 to 35.3 for women and 35.1 for men (0.2 points in women's favor) in 1983. Mathematical scores went from 37.1 for women and 40.4 for men (3.3 points in men's favor) to 37.7 for women and 39.1 for men (1.4 points in men's favor) over the same time period.[6] Norms studies of other tests reflect this same trend.[7]

The Dilemma of "Underprediction"

The differences between men and women do not disappear entirely, however. One of the most vexing issues in admissions is the frequent finding that women tend to do better in college than the test scores predict. The "underprediction" of college performance is often cited as one of the reasons why the test is biased against women. However, several issues must be taken into account before such claims can be verified.

Research has shown that some of the difference between men and women in grade-point average can be explained by the very different patterns of course enrollment at the college level.[8] Women do not enroll in college-level math and science courses to the same extent as men, and it is in those courses, more often than not, that tougher grading exists. One researcher developed an index at Dartmouth College to account for differences in professors' grading practices by ranking the average grades given in various courses. Adjusting grades by this index accounted for most of the underprediction of performance for women in a study he conducted on Dartmouth's class of 1986.[9]

Other factors also help to explain the difference in grades achieved by men and women. Women tend to have better attendance in class, do their homework more frequently, and seek help when needed—all behaviors that contribute to academic success, separate and apart from the stereotypical

notion that women simply are better behaved in class and thus are favored
by teachers.

The Math and Science Quandary

The troubling notion that persists is that women still trail significantly in the
preparation for higher-level math and science. The most recent set of National
Assessment of Educational Progress (NAEP) results shows that women have

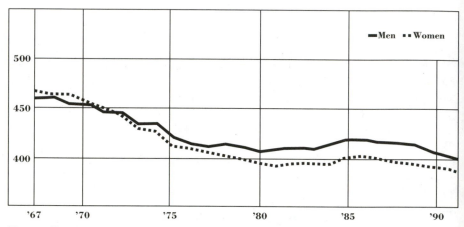

**Figure 1. Average SAT Verbal Scores for College-Bound Seniors
1967–1991**

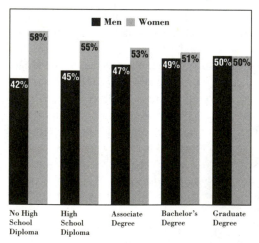

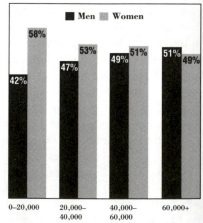

**Figure 3. 1991 Profile of SAT
Takers by Highest Level of Parental
Education**

**Figure 4. 1991 Profile of SAT
Takers by Family Income**

closed the gap in math and science to some degree, but nonetheless are behind their male colleagues.[10] For schools interested in significantly increasing their enrollments in sciences, math, and engineering, these are disturbing trends. The NAEP results also raise significant issues for the United States as a nation if indeed the demand for highly skilled, technically competent professionals continues at the pace that is predicted.

What does all the research about gender differences tell us? Conclusions are difficult to reach because the data that support many of the contentions

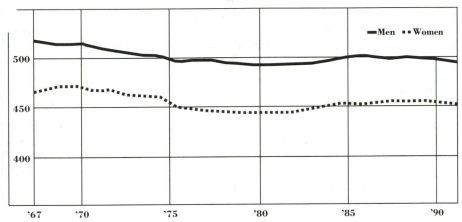

Figure 2. Average SAT Math Scores for College-Bound Seniors 1967–1991

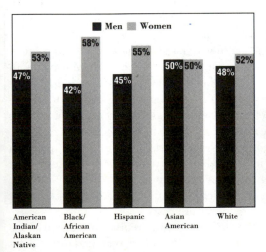

Figure 5. 1991 Profile of SAT Takers by Ethnic Group

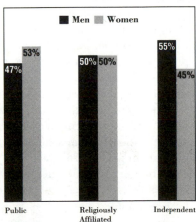

Figure 6. 1991 Profile of SAT Takers by Type of High School

about gender differences and their causes are elusive and often contradic-tory.[11] We know that the largest differences are in math or quantitative ability, especially at the secondary level and at the more difficult levels of reasoning. We also can trace a pattern of performance favoring women in the verbal areas, especially in writing. The math difference seems to be shrinking, albeit slowly, as is any advantage held on the verbal side. What is so troubling to document is why all of this is occurring. Is it course enrollment in middle and high school—or at the college level itself? What role do attitudes play and how are they influenced by the existence of standardized measurement? What about the tests themselves? How are higher education institutions supposed to react to the differences in test performance, and to course enrollment? The patterns give rise to more questions than answers.

Implications for Admission and Aid Professionals

Most colleges and universities in this country are not that selective. In a study done in 1986, fewer than 10 percent of the four-year institutions were admitting fewer than half of their candidates. Almost half of the schools admitted more than 80 percent of their candidates.[12] Yet, the emphasis in this country still seems to focus *not* on the colleges students choose, but rather on the choices being made by the colleges. The belief continues that the most important factor related to the choices made by colleges is test results. However, objective research and the professional experience of ad-missions officers suggests otherwise. In that same 1986 study, even those institutions labeled as selective did not cite one factor as the single deter-minant of admissions. Rather, several were noted as important, with high school grades and class rank as the most important, followed by test scores and curriculum, each viewed as having equal value.

The value of personal qualities has long existed in the flexible admissions processes evident in selective, private institutions. The challenge remains of communicating that fact in an era when much of what students learn about schools and colleges comes from the many "McRankings," as Dean of Ad-mission Fred Hargadon at Princeton University calls them. Such factors as initiative, motivation, persistence, or commitment to service, among others, do not fit neatly (thank heavens!) into such comparisons. Yet, these qualities play an important role not only in the selections made by the colleges but also in the eventual success achieved by the students. We have a major challenge conveying that message, particularly to those who may already have eliminated themselves from consideration.

How do we convince students that human beings really do read all those essays we ask them to write, along with the letters of recommendation? That we do consider, seriously, their level of accomplishment outside the class-room? That we look carefully at the opportunities they had available to them academically to understand how much they challenged themselves? It seems so much easier to be able to point to a test score or two, or a defined rank in class, to explain the sometimes inexplicable decision that emerges from a very selective admissions process. To fall into that trap, however, belies the time and professionalism that went into the review of the file, and unfortunately, misleads the student.

Do those nonacademic factors make up for a lack of academic performance? No, not really. What they do provide is a context for the selection committee to understand who this person is, and what kind of student he or she is. A student with very high test scores and excellent grades may not be admitted if those grades were achieved in a curriculum that lacked the challenging opportunities available or in a curriculum that became weaker in the senior year, once the "high school requirements" were met. That student who takes little time in completing the written application, providing little evidence of interest or accomplishment beyond simply what was required, will often be denied despite high scores and good grades. Or in some specialized programs, like architecture, where a match between the student's interest and the particular curriculum is important for success, a student truly aware of the particular discipline and experienced in it can emerge successfully in the competitive process despite test scores that may be lower than some others. In a selective institution, the committees have the luxury of choosing among those who present both strong performance in the classroom and interesting personal accomplishments. Thus, while academic accomplishment is necessary, it certainly is not sufficient—those other qualities of commitment, ability to express oneself, persistence, and motivation are the tiebreakers.

Perhaps it is unfortunate that some of these characteristics can't be captured easily so they could send important messages to prospective students, even as early as junior high school. For in reality, test scores play a key role in the decisions students make about their choice of schools, most likely because there is so little else to use as a benchmark. One study shows that students tend to consciously match the average SAT of the college to their own SAT scores, valuing most the schools that had average SATs within 100 points of their own.[13]

If women are consistently falling behind men in standardized-test performance because they have not taken as many of the challenging courses available to them in high school, we are creating a cycle that is self-perpetuating, and ultimately defeating. Students are pulling themselves out of possible consideration where in fact, so many of those other factors will lead not only to positive admissions decisions but also success in the program.

As admissions professionals, we must be particularly sensitive to those messages, real and perceived. The controversy in New York State over the use of test scores in the selection of scholarship winners was translated by many into a condemnation of the tests. That was not, however, the ruling of the judge. He cited the use of the tests as the *sole* criterion for selection of

scholarship winners as discriminatory because of the disparate impact that
resulted and because the test was not validated for the program's purpose.
That impact was obvious in 1987, when only 28 percent of the Empire State
Scholarship winners and 43 percent of the less prestigious Regents Scholarship winners were women, when the enrollment in secondary education
was at least 50/50. As admissions, aid, and counseling professionals, we
should have made known our concern about the inappropriate use of standardized tests as the only measure for scholarship selection. The instrument
was not designed for that purpose; to allow that kind of decision to be made
is an abrogation of our responsibilities as educators and contributes to the
undeserved negative press about standardized tests.

We also must be sensitive to the messages sent by the scores themselves.
If the same test is given to students from vastly different backgrounds and
preparation, we set up a vicious cycle where those who perform less well
continue to set their sights lower and lower.[14] As a nation, we cannot afford
to have one-half of the population shy away from the areas that demand their
participation. We know that progress for women is being made in college
enrollment; that we must now be transferred into enrollment in the sciences,
mathematics, and engineering.

In addition to being sensitive to the messages sent by such standardized
tests, there is much to be learned about the different patterns of learning
between men and women and the implications for faculties with increasing
numbers of women in the classroom. The Harvard Assessment series found
a high correlation between how students study and whether they stay in the
sciences. Those who met in small groups tended to stay in the sciences,
while those who studied alone switched away. For whatever reason, it was
found that men are more likely to study in groups, whereas women tend to
study alone.[15] Professor Light at Harvard, who is conducting this assessment
series, cites the patterns of study as a major explanation for enrollment
patterns of men and women in the sciences. That fact raises some interesting
challenges for the university faculties, as well as for those in the secondary
schools where the pipeline is established.

Where Do We Go from Here?

The demand for competent professionals in all fields, especially technical
areas requiring strong preparation in math and science, requires that we
refocus our attention on the needs and aspirations of women. We must think
creatively about our methods of instruction so that we can create an environment that fosters exploration and inquiry in all disciplines, for all students.

We must find, and use, all forms of measurement, so that women's
accomplishments and competencies are adequately assessed and we must
insure that the form of assessment does not inappropriately steer women away
from certain fields of study. And most of all, we must make sure that the

pipeline remains as open as possible, from elementary school through doctoral education, in order for us to be able to insist that the schools do not shortchange women, and we do not shortchange our society by leaving behind one-half of the population which has so much to contribute.

Notes

1. American Association of University Women. *How Schools Shortchange Girls* (Washington, D.C.: AAUW, 1992).
2. W.B. Johnston, *Workforce 2000: Work and Workers in the 21st Century* (Washington, D.C.: Department of Labor, 1987).
3. The College Board, *College Bound Seniors: 1991 Profile of* SAT *and Achievement Test Takers* (New York: College Entrance Examination Board, 1991).
4. The College Board, *College Bound Seniors: 1991 Profile of* SAT *and Achievement Test Takers*.
5. T.G. Mortensen, *Equity of Higher Education Opportunity for Women, Black, Hispanic, and Low-Income Students* (Iowa City, Iowa: American College Testing Program, January 1991).
6. H.I. Braun, J. Centra, and B.F. King, "Verbal and Mathematical Ability of High School Juniors and Seniors in 1983: A Norm Study of the PSAT/NMSQT and the SAT." Unpublished Statistical Report (Princeton, N.J.: Educational Testing Service, May 1987): 29, table 13.
7. A. Feingold, "Cognitive Gender Differences Are Disappearing," *American Psychologist* (February 1988): 95–103.
8. N.W. Burton, "Policy Issues: Women's Choice of College and College Major." Paper presented at the Annual Meeting of AERA and NCME, Chicago, April 1991.
9. C. Holden, "Court Ruling Rekindles Controversy over SATs," *Science* 243 (1989): 17.
10. U.S. Department of Education, "Trends in Academic Progress" (Washington, D.C.: U.S. Government Printing Office, 1992).
11. G.Z. Wilder and K. Powell, *Sex Differences in Test Performance: A Survey of the Literature*. College Board Report No. 89–3 (New York: College Entrance Examination Board, 1989).
12. H.M. Breland, G.Z. Wilder, and N.J. Robertson, *Demographics, Standards, and Equity: Challenges in College Admissions* (Washington, D.C.: The American Association of Collegiate Registrars and Admissions Officers, 1986).
13. N.W. Burton, "Policy Issues: Women's Choice of College and College Major."
14. G.Z. Wilder and K. Powell, *Sex Differences in Test Performance: A Survey of the Literature*.
15. T. Marchese, "Assessing Learning at Harvard, an Interview with Richard J. Light," AAHE *Bulletin* (February 1992).

19.

Gender Equity in the Classroom

MYRA SADKER, DAVID SADKER, LYNN FOX, AND MELINDA SALATA

"In my science class the teacher never calls on me, and I feel like I don't exist. The other night I had a dream that I vanished.[1]" Our interviews with female students have taught us that it is not just in science class that girls report the "disappearing syndrome" referred to above. Female voices are also less likely to be heard in history and math classes, girls' names are less likely to be seen on lists of National Merit finalists, and women's contributions infrequently appear in school textbooks. Twenty years after the passage of Title IX, the law prohibiting gender discrimination in U.S. schools, it is clear that most girls continue to receive a second-class education.

The very notion that women should be educated at all is a relatively recent development in U.S. history. It was not until late in the last century that the concept of educating girls beyond elementary school took hold. Even as women were gradually allowed to enter high school and college, the guiding principle in education was separate and unequal. Well into the twentieth century, boys and girls were assigned to sex-segregated classes and prepared for very different roles in life.

In 1833 Oberlin became the first college in the United States to admit women; but these early female college students were offered less rigorous courses and required to wait on male students and wash their clothes. Over the next several decades, only a few colleges followed suit in opening their doors to women. During the nineteenth century, a number of forward-thinking philanthropists and educators founded postsecondary schools for women— Mount Holyoke, Vassar, and the other seven-sister colleges. It was only in the aftermath of the Civil War that coeducation became more prevalent on campuses across the country, but even here economics and not equity was the driving force. Since the casualties of war meant the loss of male students and their tuition dollars, many universities turned to women to fill classrooms and replace lost revenues. In 1870 two-thirds of all universities still barred women. By 1900 more than two-thirds admitted them. But the spread of coeducation did not occur without a struggle. Consider that as late as the 1970s the all-male Ivy League colleges did not admit women, and even now state-supported Virginia Military Institute fights to maintain both its all-male status and its state funding.

Cycle of Loss

Today, most female and male students attend the same schools, sit in the same classrooms, and read the same books; but the legacy of inequity continues beneath the veneer of equal access. Although the school door is finally open and girls are inside the building, they remain second-class citizens.

In the early elementary school years, girls are ahead of boys academically, achieving higher standardized test scores in every area but science. By middle school, however, the test scores of female students begin a downward spiral that continues through high school, college, and even graduate school. Women consistently score lower than men on the Graduate Record Exams as well as on entrance tests for law, business, and medical schools. As a group, women are the only students who actually lose ground the longer they stay in school.

Ironically, falling female performance on tests is not mirrored by lower grades. Some have argued that women's grade-point averages are inflated because they tend not to take the allegedly more rigorous courses, such as advanced mathematics and physics. Another hypothesis suggests that female students get better grades in secondary school and college as a reward for effort and better behavior rather than a mastery of the material. Another possibility is that the standardized tests do not adequately measure what female students know and what they are really able to do. Whatever the reason, course grades and test grades paint very different academic pictures.

Lower test scores handicap girls in the competition for places at elite colleges. On average, girls score 50 to 60 points less than boys on the SAT. Test scores also unlock scholarship money at 85 percent of private colleges and 90 percent of the public ones. And here, again, boys generally outperform girls on qualifying tests used in scholarship programs.

The drop in test scores begins around the same time that another deeply troubling loss occurs in the lives of girls: self-esteem. There is a precipitous decline from elementary school to high school. Entering middle school, girls begin what is often the most turbulent period in their young lives. According to a national survey sponsored by the American Association of University Women, 60 percent of elementary school girls agreed with the statement "I'm happy the way I am," while only 37 percent still agreed in middle school.

By high school, the level had dropped an astonishing 31 points to 29 percent, with fewer than three out of every 10 girls feeling good about themselves. According to the survey, the decline is far less dramatic for boys; 67 percent report being happy with themselves in elementary school, and this drops to 46 percent in high school.[2]

Recent research points to the relationship between academic achievement and self-esteem. Students who do well in school feel better about themselves; and in turn, they then feel more capable. For most female students, this connection has a negative twist and a cycle of loss is put into motion. As girls feel less good about themselves, their academic performance declines, and this poor performance further erodes their confidence. This pattern is particularly powerful in math and science classes, with only 18 percent of middle school girls describing themselves as good in these subjects, down from 31 percent in elementary school. It is not surprising that the testing gap between boys and girls is particularly wide in math and science.[3]

Inequity in Instruction

During the past decade, Myra and David Sadker have investigated verbal interaction patterns in elementary, secondary, and college classrooms in a variety of settings and subject areas. In addition, they have interviewed students and teachers across the country. In their new book, *Failing at Fairness: How America's Schools Cheat Girls,* they expose the microinequities that occur daily in classrooms across the United States and they show how this imbalance in attention results in the lowering of girls' achievement and self-esteem.[4] Consider the following:

- From grade school to graduate school, girls receive less teacher attention and less useful teacher feedback.
- Girls talk significantly less than boys do in class. In elementary and secondary school, they are eight times less likely to call out comments. When they do, they are often reminded to raise their hands while similar behavior by boys is accepted.
- Girls rarely see mention of the contributions of women in the curricula; most textbooks continue to report male worlds.
- Too frequently female students become targets of unwanted sexual attention from male peers and sometimes even from administrators and teachers.

From omission in textbooks to inappropriate sexual comments to bias in teaching behavior, girls experience a powerful and often disabling education climate. A high school student from an affluent Northeastern high school describes her own painful experience:

My English teacher asks the class, "What is the purpose of the visit to Johannesburg?" . . . I know the answer, but I contemplate whether I should answer the question. The boys in the back are going to tease me like they harass all the other girls in our class . . . I want to tell them to shut up. But I stand alone. All of the other girls don't even let themselves be bold. Perhaps they are all content to be molded into society's image of what a girl should be like—submissive, sweet, feminine . . . In my ninth period class, I am actually afraid—of what [the boys] might say . . . As my frustration builds, I promise myself that I will yell back at them. I say that everyday . . . and I never do it.[5]

Teachers not only call on male students more frequently than on females; they also allow boys to call out more often. This imbalance in instructional attention is greatest at the college level. Our research shows that approximately one-half of the students in college classrooms are silent, having no interaction whatsoever with the professor. Two-thirds of these silent students are women. This verbal domination is further heightened by the gender segregation of many of today's classes. Sometimes teachers seat girls and boys in different sections of the room, but more often students segregate themselves. Approximately one-half of the elementary and high school classrooms and one-third of the coeducational college classrooms that the Sadkers visited are sex-segregated. As male students talk and call out more, teachers are drawn to the noisier male sections of the class, a development that further silences girls.

Not only do male students interact more with the teacher but at all levels of schooling they receive a higher quality of interaction. Using four categories of teacher responses to student participation—praise, acceptance, remediation, and criticism—the Sadkers' studies found that more than 50 percent of all teacher responses are mere acceptances, such as "O.K." and "uh huh." These nonspecific reactions offer little instructional feedback. Teachers use remediation more than 30 percent of the time, helping students correct or improve answers by asking probing questions or by phrases such as "Try again." Only 10 percent of the time do teachers actually praise students, and they criticize them even less. Although praise, remediation, and criticism provide more useful information to students than the neutral acknowledgment of an "O.K." these clearer, more precise teacher comments are more often directed to boys.

Who gets taught—and how—has profound consequences. Student participation in the classroom enhances learning and self-esteem. Thus, boys gain an educational advantage over girls by claiming a greater share of the teacher's time and attention. This is particularly noteworthy in science classes, where, according to the AAUW report, *How Schools Shortchange Girls,* boys perform 79 percent of all student-assisted demonstrations. When girls talk less and do less, it is little wonder that they learn less.[6] Even when directing their attention to girls, teachers sometimes short-circuit the learning process. For example, teachers frequently explain how to focus a microscope to boys but simply adjust the microscope for the girls. Boys learn the skill; girls learn to ask for assistance.

When female students do speak in class, they often preface their statements with self-deprecating remarks such as, "I'm not sure this is right," or "This probably isn't what you're looking for." Even when offering excellent responses, female students may begin with this self-criticism. Such tentative forms of speech project a sense of academic uncertainty and self-doubt—almost a tacit admission of lesser status in the classroom.

Women are not only quiet in classrooms; they are also missing from the pages of textbooks. For example, history textbooks currently in use at middle and high schools offer little more than 2 percent of their space to women. Studies of music textbooks have found that 70 percent of the figures shown are male. A recent content analysis of five secondary school science textbooks revealed that more than two-thirds of all drawings were of male figures and that not a single female scientist was depicted. Furthermore, all five books used the male body as the model for the human body, a practice that continues even in medical school texts.[7] At the college level, too, women rarely see themselves reflected in what they study. For example, the two-volume *Norton Anthology of English Literature* devotes less than 15 percent of its pages to the works of women. Interestingly, there was greater representation of women in the first edition of the anthology in 1962 than in the fifth edition published in 1986.[8]

Presence and Power

Not only are women hidden in the curriculum and quiet in the classroom, they are also less visible in other school locations. Even as early as the elementary grades, considered by some to be a distinctly feminine environment, boys tend to take over the territory. At recess time on playgrounds across the country, boys grab bats and balls as they fan out over the school yard for their games. Girls are likely to be left on the sideline—watching. In secondary school, male students become an even more powerful presence. In *Failing at Fairness*, high school teachers and students tell these stories:

> A rural school district in Wisconsin still has the practice of having the cheerleaders (all girls, of course) clean the mats for the wrestling team before each meet. They are called the "Mat Maidens."
>
> In our local high school, boys' sports teams received much more support from the school system and the community. The boys' team got shoes, jackets, and played on the best-maintained grounds. The girls' softball team received no clothes and nobody took care of our fields. Cheerleaders did not cheer for us. When we played, the bleachers were mostly empty.

Sports are not the only fields where women lose ground. In many secondary schools, mathematics, science, and computer technology remain male domains. In the past, girls were actively discouraged or even prohibited from taking the advanced courses in these fields. One woman, now a college professor, recalls her high school physics class:

> I was the only girl in the class. The teacher often told off-color jokes and when he did he would tell me to leave the room. My great regret today is that I actually did it.

Today, we hope such explicitly offensive behavior is rare, yet counselors and teachers continue to harbor lower expectations for girls and are less likely to encourage them to take advanced classes in math and science. It is only later in life that women realize the price they paid for avoiding these courses as they are screened out of lucrative careers in science and technology.

By the time they reach college, male students' control of the environment is visible. Male students are more likely to hold positions of student leadership on campus and to play in heavily funded sports programs. College presidents and deans are usually men, as are most tenured professors. In a sense, a "glass wall" divides today's college campus. On one side of the glass wall are men, comprising 70 percent of all students majoring in chemistry, physics, and computer science. The percentage is even higher in engineering. While the "hard sciences" flourish on the men's side of the campus, the women's side of the glass wall is where education, psychology, and foreign languages are taught. These gender walls not only separate programs, they also indicate social standing. Departments with higher male enrollment carry greater campus prestige and their faculty are often paid higher salaries.

These gender differences can be seen outside academic programs, in peer relationships both at college and in high school. In 1993 a national survey sponsored by the AAUW and reported in *Hostile Hallways* found that 76 percent of male students and 85 percent of female students in the typical high school had experienced sexual harassment.[9] What differed dramatically for girls and boys was not the occurrence of unwanted touching or profane remarks but their reaction to them. Only 28 percent of the boys, compared to 70 percent of the girls, said they were upset by these experiences. For 33 percent of the girls, the encounters were so troubling that they did not want to talk in class or even go to school. On college campuses problems range from sexist comments and sexual propositions to physical assault. Consider the following incidents:

> A UCLA fraternity manual found its way into a campus magazine. Along with the history and bylaws were the songs the pledges were supposed to memorize. The lyrics described sexual scenes that were bizarre, graphic, and sadistic.[10]

One fraternity on a New England campus hosted "pig parties" where the man bringing the female date voted the ugliest wins.[11]

A toga party on the campus of another elite liberal arts college used for decoration the torso of a female mannequin hung from the balcony and splattered with paint to look like blood. A sign below suggested the female body was available for sex.[12]

When one gender is consistently treated as less important and less valuable, the seeds of contempt take root and violence can be the result.

Strategies for Change

One of the ironies of gender bias in schools is that so much of it goes unnoticed by educators. While personally committed to fairness, many are unable to see the microinequities that surround them. The research on student-teacher interactions led the Sadkers to develop training programs to enable teachers and administrators to detect this bias and create equitable teaching methods. Program evaluations indicate that biased teaching patterns can be changed, and teachers can achieve equity in verbal interactions with their students. Research shows that for elementary and secondary school teachers, as well as college professors, this training leads not only to more equitable teaching but to more effective teaching as well.

During the 1970s, content analysis research showed women missing from schoolbooks. Publishers issued guidelines for equity and vowed to reform. But recent studies show that not all publishing companies have lived up to the promise of their guidelines. The curriculum continues to present a predominately male model of the world. Once again publishers and authors must be urged to incorporate women into school texts. Teachers and students need to become aware of the vast amount of excellent children's literature, including biographies that feature resourceful girls and strong women. *Failing at Fairness*[13] includes an extensive list of these resources for both elementary and secondary schools.

In postsecondary education, faculty members typically select instructional materials on the basis of individual preference. Many instructors would benefit from programs that alert them to well-written, gender-fair books in their academic fields. And individual professors can enhance their own lectures and discussions by including works by and about women.

Education institutions at every level have a responsibility to create comfortable and safe learning environments for students in and beyond the classroom. Harassing and intimidating behaviors that formerly might have been excused with the comment "boys will be boys" are now often seen as less excusable and less acceptable. Many schools offer workshops for students and faculty to help eliminate sexual harassment. While controversy surrounds the exact definition of sexual harassment, the education community must take this issue seriously and devise strategies to keep the learning environment open to all.

After centuries of struggle, women have finally made their way into our colleges and graduate schools, only to discover that access does not guarantee equity. Walls of subtle bias continue to create different education environments, channeling women and men toward separate and unequal futures. To complete the agenda for equity, we must transform our education institutions and empower female students for full participation in society.

Notes

1. M. Sadker and D. Sadker, *Failing at Fairness: How America's Schools Cheat Girls* (New York: Charles Scribner's Sons, 1994). The research for this article as well as the anecdotes are drawn from this book.
2. The Analysis Group, Greenberg-Lake, *Shortchanging Girls, Shortchanging America* (Washington, D.C.: American Association of University Women, 1990).
3. *Ibid.*
4. M. Sadker and D. Sadker, *Failing at Fairness*.
5. L. Kim, "Boys Will Be Boys . . . Right?" *The Lance*, Livingston High School (June 1993) 32:5.
6. The Wellesley College Center for Research on Women, *How Schools Shortchange Girls: The AAUW Report* (Washington, D.C.: American Association of University Women Educational Foundation, 1992).
7. J. Bazler and D. Simonis, "Are Women Out of the Picture?" *Science Teacher* 57 (December 1990):9.
8. W. Sullivan, "*The Norton Anthology* and the Canon of English Literature." Paper presented at the Annual Meeting of the College English Association, San Antonio, Texas, 1991.
9. Louis Harris and Associates, *Hostile Hallways: The AAUW Survey on Sexual Harassment in America's Schools* (Washington, D.C.: American Association of University Women, 1993).
10. J. O'Gorman and B. Sandler, *Peer Harassment: Hassles for Women on Campus* (Washington, D.C.: Project on the Status and Education of Women, Association of American Colleges, 1988).
11. M. Sadker and D. Sadker, *Failing at Fairness*.
12. B.A. Crier, "Frat Row," *Los Angeles Times* (February 9, 1990).
13. M. Sadker and D. Sadker, *Failing at Fairness*.

Retrospect and Prospect

Each day the media bring before the people of the United States an almost bewildering array of topics and issues ranging from the merely titillating to the significant. The dissonance created leads more often to inertia than to social policy and action. Arousal of public concern, focus on the problem, and corrective action do not come easily. Many problems approach the level of crisis before they become visible and receive attention.

The problems of our young people falling through the cracks of the community infrastructure, particularly in heavily populated centers, were becoming critical long before the words "at risk" were coined to classify an ill-defined pathology. Initial descriptions frequently reverted to the language once officially used in connection with juvenile delinquency. Both diagnosis and treatment focused on the "delinquent" juvenile. The young person demonstrating "abnormal" behavior was to be returned to an assumed norm through treatment, often involving incarceration.

Emile Durkheim, writing in France during the closing decades of the nineteenth century into the twentieth, made a close connection between individual behavior and the social context of which it is a part.[1] His work profoundly influenced later thinking about delinquent behavior, including that of Cyril Burt in England, who wrote in 1944:

> On an average, . . . each delinquent child is the product of 9 or 10 subversive circumstances. . . . Among personal conditions, the most significant are, first, the mental dullness which is not severe enough to be called deficiency, and, secondly, the temperamental instability which is not abnormal enough to be considered pathological. Among social conditions, by far the most potent is the family life; and, next to it, the friendships formed outside the home. . . . Between them, . . . they account for more than 50 per cent of juvenile delinquencies and crimes.[2]

In the Chicago of the 1930s and 1940s, individuals such as Clifford Shaw and Henry McKay, simultaneously working daily with young offenders and closely connected with the University of Chicago sociologist, Ernest Burgess, learned to look beyond the delinquent youth to circumstances of which that person was or had been a part.[3] Clearly, environmental factors did not explain the whole of individual deviations from accepted norms, but the ecology of interactions appeared to determine a great deal. The trajectories of lives cannot be understood and redirected when the individual alone is the unit of analysis examined out of context.

Nonetheless, the less complex explanation of individual irresponsibility as cause prevailed for decades more and is alive and well today. During my own years of educational work with incarcerated juvenile delinquents, the popular view among most of my co-workers and friends went no further than the "bad boy" or "bad girl" theory. The corrective route was hard work or harsh punishment or both.

When the words "at risk" surfaced in the 1980s to describe a condition among our young people that threatened both their present and their future, the early characterizations were very much like those prior to the ecologically oriented renaissance in the domain of juvenile deliquency. The individual was largely to blame—for a lack of moral grounding, for character weaknesses in the face of temptations (alcohol, drugs, sex, etc.), for listening to losers, and more. And deviance from legal and moral norms was commonly associated with race and socioeconomic class. Professional families in particular assumed exemption from the at-risk malaise, although disturbing news regarding their problems leaked out every now and again in most communities.

But the work of many community-minded groups, frequently with an educational orientation, fueled a much-needed change in emphasis. The alarm sounded by such organizations as the College Board, the Education Commission of the States, the National Education Association, and more, as well as reports funded by foundations such as Carnegie, Ford, and W. T. Grant broke through the dissonance-producing cacophony of the media. By the end of the 1980s, an increasingly enlightened national conversation was under way, a conversation that continues to produce promising initiatives. Nonetheless, the need for better and more comprehensive ones remains intense.

"At Risk" and the Schools

When the authors of preceding chapters were writing their manuscripts, circa 1989, the dominant attention to schools with respect to the "at-risk" phenomenon was to get children and youths at the margins into the mainstream of school life. Truancy and drop-out were rampant and exacerbated in the inner city. Large numbers in schools were struggling in the slow groups and low tracks, creating their own self-fulfilling prophecy of failure and drop-out. Once again, the focus was on individual pathology; hence, concentrate on remediation to get those at risk into the mainstream.

Although the editors of this volume recognized the importance of existing intellectual, social, and emotional factors in individual academic progress, they sought to introduce into the conversation an additional, largely ignored, perspective—that of pathology in the systemics, regularities, and organizational practices of schools. What price mainstreaming if the waters were polluted?

Analytical and research-based books such as Boyer's *High School* (1983), Sizer's *Horace's Compromise* (1984), and my *A Place Called School* (1984),[4] together with hundreds of journal articles and commission reports, had been chronicling for years some of the curricular and instructional sterility of schools in general. Instead of rescuing young people from risk, some school practices were putting them at risk. Among these practices were those that further savaged children and youths already at the edges of the mainstream, as documented by Oakes in her *Keeping Track: How Schools Structure Inequality* (1985).[5]

Since there was in the late 1980s ample documentation of issues pertaining to access to schools, we decided to concentrate primarily on issues of access to knowledge inside of schools. They ranged from conditions brought into schools by students such as poverty, race, and gender—which schools cannot change but must recognize and relate to if learning is to occur—to conditions within schools such as grouping and tracking practices, the expectations and language of teachers, curricular and instructional decisions, and more that lie within the power of educators and policymakers to change. The list and the agenda for fundamental change are long and formidable, as preceding chapters reveal.

Unfortunately, an agenda of educational improvement, however well documented and argued, is quite unlike even a less well-documented agenda of highway or postal service improvement with respect to its prospects for implementation. In regard to public works in general, there is minimal or at least tolerable robbing of Peter to pay Paul. Peter may pay more taxes than Paul, but the returns are roughly comparable; indeed Peter may get back a little more than Paul does. In educational matters, many citizens, perhaps most, resonate to the moral language of equity, justice, all children can learn, the right to learn, and, to a lesser degree, the need for "compensatory" policies. But the niceties of democratic spirit and language are quickly replaced by anger and protest when long-standing school practices perceived to be personally advantageous are threatened because, say reformers, they disadvantage the disadvantaged.

The overall academic improvement of schools squares nicely with the public's perception of the public purpose of schooling and, consequently, fits comfortably into political agendas. Words such as excellence and world-class sell well, as we have observed for a decade. But more fine-tuned school improvement agendas, designed particularly and specifically to extend access to first-rate knowledge to all, suggest to many people a taking away from some—especially me and mine. Consequently, moral educational agendas do not fit easily and comfortably into political agendas.[6] Words such as equity sell poorly on the campaign trail. Consequently, we should not be surprised by the fact that the politically driven school reform movement we continue to witness emphasizes very general improvement goals and not the fine-tuned changes required for schools to perform their democratic functions well.

Fortunately, some courageous, sound, grass-roots reform—often struggling with well-organized opposition—has been driven by moral imperatives. There can be no democracy without education, and education, in its full essence of meaning, withers without democracy.[7]

The above analysis partially explains, I think, why the moral educational agenda the chapters of this book suggest has not been picked up in any significant way in the political agenda of federal and state governments during this surprisingly sustained period of attention to school reform that began with the 1983 publication of *A Nation at Risk*. And perhaps the analysis explains in part—probably to lesser degree—the silence surrounding our book during the years since its first publication. So far as I am able to determine, its contents have been little cited in either documents of public policy or the professional literature. Virtually all of the educators with whom I have discussed some of these contents were surprised to learn of the book's existence while simultaneously expressing interest in its themes.

Did these themes touch sensitive nerves or was the book just ahead of its time? I think the answer to both queries is "yes." Have circumstances changed sufficiently to justify release of this second edition and to offer some promise of a greater impact? Again, my answer is "yes," but it is proffered more cautiously. I turn now to some of thess circumstances.

The Climate for Educational Excellence and Equity

The United States of America is in one of its longest periods of attention to school reform. This attention has abated somewhat recently as other social issues—health care, homelessness, poverty, and crime—have risen in visibility. But this is a plus, not a minus, for at least two major reasons.

The first is that we have had an orgy of unrealistic expectations for our schools. They cannot do alone what they have been exhorted unwisely to do. And, alone, they cannot do well what it is reasonable to expect them to do. The second is that the continued political attention paid to schools, albeit reduced in intensity, provides a unique opportunity to profit from mistakes—indeed, silliness—during what I hope will prove to have been only the first phase of a continuing era of school renewal. Our usual custom as a nation is to engage vigorously in a largely rhetorical, short-lived period of school reform that quickly fades into oblivion and from which few useful lessons are learned. And so, the next period of equally fruitless frothing repeats the errors of the previous one. But, given a sustained period of attention, there is the hope of not only learning some lessons about change and improvement, but also of applying them.

One exceedingly important lesson regarding a moral agenda such as the one preceding chapters address pertains to the need for moral principle and its applications to cut a wide swath. In seeking to right inequities, the agenda must offer widespread betterment to succeed. The irony here is that prospects for widespread betterment, while offering a hospitable context for change, provide only a mild stimulant for it. Outrage is a more commanding stimulant and outrage is born more often out of sharp recognition of pinpointed human hardship, suffering, and inequity than out of awareness of general malaise and the hope of general improvement. I return later to this dilemma.

What Schools Are For

During the second half of the 1980s, a funny thing happened on the rhetorical road to school reform. What schools—damned as failures—were called upon to do (should, could, and must) was blown up, taking on herculean proportions. Among other small miracles, schools were to create better jobs and put our nation at the forefront of global economic competition—and quickly. The degree to which these expectations sold well on the political campaign trail provides exceptional evidence for the need for schools to do better the only thing they can and should do well beyond providing cheap, safe, caring daily custody of the young—that is, provide comprehensive access to knowledge, provocations to thought, and the makings of civility. Had the ability to think critically been more widespread, the inflated rhetoric regarding the instrumental power of schools would have been quickly punctured. Whether, for example, Japanese schools are better than ours is a matter that will be debated indefinitely into the future. But we would have been better advised in recent years to look into the relationship between government policy and business in Japan than into its schools for plausible explanations for the rise of that country to a powerful position of global economic competition.

It is worth noting that there was no comparable pointing to the schools within Japan for their casual role in the rapid rise in the economy and a subsequent falling off. Nor was this connection made in England when that country went into economic decline. And, ironically, pundits and politicians in the United States currently are silent about the schools' role in the improved economy and polls showing a higher regard for the U.S. economy than our citizens bestowed on that of Japan just a few years ago.

No, schools do not create better jobs. Nor are they the driving force behind healthy nations. Healthy nations provide good work and good schools. Over time, of course, good education in schools develops the minds and character of a people who turn their attention to the policies and engineering characteristic of a healthy nation. So long as we flagellate the schools for failing to carry us into a robust new era, we condemn them to failure. Worse, we draw attention from what must be done to ameliorate and then eliminate malaise that inexorably erodes the very foundations of our democratic society.

The disturbing thing about schools is that they do not do well enough the only thing they can and should do—namely educate our young to be thoughtful, caring parents, workers, citizens, and human beings. The surrogates to which we look in assessing whether or not students are, indeed, being educated—marks and test scores in school subjects—correlate society scarcely at all with commonly espoused virtues such as honesty, dependability, work habits, happiness, successful marriages, and the like. The criticisms that Boyer, Sizer, and I directed at the schools addressed primarily the core of what school-based education should be about: compelling encounters with first-rate knowledge, lively discussions regarding the implications of this knowledge for daily living, the cultivation of civility in all aspects of the school environment, creative instructional and organizational arrangements to ensure meaningful participation by all students, and more. Our recommendations focused on getting rid of things, adding some alternatives, and doing everything better: downplaying the role of textbooks and workbooks to near extinction, beefing up the array of instructional methods, paying more attention to individual differences, etc. We said nothing about throwing our schools at the warts and blemishes the growing political school reform movement selected for a war-like educational crusade that was to be waged without new resources.

Several of the preceding chapters of this volume add urgency to the continuing need for schools to be more educative. They call for nothing more than the omissions, additions, and improvements that dozens of reports have recommended for years—that is, recommendations designed to make schools more effective across the board. What these chapters add to the conversation and the urgency of the agenda is the degree to which many present practices shortchange the already shortchanged: grouping practices that wall off some students from access to first-rate knowledge, instructional practices that favor only some students' modes of learning, unwitting gender and other cultural preferences of teachers that create harmful classroom dissonance, and so on. The prejudicial effects accentuate the need to address problems that careful inquiries into schools have revealed to be detrimental to the education of all students. Once again, I touch upon the proposition that the likelihood for constructive change is enhanced when the school conditions that severely affect some students affect all students substantially.

In my opinion, the chances of addressing the problems that impede the educational function of schools improve when the inflated political rhetoric exhorting them to do what they are incapable of doing well subsides—provided the importance of education and schooling are not pushed into the shadows. This is one such time. But will it be sustained?

Toward Healthy Communities

Lawrence Cremin pointed out that it is folly to seek excellence in American education without paying attention to the whole array of institutions and agencies that formally and informally educate.[8] The schools may not be the most powerful among these. The thesis posed three decades ago by Coleman still stands: the most significant contribution to a child's learning in schools is what he or she brings from home and encounters there from other homes.[9] The hours of watching television, many of them in the very impressionable pre-school years, exceed the hours spent in elementary and secondary schools by many young people. It is hard to believe that these are not powerfully educational. Barber observes that much of the good educating of schools in regard to civility and decency is countered daily in life outside of schools.[10]

Two critical implications emerge from the preceding paragraph. First, children are more likely to flourish in schools when the infrastructure of the community supports their total welfare and development.[11] Second, the educating of schools is more likely to be effective when all other elements of this infrastructure are self-consciously aware of and attentive to their own educative functioning.[12]

We have seen in preceding chapters the impact on academic performance of a societal context that assumes intellectual handicap to be a correlate of completely unrelated characteristics such as race and gender. We have seen in preceding chapters the impact of several generations of poverty. And we have read about a neglected teacher education enterprise that fails to prepare teachers for the realities they confront daily. These chapters point to malaise in the ecosystem of which schools are only a part.

The failure of the politically driven school reform effort of the past dozen years to address these matters increasingly has been revealed. The stakes of schooling have been significantly raised by the rhetoric of world-class standards and the levels of schooling to be required for entry into a vastly more demanding job market.[13] One of the goals of America 2000 was for all children to come to school ready to learn. But there were no accompanying initiatives to provide the health care and nutrition such readiness requires. Our students were to lead the world in mathematics and science even though thousands of schools lack the necessary teachers and a world-class curriculum. Our schools were to become drug-free even as drugs spilled into them from the surrounding community. The gap between rhetorical hype and realities such as these reached such proportions that they aroused moral outrage among education spokespeople. America 2000 blew away on an election day in November 1992, leaving only a vacuum to be filled by some other political agenda.

There are now clear signs in many quarters, including those of federal and state policymakers, of a concern for our young people and our communities that transcends and vastly expands in understanding and scope what was a few years ago a relatively narrow focus on children at risk as individual pathology. We are coming to see much more clearly a complex community ecosystem that is dependent for its health on the healthy condition of all of its parts, not just its schools. Schools can no more make up for chronic community malaise than they can be healthy in unhealthy communities.

We begin to see the broadening of a concern for the quality of living in this nation that began with a focus on schools now moving on to preoccupation with family stability, health care, guns and violence, social services, unemployment, child care, ethical and moral standards, and the role of the media. There are two distinct stages to be anticipated in this broadening.

The first is to ensure that the necessary agencies and services are in place and functioning to provide equitable access for all. Some of our major philanthropic foundations and corporate offices of giving are currently involved, in cities across the country, with locally initiated efforts that address components of the necessary infrastructure. The second stage is for all of these agencies to perform both service and educative functions. The second will be longer in coming, but there already has been significant progress in the health arena. The health professions have been plodding along toward a realization of a prevention model that includes a major educational component. Better health and longevity are only in part a product of medical science. The rest is the product of more and more people becoming aware of and following sound principles of nutrition, exercise, and self-discipline. This stage of advancement toward healthy communities depends on all of our institutions adopting an educational perspective in what they do.

Currently, the need for a shift toward a more educative role is most apparent in business, particularly in regard to the messages conveyed generally and in the functioning of the media specifically. Getting a message out prevails over exercising care with regard to the potential moral impact of the message. The prescience of Marshall McLuhan is confirmed one more time: the medium has become the message. [14] It is past time for the message to be for the common good.

In healthy communities, schools are healthy, too, and have no excuses for being otherwise. Being healthy means being maximally educative for all of their students. My concern now is that we will continue to label schools failures for not doing what they cannot and must not be charged to do, even as the nation's economy climbs back. This educational mission is what the several analytical, research-based books of 1983 and 1984, referred to earlier, agreed was not being adequately fulfilled. Schools will continue to lag in this mission if they alone are charged with responsibilities that require the full attention and collaboration of all community agencies. Recognizing this is a first step toward creating the context in which schools can perform their unique mission well.

Good Schools and Their Teachers

Earlier, I referred to the dilemma of effecting significant school reform when the conditions targeted are perceived as not being widespread or as outside the scope of reform initiatives. The data in support of change may stir interest, concern, or even outrage but, confined to particular persons or settings, they do not necessarily arouse national, state, or local action. Just a few years ago, this was the problem surrounding initial statements of alarm regarding children and youth "at risk." Disturbing though the data were, they pertained to "deviant" young people in deviant circumstances, not to the mainstream. As with the situation with respect to juvenile delinquency several decades ago, the problems described were representative of individual, not societal, malaise.

But there has been a profound shift in perspective. Drugs, random shootings, satanic rituals, burglary, and rape are part of the ambience of most communities. Parents are disturbed about the prospects for raising their children safely and in good schools. Test scores may remain high and dropout rates low in those schools that never have been characterized otherwise. But the concerns of the community have escalated nonetheless. The problems that only yesterday were those of someone else are now widely shared.

There is not yet, however, widespread agreement on the need for all to join in a common cause of community and school renewal. There are those who would privatize the public schools to ensure ghetto-like havens for "my children" and those of "my kind of people." This struggle for the soul of the U.S. public school goes beyond the scope of this book. Of proper concern here is the degree to which interest in good schools generally and schools that alleviate "at risk" particularly leads to one agenda, not two. Various groups may try to run away, seeking sanctuary in their self-imposed isolation, but there is no way to escape envelopment in the fabric of our civilization.

The fabric of a democratic society always is a work in progress. There is much work to do out there and some encouraging signs. These include growing recognition of the limitations of schools, deepening concern over the considerable unraveling of community stability, and increased awareness that access to schools for all is only a step along the road to access to knowledge for all. We also have a school reform movement that has been sustained long enough for there to be both some success stories and some lessons learned, and increasing recognition of the relationship between good schools and the education of their teachers. These signs and more warrant *cautious* optimism.

The Context for Good Schools

The people of this nation are reluctant to abandon their strong belief in the connection between schooling and the American dream. But there has been considerable loss of innocence in recent years. Being much-schooled does not put that desired job on a platter; nor does it ensure that the one now enjoyed will be there tomorrow. But being well educated makes one ready, with relatively little new training, for the jobs of one's choice that a robust society creates. This perspective increases the importance of education as an end in itself rather than a mere instrumentality to other ends.

Consequently, growing understanding of the loose connections between schools and the creation of jobs turns attention to the educational mission of schools: the enculturation of the young into a political and social democracy;

the fostering of efficacy in the mastery and use of knowledge and in thought. We are not yet into a national dialogue regarding what schools are for, but at least we appear to be a little less naive in regard to the inflated, misleading rhetoric that has been stretched to the limits of credibility in recent years by politicians and business leaders in particular.

There are signs of potentially productive corollaries of this more realistic perspective regarding the function of schools. One is a somewhat greater awareness of both erosion in the community infrastructure and the degree to which malaise cannot be isolated, walled off, or sidestepped. It affects us all. Another is growing understanding that missing or inadequate health, educational, and other services for some weakens the human support eco-system for all. My well-being is connected to the well-being of all. This kind of awareness is what substantially motivated the early householders to tax themselves for schools they did not need, as referred to in Chapter One. Self-interest may not be the most noble motivation for addressing the needs of others, but it may well be the most powerful.

Trends like these in the changing fabric of this democracy help to shift both policy and social engineering from individual pathology as the sole cause of tears in this fabric to a much more productive, ecological perspective. And so we find politicians scurrying to find a credible public position with respect to health care, crime and imprisonment, gun control, "safe" sex, child care, family values, and more. Although the hard and tough language of tests, standards, and accountability still dominates federal and state policy discourse regarding schools, the language of equitable access to necessary knowledge is finding an increasingly hospitable place.

These encouraging signs—and one must put on at least slightly rose-colored glasses to find them—lead us to be somewhat optimistic about the emergence of a climate in which schools can be good. There are two senses in which this can happen. The first pertains to public opinion: there are no perceptible changes, but it has become fashionable to praise schools rather than to blame them. The second pertains to genuine renewal: schools are becoming more educative for more children and youth.

Good Schools

There are good reasons that the climate of public opinion regarding our schools is improving. By tying them closely to the economy, we doomed schools to a perception of failure so long as the economy lagged. With economic signs improving, regard for the schools should increase in proportion to the blame we gave them for the economy of a few years ago. No such praise is being given. The best we can hope for is a greater distancing of schools from the economic ups and downs of the future. Should that occur, there is some possibility of a greater congruence between public opinion and how well the schools are performing their educational mission. But it is unlikely that the popular myths regarding the instrumentality of our schools will completely dissolve.

Another reason for lowering the cadence of criticism is the growing body of evidence that no precipitous decline occurred.[15] When getting better schools becomes a political mission, it is aided by depicting the schools as performing miserably so that progress can be proclaimed a few years hence simply by spotlighting some success stories or being selective in the choice of confirming data. The reality now surfacing is that the schools in many communities have been the most stable institutions during a period of rapidly changing circumstances that threaten their educative function. Instead of being perceived as the *cause* of these changing circumstances, schools are being viewed by some thoughtful observers as the *victims*. Schools become only one of an array of institutions and agencies requiring buttressing and renewal.

But this more comprehensive view of disarray in the community infra-structure must not be allowed to draw attention from the continuing need for schools to be more educationally effective. Were my colleagues and I to conduct today the massive study of schooling reported in my book, *A Place Called School* (1984), we would find some of the schools in our sample to be barely hanging together and some to be taking care of their business very well. Undoubtedly, our overall appraisal would echo what we described then: vast school-to-school differences in the amount of time students are seriously engaged in learning; primary grade grouping practices that deny some children access to first-rate knowledge; a continuation of these misguided practices in the separation of secondary school students into academic or vocational emphases and further division into upper, middle, and lower tracks that serve few students well; an excess of lecturing and telling and a dearth of hands-on and inquiry approaches to learning; teachers doing too much of the work that students should be doing; second-hand curricula too oriented to textbooks and routine assignments; teachers bewildered by the cultural diversity of their students; teachers lacking the understanding required for them to avoid stereotyping and innocently demeaning students of differing ethnic and racial backgrounds.

Two of the major themes of preceding chapters resonate with particular urgency today. The first pertains to the inadequacy of improvement strategies that have as their goal only getting students at risk into this mainstream that our research and that of others has revealed. Misbegotten practices in the mainstream of schools put some students at risk and limit the attainments of others. The second theme emerges from the first: it is the fundamental conduct of schooling that must be revitalized to the benefit of all students. The organizational, curricular, and instructional changes required are for whole school populations, not just a segment perceived to be in special need. Such changes will not eliminate, of course, a differential spread in pupil attainment. Nor will they remove all of the factors that unfairly prejudice performance, or the need to be very attentive to the special problems of the physically, emotionally, and intellectually disabled.[16]

The problem of destructive or unproductive deviancy from generally accepted norms always will be cause for concern and inquiry. But the assumption of individual pathology as the sole or even major condition to be addressed grows increasingly less viable in the face of evidence to the contrary. Years ago, a colleague and I were startled to find the degree to which students performing poorly in the early grades simply were exposed for remedial purposes to more of the circumstances under which they were performing poorly.[17] The recommendations we made were nothing more than a reiteration of what research increasingly is revealing to be desirable conditions for learning in school settings.[18] A relatively recent comprehensive study dealing with the learning of children of poverty adds to the conclusion that these desirable conditions benefit all, not just children assumed to be ready to learn. Schooling for children of poverty, like schooling for most children perceived to be dropping through the cracks, has been guided by a conception that emphasizes drill, tight control of instruction by the teacher, grade repetition, and the like. But the team of researchers studying 140 classrooms in 15 schools found that the children of low-income families profited from instruction stressing a search for meaning, using an array of techniques emphasizing the reading of stories, poems, and journals; the use of language mechanics in context; the integration of reading and writing; and more.[19]

Becoming increasingly apparent is the degree to which those school improvement agendas that are gaining a grass-roots following and attracting widespread attention are addressed to whole-school practices on the assumption that these must be changed if all children are to learn. The guiding philosophy is not one of remedial or compensatory education intended to do more of the same. Schools following Howard Gardner's concepts of intelligence seek to provide a range of learning opportunities designed to involve the active participation of all students.[20] The search is for alternatives, not a narrow array of didactics for all. Theodore Sizer has laid down a set of concepts that call for secondary schools to conduct their business quite differently—not for some students but all.[21] Henry Levin has addressed the matter of disadvantaged students by putting together a rich combination of practices derived from inquiry into learning and schooling generally.[22] The theme common to all is that the healthy educational performance of children and youth and the healthy educational conduct of schools are intimately connected. With either at risk, both are at risk.

Teachers for Renewing Schools

Chapter Fourteen advanced the proposition that today's preparation programs fail to produce teachers with the awareness, understanding, and skill necessary for dealing successfully with students from diverse cultural back-grounds and those whose ways of learning differ from classroom norms. Our research not only confirmed this, but went on to depict other shortcomings that raise serious questions about the degree to which teachers are prepared to renew their schools and make them truly educative for all.

Teachers in our sample, especially at the secondary level, identified ability to deal with students of special need as a major deficiency.[23] In later research, we found that prospective teachers listed precisely the same short-comings. Also, teachers preparing in the field of special education perceived themselves as ill-equipped to relate to parents—a deficiency reported also by those preparing for general classroom responsibilities.[24] And it was very clear that neither group of teachers perceived themselves as responsible or ready for stewardship of the school as a whole.[25]

Yet, a major implication of preceding chapters is the need for a teacher corps alert to and ready to address a host of school-wide problems that conspire to deny access to knowledge to a much larger proportion of students than that labeled "at risk." Until very recently, school reform and the reform of teacher education have been addressed separately, as though there were no connection.[26] Unless schools and university campuses are joined in a common mission, new teachers simply are inducted into the long-standing conventions of schooling. And there have been few efforts on the part of professors of education and professors in the arts and sciences to join with one another, let alone with colleagues in cooperating schools, to design and conduct coherent teacher education programs. The most popular proposals and programs on the scene continue to be those that offer even less "profes-sional" preparation and a heavy dose of mentoring by the very teachers whose shortcomings not only are well documented but are the cause of national concern. A major source of the attraction to these simple, misguided re-sponses to complex needs is that they do not cost much.

As with schools, there are encouraging stirrings. Some school-university partnerships committed to joint conduct of teacher education have been in existence for a decade. In 1986, two major reports urged joint development of professional development schools as a significant component of teacher education initiatives.[27] Some 25 colleges and universities are joined with school districts (almost 100 at this time) and partner schools (275 with the number growing) in the simultaneous renewal of schools and the education of educators. As a group, these settings constitute the National Network for Educational Renewal.[28] Similar collaborations are occurring nationwide.

There is no question that all teachers need to be prepared to relate sensitively, with caring pedagogy, to young people from disadvantaging cir-cumstances of many different kinds. This need alone calls for major redesign of pre-service and in-service education programs. And all faculty groups must include teachers who have the specialized preparation required to address the most deep-seated problems these children bring with them. There must be no lessening of attention to the socially, emotionally, physically, and mentally disabled.

Simultaneously, however, there must be continuing attention on the part of all educators, policymakers, and the general public to the design of schools that are at once excellent and equitable in the access to knowledge they provide. Schools called upon by policymakers to serve passing, partisan interests are diminished or distorted in their educative functions. Schools designed to reflect the special interests of this or that religious, ethnic, or racial group imperil the social and political democracy they are supposed to serve. Schools committed to narrowly defined curricular and instructional practices fall short of providing quality education for all. Schools staffed by teachers whose preparation failed to prepare them for the moral stewardship of these institutions are unlikely to engage in the renewing processes that changing circumstances require.

In the brief span of years since this book was first published, there has been encouraging evidence of a maturation in public perceptions of what schools can and cannot do well. There has been, too, growing awareness that increased deviance in the behavior of young people requires interventions that go beyond individual pathology to the very core of the community context. There has been improved understanding that this core cannot be addressed effectively through schools alone or quick-fix, politically driven panaceas. And there have emerged several long-term agendas and programs focused on both schools and teacher education that are driven by the moral purpose of seeking to make things better.

These developments stand in delicate balance with quite other perspectives and purposes that have little to do with equal access to first-rate knowledge for all or, for that matter, equal access to first-rate schools for all. The future of the American democracy depends significantly on which way this balance swings. The struggle for the soul of our system of public schooling is in large part a struggle for the soul of a way of life that must be celebrated daily and watched over with informed care by a citizenry that is well educated.
JOHN I. GOODLAD

Notes

1. See, for example, Emile Durkheim, "The Dualism of Human Nature and Its Social Conditions," in *Emile Durkheim on Morality and Society*, ed. Robert N. Bellah (Chicago: University of Chicago Press, 1973), 149-63.
2. Cyril Burt, *The Young Delinquent* (London: University of London Press, 1944), 602-08.
3. See Clifford R. Shaw, *The Natural History of a Delinquent Career* (Chicago: University of Chicago Press, 1931); and Clifford R. Shaw and Henry D. McKay, *Juvenile Delinquency and Urban Area* (Chicago: University of Chicago Press, 1942).

4. These three books, the first two on secondary schools and the third on both elementary and secondary schools, were cited over and over in school reform reports of the time to support the contention that our schools were inferior to those of other nations, even though all three were directed, rather, to specific changes that would make them better. See Ernest L. Boyer, *High School* (New York: Harper & Row, 1983); Theodore R. Sizer, *Horace's Compromise* (Boston: Houghton Mifflin, 1984); and John I. Goodlad, *A Place Called School* (New York: McGraw-Hill, 1984).

5. Jeannie Oakes, *Keeping Track: How Schools Structure Inequality* (New Haven: Yale University Press, 1985).

6. I am indebted to my colleague Timothy J. McMannon for his insightful separation of the political and the moral as motivations for school reform agendas (unpublished).

7. See Benjamin R. Barber, "America Skips School," *Harper's*, November 1993, 46.

8. Lawrence R. Cremin, *Popular Education and Its Discontents* (New York: Harper & Row, 1990), 51-83.

9. James S. Coleman, *Equality of Educational Opportunity* (Washington, D.C.: U.S. Government Printing Office, 1966).

10. Barber, "America Skips School," 42.

11. For a penetrating report on school restructuring in the context of a multicultural community, see *California Tomorrow, The Unfinished Journey: Restructuring Schools in a Diverse Society* (San Francisco: California Tomorrow, 1994).

12. See John I. Goodlad, *Toward Educative Communities and Tomorrow's Teachers* (Seattle, Wash.: Institute for Educational Inquiry, 1992).

13. John I. Goodlad, "On Taking School Reform Seriously," *Phi Delta Kappan* 74 (November 1992): 232-38.

14. Marshall McLuhan's most widely read book, *Understanding Media: The Extensions of Man* (New York: McGraw-Hill, 1964), was an insightful analysis of the ways in which the new electronic communications technologies were influencing (and would influence) life and culture.

15. Three analyses of the available data, in particular, raise doubts about the "shocking declines" in test scores claimed by an array of commission reports in the mid-1980s: David C. Berliner, "Mythology and the American System of Schooling," *Phi Delta Kappan* 74 (April 1993): 634-40; Gerald W. Bracey, "The Third Bracey Report on the Condition of Public Education," *Phi Delta Kappan* 75 (October 1993): 114-18; and Robert M. Carson, Robert M. Huelskamp, and T. D. Woodall, "Perspectives on Education in America," 3rd draft (Albuquerque, N.M.: Sandia National Laboratories, May 1991).

16. For an analysis of and recommendations regarding the integration of both general education for all and special education for some in schools and classrooms, as well as the need for some separate provisions, see John I. Goodlad and Thomas C. Lovitt, eds., *Integrating General and Special Education* (New York: Macmillan, 1993).

17. John I. Goodlad, M. Frances Klein, and Associates, *Behind the Classroom Door* (Worthington, Ohio: Charles A. Jones, 1970).

18. For a review of research on such topics as what to teach, how to teach, relevant knowledge about learners and learning, school improvement, school-community relations, and professional issues pertaining to teachers, see Virginia Richardson-Koehler, *Educators' Handbook: A Research Perspective* (New York: Longman, 1987).

19. Michael S. Knapp, Patrick M. Shields, and Brenda J. Turnbull, *Academic*

Challenge for the Children of Poverty, Summary Report Prepared for the U.S. Department of Education (Menlo Parkm Calif.: SRI International; and Washington, D.C.: Policy Studies Associates, 1992).

20. Particularly influential among elementary school principals and teachers is Howard Gardner, *Frames of Mind: The Theory of Multiple Intelligences* (New York: Basic Books, 1983).

21. See particularly Theodore R. Sizer, *Horace's Compromise* (Boston: Houghton Mifflin, 1984) and *Horace's School* (Boston: Houghton Mifflin, 1992).

22. Henry M. Levin, "Don't Remediate: Accelerate," *Principal* 70 (January 1991): 11-13.

23. Goodlad, *A Place Called School,* 185.

24. John I. Goodlad and Sharon Field, "Teachers for Renewing Schools," in eds. Goodlad and Lovitt, *Integrating General and Special Education,* 236-37.

25. Preparation of teachers for classroom management only and not the stewardship of schools is a theme that emerged over and over in our research on selected teacher education programs. See John I. Goodlad, *Teachers for Our Nation's Schools* (San Francisco: Jossey-Bass, 1990).

26. Zhixin Su, "Teacher Education Reform in the United States (1890-1986)," Occasional Paper No. 3 (Seattle, Wash.: Center for Educational Renewal, College of Education, University of Washington, 1986).

27. That of the Carnegie Forum on Education and the Economy, *A Nation Prepared: Teachers for the 21st Century* (Washington, D.C.: Carnegie Forum, 1986) and that of the Holmes Group, *Tomorrow's Teachers: A Report of the Holmes Group* (East Lansing, Mich.: Holmes Group, 1986).

28. See John I. Goodlad, "The National Network for Educational Renewal," *Phi Delta Kappan* 75 (April 1994): 632-38.

Index